Moscow and Muscovites

Translation of this book was made possible through generous financial support from
The Institute of Translation, Moscow, Russia
Издано при поддержке АНО «Институт перевода», Россия.

Перевод издания и создание его оригинал-макета осуществлен при финансовой поддержке
Федерального агентства по печати и массовым коммуникациям в рамках Федеральной
целевой программы "Культура России (2012—2018 гг.)"

ИНСТИТУТ ПЕРЕВОДА

AD VERBUM

Cover: *Near St. Basil's Cathedral, Early in the Twentieth Century*

This book is an original translation of
Москва и москвичи (1926), by Vladimir Gilyarovsky
English translation copyright © 2013, Russian Information Services.
All rights reserved.

ISBN 978-1-880100-82-0

Library of Congress Control Number: 2013955149

Russian Information Services, Inc.
PO Box 567
Montpelier, VT 05601-0567
www.russianlife.com
orders@russianlife.com
phone 802-234-1956

MOSCOW & MUSCOVITES

VLADIMIR GILYAROVSKY

TRANSLATED BY BRENDAN KIERNAN

Dedicated to
Lyudmila V. Kareva
1958 – 2012

Вл. Гиляровскій

CONTENTS

TRANSLATOR'S INTRODUCTION

Overview

I am pleased to present the first English translation of Vladimir Gilyarovsky's popular social history, *Moscow and Muscovites*. First published in 1926, the text covers many aspects of everyday life in Moscow from the early 1860s to the mid 1930s.[1] Gilyarovsky's self-described "chronicle" is a spectacular verbal pastiche: conversation, from gutter gibberish to the drawing room; oratory, from illiterates to aristocrats; prose, from boilerplate to Tolstoy; poetry, from earthy humor to Pushkin.

While a basic familiarity with the broad strokes of Russian and European history and culture will help readers get more out of the text, none of this knowledge is assumed. Footnotes provide context or point out consequences that may not be immediately apparent to the inexperienced eye. Period photographs and paintings complement the text and illustrate many of the book's key topics. Thanks largely to technology, inexpensive access to a colossal number of images offers opportunities for historical-cultural illustration unavailable to previous generations of translators. This is especially important because, as readers will quickly note, Gilyarovsky, to an uncommon degree, references all five senses to cast his spells. While I have to leave smell, touch, taste, and hearing to the text, I hope the photographs will help readers develop a more vivid sense of Gilyarovsky's canvas.

An 1893 map of Moscow was recreated to help readers follow the action. Gilyarovsky lived in an empire challenged by vast distances between cities; he worked

---

1. Gilyarovsky revised, expanded, and republished the book in 1936. Another version edited by G. Firsov was published in 1955 (Moscow Worker Press) with the cooperation of Gilyarovsky's son. The edition re-organized the original material and added approximately 90 pages (not included here).

in a city where harsh weather, low-quality roads, and poor lighting limited mobility; he relied heavily on uncomfortable modes of transportation, mostly oat-fueled, now consigned to museums. Writing in a world where such limits were felt, literally, in the seat of your pants, Gilyarovsky naturally shared with readers his highly developed understanding of Moscow's physical geography.

Gilyarovsky called himself a "chronicler" of life in Moscow, attempting to help later generations understand their past.[2] He focused his discussion on groups and situations he considered outside the mainstream of his day's reporting and publishing: criminals and their milieu; alcoholics and bars; prostitutes and their pimps and johns; gamblers; child labor, both its victims and perpetrators; debtors and criminal and political prisoners; scam artists and petty thieves. He also covered some of Moscow's lesser-known, yet admirable and interesting types: firefighters, university students, merchants and traders, conservatives and revolutionaries, hidden aspects of high society. In many instances, Gilyarovsky resorted to sensationalism: abandoned torture chambers and skeletons; rats and repulsive, unsanitary conditions in Moscow's food supply; the odiferous and mysterious depths of Moscow's sewers; violent crime.

Gilyarovsky was not a trained historian. As a translator and, if you will, assistant tour guide, I would like to point out a number of issues related to his methods. First, despite the special characteristics treasured by Gilyarovsky, Moscow was never *sui generis*. Readers should trust their comparative instincts; while not always a perfect analogue, Western history certainly provides useful context. Gilyarovsky's Moscow was shaped by economic, social, and political forces that can be summarized broadly as modernization. While some aspects of the dynamic were delayed or disfigured compared to the West (heavy industrialization, political liberalization), in other areas Russia was not dissimilar to other countries. This included a wave of migration from the countryside to factory work in the cities; the construction of the empire's railroads and other modern transportation and communication systems; the development of a commercial banking system; changing social and political relations as the landed gentry gave way to a commercial class untied to the earth; the increasing openness of Russia to international trade and foreign social and cultural influences; and, the growing assertiveness of secular institutions outside the Russian Orthodox Church. In all these ways, Moscow and Russia developed local answers to challenges faced around the globe. At the time, poverty, crime, child labor, overcrowding, alcoholism, and related phenomena pointed to by Gilyarovsky were as likely to plague inhabitants of New York or London as those of Moscow.

Readers should of course hesitate to take Gilyarovsky at his word in all of the marvelous scenes depicted in this broad-ranging text. He faced the same temptations

---

2. Chronicles, more or less detailed records of events, handwritten, and often copies of long lost originals, are perhaps the most important historical source for Russia before Peter the Great (1672-1725).

and professional incentives, monetary and otherwise, as any other writer. Given the nature of his reporting and writing style, much of his material simply defies normal fact checking. Gilyarovsky may have, for example, exaggerated his own role and importance in certain events. For ease of exposition and dramatic effect, he probably fabricated, in whole or in part, conversations that took place years earlier (some that he could not possibly have witnessed). He is a shameless namedropper who claims to have been privy to all types of private information: who knows where the truth lies? I suggest that readers set aside second-guessing or doubts about the historical record. Gilyarovsky's goal was not to mirror events, but to help people understand the best way he knew how: through entertaining stories. He worked for much of his life as a journalist in an industry driven by the need to sell newspapers. His years on the stage, his reputation as a raconteur, his flair for the dramatic, and his sharp wit give his prose a special flavor. If you want facts or a nuanced presentation, this is not your source.

Readers are likely curious about Gilyarovsky's political inclinations. Clearly, in his newspaper articles and the intended publication of *Slum People*, an account of Moscow's poor banned by the Russian censor in 1877, Gilyarovsky humanized the downtrodden, and in that way was palatable for the new powers. It may also have been significant that he never joined forces in any serious way with a political party. Although an examination of his relationship to the Bolsheviks and the events of 1917, and related developments up until publication, is outside the scope of this effort, a few general remarks are in order. In *Moscow and Muscovites*, Gilyarovsky makes numerous small nods to the early accomplishments of Soviet power, while painting high society, business leaders, the Orthodox Church, and other social elements with a note of scorn. Russia's liberal parties and their leaders are not even mentioned. He describes the weaknesses and foibles of a wide range of Moscow's colorful characters, but leaves the Bolsheviks alone. While claiming interest in historical buildings, he fails to mention the demolition in 1931 of one of Russia's greatest treasures, Moscow's Cathedral of Christ the Savior. Built (starting in 1839) to commemorate Russia's victory over Napoleon, the cathedral's marble was confiscated and used to decorate a Moscow metro station. A "chronicle" crafted by a clever professional to get an otherwise worthy effort into print under the watchful eye of the Bolsheviks, or political pandering to butter his own bread? Without a detailed biography that includes documented analysis of his later years, we can only guess.

Biographical Summary[3]

Vladimir Alexeyevich Gilyarovsky was born on November 26, 1855, on an estate near Vologda.[4] His father worked for a Cossack, whose daughter he later married.[5] In 1860, Gilyarovsky's father received a regional administrative position. The family relocated to the region's administrative and trade center, Vologda, when he was still a young child. Following the untimely death of Vladimir's mother, his father re-married, and the boy's life, in his own words, was transformed. French lessons commenced immediately. He was taught how to conduct himself in the drawing rooms of Saint Petersburg and Moscow. At the same time, according to Gilyarovsky's account, by the age of 12 he excelled with both rifle and shotgun, rode horseback, was a tireless cross-country skier, and enjoyed hunting and camping trips with his father in the swamps and forests near Vologda. He recalls being a difficult child. He had few warm memories of his formal education, which ended by the time he was 14.

In the early summer of 1871, Gilyarovsky, at the age of 15, walked the 100 miles from Vologda to Yaroslavl, with no internal passport and only pocket change, to find work that he had dreamed of, he said, since early childhood: being strapped to a harness and pulling boats on the Volga River. Romanticizing a brutal way of life, he wanted to be a Volga boatman, work that had started disappearing years before he started his journey. Was this anything more than a childish rebellion against his father or stepmother? A teenage assertion of independence by one of the stronger personalities Russia ever produced? The record is not clear. The situation was, perhaps, brought to a head by problems with poor grades in his Vologda *gymnasium*, but young Vladimir did not hasten home at the first sign of difficulty: laughter and ridicule for his "career choice" on the streets of Yaroslavl. Instead, he found a local group of boatmen and convinced them to give him a chance.

Gilyarovsky lived his dream in the harness, at least for a few weeks, and then moved on to work as a stevedore. By the end of the summer, Vladimir had written his father to recount his adventures; perhaps, too, he was hoping for reconciliation. Gilyarovsky senior visited, met his son, and serendipitously encountered an old friend on the docks. As a result, the boy's enthusiasms were redirected, and he ended up enrolling in the army on 3 September 1871. Probably thanks to this connection

3. Most of the biographical information here is distilled from Gilyarovsky's *Мои скитания (My Travels)*, a collection of autobiographical sketches finished in 1927. This was included in a collection of his works, *Репортажи из прошлого*, Moscow, Astrel, 2010.
4. Modern-day Gilyarovskaya Street may have been the location of his first home in Vologda proper. In Moscow, Gilyarovsky lived in Stoleshnikov Alley, in a building that now has a memorial plaque with the simple words "Vladimir Gilyarovsky, writer."
5. Cossacks, a group of East Slavic peoples with origins in the fourteenth and fifteenth centuries in the Dnieper and Don basins, originally lived in popularly democratic, semi-military communities. By the eighteenth century they were recognized for their military achievements. Later they were used in police service and to suppress dissent.

and his (unfinished) education, he entered the service as a Junker, essentially an officer candidate. Gilyarovsky did not last long in the military. After resigning his position (or being dismissed, there are alternative versions) to chase youthful visions of adventure, he wandered Russia for years. This included stints as a firefighter, factory worker, and with a circus. In 1875, on a stopover with the circus at a railroad siding in Tambov, almost by chance, he was invited to join a theater company. An actor whom he saved from a beating by a gang of Tambov street toughs took a liking to him and invited him to stay. He toured with the troupe until he again enrolled in the army, this time as a private, where he served in the Caucasus as a scout. He left the army in September 1878, and shortly thereafter returned to the provincial stage.

By the fall of 1881, 10 years after leaving home, Gilyarovsky had abandoned the theater and turned to writing. First he wrote poems for Moscow literary journals and some short notes for *Russian Newspaper*. He considered 1882 his first full year of journalism. By the time he was 30, Gilyarovsky was firmly established at *Russian Gazette* and had developed friends and acquaintances throughout Moscow's journalistic circles. In 1887, he prepared to publish *Slum People*, a collection of some of his early newspaper accounts of the frightful condition of Moscow's poor. The book had already been printed when it was seized and destroyed by the censors. In 1896, Gilyarovsky reported from the site of the notorious Khodynskoye Field disaster, in which thousands of people were crushed during celebrations of the coronation of Tsar Nicholas II (1868-1918). This article was probably his most widely read piece of journalism.

Throughout his life, Gilyarovsky enjoyed celebrating the Ukrainian Cossack blood and features that came to him by way of his paternal grandfather. In an introduction to the 1955 version of *Moscow and Muscovites*, Konstantin Paustovsky remarked that Gilyarovsky had both a Cossack soul and appearance. "Not for nothing, Repin used him as a model for one of the Cossacks writing a letter to the Turkish sultan, and the sculptor Andreyev worked from Gilyarovsky to create a bas-relief of Taras Bulba on the Gogol monument."[6] Soviet authorities used these looks in service of their efforts to formulate and propagandize a nationalities policy. His face, topped with a dramatic Cossack hat, adorned Soviet postage stamps.

In 1917, Gilyarovsky was 62. After the October Revolution, he mostly wrote about his past, primarily memoirs. Among those were *My Travels* (1928) and *Newspaper Moscow* (published posthumously), which covered the pre-revolutionary years. *Theater People*, a description of some of the famous individuals he worked with, and a behind-the-scenes look at their working world, was also published posthumously.

Gilyarovsky died in Moscow, at the age of 80, on October 1, 1935. He is buried on an estate near Vologda.

---

6. V. Gilyarovsky, *Москва и москвичи*, Moscow Worker, 1957, p. 4.

Translation & Editing Challenges

After even a cursory skim of Gilyarovsky's treasures, one might wonder why it took over 75 years for _Moscow and Muscovites_ to be translated into English. The first obstacle that comes to mind is that the work does not fit neatly into any of the academic or commercial categories used by translators and publishers, American or Soviet. While it is an account of modern Russian history by an eyewitness, even in the 1930s there were far better, more reliable primary sources for the historical questions that were considered most interesting. Indeed, most professional historiography was focused in those days more on politicians, diplomats, and policy than society and change. _Moscow and Muscovites_ has little in the way of political analysis, social criticism, religion, philosophy, or military or security matters. It is most certainly not fine literature, so ambitious young scholars in Russian language and literature would likely have considered it a waste of time. On the Soviet side, Gilyarovsky had little hope of state support. In those years, Soviet translation efforts were directed elsewhere, mostly aimed at producing series of selected classics: it is unlikely that Gilyarovsky was even considered. With nothing to offer the primary consumers of Russian-language materials, there was little incentive for a translation.

A second set of reasons for the delay in translation probably arose from a combination of politics and peer pressure: translators and publishers may not have wanted to be seen giving voice to an author who in any way could be seen as supporting the Bolsheviks. And, if an English translation of a Russian writer sympathetic to Communism faced any resistance in the 1920s and early 1930s, the Moscow show trials conducted in the late 1930s reduced the book's chances of finding an English language audience even further. While in-depth research in primary documents might add a few new or unexpected twists or complications to the translation tale, in the end Gilyarovsky's demise in 1936 left the text without a champion. It soon faded into obscurity in the West.

Translating _Moscow and Muscovites_ presented a number of challenges. Perhaps the toughest decision was how to treat the book's poetry. _Moscow and Muscovites_ leans on the genre, in places quite heavily, sometimes for added emotional depth, sometimes for a bit of humor or a change of pace. Like many Russians, Gilyarovsky was a poetry lover; indeed, his first published poem was a prizewinner.[7] In this book, he used a variety of works, quoted selectively or in their entirety, from a number of poets, including some unattributed works that most likely belong to him. He offers a wide spectrum of styles, from Shumacher's earthy humor to Pushkin's classic verse.

---

7. _Volga Boatmen_, Moscow, 1882.

I had originally planned to render all of the poetry in a simple, impressionistic style. However, the further I got through the draft translation, the more I understood just how important poetry was to Gilyarovsky. After reading a bit on poetry translation,[8] and pondering the tradeoffs among meter, rhyme, rhythm, and meaning, I experimented with a quick rendering of the amusing, four-line poem by P.G. Shumacher at the start of the chapter "Bakers and Barbers." Not completely unhappy with the result, and surprised at how much I enjoyed the process, I soon found myself working on a major, unanticipated sub-project. In the end, I translated the majority of the book's poetry in rhymed and metered text that conforms, I hope, with the sense and meaning of the original. Poetry enthusiasts are often quite passionate in their discussion and evaluation of a translation: to facilitate that process, the original Russian texts of the poems and songs are reproduced in an appendix. In some cases, for a variety of reasons, I opted for a free translation. Finally, as regards poetry translation, a personal observation: for me, the better the poet, the easier was the translation. While translating Pushkin, my pen flowed relatively freely. Translating weaker poets was never quite as easy. (Yet, of course, easier "flow" does not necessary indicate higher quality of the translation!)

In his prose, Gilyarovsky was both a journalist and a playwright. He had a nose for stories, chased down leads, beat deadlines, and quenched the public's thirst for news; thanks to years reporting on the street, he was thoroughly familiar with Moscow's character types. But he also was an actor, and his experience on the stage thoroughly informs this work. A reporter with an ear deaf to the drama found in the rhyme and rhythm of street talk, or with eyes blind to the subtleties of back-room body language and movement, could never have written this book. Vignettes with two or more characters are the heart of many of the book's most telling moments. Gilyarovsky uses chance meetings on the street, banter over card games, table talk, and other casual conversations to color his characters and tell his story. In these vignettes, one senses the timing, stagecraft, and sensibilities of a man who worked in and loved the theater. His personality, marked by an open and friendly conversational style much praised by his contemporaries, also shines through brightest in these bits.[9]

Especially because of my high regard for *Moscow and Muscovites*, it would be a mistake to hide my opinion of Gilyarovsky's prose: in places, it is weak. This may be due to poor editing, self-indulgence, or even his newspaper experience, but readers should know that Gilyarovsky, if translated in a direct fashion, would be difficult to follow. When challenged in the translation, I leaned toward readability and

---

8. K. Chukovsky, *Высокое искусство: Принципы художественного перевода,* Avalon, St. Petersburg, 2011. This version, first published in 1964, was developed over decades. For an English translation, see: Lauren G. Leighton, *The Art of Translation: Kornei Chukovsky's A High Art*, University of Tennessee, 1984.

9. It is said that most people – friends, acquaintances, near strangers – addressed him as Uncle Gilya.

understanding. I pruned sentences crippled by subordinate clauses run amok. Tense was often an issue. In cases of reported speech, English and Russian grammars are different. Unlike English, tenses do not change in Russian reported speech. I often left the original's present tense to preserve a thespian sense of "being there" that seemed vital to Gilyarovsky's illusion.

Finally, native speakers of English should know that *Moscow and Muscovites* is filled with street slang and vocabulary peculiar to old Moscow's criminal world: gamblers, scammers, thieves, convicts, exiles, prostitutes, police, and others. Regional and national accents further complicate the text. All this, combined with antique usage and elliptical speech, make *Moscow and Muscovites* a difficult read in the original for many near-native Russian speakers, and even native speakers unacquainted with the vocabulary and the times.

Remarks

This book is dedicated to Lyudmila V. Kareva (1958-2012). Lyuda (or Mila, to many) introduced me to the wonders of old Moscow in 1988-1989. Back then, she was a busy law student at Moscow State University, but took time to wander the streets of downtown and marvel with me at the city's architectural and cultural treasures. Lyuda was a dear friend and an extraordinarily private person, so I'll write no more, except to note that I am among the many that miss her daily. I would like to thank in this regard Maria Kareva, Lyuda's daughter, and a remarkable young woman. Maria offered me comfort and support when Lyuda passed away, at a time when she had her own sorrow to endure.

My translation of *Moscow and Muscovites* would never have happened without Michael R. Katz, whom I first met when I was a somewhat bewildered, potential Russian major in the early 1980s at Williams College. Michael, a tenured professor of Russian language and literature, helped me see opportunities I would have overlooked and find the path that led, with some significant wandering over the years, to the publication of this book. Michael graciously read and commented on a selected portion of this translation, for which I thank him.

Publisher Paul Richardson, a good friend since the days we spent in the 1980s sitting around various types of tables in grad school at Indiana University in Bloomington, planted the seed for this project. He even managed, in the face of fierce resistance, to teach me quite a bit about translation along the way! Any mistranslations, or other errors or omissions in the final version are, of course, my responsibility.

Nina Murray and Olga Kuzmina, both talented translators, were kind enough to read and comment on the manuscript at various stages of development. I especially appreciated Nina's expertise in the field of horses and carriages: try and find a specialist like that when you need one! I'd also like to know why she's so familiar with pickpocketing.

Karine Noack kindly and patiently proofread the document, twice, which by itself was invaluable. While her sharp eyes did find the occasional typo, her experience as a translator of four languages (none of them Slavic!), language teacher, editor, and writer informed her extraordinarily helpful comments.

Lydia Stone, a poetry translator, deserves special thanks. She played a pivotal role helping me decide how to treat the poetry in *Moscow and Muscovites*. Her insightful and friendly criticism emboldened me to attempt fully-rhymed and metrical translation. In addition to expressing my gratitude for her comments on my work here, I also thank her in advance for the hours of fun I'll have with poetry translation in the future.

This translation was funded by a grant from the Institute of Translation in Moscow, and I thank them for the opportunity their support has afforded. Dedicated to the support and promotion of Russia's literary legacy, the Institute funds numerous initiatives every year both inside and outside of Moscow.

Last and most of all, I would like to thank for their support all of the members of the Kiernan clan, stretching from Boston to Bangkok. My niece and nephew, Emily and Matthew, were always there with a kind word or a smile. Ellen and Alex, my daughter and son, contributed to this project from start to finish, even typing the odd sentence or two; most importantly, they endured, politely, and (usually) with sympathy, my constant chatter about "the translation."

Brendan Kiernan
Middletown, Rhode Island
October 2013

Editor's Note: This volume employs the transcription system used by *Russian Life* magazine, which emphasizes simplicity and readibility in English. For more information, visit the *Russian Life* website (russianlife.com). Additional efforts were made to make the text more readable for non-Russian speakers. Thus, throughout the book *ulitsa* is street, *bulvar* is boulevard, *bani* are baths, etc. In addition, for consistency, names of streets and in most cases institutions, were left in transcribed (not translated) form, with their adjectival endings in nominative form.

Red Square in the early 1900s. Lobnoye Mesto, the execution and proclamation spot, is the circular object in front of St. Basil's Cathedral, on the left.

FROM THE AUTHOR

I AM A MUSCOVITE! HAPPY is one who can say that word, including in it his entire essence. I am a Muscovite!

… Bygone times pass before my eyes…

I quote Pushkin's Pimen,[1] but I am incomparably richer: against the colorful background of a past I know well, a past already fading and disappearing forever, I see a new Moscow emerging, not by the day, but by the hour. It is expanding, pushing both up and down, up into the heretofore unknown stratosphere, and down into the Metro's underground depths, illuminated by electricity, in wondrous halls shining with marble.

The Moscow River, "clothed in granite," is now edged by shaded boulevards.[2] Broad stone staircases run down to the water. Soon, the steps will be washed by new waves: every day the Volga River gets closer to Moscow.[3]

Long ago, at the present location of this stone staircase, in the swamps across from the Kremlin, Stenka Razin was executed and his head stuck on a pole.[4] Here, where only recently, within my living memory, lay swamps, there are now paved roads, straight and broad. Uneven rows of small old houses are being replaced by new, huge apartment buildings. First-class factories are going up one after another.

---

1. The Pimen character is a chronicler in Alexander Pushkin's play, *Boris Godunov*, written in 1825, primarily in blank verse, and published in 1831, but not approved by the censor for public performance until 1866.
2. An allusion to Pushkin's poem *Bronze Horseman* and the granite-clothed banks of the Neva.
3. The Moscow Canal, named the Moscow-Volga Canal until 1947, connects the Moscow and Volga Rivers. Prisoners built it under Stalin from 1932-1937.
4. Stenka Razin (1630-1671), the Cossack leader of an uprising in Southern Russia. The execution site is on Red Square, just north of the Moscow River

The city's edges, recently rotting, have merged with the center, and are almost its equal. Nearby villages are merging into the capital. Stadiums are being built in these new areas, Moscow's coliseums, where tens and hundreds of thousands of healthy youths train their bodies, preparing for heroic deeds in the Arctic ice, the lifeless desert of Kara Kum, on the Roof of the World, and on the glaciers of the Caucasus.

Moscow is becoming part of the Plan.[5] But to build a new Moscow in place of the old, a city that for almost a thousand years was cobbled together in pieces convenient for its builders, new, unprecedented powers are needed. This became possible only in a country where Soviet power prevailed.[6]

Moscow is already on its way to becoming the world's foremost city. This we can see already.

... The future passes before my eyes...

And bygone times pass before my eyes... Even now, the past is in many ways incomprehensible to the young, and soon it will disappear entirely. If the inhabitants of a new capital are to understand the labor it cost their forefathers to build a new life in place of the old, they need to understand what old Moscow was like, and what kind of people lived there.

And so "in my older years I live anew" two lives: an "old" and a "new." The old, as a background for the new, will reflect its majesty. My work makes me young and happy, as one who survived and who now lives...

... on the border of two centuries
at the fracture of two worlds.[7]

Moscow, December 1934
V. GILYAROVSKY

---

5. Stalin's first five year plan started in 1928; these were centralized, national economic plans.
6. A soviet, or "council" was a grassroots form of representation co-opted as a fig leaf by the Bolsheviks, while in reality they ran the show.
7. *Boris Godunov: A Drama in Verse,* Alexander Pushkin, translated by Alfred Hayes, release date: February, 2004 [EBook #5089], updated: August 10, 2012.

IN MOSCOW

OUR HALF-EMPTY TRAIN STOPPED AT a darkened, outdoor platform at Yaroslavl Station.[1] We stepped out into the square, avoiding shouting carriage drivers who assaulted the well-to-do passengers and considered us unworthy of their attention. We marched, slipping and tripping, along an uneven path hidden by snow, not seeing anything either beneath our feet or right in front of us. The snow, untouched by any wind, fell in thick flakes, and through this moving veil we could at times make out some bright spots. Only after bumping into a wooden post did I realize that it was a street lamp that lit up only its own glass, covered by thick snow.

We walked with our baggage on our shoulders. Occasionally, passengers who had managed to get a cab passed. But soon even those were gone. Complete silence, not a soul, and white snow floating off into the mysterious and invisible distance. We knew only our journey's goal – Lefortovo, or, as our guide, a native Muscovite, said, "Lafortovo." "Hey, here's Ryazan Station," he declared, indicating the darkened silhouette of a long, unlit building topped with a bright round area; it turned out that this was the clock, glowing from within, showing 1:30 am.[2]

We passed other stations. We crawled through snowdrifts and marched down narrow alleys, along fences separating small wooden houses with gates locked tight. Here and there, the yellow-red of a small lamp shone through tiny windows. Darkness, silence, deepest sleep. In the distance a bell struck twice – 2:00 a.m. "That's on Basmannaya Street," my guide explained, "and this neighborhood is Olkhovets."

Out of nowhere, a rooster crowed: "Cock a doodle doo!" We were struck dumb: had the creature lost its mind? Again it crowed... Almost immediately, first in one

---

1. Anyone who has travelled on Russia's trains recognizes this scene even today.
2. Today, the area has a huge confluence of railroad infrastructure.

Red Square.

yard and then at the neighbors', roosters answered the call. Surprised by this untimely sound, dogs started barking, at first frightened, then angrily. Olkhovets came to life. Here and there lights appeared in windows. Bolts were thrown back, doors slammed, and surprised voices could be heard: "What kind of craziness is this? Two o'clock in the morning and the roosters are crowing!"

My friend Kostya Chernov burst out barking like a dog; he was good at it. Then he started howling like a wolf. We joined him. You could hear the dogs pulling at their chains, furious. By then we were marching happily along Basmannaya Street, pitch dark and completely empty. Occasionally, we tripped on posts covered by soft snow. Another square. A big streetlight illuminated something above us that looked like a window with dark and mysterious figures.

"This neighborhood is Razgulyai, and this was the home of Sorcerer Bruce," Kostya explained.[3]

That is how Moscow first greeted me in October of 1873.

---

3. James Daniel Bruce, a Scottish scientist, engineer and advisor in the court of Peter the Great. He founded Russia's first observatory and led a navigational school located in Sukharevka Tower. He was reputed to be Russia's "first Mason"; rumors associated him with black magic, likely driven by his activities in the sciences.

FROM LEFORTOVO TO KHAMOVNIKI

ON THE DAY AFTER I first arrived in Moscow, I had to go from Lefortovo to Tyoply Alley in Khamovniki.[1] I had just enough money in my pocket, two 20- kopek pieces and some lesser coins. The weather made boots useless. The sidewalks were iced over, uncleared, with large piles of frozen snow. Winter had not yet set in.

On the corner of Gorokhovaya Street, there was one and only one driver, an old man in a caftan, belted with the remains of a worn out rein, in a red sheepskin cap with a scrap of frayed rope sticking out like a feather. A pot-bellied, winter-coated horse was harnessed to a sleigh – a wooden undercarriage with a low seat in back for passengers and a board fastened in front for the driver. The reins were rope. The driver had a whip on his belt.

"All right grandpa, off to Khamovniki!"

"Where, exactly?"

"Tyoply Alley."

"Twenty kopeks."

I thought that was too much.

"Ten."

He thought that was far too little. I walked away. He moved after me.

"My final word, 15 kopeks? I gotta get a fare…"

After about 10 more steps he spoke again, "My final word, 12 kopeks…"

"Fine."

The driver lashed the horse. We slid with ease, sometimes on snow, sometimes on bare, wet cobbles, thanks to the sleigh's country-style, iron-less runners. They slid and did not cut like city sleighs; the tradeoff, at all the high and low spots of

---

1. Roughly five miles as the crow flies. Novodevichy Convent is in Khamovniki.

the humped streets the frame pitched and rolled, pulling the horse sideways while bumping the sleigh's sides against the ice and snow piled at the base of wooden posts lining the curb. You had to hold fast to keep from flying out.

The driver stole a look back. "You're not gonna run off on me are you? It happens, you know: you drive, drive and they run off through a gate – poof!"

"Where could I run? This is my first day in Moscow."

"Tsk, tsk," he complained along the way. "I wanted to use the boss's 'guitar' because the bridges to the Kremlin are clear."

"A what? A 'guitar'?"

"Well, yeah, a 'guitar.' A *koliber*." Look over there, that kind."

A strange carriage pulled by a winter-coated, small horse like ours was turning out of an alley. It truly was some kind of guitar on wheels, with a driver's seat in front. On this "guitar" rode a merchant's wife in a fur-collared winter coat, her face and legs turned to the left, and a clerk in a buttoned cap with a briefcase, turned to the right, facing us. That's the first time I saw a *koliber*, even at that time giving way to the *droshky*, a tall carriage with a body that shook while moving; its rear section sat on tall, semi-circular springs.[2] Later, *droshky* were made with flatter springs and became known as "fliers." We rode down Nemetskaya Street. The driver spoke up:

> This horse... tomorrow it's going to the country. Yesterday, at the horse market on Ilyushin Street, I bought a Kirghiz horse for 40 rubles. Gentle. Four years old. She'll last forever. Last week, a wagon train showed up with fish from the Volga. Well, Moscow traders bought some of their horses, and then charged us drivers twice as much, but on credit. Every Monday you pay three rubles. Easy, huh? That's how all the drivers get what they need. Siberians transport goods to Moscow and sell half of their horses.

We crossed the Ring Road. At Zemlyanny Embankment, there was turmoil. Down every street, drivers, coachmen, and teamsters lashed their horses and jammed in right up to the sidewalks. My driver stopped at a corner on the Ring Road. Sleigh bells rang in the distance. The driver turned to me, frightened, and whispered:

"*Caw-yers*! Look!"[3]

The sleigh bells were close. Steps and shouts could be heard. Coming from Sukharevka Street, two beautiful, matching red *troikas* tore wildly down the Ring Road. Both had long distance drivers in hats with peacock feathers. They were clicking and whistling and swinging whips. The *troikas* carried identical passengers: on the left a gendarme in a grey cloak, and on the right a young man in street clothes. The speeding *troikas* flashed by and the street resumed its usual appearance.

"Who was that?" I asked.

---

2. *Droshky*, from the Russian verb дрожать (*drozhat*), to shake.

3. Courier (курьер): the old driver does his best to pronounce this French cognate, *courrier*.

Lubyanskaya Square, the capital's busiest and smelliest square. The watering fountain is visible on left.

"Gendarmes. Hauling from Peter to Siberia.[4] Probably some sort of important prisoners. Novikov, the son, is driving the first one. That's his best *troika*, a *caw-yer*. I was parked next to Novikov on the square and got an eyeful."

The gendarme had a huge moustache. Next to him sat a pale Lithuanian, maybe 19 years old. The scene reminded me of Nekrasov, a living illustration of his poetry.[5]

"They're being taken to exile in Siberia. They went up against the tsar," explained the old man in a whisper, turning and leaning toward me.

At the Ilyinsky Gate, he pointed out the broad square. There were dozens of carriages hitched to mangy, yet powerfully built horses. Ragged drivers and sleigh owners milled around. Some haggled with potential customers, some were seating passengers: off to Ostankino, to Krestovsky Gate, and Petrovsky Park, to which the sleds had set routes. A church choir was boarding; the singers arguing in bass and treble could be heard clear across the square.

"Maybe going to a wedding or a funeral," my driver explained, and then added; "now we'll go to Lubyanka and water the horse. Give me a kopek: water is on the passenger's fare."

I did as he required.

---

4. Peter is used as slang for Petersburg even today.
5. Nikolai Alexeyevich Nekrasov (1821-1877) was a Russian poet, writer, critic and publisher. The intelligentsia acclaimed his poems about Russian peasants.

"There they are, the cursed! They don't let folks with their own buckets get to the spigot. You have to pay the guard in the shack a kopek. They split the money with the bosses."

Lubyanskaya Square is of one of the city's hubs. Across from Mosolov's (on the corner of Greater Lubyanka Street) is a market for antedeluvian rental carriages that had been used to transport the dead. In the same place, some better-looking carriages were parked, rentals for visiting traders and dealers without their own rides. The entire sidewalk, from Myasnitskaya Street to Lubyanskaya Square, across from the drivers' Gusensky Tavern, was filled: horses, muzzles to the street, carriage to the sidewalk. Feedbags covered their muzzles, or nets with hay poking out hung from a rig. Horses ate while their masters drank tea. Thousands of sparrows and pigeons flitted fearlessly beneath the horses' legs, pecking oats.

Drivers ran out of the tavern to the fountain, blue shirts unbuttoned, with buckets. They paid the guard a kopek, dredged water with a dirty bucket, and gave it to the horses. They threw themselves on pedestrians, proposing their services, praising their horses, addressing each, and judging by their clothes, called some "Trader," some "Your Health," some "Your Grace," and some "Your Excellency"!

Noise, hubbub, and cursing became one loud roar covering peals of thunder from carriages, carts, and wagons, while water carriers crossed the cobbled path through the square. Lines of water carriers waited, circling the fountain, waving ladles and buckets on long poles, scooping water, and filling their barrels above the sculptor Vitali's bronze figures. [6]

Across from the Prolomny Gate, dozens of drivers sat like statues on their seats, then, as if on command, rushed to surround some customer who'd come looking for a cart. They shouted, they cursed. In the end, by consensus, they set a price, even though only one driver would be hired, and then only one way. But for the customer the deal wasn't done yet, and he could hire a driver that gave a better price. The drivers circled-up, and each threw a marked kopek into a hat. The customer drew a coin – someone's good luck – and left with its owner.

While my driver waited in line for a bucket, I took a good look at everything and was struck by the bustle, the noise, and the general disorder of Moscow's busiest square. Also, as an aside, its worst smelling.

We went down the hill and around roped-off Theater Square, then through Hunter's Row and Mokhovaya Street. We went up the hill along Vozdvizhenka Street. On Arbat Street, a carriage with huge springs and a coat of arms thundered past. A grey-haired lady sat inside. On the sideboards, next to the driver, stood a footman with sideburns, in a top hat with a ribbon, and a uniform with large, bright buttons. At the back of the carriage, on toeholds, stood two

---

6. Ivan Petrovich Vitali (1794-1855), a Russian sculptor of Italian descent from Saint Petersburg. His best known work, mentioned in the next chapter, is in front of the Bolshoi Theater.

more footmen, clean-shaven, in long coats and top hats with ribbons. Trailing the carriage, hitched to a trotter, a government dandy proudly sported a beaver-collared cloak and a feathered tricorn hat, barely able to fit his ample body onto the narrow seat, which at the time was called an egotist.

THEATER SQUARE

TRAMS RUMBLED. ALL LIT UP, the square seemed to move and suddenly stop, as thousands of people turned their heads: squadrons of planes raced across Moscow – at times like a flock of geese, at times shifting their formation like bits of glass in a kaleidoscope. Next to me, near the entrance to the Maly Theater, sat the only bronze building owner in Moscow, wearing the same rabbit-hair robe that warmed him while writing *Wolves and Sheep*.[1] On the wall near the entrance, I saw an advertisement for this play and was carried off to the distant past.

Sinking its iron wheels into uncleared snow, dipping into ruts, an ancient theater carriage crawled up to the theater's entrance. A driver in a colorful caftan and hat, with a bandaged cheek, swayed on his bench. He clicked, then tugged the reins on a pair of dappled nags that may never have seen a groom, the kind of horses about which Pasha Bogatyrev, a singer popular at the time, crooned tearful ballads:

You, too, once were fine steeds
Your drivers, tempted to speeds...

In the 1880s, Theater Square's girlish innocence had to be compromised. Here's why. The clear-watered Neglinka River[2] had been captured in a steel pipe and flushed through a substandard sewer system, sluicing filth into the Moscow

---

1. The Maly Theater, literally "small" theater, as opposed to the Bolshoi or "grand" opera house, was founded in 1806 and has operated at its current site since 1824; Gilyarovsky refers to a statue of Alexander Nikolayevich Ostrovsky (1823-1886), who wrote 47 plays, many of which are still performed frequently.
2. The Neglinnaya River (also variously called Neglinka, Neglinna, Neglina, Samoteka) is an underground river in central Moscow, a tributary of the Moscow River. In ancient times it flowed naturally from north to south through the center of the city, approximately five miles. It flooded as recently as 1973.

Theater Square and the Bolshoi Theater, early 1900s. The Maly is just out of the frame on the right.

River and infecting its water. Over the years, the pipe collected debris but was never cleaned, and after every major downpour water filled the streets, squares, and ground floors of buildings on Neglinnaya Street. Afterwards, the waters would recede, leaving foul-smelling silt on the street and sewage-filled cellars. It was like this for years until anyone thought to find the reason. As it turned out, bends in the pipe (there were two, one under the corner of the Maly Theater and another on the square, under a fountain decorated with figures by the sculptor Vitali) were clogged with city trash. Natural subsurface swamps surrounding the square had nowhere to go.

They began reconstruction of Neglinnaya Street and they discovered a mess. Piles had to be driven into the square. They placed three tall posts in the ground, trucked in a 600-pound cast-iron pile driver, lowered it into place – and burst out in song! Crowds of people hurried to listen.

"Hey, let's sing *Dubinushka*, hey let's do *Green*."[3]

The work gang raised the cast iron giant and drove a pile. The more people that gathered, the livelier the workers; like actors, they loved to sing and play to a good crowd. As the performer gathered energy, he sang about whatever he saw. He glimpsed a plump, respectable matron, and in a falsetto, articulating each word, belted out:

---

3. *Dubinushka* is best known in the United States as the *Song of the Volga Boatmen*, about harnessed laborers who dragged ships up-river. In the United States, cartoons popularized the tune, which took on a variety of clever lyrics.

The matron wore a dress so long,
But out from under came a...[4]

He concluded with a rhyme coarse enough that the respectable matron, faced with the ensuing catcalls and laughter, would rather have fallen through the earth. The singer then saw a young dandy in a top hat:

The dandy's shirt, so white in color,
But the tailor knows, he has no other.

Spring flood in the capital.

The crowd roared, and the crowd grew. The singer was done, but the gang boss demanded, "Come on and try, Pimples, give us another!"
The singer dusted himself off and added:

While in the yard barks a mutt,
The boss man sits and rubs his gut!

---

4. This is what is known as a *chastushka*, a two to four line, typically light-hearted (and often saucy) song.

The crowd laughed.

"All right, Pimples, time for lunch."

They sang *Dubinushka* while they were driving piles in the same spot, in the unseen depths, where the subway now runs. A subway had been discussed in the Moscow City Council more than once, but without conviction. The City Fathers felt that the theft and bribery involved would lead to such a "Panama" that no amount of money would ever be enough.[5] "They will steal everything; nothing sensible will come of it." Some old priest told his flock one Sunday that, "for our sins we will be sent to Hell."[6] "Sinners" believed him and were frightened at the prospect of underground tunnels. In any event, armed only with a song, and no technology, it *would* have been a good idea to get out of town.

---

5. A French company's effort to build a canal across the Isthmus of Panama, starting in 1881, failed miserably. Bonds sold to finance the effort, touted by the company and many others as fail-safe, became worthless.
6. Literally, here, "the Underworld."

KHITROVKA

KHITROV MARKET SOMEHOW ALWAYS SEEMED to me like London, a place I had never seen. But London always seemed to me the most mysterious place in Europe and Khitrov Market, doubtless, was the most mysterious place in Moscow. It was a spacious square in the center of the capital, close to the Yauza River, surrounded by hard-used stone buildings. It was lowland, reached by descending through alleys, like following streams into a swamp. The place fogged constantly. Especially toward evening, when it was a bit dark, or after a rain, you'd look down from the top of an alley – terror seized a clear mind – the cloud moved! You walked down through the alley into a writhing, rotten pit.

Crowds of street people wandered through the gloom, moving in and out of sight under lamps obscured by evening mist as thick as steam in the *banya*.[1] Food vendors sat in rows on enormous cast iron or fired clay benches with spoiled sausages sizzling on iron braziers, and hot broth, most often called "Dog's Delight." The "gourmets" of Khitrov Market loved to treat themselves to discarded food. "This was a grouse!" drooled some has-been. Less demanding folks ate rotten potatoes with spoiled *salo*,[2] cheeks, throat, or lungs wrapped in tripe with the unwashed greens contained in the stomach, or a small piece of sliced poultry known as a "grouse."

All around, clouds of steam rushed out of the briefly opened doors of shops and taverns and mingled with the gloom, which of course was fresher and clearer than the air inside, filled with tobacco smoke, the slightly corrosive stink of foot rags, human breath, and over-warm vodka. Two and three story buildings around the square were filled with flophouses, where, in all, ten thousand people could find spots for

---

1. A *banya* is a traditional Russian steam bath. Gilyarovsky has much more to say on this topic in the eponymous chapter that begins on page 264.
2. *Salo*, sliced animal fat, is still served (salted, smoked, fried, etc.) throughout Russia.

Khitrov Market and the pavillion.

the night. The owners of these buildings earned enormous profits. Lodgers paid five kopeks per night, but a "room" went for 20 kopeks. Under the bottom bunks, which were a bit over two feet off the floor, was a spot for two; the top and bottom shared a hanging reed mat. The space two and a half feet high and four feet wide was a "room" where people spent the night with no bedding except their own rags.

Groups of workers arrived at Khitrovka and went directly to find places under a huge pavilion. Mornings, contractors showed up and led groups of laborers off to work. After noon, the pavilion was controlled by the Khitrovka Market regulars and street traders: the latter bought up anything they could get their hands on. Wretches sold their clothes and shoes, took them right off, and in place of their boots put on *lapty*[3] or sandals pieced together from shoe leather scraps. They exchanged their clothes for knee-length rags, their bodies showing through.

Flophouses went by the names of their owners: Bunin's, Rumyantsev's, Stepanov's (then Yaroshenko's), and Romeyko's (later Kulakov's). Rumyantsev's had two taverns, Exile, and Siberia, and Yaroshenko's had Hard Time. The names, of course, sound gritty, but were accepted around Khitrovka. Exile served the homeless, the poor, and street traders. Siberia was a step up: thieves, pickpockets, and fences. But Hard Time was in a class by itself, a den for the wild and drunken depraved, a market for thieves and runaways. A "round tripper" returning from Siberia or prison would never pass by this place. A new arrival, if he really was "in the business" was greeted here with honor. He was "put to work" immediately. Police records confirm that the majority of escapees from Siberia were arrested in Moscow, right there in Khitrovka Square.

In the last century, Khitrovka was a sad spectacle. There was no light in its labyrinth of alleys and intersections, or in the sagging, half-destroyed stairways leading to every floor of the flophouses. Locals could find their way while strangers had no reason to be there. In truth, no lawful authority dared trespass in those murky depths.

All of Khitrovka Market was run by two local cops, Rudnikov and Lokhmatkin. The "riff-raff" truly feared only these cops' heavy fists, and the "professionals" were friendly with both of these representatives of authority. On the way back from a Siberian labor camp, or after escaping from prison, they first went to pay respects to the two cops. Both knew all the criminals on sight, having studied them throughout a quarter century of ceaseless toil. Besides, there was nowhere to hide from these two: and, in any case, their neighbors would report that so and so had returned to such and such an apartment.

Khitrovka's ruler stood at his post drawing on a pipe and saw that someone, hiding their face, is pushing their way through the square along the wall.

"*Boldokh*!" thundered the cop.[4]

The figure, tearing off his hat, approached.

"Hello, Fedot Ivanovich!"

"Where are you coming from?"

"From Nerchinsk. Just crawled in yesterday. Please pardon me, I still..."

---

3. *Lapty*: traditional footwear woven from strips of bark, see photo, opposite page.
4. *Boldokh* is slang for someone just returned from exile or prison.

"Just so... Look at me, Seryozha, you had better behave like a schoolboy, or else..."

"I haven't heard anything yet... My people..."

Major Case Detective V.F. Keizer once asked Rudnikov, "Is it true that you recognize on sight all of the criminal fugitives in Khitrovka, but don't arrest them?"

"That's why I've been able to stay at my post for 20 years, otherwise I wouldn't have lasted a day. They'd have knifed me.[5] Of course I know them all."

The Khitrovka regulars "flourished" under such rule. Rudnikov was one of a kind. Even runaways from the labor camps considered him fair, and for this reason alone he was not killed, though he sometimes was hit and wounded making arrests. They did not hurt him in anger, but only to save their own hides. Each had his own task: one caught and jailed, one hid and ran. Such was the logic of exile.

Poor women at the turn of the century, wearing *lapty*.

All of Khitrovka feared Rudnikov like fire:

"If you give him a chance, he'll grab you."

"If they order him, he'll find you."

In 20 years as a cop among street people and fugitives, Rudnikov worked out his own special view, "An exile, a thief, a poor man, a bum, they're all people. Everyone wants to live. Otherwise, what? If it was me against them? Could you catch them all? Catch one, others will show up. You have to live life!"[6]

While roaming the slums as a crime reporter, I often ran across Rudnikov, and was always amazed by his ability to find clues where it seemed there was nothing. I remember one of our typical meetings. On a rainy September evening, I was with my friend, the actor Vasya Grigoriyev, visiting acquaintances on Pokrovsky Boulevard. Around 11, we were getting ready to leave when we learned that Grigoriyev's summer coat had disappeared from a hanger. Judging by the evidence, a thief had crawled in through an open window, put it on, and walked out the door. The neighbors' doing. From Khitrovka. This had become commonplace.

---

5. The verb here, пришить, in criminal slang means "to stab."
6. As Rudnikov sketches a philosophy, his uneducated speech stands out.

"They forgot to lock the window," said the old cook.

Vasya almost cried – the coat was new. I comforted him, "If they were from Khitrovka, we'll find it."

We said goodbye to our hosts and went to the Third Precinct of the Myasnitskaya Division. An old, mustachioed desk officer, Colonel Shidlovsky, was in the habit of staying at the precinct until midnight; we found him and told him of our misfortune.

"If it was our local boys, we'll get the coat in no time. Call Rudnikov. He's on duty!"

An enormous, athletic figure with a grey moustache and fists the size of watermelons appeared. We gave him the details on the theft.

"Locals! We'll find it straight away. You should come with me, but let him stay here. You'll recognize the coat?"

Vasya set to waiting, and Rudnikov and I went to Khitrovka, to Bunin's. Rudnikov summoned the night watchman. They whispered.

"Well, there's nothing here. Let's move on!"

Pitch black. Grime. Only the windows of the Hard Time tavern glowed dimly. Red flames gleamed through the sooty glass while mist rushed out now and again through the door. We got to the courtyard at Rumyantsev's, went straight up to the second floor, and turned left toward the first door.

"26!" shouted someone, and everyone in the flophouse jumped into motion.[7]

In the far corner, a window opened, and, one after another, three loud blows rang out, as if a sheet-iron roof had fallen.

"'Signaling," Rudnikov explained and shouted across the room: "Don't be afraid, devils! I'm alone. I'm not going to arrest anyone. I'm just stopping by..."

"Why scare us for nothing?" a red headed brute took offense. He had the look of a soldier and had been getting ready to jump out the window onto the roof of a shed.

"I'll give you one right in the mug, Stepka."

"For what, Fedot Ivanovich?"

"Because I didn't tell you to come up to me in Khitrovka. Go wherever the hell you please, just stay out from under my nose. They're looking for you. A second escape... I won't be able to do anything."

"I'm going... Look, over there, my 'kitten' just called..." and he winked at a girl with a black eye.

"Beat it. Get the hell out of here! Out of my sight! And who was signaling in the window? A greenie? Hey, *boldokh*, answer!"[8] Silence.

"Who was it? I'm asking! Why are you silent? What do you think I am, a detective or something? Well, was it a greenie? Talk! Come on, I saw his bad leg."

---

7. In criminal slang, "26" is code for "Watch out, an overseer/cop is coming!"
8. Escapees from prison or those recently back from Siberia were also called "greenie".

The *boldokh* was silent. Rudnikov wound up and gave him the cruelest possible slap in the face.

Getting up off the floor, through tears, the *boldokh* said, "You could have asked me right away, instead of all this blabbing… Oh well, it was a greenie!"

"To hell with him! If he turns up, tell him I'll arrest him. Tell him to clear out. Understand me, devils. If they order me to come back and search, I'll only arrest one of you. And if they don't send me, it's your good luck, sleep the night. I'm not here to bother you. Run upstairs and tell those fools not to signal from the window, or the third floor will take a beating too. I'm going up. Is he home?"

"He's asleep, I guess!"

We stepped into one of the upstairs "rooms." The same thing happened there: the window opened and a figure flashed by and disappeared into the air. The *boldokh* hadn't yet alerted this "room." I ran to the open window. Below me yawned the courtyard, a figure crept along the wall. Rudnikov looked below.

"That's Stepka Wayvin! They nicknamed him Wayvin because he is the best at signaling from the roof."

"Him?"

"That's Vaska Churkin's brother, Chamber Pot, not Wayvin," came a deep bass voice from under a bunk.

"Well, no, that *is* Wayvin. And is that you Lavrov? Come out from under there, show yourself to the gentleman."

"This is our deacon," said Rudnikov, speaking to me.

From under the bunk crawled a barefoot man in a dirty, woman's shirt with short sleeves that showed off a powerful neck and huge shoulders.

"Bless you, Fedot Ivanovich, Bless you!" thundered Lavrov, but after taking a shot in the puss, he crawled back under the bunk.

"He was in the cathedral choir, a seminarian. See what he's come to? Quiet down you devils!" Rudnikov shouted, and we started up the narrow wooden stairway to the attic. Downstairs, the deacon continued intoning a blessing.

Up we went. Darkness. We stopped by the door. Rudnikov tried it – locked. One huge fist knocked, and the door shook. Silence. He knocked harder still. The door cracked open the width of the little iron chain, and a tenant appeared, a fence.

"What do you want? Who are you?"

A fist was raised, someone squealed, and the door opened.

"Why the rough stuff? I'm human too."

"Well if you're human, where is the coat that Choir Boy Sasha brought you today?"

"Why are you bothering me at night? Nobody brought me any coat."

"If you'll just step back, I'll take a look," Rudnikov said to me, and while the door was closing, cries again could be heard. Then, everything went quiet. Rudnikov came out carrying the coat. "Here it is! The cursed devil hid it in the bottom trunk and piled five more trunks on top of it."

That was Rudnikov.

Sometimes there were police sweeps, but they just gave the appearance of a search: police would surround a building, calmly and methodically arrest the riff-raff, but the real, seasoned crooks never fell into the trap.

The police never butted into Kulakovka. Kulakovka was not one building, but a row of houses in Kulakov's vast holdings between Khitrovka Square and Svininsky Alley. The first building, its narrow side facing the square, was called The Iron. A most gloomy row of three-story, foul smelling buildings was called Dry Ravine, and all taken together were called The Pigsty. It belonged to the well-known collector Svinin, and the alley was named after him as well. This was also a source of nicknames for the inhabitants, known as Irons and Wolves of the Dry Ravine.

Periodic sweeps netted petty crooks, those without internal passports, the poor, and those refused residency. The very next day they were sorted out; those without passports or permission to live in Moscow were sent back through transfer prisons to their legal residences, usually in nearby regions, but they were back in Moscow in a week. They would arrive in a convoy somewhere like Zaraysk, sign-in at the local police station, and head back that night. The poor, and petty crooks who turned out to be Muscovites or from its suburbs, would be back on Khitrovka the next day, only to go about their usual affairs until the next sweep.

What could they do in some quiet little town? No "jobs." Everyone was afraid to let you stay a night, and there was no place to pay for a bed, so they went to Moscow and caroused on Khitrovka. In the capital, you could steal, abuse charity, and rob flophouse newcomers; after luring some inexperienced, homeless wretch from the street, you'd take him down into an underground passage, bash him in the side of the head, and strip him naked. Only in Moscow could you have such a life. Where else could they go with a "wolf's" passport?[9] You couldn't find work; you couldn't find a place to sleep.

I studied the slums for many years and often visited Khitrovka Market, made friends there. They never held back around me and called me "newspaper guy." Many of my literary colleagues asked me to take them to Khitrovka and show them the slums, but none of them ever agreed to go into Dry Ravine or even The Iron. We'd walk past the gate, go down a few steps into a dim underground corridor, and they would ask to go back.

Khitrovka made no bigger impression on any writer than on Gleb Ivanovich Uspensky.[10] Working at the *Russian Register*, I often met with Gleb Ivanovich. We

9. Slang for a passport without a valid residence stamp. Russia has used internal passports in one form or another since the fifteenth century to control vagrants, the poor, and the peasantry.
10. Gleb Ivanovich Uspensky (1843-1902), known mainly for his short stories was praised by Tolstoy, Chekhov, and Gorky.

spent a good deal of time together, both as a pair and in groups, dined together, and shared evenings. Once, Gleb Ivanovich and I were having lunch, and over a glass of wine the conversation turned to the slums.

"Oh, how I would like to see the famous Khitrovka Market and people who have 'crossed the Rubicon' of life. I'd like to, but I'm afraid. It would be great if we went together!"

I, of course, was happy to do this for Gleb Ivanovich, and after seven that evening (this was in October) we pulled up to Solyanka. We left the carriage and set out on foot through the dirty square, cloaked in an autumn fog, through which flickered dim tavern windows and street vendor lights. We stopped for a moment near the vendors. Half-clothed street people would run up, buy some stinking food, argue without fail over a kopek or the size of a portion, eat, and run off to a flophouse.

Food vendors, those surviving scraps of existence, all sweaty and dirty, sat on their spots, warming the food with body heat to keep it from cooling, and yelling in a frenzy, "N-n-n-noodles! Fresh jell—ied beef! Boiled pork!"

"Hey, old soldier, beat it or I'll cut your throat for spare change," croaked a rough looking older woman with traces of youthful mistakes showing on her pock-marked face.

"My throat you say? Where's your nose?"

"Nose? What good to me is a nose?"[11]

Then, in another voice, she sang out, "Hot kidneys and spleen! Scraps!"

"Well, give me a bit of everything, seven kopeks worth."

The vendor stood, opened the big, greasy pot cover, and with dirty hands pulled out a portion and put it in the customer's palm.

"Stir up a kopek's worth," ordered a tramp in a military cap with a pin.

"What misfortune! What misfortune!" whispered Gleb Ivanovich, following it all with keen eyes while fearfully leaning toward me.

"Now, Gleb Ivanovich, let's drop by Hard Time and then go to the Exile, and then to Siberia."

"What do you mean Hard Time?"

"In Khitrov slang it's the name of a tavern. This one right here!"

Past the vendors, we came to the narrow door of the small tavern at Yaroshenko's.

"Should we go in?" Gleb Ivanovich asked, taking me by the arm.

"Of course!"

I opened the door. Out rushed a rank smell and an unholy racket. Noise, cursing, fights, the stink of dirty dishes. We were heading to a table when a woman rushed right at us, heading for the door, shrieking, with a bloodied face. Following right behind was a huge lug shouting, "Ugly cuss!" The woman made it to the street, but

---

11. The missing nose is perhaps the result of street crime, or could be a sign of an advanced case of syphilis, for which there was no effective treatment anywhere until penicillin became available in the 1940s.

Gleb Uspensky.

her man had already been stopped, and was lying on the floor. He had been "pacified." This took a matter of seconds.

In the cloud of mist condensed by the cold, no one paid us any attention. We sat at an empty, dirty table. Up walked a familiar buffet attendant, a future millionaire and real estate maven. I ordered half a bottle of vodka, and a couple of hard-boiled eggs to go with it. This was all that I ever ordered in the slums. I wiped the glasses with a clean piece of paper, poured the vodka, peeled an egg, and clinked glasses with Gleb Ivanovich, whose hands shook and eyes showed fear and discomfort. I tossed down two glasses of vodka, one after the other, and ate my egg while he just sat and watched.

"Drink!"

He drank and started coughing.

"Let's get out of here... This is horrible!"

I forced him to peel an egg. We each had a glass.

"Who is that over there?"

At a table in the middle of the room, a young lad, dark-haired with a clean-shaven head and beat-up nose embraced a young woman, and then sat entertaining her. Near the couple, a former bouncer, now a drunk, a huge man with a bull's neck and a chubby, effeminate face, barefoot and in a rag that somewhat resembled a shirt, yelled in a thunderous bass, "Bless you!"

I explained to Gleb Ivanovich that this "fine young lad" was on a bender.

He kept pleading, "Let's go."

We settled up and left.

"May we pass, madame?" Gleb Ivanovich politely asked a woman, wet from the rain and slush, sprawled on her hands and knees on the sidewalk.

"Go to hell," she said. "Looks like you're a prisoner of your fancy boots."

The hoarse, angry woman spat out a tale about someone else with fancy boots whom she had set straight with strong language. She tried to get up, but lost her balance and collapsed in a puddle. Gleb Ivanovich grabbed me by the arm and dragged me into the square, empty and covered with puddles, reflecting the glow of a lonely street lamp.

"That pearl of creation is a woman," Gleb Ivanovich thought out loud.

We walked. A sad-looking tramp stopped us and stuck out a hand for money. Gleb Ivanovich reached into his pocket, but I stopped him, and, taking out a one ruble note, I said to the tramp, "I'm out of change. Walk on over to the stand, buy five kopeks worth of cigarettes, and I'll give you money to stay tonight at a flophouse."

"I'll run right over," he mumbled, and traipsed in worn out boots through the puddles in the direction of a booth a short distance away. He disappeared in the fog.

"Careful to bring the cigarettes back here, we'll wait for you!" I shouted in his tracks.

"All right," I heard from out of the fog. Gleb Ivanovich was standing and laughing.

"What's that for?" I asked.

"Ha-ha-ha, ha-ha-ha! Oh, he'll bring the cigarettes all right. The change too! Ha-ha-ha!"

That was the first time that I heard such laughter from Gleb Ivanovich.

But he hadn't even finished when steps slogged through the puddles and my messenger, breathless, appeared and opened a huge hand, black with filth, on which lay the cigarettes, some bronze and a flash of silver.

"Ninety kopeks change. I took five for myself. And here are 10 cigarettes, 'Daybreaks.'"

"Well, just a moment. What is this? You came back?" Gleb Ivanovich asked.

"How could I not deliver? What, would *I* run off with someone else's money? What am I?" the tramp confidently began.

"Fine... fine," mumbled Gleb Ivanovich.

I gave the tramp the bronze, and intended to take the silver and the cigarettes, but Gleb Ivanovich said:

"No, no give him all of it. Everything. For his astonishing honesty. After all, that's..."

I gave the tramp the change, and, surprised, he said only one thing, "You fine gentlemen are touched! How could I steal from someone who trusted me?"

"Let's go! Let's get out of here. We won't see anything better anywhere. Thank you." Gleb Ivanovich turned to the tramp, bowed, and quickly dragged me off the square. He refused the rest of the flophouse tour.

I took many of my writer colleagues to the slums, always successfully. I only failed once, and that was a special case. The fellow was brave, experienced, and unafraid of The Iron, the Wolves of the Dry Ravine, or Hard Time, all the less because he had been in a real Siberian labor camp. This was none other than the famous P.G. Zaichnevsky, secretly escaped from exile to spend a few days in Moscow. Just the night before, Gleb Ivanovich had told him about our tour, and he was burning with curiosity. It was a pleasure for me to spend time with such a well-matched companion. Near midnight we walked briskly along Svininsky Alley, taking a shortcut to The Iron, where we continued our drinking after Hard Time, which had closed at

11. Suddenly, we heard marching boots: in front of us a squad of city cops was turning out of Solyanka. We moved onto the square as fast as we could, and saw police flowing from every alley and surrounding the buildings: a flophouse raid.

My companion's hands shook.

"What the hell?... It keeps getting worse!"

"Don't worry, Peter Grigoriyevich, move with confidence!"

We quickly crossed the square. Podkolokolny Alley, the only one without police, led out to Yauzsky Boulevard. The buildings' sheet metal roofs were booming. "Hard core criminal elements" were crawling through the attics out onto the rooftops and clinging like bandages near the chimneys, knowing that the police wouldn't climb out there.

The next day, Peter Grigoriyevich was joking with a group of us, saying how frightened he was of the crowds of police. However, it had not really been a laughing matter: instead of the rough Hard Time tavern, he risked ending-up back in Nerchinsk!

Even in daylight, it was dangerous to enter Kulakovka – its hallways were dark as night. Once I was walking through an underground passage in Dry Ravine, struck a match, and saw to my horror the head of a living man sticking out of the stone wall, the smooth stone wall. I stopped, and the head yelled, "Put that match out you devil!" Then, mostly to himself, grumbled "They just keep going past!" My companion blew out the match and dragged me ahead. The head said something else to our backs. A disguised entrance to a secret underground hideout was something that, never mind the police, the devil himself couldn't find.

In the eighties, I witnessed a scene at Romeyko's. One summer day, around three o'clock, I dropped by Hard Time. Everything was in full swing. I sat with a source of mine, Kirin. The place was crowded with "tomcats" and their "kittens." Suddenly a "tomcat" flew through the door and shouted, "Hey, anyone with a warrant! 26!" Everyone jumped up and got ready to leave, but I waited for more.

"Someone was killed at The Iron. They sent for the cops."[12]

"Careful, they'll be coming here!"

A huge, dark-haired man was first to run out. Sticking out from under a worn hat, the right side of his forehead was covered with bangs much longer than those on the left. In those days, labor prisoners had their heads shaved, so I could understand why he had to hurry. Maybe five other men ran out, leaving their kittens to pay for the hospitality.

I grew curious and hurried to Romeyko's, to the door facing the square. In a second floor apartment, in the middle of a crowd, a man lay face down in a puddle of blood, dressed only in a shirt and tooled and polished knee-length boots. A knife

12. For "get ready to leave," Gilyarovsky uses the colorful expression навострили лыжи, "packed up their traps."

stuck out of his back, sunk to the hilt near his left shoulder blade. I had never seen such a knife: a large, gleaming bronze handle, monstrously designed, jutted out of the body.

The victim was a tomcat.[13] The murderer avenged a woman. The murderer was never identified.

"Everyone gawked, no one talked."

"He's a good man," they said.

While I collected the information needed for the paper, the police arrived with a local doctor pressed into service, the much-admired D.P. Kuvshinikov.

"A skilled strike! Straight to the heart," he pronounced.

The police started to fill out their report. I walked up to the table to speak with Kuvshinikov, whom I had met through Anton Pavlovich Chekhov.

"Where's the knife? Where's the knife?" The police started getting agitated.

"I saw it just this minute. I saw it myself," yelled the doctor.

After no small amount of searching, the knife was found: in all the fuss someone in the room had pulled it out of the body and placed it behind a bottle in the tavern next door.

Bunin's was cleaner than the others because its door was on the alley, not the square. Many long-time Khitrovka regulars lived here, getting by on day work such as chopping wood, clearing snow, or, for women, scrubbing floors, cleaning house, or washing laundry. Professional beggars lived here, as did masters of various trades who had ended up in the slums for good. Most were tailors, called "crabs," because after drinking through their last shirt, they were naked and never left their bunks. They worked day and night sewing clothes for the market, always hungover, in rags, and barefoot. Often, the pay was good. At midnight, thieves with bundles might barge into some "crab's" apartment and wake the place up.

"Hey, get up guys, you have work!" a manic fence would yell.

From bundles they took out fur coats, fox-fur stoles, and a mountain of various clothing. Cutting and sewing started at once, and by morning the traders would show up and carry off armloads of fur hats, vests, caps, and pants. The police were looking for coats and stoles, but they were gone: in their place were hats and caps. The fence of course, played the most important role because he bought the goods and, frequently, was the gang's boss.

Traders made the largest and most dependable part of their income from selling liquor. You could buy a drink at any apartment. In the walls, under the floor, in thick table legs – everywhere there were stashes of wine watered down for flophouse customers and their guests. During the day one could get pure vodka poured in taverns and bars, but at night vodka was sold in sealed containers. In the heart of Bunin's

---

13. "Tomcat" is slang for a pimp. "Kittens" are their prostitutes.

courtyard they had their own "*shlanboy*."[14] The yard was lit at that time by one weak, kerosene lantern. A glow barely escaped its dirty glass, and the only window, the one with a white curtain, was lighter than the others. Someone needing a drink would go to the window and knock. A small slot would open. A hand was stuck out the window, palm up. The customer would pay a ruble and a half. The hand would disappear and in a moment reappear with a bottle of Smirnov's, and the slot would slam shut. One deal, no words.

The silence in the courtyard was total. You could hear from a distance drunken singing and cries of "guard," but no one helped. They would strip someone, take their shoes, and leave them naked. Now and then, in the alleys right next to the square, corpses were picked up that had been murdered and stripped. They sent the dead to the Myasnitsky Police Morgue for official autopsy, and occasionally to the university.

I remember that I once dropped by Professor I.I. Neiding's anatomy lecture hall and found him teaching a class of university students. On the slab lay a corpse found at Khitrovka Market. After examining the body, Neiding announced, "No sign of a violent death." Suddenly, out of the group of students, appeared the lecture hall's old night watchman, the famous Volkov, who helped students prepare for exams, and did it remarkably well. "Ivan Ivanovich," he said, "what do you mean no signs? Take a good look, he got it in the neck," he stage-whispered. He turned the body over and pointed out a fracture. "No, Ivan Ivanovich, there's never been a case where they sent someone over from Khitrovka who had not been murdered."

Many of those born in Khitrovka were orphaned. Here's an incident from the 1880s. One foggy autumn night in Bunin's courtyard some people on their way to buy vodka heard moaning from a trash heap. They saw a woman "settling accounts" with a child. Children were worth money in Khitrovka: the poor rented them out when they were weaned, almost an auction, really. Some dirty wench, often with the symptoms of a horrible sickness, would take an unlucky child, stick a chunk of bread wrapped in a dirty rag in its mouth as a pacifier, and drag him off to a frigid street. The child lay in her arms the whole day, cold and dirty, slowly poisoned by the pacifier, and moaning from cold, hunger, and the constant ache in its stomach. All this was to rouse sympathy in passersby for "the poor mother of an unfortunate orphan." There were cases where a poor infant perished in the morning in a beggar's arms, and not wanting to lose a day, she would carry the body until the evening, begging. Two year olds were taken by the hand, but by three they had learned to work the crowd. In the last week of Lent, an un-weaned infant with a loud cry went for four kopeks per day, a three-year-old for 20 kopeks. Five-year-olds worked by themselves and brought home to their fathers, mothers, aunts, and uncles 20 and sometimes

---

14. A slot with a sliding door, through which alcohol and money were exchanged anonymously.

even 50 kopeks "to water their souls." The more children in a family, the more their parents demanded, and the less passersby gave.

When begging, the children removed their winter shoes and gave them to a lookout around the corner, while they loitered near taverns and restaurants, barefoot in the snow. They needed to get money any way possible so they could go home with 20 kopeks and avoid a beating. Young boys stood lookout while adults stole, and at the same time learned the adults' "trade." Typically, barefoot boys born in Khitrovka lived there until their hair greyed, only disappearing for a time to go to prison or be exiled. That was the boys.

Girls were in a much worse position. They had one option: sell themselves to drunken degenerates. 10-year-old, drunken prostitutes were not uncommon. They spent most of their time in The Train Car. This was a tiny, one-floored wing of a building deep in Rumyantsev's courtyard. In the first half of the eighties, a great beauty lived there for some time, and became known as The Princess. She occasionally disappeared from Khitrovka, spending time, thanks to her beauty, as a kept woman, or in "luxury" whorehouses. She returned every time to The Train Car and drank through all of her savings. At Hard Time she sang French *chansons*, and danced the fashionable *caucha*.

Among her "callers" was Stepka Wayvin, a cousin of the well-known criminal Vaska Churkin, who was glorified in an eponymous novel. But Stepka was cleaner than his cousin, and talked about him suspiciously: "Vaska? A bad liar! A petty thief!" Once, the police arrested Stepka and sent him to a transfer jail, where they handcuffed him and put him in leg irons. The guard proposed: "I'll remove the leg irons if you promise not to run." "It's your duty to jail us," Stepka replied, "and our duty to run. I will not give my word. You can depend on a prisoner's word, and I already gave it." Shortly thereafter, he escaped by climbing a wall. He went straight to The Train Car, to The Princess, whom he had promised to see again. A jealous scene ensued. Stepka beat The Princess half to death. She was sent to the Pavlovsky Hospital, where she died from her wounds.

IN MOSCOW'S 1826 MUNICIPAL ADDRESS book, on the list of building owners, one could find "Svinin, Pavel Andreyevich, General Counsel, Pevchesky Alley No. 24, Myasnitsky Region, Corner of Solyanka Street." Pushkin sang Svinin's praises: "Svinin, The Great Russian Beetle."[15] Svinin was a well-known figure, a writer, an art collector, and a museum owner. As a result, the city renamed Pevchesky Alley "Svininsky."

On the corner opposite Pevchesky Alley, like a castle circled by a high fence, stood a large residence with servants belonging to Major-General Nikolai Petrovich

---

15. Beetle was slang for touts at the track. This address is in what appears now on maps as Pevchesky Alley.

Khitrov. At the time, the alley opened onto a huge, overgrown lot, crisscrossed by ruts, a long-standing haven for vagrants, who considered it "free space." Khitrov owned the empty "free space" all the way up to what is now considered Yauzsky and Pokrovsky Boulevards, at that time both formed what was known as White Town Boulevard.[16] On this boulevard stood another building belonging to Major General Khitrov, No. 39. This was where he lived, and at No. 24, next to the "free space," were his servants, stables, root cellar, and basements. Khitrov Market developed on this enormous property, and was named in honor of this wild homestead's owner.

Svinin died in 1839, and his extensive holdings and grand residences went to the merchant family Rastorguyev, which owned them until the October Revolution. An education society acquired Major General Khitrov's residence to make apartments for its staff, then resold it in the second half of the century to the engineer Romeyko. The city bought the empty lot, still occupied by vagrants, for a market. The building required expensive repairs. The neighborhood, a dangerous place, didn't inspire potential tenants, so Romeyko turned the building into a cheap hotel: profitable, with no expenses.

For decades, Khitrovka's terrible slums loosed horror on Muscovites. And for decades the press, the city council, and the city government, right up to the Governor-General, took measures calculated to destroy this den of criminals. On one side of Khitrovka sat the shopping street of Solyanka and the Opekunsky Council Building. In the other direction, Pokrovsky Boulevard and the alleys next to it had mansions belonging to Russian and foreign merchants. Here lived Savva Morozov, the Korzinkins, the Khlebnikovs, the Olivyanishnikovs, the Rastorguyevs, and the Bakhrushins. The owners of these residences were upset by their frightful neighborhood, and took all possible measures to destroy it, but neither thundering speeches in the city council nor expensive measures taken by the city government accomplished anything. A hidden spring pushed back all the attacking forces and nothing happened.

One of the Khitrov homeowners had a hand in the City Council, another knew someone in the Governor-General's office, and another held a top-level position in a charitable organization. But only Soviet power, one order from the Moscow City Council run by the Soviets, removed a tumor that had been considered incurable under the old regime. In one week in 1923 they cleaned out the entire square and the ancient criminal dens around it. In a few months, they made the slums over into clean apartments and settled them with both blue and white-collar workers. The worst slum, Kulakova, with its underground hideouts in Dry Ravine, along Svininsky Alley, and the enormous tavern The Iron, was torn down to its foundation and

---

16. Белый город ("White Town") was the territory of Moscow inside the outer white walls of the old city's defenses but not including the Kremlin or Kitai City. Catherine the Great ordered the wall demolished and replaced by a chain of boulevards that later became known as the Boulevard Ring.

rebuilt. Its replacement was identical, but clean. There were no discarded papers, or rags, or broken windows leaking air filled with moisture and a drunken roar. Look at Orlov's now, with its apartments for low income professionals and a place for newcomers to spend the night while searching for day work. Next door are the enormous Rumyantsev buildings, in which there had been two taverns, Exile and Siberia. Further on at Stepanov's was Hard Time, once belonging to the famous protector of runaways and exiles, Mark Afanasyev. Later, it went to his henchman, Kulakov, who lied and swindled his way to ownership of the property much like his former boss.

Hard Time no longer has a door that, when open, belches mist, wild song, the crash of dishes, and the roar of knife fights. The windows of Bunin's, right next door, now shine. Thousands of street people no longer crowd the square, sit at vending tables dirty and stinking of fish, spoiled bullion, and innards. Clean-cut people stroll by, children play. But until just recently, 24 hours a day, the square teemed with street people. Toward evening, drunks with their "kittens" loitered and shouted loudly back and forth. Blindly, cocaine addicts of both genders and all ages swayed along after sniffing their drugs. Among them were teenage girls, born and raised right here, and half-naked young men, their companions. These troublemakers would show up at the market, bunch together, lurch toward a vendor, knock over his display, sometimes even smashing the booth, grab up the goods, and disappear in all directions.

"Railroaders" were considered a step up. Their method was to sneak bags and suitcases from luggage racks on long boulevards and in quiet alleys and dark stations. There were "window boys," agile and flexible kids who could crawl in through even tiny train windows. There were "curtain boys," capable of silently going through the pockets of a person in a buttoned coat, then screening themselves off and disappearing in the crowd. And covering the whole square, the poor, the poor. At night, from the underground passages of Dry Ravine, "business kids" would crawl out with pistols and knives. Even the "night tailors" got into it, perhaps grabbing a hat off a pedestrian or luring a fellow Khitrovka beggar with a scrap of bread, then stealing his money. Nights could be terrible on the square, where drunken song mixed with the shrieks of beaten kittens and cries of "guard." But no one risked helping: undressed, barefoot, or naked, they were left alone, or might be beaten for being somewhere they shouldn't.

The police guardhouse was always quiet at night, as if it wasn't even there. For about 20 years the city cop Rudnikov, discussed above, ruled there. Rudnikov was uninterested in unprofitable nighttime calls for help, and the guardhouse door stayed locked. Epifanov, a writer for *Entertainment*, once decided to study the slums, but he got drunk and ended up lost. In the square, he was stripped naked. He walked straight to the police guardhouse. He knocked, roared, and shouted "guard," but in the end he went home naked. The next day, he showed up at *Entertainment*, asked for compensation for the theft, and described the end of his journey: an enormous cop had hopped out of the guardhouse barefoot and in his underwear, thinking that Epifanov was a local. The cop had grabbed Epifanov, turned him around backwards, and given him such a kick, barefoot, that he flew into a puddle.

Rudnikov feared nothing and no one. For Rudnikov, even Ivan Petrovich Kulakov was nothing, a man who with all his millions was feared even by the police because, "the Governor-General shook his hand when they met." Rudnikov walked right up to Kulakov one holiday and, after palming a 100 ruble note, rumbled,

Khitrov residents.

"Johnny, are you joking? Maybe you forgot? Huh?" Kulakov, who at that moment was receiving holiday guests in his own home in Sininsky Alley, in a decorated uniform, started shaking, and babbling. "Excuse me, please, my dear Fedot Ivanovich." He gave Rudnikov 300 rubles. Rudnikov, and his guardhouse, are long gone.

The buildings around Khitrov Square were divided into apartments, either one big room or two or three smaller rooms with cots, sometimes stacked, where the homeless spent nights without regard to gender or age. In the corner of the room, a small section was screened off with thin boards, or sometimes just a cheap cotton curtain. This was where the leaseholder and his wife lived. The leaseholder always was a simple retired soldier or peasant, and always with a "clean" passport, since it was otherwise impossible to get formal permission to be a leaseholder. Leaseholders never lived alone; they always had a wife, but never a legal marriage. They left their lawful wives back in their villages in the countryside, and in Moscow they had roommates, female aborigines from Khitrovka, often without passports. Every leaseholder had his favorite type of tenants: some liked robbers, some thieves, some "brown trash," and some simply preferred their brothers in poverty.

Wherever there are poor people, there are children – future convicts. Anyone who was born in Khitrovka and grew up in its horrible conditions would end up in prison. Exceptions were rare. The poor were the most well-intentioned part of Khitrovka's population. Many were born and grew up there, and whether because of their poverty or their hopelessness, became thieves or muggers, and remained just as poor, since there was no way to change trades. These were not the type of poor who have accidentally lost their means of existence, the kind we see on the street. That type of person would hardly steal enough for a piece of bread or a place to sleep. Khitrovka's poor were another sort.

At Rumyantsev's, for example, there was an apartment of "pilgrims." Huge, simple men with dirty beards, bodies swollen from hard drinking; greasy hair hung down to their shoulders. Never in their lives had they even come close to a comb or a bar of soap. These were monks of a non-existent order, pilgrims who spent their lives around Khitrovka walking to and from church walls, or back and forth to merchants along the Moscow River.

After a night of drinking, a frightful-looking man gets out of his bunk, asks for a glass of *sivukhi*[17] on his tab with the leaseholder, puts on a cassock, a knapsack stuffed with a rag over his shoulders, a skull cap, and barefoot, sometimes even in the winter snow as proof of his piety, marches to a cathedral. What kind of lies won't such a pilgrim tell the ignorant merchants' wives? What won't he dump on them to save souls?! How about a splinter from the Lord's tomb, a piece of the ladder that Jacob saw in a dream, or, fallen from the heavens, a piece of John the Prophet's chariot?

There were poor folk who gathered near the booths, taverns, and rows of traders: their "service" lasted from 10 in the morning until five in the evening. This group, and another group that rushed from church to church, known as "hand-to-mouths," were the largest. In the latter were women holding breast-feeding infants, rented for the day, or sometimes simply clutching a log wrapped in a rag that they would tenderly croon at while begging for "a poor orphan." Here there were both real and fake blind people and wretches.

There were aristocrats too. Some lived at Orlov's, some at Bunin's. Among them were government bureaucrats, former military officers driven from the service, and defrocked priests. They worked collectively, dividing Moscow's buildings into lists. They would place down in front of them the Moscow address book and calendar. A beggar-aristocrat might take, for example the right side of Prechistenka Street with its alleys and write 20 tear-jerking letters, not leaving out any of the 20 homes deserving attention. After mailing the letters, the next day they would walk to the addresses. An aristocratic figure wearing a nice, but rented, suit would ring the front bell. Responding to the doorman's question, they would say, "A letter was sent yesterday by city mail. An answer is expected." They would walk away with an envelope containing money, a ruble or more.

Apartment No. 27 in the wing of Yaroshenko's facing the courtyard was called Scribbler and was considered both the most aristocratic and humble apartment in all of Khitrovka. In the eighties, a "king" and "queen" lived there, a blind old man with a toothless old woman, his wife, to whom he dictated letters to philanthropists, his old acquaintances, and occasionally received donations sufficiently large to help feed the scribblers. They called him "Your Excellency" and treated him with respect. His surname was Lvov, he had documents that placed him among the gentry, but

---

17. A home-made alcohol usually with impurities.

claimed no title; the scribblers called him a prince and, following this lead, so did all of Khitrovka. He and his wife were hopeless alcoholics, but when they were sober conducted themselves with dignity and appeared quite respectable, although the prince wore old rags and the princess a simple dress mended with colored patches. Eventually, relatives from out by the Volga came to visit and took them away, to the great disappointment of the scribblers and the poor neighbors.

An embittered alcoholic also lived there, a lawyer and former state councilor[18] and judge, for which the Khitrovka locals, who had appeared at his bench more than once, nicknamed him "Chained," alluding to the fact that, when carrying out their official duties, judges wore a gilded chain. On the next cot slept his friend Dobronravov, at one time a promising writer. He published love stories in small newspapers as well as sharp, revealing features. One of these features led to his exile from Moscow at the demand of its target: manufacturers. Dobronravov kept on his person, like a holy relic, a newspaper clipping of the article that destroyed him. It was published under the title, "Blessed." He lived for a few years in some remote little city in the far north, showed up in Moscow at Khitrovka, and settled permanently in this apartment. He appeared very respectable and in moments of sobriety he merited attention. Here are the lines for which the author of "Blessed" was exiled from Moscow.

> Please come… look here. Merchants are crafty. Gangsters and dandies can't go drinking and take time off for hunting, but thanks to both prison labor and factory workers, a millionaire manufacturer can. He's got a dashing look about him. He called forth from the bare earth a five-story building. Thousands of people work for him alone. They work, they sleep, and they suffer. These people are born to factory work, will accept any misery, and turn into skin and bones, as long as they can pour alcohol into their faces. With a poor diet and torn clothes, even young workers are betrayed by their bodies.

Heart felt!

> Irresponsible bosses wander around the factory; they don't allow time off even for food shopping; they'll say something like, "If you want onions, send your youngest son to get them with scrip at the factory store. They say the prices there are fine."

Fine but the goods are spoiled!

> If your body craves a drink or a smoke it's not your fault. Run back down to the factory

---

18. State councilor was included in Russia's official "Table of Ranks" and its holders typically served at the level of vice-governors or vice-department heads. The rank was the equivalent of a brigadier general in the army.

store and drink the house wine. They won't pour the better stuff as freely. It's not a good idea, but they'll sell as much as you can drink on a tab.

In the city, the boss is like a Count. Everything is designed to his advantage, there are charges on both profits and goods, and so no matter which way you turn, you have to ante up. He takes a percentage of sales. Wherever you look, he takes a cut. People protect their own. No one has it better anywhere!

Next to the scribblers' was an apartment used for moonlighting. In the old days, typesetters made big money on "piece work." They even made it sound like they were performing an act of charity: "Where can a naked, barefoot person go?! Whatever you pay, they'll drink it right up!"

THE DEMOLITION OF SVININ'S TAVERN, The Iron, and all of Kulakovka, began in the first days of the October Revolution. In 1917, every last tenant in The Iron outright refused to pay fees to the leaseholders. The leaseholders, seeing that there was no one to turn to, gave it all up and returned to their villages. In response, the tenants' first act was to break apart the leaseholders' things and tear up the floorboards, where they searched for vodka hoards. They tore out the very wallboards, which were burned in stoves. When authorities arrived to see the tenants, everything wooden, including the rafters, had been stripped for firewood. The buildings, without roofs, windows, or doors, continued to shelter the hardest cases. The underground hideouts, however, remained untouched. The "professionals" still went out prospecting at night. The "night tailors" stayed in the dark during the day. The former attacked far from their home bases, the latter robbed drunks and people caught alone in the underground passages, as well as the poor, their own people really. They came out in the evening onto Khitrov Square, and later went to Staraya Square to rob vendors.

During the hungriest days of the Civil War, the authorities had to ignore Khitrovka. Walking down Solyanka Street with bundles or packages was risky, even during the day, especially for women. Hooligans would swoop in, grab bundles out of people's hands, and escape into Svininsky Alley, where in full view of pursuers they would disappear into the mute brick heaps. Pursuers halted in astonishment, and suddenly they would be hit with bricks. No one knew where they came from. One, a second... Sometimes passersby saw a bit of smoke coming out of the garbage. "The Iron's customers are cooking lunch!" In the evenings, shadows flickered. People with teapots and buckets walked to the river and returned quietly: they were fetching water.

But there came a time when the Moscow City Council liquidated Khitrov Market in just a few hours. Completely by surprise, police surrounded the market, and were posted in all the alleys and near each building entrance. Anyone could exit the market; no one was allowed to enter. Residents had been fore-warned about the eviction, but none of them ever even gave a thought to leaving. After surrounding the building, the police asked everyone to move out, announcing that they could leave freely, that no one would be arrested, and that they would have a few hours reprieve, after which "measures would be taken." When all was done, only a few destitute invalids remained at Rumyantsev's.

SAILOR OF THE HIGH SEAS

IN MOSCOW, AT THE BEGINNING of the eighties, there lived a much-respected actor and drama translator, N.P. Kireyev. He worked at the People's Theater on Solyanka Street, and in the Artists' Circle. His sister, O.P. Kireyeva – they both worked at the People's Theater – also worked as a midwife at the Myasnitsky Clinic, and was a favorite in the neighboring slums of Khitrovka Market, where everyone addressed her respectfully by first name and patronymic. She understood much about the dirty, poor folk and thieves who stayed at the filthy flophouses, especially if, by chance, children had been born to a married mother, and therefore could not be taken into the safe house, which had been built exclusively for illegitimate and abandoned children. The police doctor was of a mind with Olga Petrovna, a boon to the people of Khitrovka, and was described in brief in Chekhov's short story, "The Jumper." D.P. Kuvshinikov chose this area consciously, to serve the poor.

O.P. Kireyeva was a family friend of ours, and her small daughter Lelya spent time with us. My wife and I were guests at her small apartment on the third floor of a dirty, yellow building under a watchtower. Below was a large apartment for the doctor, where I sometimes spent Saturdays, when Sofia Petrovna, the doctor's wife, a passionate fan of literary types and artists, arranged small get-togethers at which there were readings, or guests drew, and afterwards ate dinner. A.P. Chekhov and his brother Nikolai, a painter, as well as I. Levitan,[1] spent time there. In a word, our whole little circle of "beginners" attended. However, our younger members did not always find it to their well-fed tastes.

One day I dropped by to see Olga Petrovna. She was cleaning, in a small tub, the ulcer-covered little arm of a two-year-old child lying in the arms of a poor, dirty

---

1. Isaak Ilyich Levitan, painter (1860-1900), a master of the "mood landscape."

woman, about 40 years old. Two of the boy's fingers, the middle and ring, were completely corrupted. The boy quietly burbled and widened his eyes on sight of me: his right eye was green and the left brown. The woman complained coarsely to no one in particular, "His father's been sent to hard labor, the freeloader. A choking would be too good for him."

I went into the next room where a samovar steamed. On my return, Olga Petrovna told me a typical Khitrovka story: a destitute soldier's wife was found on the floor of a trash room, where she had given birth to this very child. By the time they summoned Olga Petrovna, the mother had died. The boy was legitimate, so they would not take him at the children's home. A poor woman came and took him with her to beg. On Christmas, she got drunk, fell asleep, and two of his fingers were frostbitten. The wounds festered for some time. She did not have him treated because the wounds helped her get more money. When he held the infected hand out to passersby, touched in the heart, they would give. Once, Sasha Kocherga stumbled across the police, and they sent her to the precinct and from there to Olga Petrovna, who knew her well from treating her.

He was a sickly child. Until he was three, they passed him off as a breast-feeding baby. One time they were caught: they asked Effenbach, the head of detectives, as he was walking by, to help a breastfeeding baby. "Breastfeeding, you say? He looks a little big for that." The little one stuck a tiny hand out of the rags as if making a rude gesture.[2] "What's it to you. What kind of jerk are you? Go to…" It ended with a trip to the police station, whence the child was taken to the flophouse, and Sashka Kocherga was sent, due to her illness, to Myasnitsky Hospital. She was never seen again.

Soon they started to lead Koska out by hand to beg: he became a "foot soldier." Grandfather Ivan, an old man from the flophouse who had cared for Koska's mother, taking her with him in the summer to pick mushrooms, looked out for Koska. His mother had died, and he had been born, on February 22, which is why Grandfather Ivan had him christened "Kasyan."[3] The old man later called him "Kasyan the Truthful" because of a peculiar character trait: he never lied. And the old man was just like him. "You have to live by the truth, you can't get by with lies," he would reproach Sashka Kocherga, and Koska listened and minded.

For three winters, the old man led Koska by the hand to church doors, and summers took him to Sokolniki and farther, to Losiny Island for mushrooms, and thereby they managed to feed themselves.[4] Here, Koska learned about his mother. During winters, she had done laundry in the flophouses, where she received letters

---

2. Gilyarovsky is referring to a well-known, rude hand gesture. Given the condition of the child's fingers, the mistake is understandable.

3. Kasyan is considered a saint by the Orthodox Church, but folk wisdom said otherwise. On his saint's day, some people stayed inside until sunset, and kept their livestock inside as well, fearing the animals might "attract Kasyan's eye."

4. Sokolniki, from the Russian word *sokol*, or falcon. The tsar's falcon training grounds were there.

Myasnitsky Police Station.

from her husband, a soldier, serving somewhere near Tashkent. During summers, she picked mushrooms and brought them to market at Hunter's Row. When Koska was turning six, the old man died in the hospital. Koska was left alone. He was young, spirited, and clever, and life in the forest had hardened him and made him strong. He started to beg "barefoot" at night near restaurants. He would stand in the snow barefoot, but a friend would be waiting around the corner with warm boots. Later, he took up with pickpockets, and started to work Sukharev Market and sleighs, but he never picked a pocket. He was only a "runner," that is they gave him wallets and he ran away. They trusted him: he would never take a kopek. Later, he stood watch. But a cop only had to ask, "What are you up to, kid?" and he would tell the whole truth, "I'm standing watch. Our guys are over there stealing from a booth." The thieves would beat him for telling the truth, but he never stopped. Why the truth lived so strongly in this child, no one knew. The deceased old mushroom picker had this explanation for his favorite's trait: "I call him Kasyan because he doesn't lie. Someone like him is born only once in three years.[5] Kasyans are always truthful." Kasyan heard his words often and became even more truthful.

When the old man died, Koska was driven from the flophouse, and took up with a group of homeless runaways that frequented the markets in gangs, slept in dumps, in the empty cellars under Red Gate, in the towers on Staraya Square, and, in the

5. The old man may be making a confused reference to leap year, because Kasyan's Day is on February 29.

summer, in the park in Sokolniki when it was warm and "every little shrub offered a place to sleep." Their favorite spot was near Sokolniki, on Shiryayev Field, where stacks of thick, cast iron pipes were stored for the sewers under construction in Moscow. Adult vagrants and homeless young thieves lived there. In the pipes were wood shavings, hay, mats, paper advertisements torn from posts, and rags. This was where the vagrants slept.

Koska and his gang lived here. Later, they moved as a group to the Balkan area, where they stayed in an unused, old water pipe. Thus the vagrant, young toughs, busy with petty theft so they could eat, settled-in and stayed. Many of them ended up in the Rukavishnikov Correctional Shelter,[6] many were sent home. But the gangs grew and grew, fueled by the slums, where the poor multiplied, and by runaway young apprentices, escaping unbearable lives with Moscow tradesmen. These boys had to endure a drunken cobbler's repeated blows to the head with a wooden tool handle, and other similar forms of "instruction," which had become deeply ingrained in business practice. Young boys were brought from the countryside to be trained for a year just to avoid the expense of feeding them. But not all of them could endure five years of servitude, a starvation diet, and beatings. A young one might see free kids on the street and join them, running off to the slums, because he feared neither the cold, nor hunger, nor prison, nor beatings. Sleeping in a garbage pit or a cellar is no worse than sleeping like a dog in a master's cold entrance hall. Here, you slept as much as you could, until your belly asked for food, and no one would wake you in the dark with a kick and abuse: "What are you sleeping for, you bastard! Get up, you freeloader!" the master's wife would shriek. So a 10-year-old "freeloader" would start his workday dragging a huge basket, bigger than himself, barefoot through the snow or mud to the garbage heap.

Olga Petrovna was fated to see her patient one more time. He was working as a lookout at the station on Strastnoy Boulevard, and was waiting for a handoff. He saw Olga Petrovna making her way across the square, saw the gang crash into her, force her medical bag from her hands, and how she grabbed for it and burst out yelling in a desperate voice. In a flash, they gave the bag to Koska and he sprinted off, not to the agreed spot, the Polyakovsky Garden on Bronny Boulevard, where the guys usually "split the pot," but off along the boulevards to Trubnaya Square, and then to Pokrovka, and from there to the Myasnitsky Clinic, where he sat by the gate, a bit out of the way. He hid the bag under some rags and waited. Olga Petrovna appeared, walking, but swaying a bit. Her eyes showed she'd been crying. She went through to the gate and across the courtyard. He went in behind her, caught up on the narrow stairs, and said:

"Olga Petrovna."

---

6. The Rukavishnikov Center, Moscow's first corrective work institution for underage lawbreakers, opened in 1864 under the leadership and with the funding of N.V. Rukavishnikov.

She stopped.

She asked, crying, "What's wrong Koska?"

"Olga Petrovna, here is your bag, everything's fine, all in one piece, not a speck of dust was touched."

"That was the happiest day of my life, my whole life," she told me.

It turned out that, aside from her medical instruments, the bag contained clinic funds and documents. The loss of the bag would have meant the end for her: arrest!

"Koska pushed the bag into my arms and disappeared. When I hurried after him out into the courtyard, he was past the gate and had run off."

A year later, she showed me the only letter from Koska, in which he informed her – the letter was dictated – that he had been forced to run away from his buddies, "because I had deceived them and could not tell them the truth. I climbed onto the undercarriage of a train car and escaped to Yaroslavl. That summer, I ended up in Astrakhan,[7] where I work in the fish factories, and they've promised to take me on a ship. I learned to read."

This was the last news from Koska.

Olga Petrovna died long ago.

1923. I'M ON MY WAY to my apartment building's office. At the door, I bump into someone in a black cape and sealskin cap.

"Excuse me."

"Pardon me."

He raised his left hand, holding the door, and I plainly saw only two fingers stretching out, the index finger and pinkie, no middle fingers. He had a smiling, kind, clean-shaven face, and those fingers.

We excused each other and went our separate ways.

In the manager's office, I was sitting.

"Did you just pass an interesting man?"

"Yes, he was missing fingers on one hand. As if he's making a rude gesture."

"Who cares about the fingers? Did you see his eyes? One green, the other brown, and both smiling."

"One of our tenants?"

"Unfortunately, no. He came by to refuse a room. Three days ago I showed him No. 6, all according to procedure, and today he said no. What a polite man! He's been called back to the Far East, to the fleet. He only just got here. He's a sailor, spent his whole life at sea. America, Japan, India. One of ours, an old time revolutionary, since 1905. Distinguished. Such letters of recommendation! Sorry to lose such a good tenant. We might have made him chairman."

---

7. A port city in southern European Russia on the left bank of the Volga River near where it joins the Caspian Sea.

"Interesting?" I ask.

"Yes, very. Here's what I remember. I gave him the form, he filled it out. I read it and had some doubts."

"It's all true," the sailor said. "Everything is just as I wrote. I'm unable to lie."

The manager handed me the form. I read in the blanks:

Kasyan, Ivan Ivanovich, 45 years old.
Place of birth: Moscow, at Romeyko's on Khitrovka Square.
Mother: Impoverished soldier.
Father: Unknown.

At the top of the form, next to the blank for "Occupation" was written: Sailor of the High Seas.

SUKHAREVKA

SUKHAREVKA SQUARE IS A DAUGHTER of war. Smolensk Market is a son of the plague. Smolensk Market is 35 years older than Sukharevka. After the Moscow plague, the government decreed that second-hand goods could only be sold at Smolensk market and, in an attempt to avoid spreading the disease, only on Sundays.[1] After the war of 1812, as soon as Muscovites began to return to Moscow and look for their looted property, Governor-General Rastopchin decreed that "all items, from wherever they were taken, are, as of this moment, the permanent property of their possessor, and owners may sell their items, but only once per week, on Sunday, in only one place, namely the square across from Sukharev Tower." That first Sunday, mountains of looted goods flooded the enormous square, and Moscow poured in too. This was the ceremonial opening of the timeless Sukharevka Market.

The Sukharev Tower was named by Peter the Great in honor of Sukharev, who stood alone with his troops, loyal to Peter during the Revolt of the *Streltsy*.[2] The ancient Sukharev Tower stood tall with its enormous clock. It was visible from some distance. Its upper stories had huge cisterns for an aqueduct supplying Moscow. Many legends circulated about Sukharev Tower: Sorcerer Bruce[3] turned lead into gold there, the "Black Book," written by the Devil, was kept in its hiding places. There were hundreds of legends, each one sillier than the next. On Sundays, a market seethed near the tower. All of Moscow came, as well as peasants from near the city, and folks from the provinces.

---

1. The Moscow plague: an epidemic of bubonic plague that swept central Russia from 1770-1772.
2. *Streltsy*, literally shooters, established by Ivan the Terrible around 1550 and armed with arquebuses, an early muzzle-loaded firearm. In Moscow, among other duties, they guarded the Kremlin. Following the victory over his sister in 1689, Peter gradually eliminated, and in 1698 crushed the *streltsy*.
3. See footnote page 22.

Across from the huge Sheremetevsky Hospital, hundreds of booths sprouted, put up during the night for only one day. From dawn to dusk, an ocean of heads bobbed on the square, leaving only narrow paths in both directions at the widest point of the Garden Ring. People thronged the square; each had his own goal. In the old days, Muscovites came to look for stolen property and not without success because, for ages, Sukharev Tower was the place to sell stolen goods. A thief working alone would drag items here that had been "washed" in the underground. Fences delivered entire cartloads. Things were sold cheaply at Sukharevka, "due to circumstances." Sukharevka lived for such "circumstances," often unhappy ones. A Sukharevka trader would buy goods after a domestic tragedy, when they could be gotten for nothing, or he would "take something off the hands" of someone who knew nothing of its value, or, out of nowhere, a trader would take on a "partner," and this "partner" sometimes smelled of smoke, or sometimes was blood-spattered. Always, there were bitter tears.

Buy for next to nothing and sell for cheap. Sukharevka's motto was, "Turn one kopek into five." Some were driven here by need, some came for the thrill of a profit, others for sport, once again with the slogan "turn one kopek into five." Someone might bring his last pieces of clothing and sell them for next to nothing out of dire need; dealers would surround him, practically tearing things out of his hands. Then, right there in plain sight, they would resell them at three times the price. A thief would sell his booty to these same dealers for practically nothing, just to move it faster. A customer might come here for necessities with his last ruble, thinking he would get a good price, but in the majority of cases he was swindled. There was a reason why, when talking about clothing, furniture, and such, there was a saying, "a Sukharevka job."

Moscow's wealthy came here searching for the same thing, to "turn one kopek into five."

Over the course of many years, I walked for hours on the square, frequented Bakastov's tavern and others, where, starting in the morning, thieves and vagrants got hustled playing billiards or cards. I became acquainted with these people and studied various aspects of their way of life. Most frequently, I went to the quietest tavern, a pit called Grigoriyev's that was frequented by the most frugal of the Sukharevka crowd. There was no gambling, so no thieves.

Grigoriyev and I became friendly when he was still a young man, a polite and learned autodidact. His wife, refined, worked at the till taking payment and jingling bronze tavern tokens thrown down by quick Yaroslavl waiters in white shirts. I usually sat to the right of the entrance, at the manager's desk, and talked for hours with Grigoriyev. Now and then his son, a first-year gymnasium student, would run up to the table, gleefully show us a book he had bought on the square (he enjoyed

Sukharevskaya Tower, left, built under Peter the Great, was an important Moscow landmark in Gilyarovsky's day.

Above, right, the view from the tower of the square below. Sheremetev Hospital is the curved building on the left.

travelogues), take some money and quickly disappear, only to show up again later with a new book.

All around, in the low-ceilinged, smoky rooms, guests roared, and toward evening were a bit tipsy. Among them were vendors with small items. Poor folk, slipping drunkenly, wandered among the tables. Cups held by monk alms collectors clinked. A tramp might run in, down a glass of vodka, and try to run off without paying. The waiters would detain him, causing a scene. They would call a city cop, fat and self-important, from his post. Realizing what was happening, he might spit and walk away grumbling, "For five kopeks they're distracting city government!" Occasionally, detectives would come in, but there was nothing for them to do. Grigoriyev pointed them out and spoke about them a great deal. Much of what he told me came in handy later.

Grigoriyev had a large and impressive library that he had acquired exclusively at Sukharevka. His son, while a university student, took part in the 1905 revolution. He was shot by tsarist troops. His body was found in the courtyard of the Presnensky Medical Clinic, in a pile of corpses. Grigoriyev could not endure this, and died. It should be said that earlier Grigoriyev had been considered "unreliable," at times fought openly with the police, and hated detectives.

Before 1881, there were no genuine detectives. The detective bureau as an institution was established in 1881. Earlier, only two senior officers were considered detectives, Zamaysky and Muravyov. They had assistants, petty thieves implicated in small crimes and pressured to help solve serious crimes and catch important criminals. Aside from these two, there was only one detective well known at the time, Smolin, a clean-shaven, sturdy old fellow entrusted with the most important cases. Sukharevka was the center of his activities, and from there he spun webs in all directions. Only he knew all the details. He was known as the Governor of Sukharevka.

For decades he lived at No.1 Meshanskaya Street in his own small, two-story home with an older woman for a servant. Aside from flies and cockroaches, there was only one other living creature, a huge tortoise that had grown old with him, and whom he fed by hand, and put on his knee. She would rub her head against him with knowing eyes. He lived completely alone – everyone knew. There were many valuables, but he feared no one. Behind him, like a mountain, stood the thieves and vandals who protected him, just as, when possible, he protected them. No one visited him in his private living quarters: he received visitors only in a reception room. He befriended thieves, vandals, and, principally, card sharps whom he met in gambling houses, where his presence was ignored. He knew everything, saw everything, but said nothing. If the bosses ordered him to investigate some sordid theft, especially from someone well known – well, he'd search until the thieves gave themselves up.

There was one curious story about him: a bronze cannon, weighing maybe 300 pounds, was once stolen from the Kremlin. The bosses ordered him to find the cannon within three days. He got all of the thieves on their feet. "Get me that cannon! Dump it at Antropov's garbage pit in the tall grass. That cannon had better turn up tomorrow where I've ordered." The next day, a cannon had actually been left at the designated spot. The bosses moved it into the Kremlin and put it up on its former place by the wall. Smolin received thanks. Years later, it was learned that a second cannon, from the other end of the Kremlin wall, had been stolen for Smolin by the obedient vandals and taken to Antropov's. That was the one he "returned" to the Kremlin. The first cannon vanished.

Smolin died in old age without an heir. Only the tortoise outlived him. When they compiled an inventory of his possessions – and in those days not everything ended up on the list – in his bedroom were found two buckets of gold and silver watches, watch chains, and cigar cases. Thieves and pickpockets worried: "How much of our loot was lost?! After all, it was *our* loot. If only we could have known that Andrei Mikhailovich was going to die, we could have taken it with our bare hands!"

Detective Smolin spent decades on the street. In Sukharevka, there were many legends about him. Even before the Russo-Turkish war,[4] in Zlatoustensky Alley, a wealthy, elderly Indian man lived completely alone at Medyntseva's. No one knew

---

4. Reference is to the Russo-Turkish war in 1877-8 between the Ottoman Empire and an Orthodox coalition led by Russia.

what sort of man he was. Some said he traded with the East, some said he dealt in bonds. There was a basis for both claims. Eastern people came to see him occasionally, and he was cloaked in deep secrecy. In general, the Eastern people lived at that time near Ilyinka and Nikolsky. He lived in an alley of the type where during the day trade took place and at night not a soul could be seen. Well, whose business was it? An Indian lived there. Many of them lived in Moscow.

The Indian was found dead in his apartment. Everything seemed in order: there was no trace of a theft. In the corner, on a table, sat a small, solid gold Buddha; the locks were not broken. The police arrived to look for criminals. They took suitcases full of valuables to the strong room at the Sirotsky Courthouse. Diamonds, pearls, gold, jewelry – huge amounts! An announcement about a search for heirs was printed. Sales took off at Sukharevka. Jewelry was bought in heaps... pearls... diamonds.

The case of the strangled Indian foundered when no suspect was identified. Finally, after almost two years, a legal heir appeared, also an Indian, but who dressed as a European. He had his own money, did not mention an inheritance, and his only goal was finding his uncle's killer. He was immediately put into the protective care of the police and Smolin. The first thing Smolin did was introduce him to the Easterners Pakhro and Abaz, and let the Indian visit various petty card hustlers to look for clues – they taught him to drink and play the latest games. They confused and confounded the young man. One fine day, he left the gambling house for home and disappeared, just like that. It was talked about for a while, and then forgotten. Many years later, in a friendly conversation with the polymath N.I. Pastukhov, I mentioned the Indian. It turned out that Pastukhov knew quite a bit. He was a writer at *Modern News* when the Governor-General forbade anyone from even mentioning the Indian.

"Who was this Indian?" I asked.

"An unsolved case. They say he was a fugitive leader of the Indian 'Thugees.' "[5]

"Why did Governor-General Zakrevsky forbid anything to be written about him?"

"Because a solid gold Buddha decorated Zakrevsky's bedroom."

"Can it be that Zakrevsky was a Buddhist?"

"Can it be otherwise, since the day they brought him the gold Buddha from Sukharevka?"

Not a tall man, with broad shoulders, a clean-cut face, shaven head, in a worn black coat and a cap with a cardboard brim, Smolin could move unnoticed through Sukharevka. Thieves disappeared when he arrived. If they spotted him, they knew that he'd already noticed them, and, seeing a convenient time, approached him.

---

5. *Thugees*, or thugs, from the Hindi word for thief: wandering bands of professional assassins targeted for eradication by British colonial forces in India in the 1830s.

A red-haired, well-dressed pickpocket, Pasha the Grouse, was on the prowl in the crowd and wanted to hide, but the detective's eyes held him. After completing a circle, the Grouse was close enough to Smolin to put something in his pocket.

"The Carp is here... with his girl. He lost... he's up to no good."

"Is he with Annushka?"

"Yes, sir. Yurka got involved with a group in Zamaysk. Players with money. They bought out the old-timers, Vyun, Goliath, Vatoshnik, the Finger, and even the Heron himself! They're nosing around over there, look!"

They dropped out of sight and quickly disappeared. Smolin transferred a silver watch to his pants pocket. From a distance he saw a tall woman in a colorful kerchief in the middle of the crowd, and next to her the Carp's goat-like beard. The woman caught sight of Smolin and whispered something to the bearded one. In a moment, the Carp was standing, with no sign of recognition, near Smolin.

"Today I got stripped to my kidneys. I was at Vaska the Dark's place and lost."

"Don't worry, you'll just have to thieve more fiercely!" The Carp put a wallet in Smolin's pocket.

"Did Annushka work out?"

"She... I myself don't know..."

"What's up with the Heron?"

"Frankly, I'm in tears that I didn't go by there today, but decided instead to go see Vaska the Dark. What a scene it must have been! They took six thousand from Sashka, the one from The Iron."

"Sashka? He was exiled to Siberia!"

"What!? He's been in Khitrovka all winter. He wasn't well. Mark Afanasyev took care of him. On Thursday, they say, he had some luck over in Guslitz. With an accomplice he scammed a merchant. The guy lost six big ones as if they were a kopek. The Heron cleaned up. Arkhivarius cleaned up. Nazarov decided the split."

"Raspluyev!"[6]

"Yeah, there he is standing by the tent with the Heron. Alexei Mikhailovich, I gave you my first catch today. Give me even just a kopek for good luck."

"Here. Live it up!"

He gave back the wallet.

"Well thank you! I won't forget this for the rest of my life. After all, honor is more important than money. Now I'll win everything back! Yes! They took Sasha for everything right down to his last kopek. In the morning, they gave him a 100-ruble bill and he went straight to the station and boarded an outbound train. Heron is starting up a new gaming house, a nice one."

Smolin walked up to the Heron.

---

6. The street name comes from a character in a play, *Krechinsky's Wedding* by A.V. Sukhovo-Kobylin.

"Congratulations on your score. Will you invite me to the housewarming party?" The Heron's jaw dropped. "Sashka himself was taken for six thousand today. So, when's the party?"

The Heron was dumbstruck.

"Heron! What's that you've got there? Portraits of Polish nobles? Why do you need those?"

"For fools, Andrei Mikhailovich, for fools. I'll hang them in my guest room and pass them off as my ancestors. Anyway, please, if you would be so kind, come by on Thursday to the same old spot on Tsvetnoy Boulevard. Above my old apartment, I rented a first floor..."

"Did you see Sashka off to the Volga?"

The skilled detective grabbed the Heron and went over to the jewelry tents, where card sharps turned their winnings into gold bars so they could lose everything again at the tables. He spoke with everyone, amazed everyone with his knowledge, and squeezed more out of them.

"Who's that dandy standing with Abaz?"

"Some goose from Peter... what's his name...?"

"Kikhibardzhi? Why's he here?"

"He's working a scam on some merchant. They're staying in a 40-ruble suite at the Slavyansky Bazaar.[7] Karaulov is with them."

Smolin moved like a shadow.

He spotted the Mosquito.

"Well, how's the counterfeiting business?"

Smolin knew everything. It's not that he knew where things happened, but knew what *would* happen and where. He knew but would stay silent until the boss caught him at it.

ALMOST NO ONE FROM THE powers that be had ever been to Sukharevka, except N.I. Ogaryov, the famous Moscow Chief of Police, who had the only chest-length, black moustache on the force. Occasionally, on Sundays, he was part of the crowd bustling around the antique dealers' tents. From time to time, in the tents, he would buy a wall clock. He always paid cash, and the traders, perhaps for him alone, never overcharged. He had a passion for wall clocks. His apartment was filled with them, and they struck without pause in various tones, one after another. He also collected police caricatures from around the world. One of his rooms was practically wall-papered with them. He was supplied with them by booksellers and the Censorship Committee, which confiscated such publications.

---

7. A famed hotel and restaurant that opened in 1873, Slavyansky Bazaar was the site of the historic marathon meeting of Konstantin Stanislavsky and Vladimir Nemirovich-Danchenko, which led to the formation of the Moscow Art Theater. The hotel was closed after the revolution, and the restaurant burned down in 1993.

Sukharevskaya Square, circa 1905.

Ogaryov prized one caricature, a drawing of a wooden fence; in the distance were a watchtower with signal balloons deployed and a red flag flying (assemble all troops). Bright clothing was hanging on the fence. An angry dog stood on its hind paws, scrabbling at, but not quite reaching, the clothes. The caption: "Too far for Arapka."[8] (At that time, in Petersburg, Trepov was the Chief of Police and, in Moscow, Arapov.) "What idiots," commented Ogaryov. Well, who would have guessed what followed? Such a gibe, by itself, would have gone unnoticed. I saw this issue of the magazine *Alarm*, but did not pay it any attention until the Moscow police began to confiscate it from newsstands. They spilled the whole thing.

In those days, the market had as many as 30 booksellers. You could get anything you wanted. If you could not find one volume of a sold-out series, you would just order it, and by the following Sunday they would get it. Even the rarest books could be found there. Bibliophiles never missed a Sunday. How the booksellers prepared for these days! Six days they rushed around looking for goods in private homes, country estates, attics, or buying entire libraries from heirs or bankrupt bibliophiles. "Troopers" would buy up books everywhere and resell them to the booksellers, gathered in the taverns on Rozhdestvenskaya Street, Great Kiselny Alley, and Little Lubyanka Street. This was a wholesale book market, perfected at Sukharevka, where every wholesaler knew every bookseller, and every bookseller knew every wholesaler: what he needed and how he paid. Professors I.E. Zabelin, N.S. Tikhonravov, and E.B. Barsov, were accorded special honors among the booksellers.

8. Both Goncharov (*Oblomov*) and Chekhov (*The Cook's Wedding and Other Stories*) used the name "Arapka" for a pet, so it probably was not uncommon and the jibe might have gone unnoticed.

Children working the streets, selling their wares.

Booksellers loved impoverished students and did them all sorts of favors. A group of university students would shop together, say five of them, and pool their funds to buy one book or compilation of lectures inexpensively. They all would study the one copy. Or, together, they might rent a book, paying five kopeks a day. Booksellers let students have books without a deposit, and students, in their turn, never lost them.

Booksellers and antique dealers (the latter were called "junkers") were Sukharevka's aristocrats. Their spot was close to the Spassky Barracks. Here, they were not crowded, like those in the middle of the square and the customers were a little better scrubbed. They were collectors and library agents, mostly from well-known merchant families.

All the booksellers knew one collector who every Sunday rooted around in their tents and and the books piled on mats on the ground. When he died, he left behind a valuable library. Without exception, he always paid as follows: say he agreed to buy a book priced at five rubles for two, having squeezed everything possible out of the bookseller, and reached into his pocket. He would take out two wallets, remove a ruble from one, pour out all the coins from the other, and hand over one ruble and 93 kopeks. "I'm short seven kopeks. You'll get it." The booksellers knew this scam, and knew that no matter what he'd never pay up. They let it go. Once, a bookseller asked him, "Doesn't it bother your conscience to squeeze a brother for a few kopeks?" "You don't understand anything! Think about how much I can get in a year!"

The booksellers had another eccentric customer. For a long time an elderly servant came to Sukharevka with a ruler in his hands and asked for books with good bindings that had to be a certain size. He did not care about the price. His crazy master was paralyzed and unable to get out of bed, and was building a library that soothed him just by its appearance.

In this "aristocratic" section of Sukharevka, antique dealers' tents alternated with booksellers'. Peter Ivanovich Shukin was a respected customer of the antique dealers. He himself rarely came to Sukharevka. They brought goods to him at home. The door to his office on Ilyinka Street, at a warehouse, was closed to everyone else, but always open for antique dealers. Dealers with huge sacks would pour into the warehouse and were immediately brought to the office unannounced. In seconds, Peter Ivanovich would be enveloped in a cloud of dust, digging through piles of stuff from the bags. He would select all the best pieces. The leftovers would show up in Sukharevka's tents or on nearby mats.

Behind the tents, toward the street, second-class peddlers put out mats to display all possible types of attic junk: a broken bronze doorknob, a part to a candleholder, a piece of an antique candelabra, worn-out dishes, a protective cover for a small book. Enthusiasts dug through the goods and always found something to buy.

From time to time, the owner of a bell factory came by the mats and picked out pieces of the best bronze, which he sent immediately to his factory. Then he would visit antique dealers' tents and pick out silver and bronze salvage. Once, I asked him what he was buying. "The sound of silver!"

Here is what passed for entertainment in Sukharevka: "They're casting a bell!" Whispering would start at Sukharevka – and right away in the entire market and across the whole city wild rumors and lies would circulate. It's not only that strangers repeated the rumors, but that each tried to lie more cleverly. But a lie's main character, time, and place would be given exactly.

"Did you hear what happened this morning? A whale beached itself under Kamenny Bridge. What a crowd..."

During a quick chat, someone might say that the doorman's wife had borne triplets – all with foal heads.

"Spassky Tower just collapsed! The whole thing! The clock too! Only the spire can still be seen."

A new arrival might believe such a tale, but a genuine Muscovite would listen, not even hint that he knew it was all lies, not smile, and would add something wilder. Such was the custom: "They're casting a bell!" For hundreds of years it was thought that the wider a tall tale was passed around, the better sounding the bell.

They would meet later: "Why did you say that the tower collapsed? I ran over there and it's standing right in place."

"At Finlandsky's factory they're casting a bell! Ha-ha-ha!"

In the eighties, when newspapers became common in Moscow, they were filled with advertisements by bell factories. Sukharevka ceased its tall tales, which at the time had served as advertising. But bell factory employees unfailingly came to

Sukharevka and bought "scrap silver." The antique dealers liked their business because they did not try to "turn one kopek into five." This was a customer with a
strictly defined goal – to buy "the sound of silver," but not "turn one kopek into
five." Similar to him was one other "teapot," who never missed a Sunday, did not
worry about kopeks, and bought up china, crystal, and paintings.

Among the amateur collectors there were only a few experts, mostly on crystal,
silver, and china. The majority of customers dreamed of buying, for "nothing," a
genuine Raphael that they could re-sell for thousands, or acquire "from the source"
a stolen diamond necklace for 50 rubles. So what if the Rafael turned out to be
a homemade reproduction or the necklace to be glass? The customer would go
back to Sukharevka anyway with those same dreams and search until death itself
to "turn one kopek into five." He had nothing, neither education nor expertise,
nothing except Daddy's fortune and the knack for acquiring money. Such customers
would bargain to the point of tears for kopeks, and be ecstatic that they succeeded
in buying a statuette of a nude woman with a broken hand and damaged nose. They
assured their acquaintances that they had bought it for nothing.

"It's Venus de Milo's niece."

"What?"

"But where is its arm? And you're blabbing about it!"

These types would be insulted to boot! Then they would dicker with the taxi
driver over kopeks. There were many like this at Sukharevka, but genuine antique
lovers also visited, those who bequeathed rich collections that later became national
treasures. But many of these treasures vanished. Everything was done quietly, the
Sukharevka way. All these dealers and enthusiasts were tight lipped, as if they had
bought something stolen. Buy, hide, and keep silent: these were their methods. All
operated independently and secretly.

Once there was a case when all of them, like a pack of hungry wolves, or, more
exactly, like a flock of timid crows, descended on a huge treasure. This was in the
eighties, when the famous Moscow collector M.M. Zaitsevsky died. He had spent
more than 40 years collecting fine art rarities, manuscripts, parchments, and first
editions of books. For half a century he was known by all at Sukharevka. For decades, his enormous wealth was spent on a private museum that in the fullest sense
was his entire life. He had forsaken the world to chase "the latest antique bauble,"
and never gave up. He would pursue some silver cover for a cup with passion and
patience until it was acquired.

I was acquainted with M.M. Zaitsevsky, but it was difficult to convince him to
show his collection. He, alone, would admire his treasures, carefully keeping them
from others' eyes. Forty years have passed, but the rarities found in these four spacious rooms in his home on Khlebny Alley still shine before my eyes. The walls were
thickly covered with antique paintings. The place of honor was given to a painting

of Saint Hieronymus.[9] This was an original by a marvelous artist. Some experts attributed its brushstrokes to Luca Giordano. Next to this painting hung two enormous paintings from the Flemish school, depicting a ruler's ceremonial departure from a feast. Next was Le Sueur's *Christ with Children*, then a painting by Adriana Stade, and many other works from past centuries.

In the next room, there was an enormous collection of the rarest icons, starting with an icon in the style of the Stroganov School,[10] and ending with works that had remained intact practically from the days when Christians were persecuted in Rome. Here, there was also a collection of crucifixes. In among them was a painting titled, *Prayer by the Leader of Moscow's Streltsy*, by Matthew Timofeyevich Sinyagin.

A third room was dedicated to portraits on ivory and metal. A portrait of Catherine II, formed out of German letters visible only with the aid of a loupe, spelled out the complete history of the Russian monarchy. Two other oil portraits were of Count Orlov-Chesmensky.[11] In one, the Count was mounted on his horse, Bars, and in the other, by Svirep, in a sleigh. On a table nearby there was leather riding tack, inlaid with turquoise by Svirep. Further, there were hundreds of clocks, horns, chalices, plates, and, in the midst of all this, a statue of Yermak Timofeyevich,[12] whose chest was fashioned from an entire enormous pearl. It stood on an extremely rare eleventh century silver platter.

Listing everything that was in these rooms would be impossible. In the yard, moreover, was a spacious barn filled with large-sized rarities. Here too was his library. In the first edition section was a copy of *The Teachings of Thomas Aquinas*, published in 1467 in Mainz, by the Schaefer Publishing House, founded by a companion of the printing press' inventor, Gutenberg. In the manuscript section were two enormous tomes on parchment with hundreds of drawings embossed with gold leaf. One was Boccaccio's *Decameron*, written in French in 1414.[13]

After the owner's death, his heirs did not open the rooms to the public, but instead displayed some of the items for a time at the Historical Museum. Later, they decided to sell the entire collection, a step required for the division of the estate. Learned archeologists, academics, and museum curators were amazed by the rarities, appraised them highly, and comforted one another when their funds were insufficient to acquire anything for their vaults. The museum stood open for private collectors for three months, but sold nothing aside from a few trifles. Private Moscow experts, raised in the Sukharevka tradition of "turn one kopek into five,"

---

9. Hieronymous is commonly referred to in the West as Saint Jerome, first translator of the Bible from Greek to Latin.
10. Named after a wealthy merchant family that funded the arts, the Stroganov School was known for diminutive works with rich details and is thought to have been influenced by styles from as far away as India and Persia.
11. Count Grigory Orlov, Catherine the Great's lover and, later, preeminent advisor.
12. Yermak Timofeyevich (1532-1585), historically recognized as the Cossack who conquered Siberia for the Russian Empire.
13. *The Decameron* was written in Italian and finished around 1351. Gilyarovsky must be referring to a reproduction.

visited in flocks but bought nothing. There were antique peddlers, rag dealers from Sukharevka, and collectors hurrying to skim the cream, or putting together collections to crow about in front of their friends, or buying up valuables to move money from one pocket to another, or disgraceful bargain hunters looking to "turn one kopek into five." Pretending to be experts, they had to strain to leash their eyes, which, at the first sight of treasure, darted around like those of a thief at a fair. When they caught sight of something truly rare and enormously valuable, they would raise their heads and say casually: "Hmm, yes. This isn't terribly uncommon! I might as well take it. Let it lay around at home. I'll pay 200 crisp rubles."

That is how they appraised an enameled jewelry box that was priced at seven thousand rubles. The usually taciturn rarities dealers on Sukharevka started talking about this box on a Sunday. Someone who had offered 200 rubles the day before sent an agent to buy it for three thousand. But the heirs did not give ground. Sukharevka, insulted that you could not buy anything for nothing from this museum, started "casting a bell." For a few Sundays, among the antique dealers it was said that the best pieces had been sold, that the heirs needed money and were making deals for practically nothing. But this did not help the Sukharevka locals "turn one kopek into five." One fine day a poster appeared on a door, announcing that Sukharevka's traders, antique dealers, and those from two side streets (they were named) should not bother to call at the museum.

I know nothing of the fate of the museum and its valuables, but I do remember the museum owner's son, V.M. Zaitsevsky, an actor and storyteller, who enjoyed in his day some success on the stage, lived on only a poor actor's earnings, and died at the beginning of the century. He had a stage name and his friends, whom he would help generously in times of need, knew him simply as Vasya Dneprov. That he was a Zaitsevsky, they had no idea. For some reason, he dropped by to see me once with a book of poems and stories that he had published and performed on stage. The volume was titled, *In Half*. He did not catch me at home, and the next day called on the telephone to ask if I had received it.

"Thank you," I answered. "It's a pity I was not home. By the way, tell me, is your father's collection intact?"

"Eghh... It was snatched up! All that remains is a portrait of my father, and even then I had to buy it this winter at Sukharevka."

ANTIQUE SHOP OWNERS WERE UNFAILING visitors at Sukharevka. There was one who would appear at dawn, sit on a box, and watch as goods were set out. He would sit and watch, but let him catch sight of something interesting, and he would snatch it up right away before the hobbyists and collectors, and later would sell it to them for three times the price. Often, the dealers drove him off:

"Get away, don't bother me, let me set up!"

Scenes from Sukharevka Market. Above, getting measured for a suit; a guitar seller.

"Later! Later!," he would always answer with one and the same word, and sit as if frozen.

The traders called him just that, "Later."

Vladimir Yegorovich Shmarovin also loved getting to Sukharevka early. He was considered the Popov factory's expert on painting and china. He sometimes bought silver cups, from which we drank his booze, or old inexpensive brass, or bronze earrings. He had an encyclopedic knowledge of antiques, and it was impossible to deceive him, although fake china was common, especially copies of Popov. These were manufactured abroad, whence agents would bring their goods. At Sukharevka, there was one booth that specialized in foreign-made, fake Popov china. This happened to all types of products.

Inexperienced coin collectors often bit on a Sukharev-style lure. A silver row of dealers' windows stood filled with antique coins. Moreover, on glass traveling cases dealers sold coins. For three or five rubles they would sell rare paper currency from the time of Alexei Mikhailovich[14] and enormous counterfeit, four-cornered bronze rubles made in Moscow or Kazan.

Raphael, Correggio, and Rubens were forged. You could buy as much as you pleased. This was especially interesting for the most inexperienced bargain hunters looking to "turn one kopek into five." Genuine experts were never even shown these, but the product moved all the same.

There was one interesting event. A woman came to the booth of one particular dealer, looked at the paintings for some time, and stopped at one with the signature "I. Repin." On it was a price tag, 10 rubles. "Here are 10 rubles for you. I'm taking the painting. But if it's not genuine, then I'll bring it back. I'll be at some friends' today where Repin is having lunch, and I'll show it to him." The woman brought the canvas to her friends' and showed it to I.Y. Repin.[15] He laughed. He asked for a pen and wrote underneath the painting. "This is not a Repin. I. Repin." The painting wound up back on Sukharevka and was sold, thanks to Repin's autograph, for 100 rubles.

Old time Sukharevka covered an enormous area: 5,000 square meters. All around Sukharevka, except for the Sheremetev Hospital, the buildings contained taverns, beer halls, shops of all kinds, and retail trade and services – cobblers and dressmakers who would practically drag in customers. In the nearest alleys, furniture was stored and put out on the square on Sundays.

Principally, in those days Sukharevka was a mob scene and a complete mess. These are two image-filled phrases: people crowded together all day long in one place, and bumped into all comers so rudely that later they hurt everywhere. Or a mess: endless rows of mats on the ground covered with cheap goods traded willy-nilly. One person sold used shoes, another displayed scrap iron, another guy matched keys to locks and immediately cut a replacement if the key didn't fit. Pickpockets covered the square and prowled, teamed with their "screeners": they surrounded, screened, and picked. Yell "police," and no one would listen, but let someone check their pocket and find it empty, and they would sing out, "Police! I was robbed!"

Pickpockets moved in gangs. Counterfeiters and their accomplices moved in gangs. There were money trader gangs and gangs of speculators. At Sukharevka, a lone scammer could do nothing. And so many types of crooks! Take even just

14. Tsar Alexei Mikhailovich, ruled 1645-1676.
15. Ilya Yefimovich Repin (1844-1930), one of Russia's most celebrated painters.

"the players." On every convenient little corner three or four would sit right on the sidewalk and start a three-card game – two black cards, one red. You had to guess which was red. Or a game of "strap": a leather strap would be wrapped around a hoop, and you had to throw a nail so that it remained inside the strap. But no one ever guessed which card was red, and the nail never stayed inside the strap. Hands can be amazingly adroit.

Dozens of gangs of "players" moved around Sukharevka, and hundreds of simpletons wanted to win but were swindled out of their last kopek. Another game was played on a booth's counter with buckwheat grains: young boys were most attracted to this one in the hope of eating the grain for nothing with a bit of Lenten oil. Further on might be a crooked lottery; nearby, its organizer.

There were bigger scammers. Let's suppose that a man comes to sell his only fur coat. A gang of buyers immediately surrounds him. Each one bargains, each one states a price. Finally, the prices converge. A buyer slowly reaches into his pocket, as if to get money, and hands the purchased item to his neighbor. Suddenly, behind the man there is a noise, everyone looks over, and the seller also glances in that direction. The coat, in that instant, is passed from hand to hand and disappears.

"What about the money? Hand it over."

"Whaaa-t?"

"The money for the coat."

"What coat? I didn't see anything!"

All around: laughter and noise. The coat is gone and there's no one to answer for it.

There was a gang of bait and switch artists: they would sell a gold watch, and the customer could even test it, or a genuine diamond ring, but when the customer got home he could see that the watch was brass without a movement, and the ring was cheap metal and glass.

Let's suppose further that Krechinsky himself did it.[16] Sukharevka is more masterful than Krechinsky. How long does it take to switch out a watch or a broach?! But to turn the trick with a dozen pairs of pants? Only at Sukharevka. It was accomplished like so: two older boys would walk through the crowd with bundles of pants over their shoulders, brand new, just sewn, and carefully folded.

"How much for the pants?"

"Four rubles. But look at what a good product. I lucked into a piece of English cloth. I got 36 pairs out of it. He bought a pair, and he bought a pair. They just left."

The customer looks at the second vendor.

"For three rubles I'll take a pair."

"What!"

---

16. The reference here is to *Krechinsky's Wedding*, a play by A.V. Sukhovo-Kobylin. Krechinsky borrows a diamond pin from his fiance and then pawns a replica to resolve debt problems.

"A pair for three rubles. Will you take it?"

"Four. But look here, if you want, take the whole dozen for three crisp rubles each."

The customer's eyes sparkled: no matter whom you asked, they would buy for three and sometimes four rubles... He looks carefully at both of the vendors and counts – right, a dozen. And someone else is bargaining with the other vendor close by. They agreed on the discount. The buyer handed over the money, the vendor bound the pants with a string, Someone unexpectedly tapped the buyer on the neck. He looked around.

"Excuse me. I mistook you for a friend."

The buyer takes the bundle and leaves. He carries it home. It turns out that there's one pant leg on top, another on the bottom, and between them rags. They switched packages while he wasn't looking. The trader "turned one kopek into five"!

Near the food vendors, sitting in rows selling stinking, hot meals, there were fewer crooks. Homeless children rushed about, small time pickpockets and train thieves, pulling travelers' handbags out of train cars through narrow windows left open for air. The hot food area was their favorite spot, their market. Spoiled sausage on a grill, broth, scraps, dirty platters; old women standing on clay warmers and holding boiled potatoes. Suddenly, a downpour. Goods are rolled up in mats, a mess. People who can save themselves stand under the tower. Only the hot food vendors are motionless. The old women raise the back hem of their skirts and use them to cover their heads. Blue sky appears again in a few minutes and the crowd is back teeming in the market.

During and after the rain, shoes sell exceptionally well. They succeeded in dragging a government clerk in a badly worn cloak into a booth. For some time, two vendors tore him in two, one at his right arm, and one at his left. For two rubles, the clerk bought a pair of used shoes, put them on, and left, winding through the puddles. The vendors wagered:

"He won't make it!"

"He'll make it!"

"Put a couple of beers on it?"

"How long?"

"Fifteen minutes."

"Done."

"No, he's gonna get a shave."

The clerk sat down on a crate near the tower. An unshaven, filthy barber winked at a shaggy young boy, who grabbed an unwashed oil jar, ran off, scooped up some water from a puddle, and handed it over.

"A shave here costs three kopeks, and a haircut five."

In the mornings, when there weren't any clients, the boys practiced their trade on soldiers whom they shaved for free. An untrained street kid would hack up some unlucky fellow's hair, but he would sit there because his orders said: "shave your beard, cut your hair, go nowhere." In a week, the soldier would ask for another shave.

"Well, fuzzy, have a seat!" The Moscow Figaro invites him to the crate.

I loved to stop and watch this shouting horde for a bit, and occasionally, on a whim, respond. You walk along the sidewalk by the booths and someone quietly grabs you, "If you please, sir, we're selling out!" They pull and pull. Whether you want to or not you're going to the booth. And there, standing around, are the other participants; each does his job and recites his lines. The rehearsal of roles and execution are marvelous. They force you to look at everything, and try everything on: a fur coat, a jacket, a shirt.

"But I really don't need anything!"

"Now, you don't need it. Later, you might. Can't hurt to know where to go. Nothing but good can come of this. Maybe a friend will need something. Now you know where you can shop. And what a good product. You've been convinced by your own eyes."

A barker shouts on the street near a booth. A stern-looking woman walks by.

"Madame! We're selling out! For your spouse, a coat, for your children, shirts, ma'am."

The woman walks right by, self-importantly. The barker's tone changes.

"Madame, madame! Might you want something or other in a pair of pants?!" the barker yells at her back, with laughter all around. Then, he spots new arrivals.

What characters! I knew one of them. He would ask his boss for vacation and go for Holy Week and Easter Sunday to the sideshow at Devichy Field to work as a barker. He was near 40 and stayed with the kids of one of the bosses. He was called Yefim Makariyevich. Not the common but too familiar shortened version, Makarich. It was Makariyevich, out of respect. Dependable and respectable at the counter, in the sideshow he was unrecognizable, with a fake grey beard. He would roar out across the whole field:

"Hu-rrrrrraaaaaaaahhh! Let's get started! We have Yulia Pastrana, a grandniece of the monk-sleaze. Look through the peephole on the side of the exhibit. She's dressed all in silk!" And on and on...

The crowd couldn't believe its ears. They ran over from all the shows to listen to Yushka the Comedian. I too was wide-eyed, standing in the dark and the crush of the crowd, looking up. He wiggles his grey beard and pokes fun at the audience. Suddenly he points a finger at the crowd and shrieks out:

"What are you doing rooting around in a stranger's pocket!"

Everyone turns their heads, but he's moved on; he's spotted some old crow and turns to her.

"You are a fool, a fool! Where do you get off, messing for no good reason with black magic… Hey, you nine-legged waitress from a garbage pit!!! Hurr-aaaaaaah! Let's get started! Let's get started!"

He tears off the beard, waves it above his head, and disappears below. In a minute, he jumps up again, putting the beard on as he goes:

"A-hum, a-hum!! Respected audience, half-respected audience, and those who don't care! Hurry up, we won't start without you. Don't die before you see our show!"

Suddenly, as the laughter recedes, he makes a serious face and puts a hand to his ear. The crowd freezes.

"Oi-oi-oi! There's no way they started yet! Hurry kids!"

The sideshow where Yushka worked was always packed. Once, chatting with him over a cup of tea, I expressed amazement at how adroitly he managed the crowd: He answered: "What is a crowd? It's a herd of sheep; wherever the goat walks, they follow. You can turn them any way you want. But try it at Sukharevka! Try to sell a wild dog, or even tougher, sell fancy clothes to someone from the steppe. Force him to stop at your booth and convince him to buy something he doesn't need. This, brother, is not like the crowd in Devichy Field, this is a hundred times worse. In 30 years at Sukharevka, no one has walked past my booth. You are the crowd. I could convince a crowd of people to swim in the winter!"

Sukharevka was its own special world, never to be repeated.[17] All of it is contained in one anecdote: one of the frequent visitors to the Shmarov art scene, a painter-restoration artist, returned one Sunday from his *dacha* and went straight from the station, as was his habit, to Sukharevka, where he purchased a magnificent, antique vase to complete a matching pair. You can imagine an art lover's joy at acquiring such a treasure. At home, a servant greeted him and reported that the day before his apartment had been robbed. He had bought his own vase!

---

17. Sukharev Tower was torn down by the Soviet government in 1934, allegedly because it constricted traffic.

NEAR THE KITAI CITY WALL

THE CONSTRUCTION OF MOSCOW'S KITAI City Wall, dividing Kitai City from White Town, dates to the mid-sixteenth century.[1] Ivan the Terrible's mother, Elena Glinskaya, named this part of the city Kitai City in memory of her homeland, Kitai Town in Podolia. In the beginning of the last century, in 1806, P.S. Valuyev wrote:

> Abuse of the Kitai Wall has put it in an embarrassing condition. Clerks' offices were built in its towers; in some places, unsightly stalls were installed against the wall, in others there are root cellars, storehouses, and stables... Earthen fortifications, bastions, and trenches, later additions to the wall, further complicate the problem, blocking drainage. Filth infects the air. This abuse started before the capital moved to Petersburg. Stone and wooden booths were built along the entire wall around Kitai City.

Later, just before the War of 1812, insofar as was possible, the wall was restored. On the outer side, all abutting construction was demolished. The inner side of the wall remained untouched. On Staraya Square, between Ilyinsky and Nikolsky Gates, Tolkuchy Market opened. In the mid-1880s, the market was still at its height. V.E. Makovsky captured it magnificently on canvas, a work still located at the Tretyakov Gallery. The market was shut down in the 1880s, but traces remain even today. In the city center it spawned a slum that Soviet authorities destroyed. There were booths built against the wall all the way to Varvarsky Gate, and on the outer

---

1. The Китай-Город ("Kitai City") Wall was built of stone in 1535-8, and is not related to the modern word Китай ("China"). Instead, historians tend to agree that the name derives from the old Russian word кита, which refers to fortifications made from woven and bound tree limbs, backed with dirt. Белый город ("White Town") was the territory of Moscow inside the outer white walls of the city's defenses (roughly the line of the current Boulevard Ring) but not including the Kremlin or Kitai City.

Views of the Kitai City Wall at the end of the nineteenth century.

side to Lubyanskaya Square, with its tavern hideouts and the well-known apartment building Shipovsky Fortress.

During and after the time of Catherine the Great, a building here housed N.I. Novikov's publishing company. He printed his own titles. The building was knocked down when they closed the market, and later, in the first half of the last century, a new building went up belonging to General Shipov, a well-known, wealthy man with influence in the capital. He was a real original: he took no payments from his tenants, allowed them to bring in as many people as they pleased, and kept no records, not only of passports, but not even of the people who lived there. The police didn't dare so much as peep at the General, and soon the building was filled with escaped thieves and vagrants from all over. They were armed to the teeth, and brought the fruits of their nighttime labors to fences who had also settled in the building. At night, it was risky to walk through Lubyanskaya Square.

The inhabitants of Shipovsky Fortress could be divided into two categories: one, runaway serfs, petty thieves, poor folk, children running from their parents or employers, students, those from the juvenile division of the prison system, various Moscow types, and peasants from nearby villages without passports. This entire jolly, drunken tribe was here seeking refuge from the police. The second category included depressed, morose people who associated with no one and, even on the roughest bender, drunk as never before, they would never reveal their names, nor even a single word about their past. None of the people around them would dare ask any question even distantly related to their past. These were experienced criminals, deserters and escapees from hard labor in exile. They recognized one another on sight, like people bound together by a secret link. People from the first category knew who these people were, but kept silent, scared stiff, and would not betray the secret by word or glance.

The first category of Shipovsky Fortress' inhabitants left the building during the day to tend to their affairs, and in the evening they got drunk, then slept. The second category slept during the day and "worked" at night, in and around Moscow, on the estates of both lords and merchants, in the warehouses of wealthy men, and on busy roads. Their work smelled of blood. In the old days they were known as "Ivans" and later "working boys." The police once surrounded a building after midnight for a raid, and blocked the entrances. The Ivans, returning with their night's haul, noticed something wrong, divided into groups, and waited in the garden. When the police rushed the building, armed Ivans attacked them from behind, and a scuffle ensued. The police, entering the building, met resistance from the "night tailors" inside, and an attack from the Ivans from the outside. The police ran in shame, badly beaten and hurt, and forgot about new raids for quite some time.

The Ivans would show up with stolen property in enormous bundles, and some-times an entire load of household goods hauled by a horse, often stolen by beating someone who had been riding past. They would wait for morning, and then take their loot to booths that opened at dawn on Staraya and Novaya Squares. At night, it was impossible to approach the booths, as they were guarded by enormous, chained dogs. Entire cartloads vanished without a trace into these booths, built against the Kitai City wall, where there were hiding places impossible to find in the dark cellars.

The booths were dark even during the day, making it impossible to see inside. It appeared, from the goods on display outside, that each of these booths had its own specialized, unattractive trade. One sold cheap furs, another reconditioned shoes, a third wool and papers, a fourth rags, and a fifth iron and brass scrap. But this was only a convenient front, a decoration that hid the essence of the matter. These booths accepted anything carried or carted there, from silver spoons to samovars, from china cups to tombstones. Once the police found there a 300-pound brass cannon stolen from the Kremlin.[2]

During the day, the booths worked a retail trade with pickpockets and petty thieves, taking everything from gold watches to handkerchiefs, or a hat torn off someone's head. At dawn, they bought wholesale, by the sack-full from Ivans – nightly booty sometimes stained with wet blood. After getting their money, the

---

2. See anecdote, page 62.

Ivans went to feast at their hideouts, their beloved bars and taverns, to Hell at Trub-naya Square or to The Poles' Tavern. Petty thieves and con men met in these dens at night, and Ivans toward morning, sometimes not even stopping by the booths at the wall, but going directly to the taverns, to secret rooms, where they divvied-up loot and sold it directly to the tavern owner or special fences.

In the days of Shipovsky Fortress, the main criminal hideout was near the Yau-za River, The Poles' Tavern. It was filled with separate rooms used for dividing and fencing stolen goods. Former human beings, who feared nothing and thought nothing through, gathered here. In one of these rooms, during the division of a large score, four robbers killed one of their own to take his share. Later, right there in the attic, two legs were found, cut clean off, still in boots. After the split, they would start drinking with women or gambling. Serious Ivans were not distracted by drinking or women. Their passion was gambling. Here, they played Fortune, Fate, and of course, there were card sharps.

The Poles' Tavern prospered until the Fortress was emptied, but not by the police. The Imperial Philanthropic Society acquired the building after the death of the overly-philanthropic General Shilov. The Society dealt with the old, free-wheeling tenants in a decidedly un-philanthropic way. Police and military forces summoned to aid the society were positioned for an assault. Old timers who re-member that night said: Soldiers surged through the dark and into the building's silence and murk. They entered the first apartment, darkness, a foul smell, a mess, mats on the floor, hay, rags, firewood. It turned out there were only two people in the entire apartment, the leaseholder and his young son. In a second it was the same story. In the third, there was half a decanter of wine on the table, some bread crusts and cucumbers, but not a single tenant. There was a soldier at each exit – nowhere to run. They dug through the barn, the root cellar, and a storeroom and found only a few people, quiet as stumps.

Only morning and the first rays of the new day unlocked the secret: when the sun rose the roof was completely filled with men, sitting and reclining. They were removed but not arrested, simply driven away. They rushed in crowds to the banks of the Yauza and then to Khitrov Market, where a row of flophouses had recent-ly opened, and rented beds. Shipovka's inhabitants from the first category settled there, but the Ivans scattered at first, then appeared on Khitrovka and settled into the cellars and secret rooms at Romeyko's Dry Ravine.

The Philanthropic Society partially renovated the building, and then let back in the same kind of trash, but with passports, and just as closely connected with the market. The building was filled with tailors, cobblers, traders, second-hand dealers, and fences. Apartments were rented by tailors with a particular specialty: "crabs," employed by bosses with licenses for trade work. They were called "crabs" because they sat "like crabs under a rock" in their dens, drinking until their last shirt was sold.

Shipov's never changed its name or its essence. Earlier, it had been filled with robbers, and now it was filled with legally registered "merchants." Guaranteeing the disappearance of any trace of a crime, theft or mugging, these "merchants" made evidence a permanent source of income, buying and altering stolen goods. It can be said with confidence that not one building owner received as reliable and high returns as the apartment renters and the fences.

In this enormous, three-story building, with the exception of a few booths, snack shops, and the bar on the lower level, as well as a tavern-hideout, all the rest of its square footage was occupied by small, dirty apartments. They were jammed full of traders with their help, or simply additional tenants. Apartments were almost all rented in a woman's name, and "husbands" would live with them: a tailor, a cobbler, a locksmith. Each apartment was divided by small barriers into corners and cots. Such an apartment would have three or four "rooms" that housed 30 people, including children. Summers, at five a.m., and winters, at seven a.m., everyone in the apartment would be on their feet. After a quick bite, the bosses and tenants, grabbing in their arms bunches of old clothes, and jamming thick wallets into their breast pockets, dirty and rough looking as they were, would run to the market and their trade. Leaseholders themselves worked from dawn to dusk. And their tenants did the same. Even young children and the elderly ran into the streets and sold matches and single cigarettes rolled on the spot out of who the hell knows what.

Once a week, renters would make a willy-nilly effort to tidy-up the apartment, or at least pretend that they were cleaning. The apartments were impossibly filthy and could never truly be cleaned. But there were renters who never, or with rare exception, not more than twice a year, cleaned their apartments, which were always full of thieves, drunks, and prostitutes. These renters also sold stuff, but came to the market later, toward evening, since by that time they had gotten drunk with their "partners."

The first category of traders arrived at the market at first light with their husbands and roommates, and immediately loaded-up on fresh stock, bought second-hand right there, and swindled customers with it. They surrounded customers, and everyone would hold out what they had, a suit jacket, pants, a cape, underwear. All of it was torn, smelly, and seemed to crawl at first touch. Galoshes or boots would turn out to be glued together and badly dyed; a black coat would turn out to be grey-brown-purple, after the first rain a red stain would appear on a cape, one side of a frock coat would turn out to be blue, the other yellow, and the lining green. Underwear fell apart the first time it was laundered. All these were "productions" of the first category of Shipov's traders, who had "passed the exam" in the trade.

Just before dawn, traders and clothes merchants from the first category appeared on the square as did fences from Shipov's. Among those wanting to sell were the capital's poor: a fired government clerk brought his last cloak with a dog fur collar; a poor student sold a frock coat to pay for coal; a hungry mother sold her child's pillow and blanket; and a bankrupt merchant's wife, once wealthy, fearfully offered a samovar to buy food for her husband, who was in debtor's prison. Bitter necessity made these sellers the most profitable for the market's hawks. Like a flock they circled the victim, showered him with taunts, and frightened him with pointed remarks and threats. In the end, they got him to panic.

"How much?"

"Four rubles," answers a confused student, who had never even seen such a market.

"Hah! Four?! How about one?"

They surrounded him, felt the cloth, laughed and insisted on one ruble. Each threw in a caustic word:

"Junk! Not worth buying. Someone else will come along."

The student has turned all red, with tears in his eyes, and they keep tearing at the coat.

The hungry mother cries.

"Maybe she's sick?"

The trader, draped in a dirty rag he's just bought, suspiciously pushed away the blanket and pillow, as if he might get infected, proposing a fifth of the named price.

"It's probably stolen," remarked an older dealer, offering the merchant three rubles for a samovar worth 15. Another spitefully added, seeing that the poor wretch was dumb from fright, "maybe we should call the cops."

Such tactics always worked: the confused student, the grief-stricken mother, and the merchant woman surrendered their things for only a fifth of their value. Only the clerk, experienced with some of these tricks, held his own, and even stood up for the others, whom the punks intended to cheat. In the end, he sold his cloak with a dog fur collar for an appropriate price, which the toughs gave him just so he wouldn't raise any flags.

This describes the earliest part of the morning, when the second category was still hung over. But these folks also crawl out of their holes. The mix of people on the square changes, the hours for fleecing the poor give way to the hours for taking advantage of the flaws and weaknesses of human nature. A crowd of drunks gather, having dragged with them both their own and others' things, just to get enough money to take care of their hangovers. These sellers are more fitted to the toughs of the second category. Another form of the hunt has been worked out for them because these sellers are without conscience, without fear; you can neither frighten them nor even get in a word. For every word they have 10 in response. They'll bring up their parents and great grandmother. The toughs surround an uncertain seller. They begin to look an item over, examine it from all directions, look at it in the light, and get to business proposing a price:

"Two rubles? One and a half! Look yourself, it's not worth more."

"I said two, not a kopek less!"

"Take a bit off, you stubborn devil!"

"Two!," he answers sharply and imperiously.

"Well then, take the money. What can I do with you!?" as if unwilling, the trader says, hurriedly hands the seller a pile of change, and tears the purchase from his hands.

The seller starts to count the money, and instead of two rubles it turns out there are one and a half.

"Hand over half a ruble! I sold it for two after all." The trader stands, unruffled.

"Give it back!"

"Well take it, little flower, take it, after all, we won't grab it by force," the trader says. But suddenly, with a shout of horror, "Where did it go? Oh, saints, we were robbed, in the light of day, robbed!"

With these words, he disappears in the crowd.

Thirsting to cure their hangovers, people grabbed at the first offer just to get their alcohol faster – they were burning inside!

Beginning at noon, people who didn't really want to buy anything started to appear. Pretending to shop, they entered booths attached to the Kitai City wall on Staraya Square, where, with the exception of two or three places, everyone else is busy fencing stolen goods.[3] On the corner of Novaya Square and Varvarsky Gate, was the booth of the Old Believer S.T. Bolshakov, who traded in antique books and icons painted before the time of Patriarch Nikon.[4] Scholars and writers often came by. There were university professors and academics. Next to Bolshakov were two other antique booksellers and, farther on, before the market was shut down, you could find black market goods in any of the booths.

The market covered all of Staraya Square between Ilyinka and Nikolskaya Streets, and part of Novaya Street between Ilyinkaya and Varvarka. In one direction was the Kitai City wall and in the other a row of tall buildings occupied by commercial enterprises. On the upper floors were offices and storage space, on the lower floors there were dress and shoe shops. All these goods were cheap, and they were mostly Russian: fur coats, jackets, pants or an overcoat and suit and frock coat combinations, sewn with large stitches for average folk. There was, moreover, "fashion" with pretensions to *chic*, sewn by the same tailors. There were shops with

---

3. The Communist Party's Central Committee was later headquartered on Staraya Square.
4. Old Believers separated from Russian Orthodoxy in 1666 in protest over reforms made by Patriarch Nikon. Old Believers continue the liturgical practices of the pre-reform church.

Selling along the Kitai City Wall.

ready-made clothing. Here, just like on Sukharevka, customers were dragged in. Near the entrance, there was always the racket of barkers, who grabbed pedestrians by the lapels and dragged them from the sidewalk right into the shop, not paying attention to whether they needed ready-made clothes.

"I don't need clothes!," objected a merchant or a clerk to two young men grabbing his arm.

"If you peas, Your Healthfulship," or to the clerk "Your Exuberance," anything, just so long as they look at the goods.[5]

Neither of them would leave him alone, and each would drag him in his own direction. And once they succeeded in dragging someone into a booth, they would talk the ear off of the poor unfortunate, torture him with measurements, urge him to buy, if not for himself, then for his spouse, his children or even his taxi driver... The "barkers" were great masters of their craft. "Just drop into my shop, you don't have to need anything! I'll convince you," a good barker would say. And he really would convince them. The same type of barkers worked the booths with ready-made shoes on Staraya Square. In both places, they specialized in low-quality footwear made elsewhere, boots and shoes made mostly in Kemerovo.[6] In the seventies, paper shoe soles were widely used, despite the fact that leather was comparatively inexpensive, but the craftsmen and the sellers both did business with the slogans: "Turn one kopek into five!" and "Don't scam, can't sell."[7]

Of course, average people suffered the most, and swindling customers with "barkers" was easy. Someone might buy boots with his last money, put them on, walk two or three streets through puddles and rainy weather, and watch as a sole

---

5. Mangled language and salutations, either from ignorance or attempted humor.
6. Nearly 2,000 miles east of Moscow, as the crow flies.
7. Не обманешь – не продашь.

Trees grew atop and out of the wall.

came loose, and instead of leather, paper stuck out of the boot. He goes back to the booth... The barkers know why, and when he complains, they toss words around that make him out to be a blackmailer: "You came," they say, "to sell some junk, bought a pair of boots at the market, and now you're accusing us. What booth did you buy them in?" The unhappy customer stands, panicked, looking around at all the booths. The curtains and exits are all similar, and each has a crowd of "barkers." The customer bursts out crying and walks away accompanied by hoots and jibes.

In the sixties, there was a Chief of Police in Moscow, Luzhin, an enthusiastic hunter who kept a kennel near the city. One of his men bought a pair of boots with paper soles on Staraya Square, and complained to him. The man told him how and where the traders got their goods. Luzhin sent him to learn the details. He reported that early that morning several loads of boots from Kemerovo had been delivered to the largest retailer on Staraya Square. Luzhin, with a squad of police, rushed over and quietly surrounded the warehouses. He had said nothing to the local authorities, to prevent them from tipping off the merchant. Luzhin arrived just as they were unloading the delivery. Everyone was arrested: warehouse owners, their agents, the fences who had arrived with goods from Kemerovo, and the shoe sellers. After sealing the goods and the warehouse, Luzhin sent the arrestees to police headquarters, where they were paroled, including the warehouse owners and the traders from Kemerovo.

The merchants swore up and down that they would never trade such goods in the future, and the ones from Kemerovo, after a harsh flogging, pledged that not only they, but their children, grandchildren and great-grandchildren would refuse, at risk of a curse upon their families, to use paper soles. Indeed, Kemerovo worked honestly, and not a word about paper soles was heard until the war with Turkey in 1877-1878. Their children and grandchildren were "drawn into a bad deal," as they explained in court, as suppliers to the army, that placed enormous orders for boots with the paper soles. Soldiers climbed through snow in the Balkans and Caucasus in shredded boots and died of fevers. After that, paper soles returned to Sukharevka, Smolensk Market, and small shops according to the traditional slogans, "Turn one kopek into five," and "Don't scam, can't sell."

Only after the destruction of the market at the end of the 1880s was Staraya Square cleaned up, and Shipov's assumed a relatively orderly appearance. In 1926, Moscow's Public Services Department restored the Kitai City Wall, a monument of Old Moscow, to the way it had appeared five hundred years earlier, when it served as a defense from enemy attacks and was not yet in the poor condition seen by later generations. One is reminded of the immortal Gogol: "More than 40 cartloads of every type of garbage were dumped next to the wall. What a disgusting city. All one must do is build any kind of monument, or even just a wall – who the hell knows where the trash comes from?"[8] This was the condition of the Kitai City Wall just before it was demolished in 1934. In many places the wall had disappeared entirely, and in others it had sunk two meters into the ground. Squatters vandalized the towers. They set up housekeeping on the wall: no *dacha* needed!

Next to the ancient towers,
Old walls, their tops almost pastures.

Trees visible in Lubyanka, Varvarskaya, and Staraya Squares grew out of cracks in the wall.

---

8. Nikolai Gogol (1809-1852).

SECRETS OF NEGLINKA

TRUBNAYA SQUARE AND NEGLINNAYA STREET, almost all the way to Kuznetsky Street, flooded so badly after every heavy rain that waterfalls splashed out of shop entrances and into buildings' lower floors.[1] The never-cleaned pipe carrying the Neglinka River, which led from Samoteka under Tsvetnoy Boulevard, and along Neglinnaya Street, Theater Square, and under the Alexandrovsky Garden all the way to the Moscow River, could not hold enough water during rainy weather. This was disastrous, but the "city fathers" paid not the slightest attention.

In ancient times, the Neglinka River flowed here. In the days of Catherine the Great, the river was locked into an underground pipe: a scaffold was built into the riverbed; they covered it with a layer of gravel, put down a wooden base, installed drainage for street water, and built a sewer beneath the streets. In addition to "legal" drains for storm and household water, the majority of wealthy building owners installed secret underground pipes for draining filth into the Neglinka instead of carting it away in barrels the way it was done all over Moscow before the sewers. All the filth went into the Moscow River. The police were aware of this, as were abutting building owners, but they all, it would seem, thought: "we didn't start it; it's not for us to stop it!"

Having been underground in Moscow in the shafts of artesian wells, and having read the description of Paris's underground sewers in Victor Hugo's *Les Misérables*, I decided that I would explore the Neglinka no matter the cost. This was a continuation of my ongoing study of Moscow's slums, with which the Neglinka had a connection, as I had been forced to learn in the lairs of Grachyovka[2] and Tsvetnoy

---

1. The distance along Neglinnaya between Trubnaya Square and Kuznetsky Street is less than half a mile.
2. Grachyovka was a slum and crime-ridden area surrounding Trubnaya Square.

1909 flood on Neglinnaya Street.

Boulevard. It wasn't difficult to find two brave men who agreed to take this journey with me. One of them was a passport-less plumber, Fedya, supplementing his day job, and the other, a former janitor, dependable and thorough. The janitor's job was to lower a ladder and help us descend into the sewer between Samotek and Trubnaya Square, and later meet us at a nearby drain and lower the ladder for our exit. Fedya was to accompany me in the underworld and hold the light.

On a hot July day, across from Malyushin's near Samotek, we raised the grate on the drainage shaft and lowered the ladder. No one paid any attention to our operation; everything was done quickly. We raised the grate, lowered the ladder. A foul smelling mist rose from the opening. Fedya the Plumber crawled in first: the opening, damp and dirty, was narrow, the ladder stood almost vertically, and his spine scraped against the wall. Water splashed and his voice, as if from a crypt, could be heard: "You climbing or what?" I pulled up my hunting boots, buttoned my leather jacket, and started down. My elbows and shoulders bumped the walls. I had to hold tightly onto the dirty rungs of the shaking ladder, steadied by the worker standing above. With each step down, the stink was stronger. It became horrible. The sound of splashing and dripping water could be heard. I looked up. I could see only a rectangle of blue, clear sky and the face of the worker holding the ladder. A cold, bone-chilling damp seized me. Finally, I got to the last rung, and carefully putting my foot down, felt water flowing past the tip of my boot.

"Come down with confidence, stand still, it's not too deep here," Fedya told me in a quiet, tomb-like voice.

I stood on the bottom as cold water soaked my hunting boots.

"I can't light the lamp, my matches are wet," complained my companion.

I didn't have any matches. Fedya climbed back up.

I stayed alone in the hidden tomb and walked up to my knees into swirling water, maybe 10 steps. I stopped. Gloom surrounded me, impenetrable gloom, the complete absence of light. I turned my head in all directions, but my eyes could make out nothing. I banged my head against something, raised my hand, and fingered a wet, cold, bumpy stone wall covered with slime. I nervously pulled my hand away. I was even scared. It was quiet and only the water burbled below. Every second of waiting for the worker with a light seemed to me an eternity. I moved just a bit farther and heard a noise similar to the roar of a waterfall. In fact, right next to me, a waterfall gurgled, dripping millions of dirty drops, barely lit by a pale yellow light from a pipe opening into the street. This turned out to be a drain for run-off from an opening in the wall.

I did not hear Fedya coming up from behind until he nudged me in the back. I turned. He held a lamp and five tapers, but their flames, which would have been bright anywhere else, seemed here like tiny, dim red stars. They illuminated almost nothing and could not win back even a foot from the gloom. We moved ahead in the deep water, avoiding occasional waterfalls from street drainage burbling at our feet.

Suddenly, there was a frightening rumble like a falling building. I shuddered involuntarily. It was a cart moving past above. I remember a similar rumble on my trip into the shaft of an artesian well, but here it was incomparably stronger. More and more frequently, carriages thundered above. With the lamp, I examined the underworld's damp, slimy walls. We moved forward for some time, in places plunging into deep mud or a foul smelling liquid filth from which no one could have climbed. In places, we had to crouch because deposits of mud were so high it was impossible to walk upright. We had to hunch over and, even then, the whole time I scraped against the top of the vault with my head and shoulders. Our feet sunk into the mud and from time to time would strike something solid. Everything was filmed with liquid filth, so we couldn't make anything out, and we weren't sure we wanted to. In the stink, we walked to the first shaft and bumped into the lowered ladder. I raised my head and rejoiced at the blue sky.

"Still in one piece? Climb out!" a voice trumpeted from above.

"We're going to walk some more. Lower the ladder at the second opening from here."

"Well then, why not? If you want to look, then look."

I ordered him to move the ladder ahead two openings; up it crawled. I liked seeing the blue sky, but after a minute, sinking above my knee into mud and debris, and crawling through street trash, we moved ahead. Again, above us was a rectangle of clear sky. After a few minutes we ran into an incline under our feet. There was an especially thick buildup of mud here and, apparently, it had buried something. We crawled across the pile, illuminating it with the lamp. I dug around with my foot, and under my boot something felt a bit springy. We walked on past the mud. In one of the piles, I saw a dog's corpse, huge, and half-covered with slime. It was especially difficult to get past the final debris pile obstructing the exit to Trubnaya Square, where the ladder waited. Here, the mud was especially thick, and it was slippery underfoot the entire time. It was awful even to think about. But Fedya burst out anyway, "I'm sure of it: we're walking on dead people." I kept silent. I looked up to where the blue sky shone through the iron grate. One more section, and waiting for us were an open grate and a ladder leading to freedom.

MY ARTICLES ABOUT MOSCOW'S SEWERS were a sensation. The City Council ordered the reconstruction of Neglinnaya Street, and the project was assigned to an engineer whom I knew, N.M. Levchayev. He was a well-known outdoorsman with whom more than once I had hunted winter wolves. During construction, I descended with him to the Neglinka River near the Maly Theater, where the main line turned. The riverbed was so clogged at the bend with all kinds of junk that water hardly trickled in a narrow stream over the top; this was the primary reason for the floods. Finally, in 1886, the Neglinka was rebuilt. A reporter's remark had done its task. Levchayev hired my desperate companion Fedya as a workman, somehow got him a passport, and later made him a work gang boss.

TEN YEARS AFTER LEVCHAYEV'S RECONSTRUCTION, mud and thick filth had clogged the bend in the mainline under Kitaisky Drive near the Maly Theater. During the war, the floods were so strong that they filled the lower floors of buildings and shops. The sleepy city manager took no measures at all – the City Council would not approve it. Only in 1926 did the Moscow City Council, under the Soviets, take up the problem of the Neglinka. After uncovering the river starting at the Maly Theater, where the foundation was being undermined by water, and continuing halfway to Sverdlovskaya Square, the littered riverbed was once again cleaned and the flooding ceased.

I once was walking along Neglinnaya Street when, across from the State Bank, I saw a wooden hut surrounded by a fence. I went inside and met an engineer, the project manager. He knew me and agreed when I requested to see the work. In the middle of the hut yawned a narrow opening with the top of a ladder protruding. I started down, but my winter coat was in the way. I did not want to miss the chance to get an interesting article for *Evening Moscow*, where I worked at the time, so I took my coat off and descended in my suit jacket.

The familiar underground corridor was lit by electric bulbs dimly shining through the gloom. The gutter was covered by a wooden walkway, and during thaws it flooded in places. The project was almost done. All the muck had been removed, and the sewer had been put back in order. I walked as far as the Maly Theater and, chilled to the bone, feet wet, and tired of the smell, I crawled up the wet ladder. I put on my winter coat, which didn't warm me, and headed to the newsroom, where I wrote my description of the construction and recalled my journey into the sewer long ago. The next day, I read my article in bed with a high temperature from the flu, and in the end went completely deaf in my left ear. Later, my right ear also showed signs of damage. This was the postscript to my underground journey 40 years earlier into the Neglinka abyss.

NIGHT ON TSVETNOY BOULEVARD

A HOLE IN A POCKET. What could be more insignificant? Exactly this kind of small hole, not noticed in time, turned out to be the start of an adventure. It was August of 1883 when I returned to Moscow after a five-month absence, and devoted my-self to literary work. I wrote poems and other trifles for *Alarm*, *Entertainment*, and *Fragments*, articles on various questions, and wrote accounts of horse races for the Moscow papers. Among my acquaintances from the track were representatives of all ranks and positions. I had to meet people from the darkest professions, but always elegantly dressed and talented handicappers. I made an effort to maintain these rela-tionships: thanks to them, I picked up interesting tips for the newspaper and some-times found my way into secret gambling houses, where my presence was tolerated, and where I met many people who had been accepted into high society, and were even members of clubs, but in reality were card sharps, con artists, or sometimes gang leaders. I could write an entire book about this world. But I will limit myself to reminiscences about one stalwart racing fan, a blond dandy with a full mustache who owned a prize-winning trotter.

The day that the problem with the hole occurred, the stalwart fan approached me at the track. Should he enter his mare in the next event, did she have a chance? Near the exit, after the races, we accidentally met again, and he suggested, on ac-count of the rain, to take me to my home in his carriage. I refused, saying that I was headed for Samotek and it wasn't on his way, but he convinced me, and after letting the driver off, feverishly sped to Samotek, where I dropped in to see an old friend, the artist Pavlik Yakovlev. On the way, we chatted the entire time about horses. He considered me a great expert and therefore respected my opinion. I left Yakovlev's around one in the morning and trudged off in my high boots down the muddy path in the median of Tsvetnoy Boulevard. By force of habit, in my right pocket, I grasped a small knife, a gift from my friend Andreyev-Burlak. This caution seemed unnecessary: there was not a living soul around:

A light autumn rain
Drifts through the mist.

The night was impenetrable. There was not a single street light anywhere because, according to the city calendar, on those nights when the moon was visible, lamps were not lit, and this night, according to the calendar, was lunar. That night, also, there was mist. It gathered above the bushes, and hung on trees, turning them into specters. Only on such a night could one walk calmly along this boulevard not risking robbery or death at the hands of the regulars, who left their slums in Grachyovka and Arbuzov's Fortress, a huge, formerly nice building located on the boulevard.

Most intimidating was Lesser Kolosov Alley, coming out from Grachyovka onto Tsvetnoy Boulevard, completely filled with johns for the last call at the whorehouses. The entrances to these buildings, where they met the street, were certain to be lit by a red lamp. The dirtiest secret dens of prostitution were in these quiet courtyards, where no lights were allowed and where windows faced away from the street. Typically, no dogs were kept in these courtyards. The women who lived here had lost all resemblance to human beings, and their tomcats, hiding from the police, were the kind for whom it was risky even to enter Khitrovka's flophouses. At night, the tomcats went out on Tsvetnoy Boulevard and Samoteka, where their kittens rolled drunks. Either they invited drunks to their hideouts, or the tomcats, who followed closely on the heels of their "ladies," took care of them right there. Muscle was recruited for crimes from distant slums, and the police never even looked in their direction. If, because of the bosses, usually the procurator, raids were actually carried out, then "the managers" knew about it in time, and, despite the "surprise" raids, they never found what they were looking for. The women in these apartments, mostly former prostitutes, were fictitious leaseholders. The real leaseholders were their lovers, escaped criminals wanted by the police, other scammers, or thieves who had not yet been caught.

Card sharps and gambling bosses, in the worst buildings, had secret rooms, so-called "mills." They were used for scamming thieves and robbers. They frequented the slums to satisfy their thirst for risk while certain there wouldn't be any distractions or bystanders. A card sharp's associates or game organizers only had to get a whiff of money in the hands of some thief after a successful job, and they would start hunting. On a pre-arranged day, they would invite him to the "mill" to play a deck or two. There were no real games at the "mills": at the appointed hour a finely tuned company of card sharps had assembled. A dealer – someone to do the job – was invited. He could deal any card needed, and the gambling thief's money would go to the sharps. "Mills" were run for this task. During the day, when the "mill" was not filled with "businessmen," every kind of dirty game was played, and provided a dependable income – the banks were paying 10 percent. Career criminals, out of caution, did not frequent the larger "mills," run out of luxury apartments. There were dozens of such "mills" at the time on Moscow's main streets.

THE 1880S SAW THE GREATEST flowering of such establishments. At the time, slum owners seemed most well-intentioned from a political standpoint, and enjoyed a special degree of support from the police, whom they paid well. The political department did not consider them "dangerous to the state" and even protected them, right up to the owners of the slums and "mills," who helped with security when the tsar came through the area. At the time, the police were busy only catching "unreliable" elements inclined toward revolution, whom they arrested and exiled by the hundreds. The slum world of Grachyovka and Tsvetnoy Boulevard flourished.

I marched in silence among the misty specters and suddenly felt a strange pain in my left foot near the ankle. The pain eventually became strong enough that it forced me to stop. I looked around for a place to sit and adjust my boot, but no bench was in sight and the pain in my foot was unbearable. I leaned up against a tree, tore off my boot, and immediately discovered the reason for the pain: my small knife had fallen from my pocket into my boot. After returning the knife to my pocket, I started to put my boot on, but heard steps in the puddles and a quiet conversation. I hunkered down behind the tree. From the direction of Bezimyanka, three people, holding each other up, were silhouetted by a circle of light from a red lamp.

"I'm freezing, let's rest… it's not fit for a dog on this street."

"Oh you skinny weakling. Alright, let go."

The furthest of the group bent forward and carefully lowered the middle one to the ground.

"They're helping a drunk," I thought.

I got a good look at an enormous man in a coat and, next to him, a hunchbacked figure. He shook his hand and blew on it.

"What a giant, stretched both my arms." The big one lay flat in a puddle.

"Fokach, let's dump him here or maybe in the bushes right over there."

"This is too close to the police guardhouse, you simpleton! Tomorrow they'll be kicking around under every shrub."

"Into a pipe would be a better idea and 'ends in the water."

"If we're doing it, let's do it quietly. Grab on! Now you can use your arms." The big one took him by the head, the small one by the legs and carried him like a log.

I followed behind, in the grass to avoid noise. The rain stopped. The water burbled, flowing through the gutter next to the sidewalk, and with a gurgle fell through

Gorodovoy - Moscow beat cop.

an iron grate into the collector shaft for the underground Neglinka. Right next to it, the "laborers" stopped and threw the body onto the stones.

"Raise the grate."

The small one bent forward and then straightened up. "It's slippery, I can't."

"Oh, you rotten scrap of flesh!"

The giant tore out the grate and moved it aside. "Aha," I thought, "here's what 'ends in the water' means." I stepped into the bushes, steadied myself, and yelled across the whole boulevard, "Over here, guys! Grab them!" Pulling from my pocket a police whistle, which I always carried just in case, racing through the slums I gave three long, sharp, whistles. Both criminals at first took off down the sidewalk, and then crossed the street and hid in an empty lot's bushes. I ran up to the prone figure and felt his face. The beard and moustache were shaven. A large strong man. Shoes, pants, vest, and a white spot on his starched shirt. I took his hand and he moved his fingers. Alive!

I gave one more triple whistle and received instant replies from two directions. I heard hurried steps. A janitor was running from the next building, and, from the boulevard, a city cop. I hid in the bushes to confirm that they saw the man by the grate. The janitor ran along the sidewalk right into him and started whistling. The cop ran up. Both bent over the prone man. I wanted to walk over, but once more felt pain in my foot. The knife had fallen through the hole again. This decided it: there was no reason to take a risk, I would find out the next day. I knew that side of the boulevard belonged to the first precinct of the Sretenskaya Division. The other side of Bezymyanka, where they dragged the body from, belonged to the second precinct. I hailed a cab on Trubnaya Square and headed home.

At 10 the next morning, I was at the Sretensky watchtower in the office of the precinct captain, Larepland. I was well acquainted with him and had more than once gotten information from him for the papers. He had one weakness. A former cantonist, he had served for 10 years in the Moscow police, rose from a street cop to captain, received the rank of collegial assessor, and was happy when he was appointed a captain even though he wore the stripes of a civil organization.[1]

"Captain, I just received information that last night a murder victim was found on Tsvetnoy Boulevard."

"First, no murder victim was found. We did pick up a drunk who was mugged on Grachyovka, dragged into my precinct, and abandoned. That's how thieves do it – so there are fewer problems for both them and us. Who needs to go searching in someone else's precinct? No one can prove that he was dragged here. That's the first thing. Second: a most humble request to you not to write a word about this for the papers. I didn't even write a report, and closed the case myself. How you found out – I give up! No one knew except the officers who found him and the victim. And he asked me himself for the case to be closed. No, no, please do not write anything, or you might undermine my authority. I did not report it to my commander." Larepland told me that they brought in an unconscious drunk, an almost naked man whom they had picked up off the sidewalk from a puddle.

"Initially, we thought he was dead, so we put him in the morgue with the bodies of two drunks, but he started moving and talking. He fell asleep right away once we put him in the reception area. They left him alone, and I spoke with him this morning. Turns out he's a wealthy German, his brother works in the Vogel office. They just came for him. The brother arrived in a carriage and took him away. The German was out last night for a good time, wound up in a dive when girls dragged him in, and there they put "*malinka*" in his drink,[2] took everything, and dumped him into my precinct. That's the way it is sometimes. Captain Kapeni (also a cantonist) is a friend, and, well, we closed the case. An open case will do no one any good; anyway, nothing will change. Anything else will only cause trouble. He's lucky to be alive. He showed signs of life just in time. A young, good looking German, ended up drunk in a den of criminals, they forced him to drink beer with girls. All he remembers is that they all drank out of beer glasses, but they served him in a glass mug with a metal lid, topped by a decorative bird. That was the only thing he really remembered.

I promised to write nothing about this event and, of course, did not say anything to the captain about what I saw that night. But I then decided to study Grachyovka, which was so similar to Khitrovka, Arzhenovka, Khapilovka and the other slums that I had often visited.

---

1. The cantonist system mandated military conscription of Jews and other targeted minorities. It was instituted in 1827, and boys as young as 12 were forced to serve a 25-year term in the Russian army. In 1856, Tsar Alexander II abolished the system. During its existence, tens of thousands of boys had been forced from their homes, faced the worst kinds of military hazing, and endured religious persecution and the threat of forced conversion. Many never returned home.

2. *Malinka*: criminal slang for a strong-acting sleeping powder or a narcotic used for euthanasia. Also slang for a mixture of beer and vodka.

BEER MUG WITH AN EAGLE

ONE FREE EVENING I ENDED up in Grachyovka. I had listened to a Hungarian choir at the Crimea tavern on Trubnaya Square, where I met some cardsharps – perpetual visitors at the track – and a familiar merchant or two. I walked past Grachyovka's whorehouses, not the official ones with a red lamp, but the ones nestled in the cellars and dark, dirty courtyards, and stinking dumps of Kolosovka, or Bezymyanka as it was sometimes called. Around midnight, this alley, where the air was especially malodorous, simmered with its usual noise, including the sounds of an out-of-tune piano, violins, and at times, harmonicas. When the doors opened under the red lamp, drunken songs could be heard. In one of the distant, dark courtyards, light from the windows barely penetrated and blurry shadows moved about. Whispering could be heard, and then, unexpectedly, a woman's shriek or hopeless cursing. In front of me was one of the slums where they lured drunks, robbed them clean, and dumped them in an empty lot. Women stood near the entrances posing in "living paintings" and called out to roaming drunks, promising all of life's joys, including cigarettes, for a flat fee: five rubles. When I crossed the yard and walked up to the entrance, I heard an invitation in French, and again in Russian.

"Visit with us, we're having fun!" A tall woman separated herself from the wall and dragged me by the hand down the stairway.

"We have vodka and beer."

We went in. We could see a weak, reddish light through the steam and smoke. Cacophony. Under a black ceiling coated with smoke was an enormous room with three tables. On the wall close to the door hung a crude lamp whose black column of smoke fanned out like a crow across the top of the room, merging imperceptibly with a ceiling already black with grime. On two of the tables were exactly the same type of lamp, empty bottles, and scattered scraps of bread, cucumber, and fish. At the far table, next to the window, a fierce card game raged. A fleshy, red-headed *bogatyr*[1] with a trimmed beard, wearing a coat, dealt. Rolled-up sleeves revealed enormous fists in which a deck of cards almost disappeared. Pale bums, with the gleaming eyes of gamblers, crowded around.

"Seven points."

"I have a fiver. Put it on P."

"25 from the five," could be heard from the players. Further on, through the open door, an identical room could be seen. A table also stood at the far end with two candles. A card game was underway there, too. In front of me, at a table without a lamp, an unshaven, pale man in a uniform jacket was embracing a drunk broad who, in a falsetto, recited:

I ate a roll and had some drink,
But I forget with whom, I think.

An exhausted young man who looked about 17, in polished boots, a Hungarian cloak, and with a new cap on his head, was banging the bottom of a water glass on the table, arguing fiercely with a small, disheveled man:

"Listen you..."

"Listen to what? To what? We do the job, we split the loot."

"That's the way it is, you mope. You're the picker, I'm the screen. You get the wallet, and I get the watch. The wallet has 20 rubles in it!"

"The watch worked well, must be foreign made."

"I got 50 rubles for it."

"You're laying it on a bit thick."

"Honest! May I drop dead if it isn't the truth."

"Where'd it all go?"

"The good life! Here are my new spats, and look at this hat. My pockets are empty."

"Look at the dandy who just walked in, Oska."

The well-fed young man looked at me and I could hear his whisper.

"He isn't a detective is he?"

"All you see is detectives!"

"Noooo! It's just that the old guy looks tough."

"Well, we'll just find out."

He turned to the "lady" who had brought me here:

"What do you say, you drunk? Brought a reference with you?"

---

1. *Bogatyr:* a heroic type, massive and strong, found in Russian folklore. Reference is to his size, not heroic qualities.

My "Colonel" turned her stern, thickly-plastered face to the speaker, blinked her large, dark, sunken eyes, and shouted:

"My lord wants to drink. Sit down, sit down! *Je vous prie.*"[2]

"Sit down, you'll be a guest. If you buy some wine, you can be the host," shouted the bearded dealer, shuffling the cards. I sat down next to Oska.

"Lord, buy some wine, treat your Colonel," said the young man in the Hungarian cloak.

"If you please."

"If you're willing to part with a crisp ruble you can treat everyone. The baron over there has a headache."

A man in a uniform coat feverishly flew over and hurriedly said: "Baron Dorghauzen, Otto Karlovich. I ask your respect and assistance." His leg shook inside his pants.

"Are you a baron?" I asked.

"Ma parole! I give my word. A baron and a governor's secretary. I was born in Liflyandia, went to school in Berlin. In Moscow, I got caught up with the wrong circle and ruined myself with drink, lost everything... lend me 20 kopeks. I'll go and double it at the gaming table. Until we meet again."

"If you please!"

In a moment, his commanding voice could be heard:

"The club is here... I have it... I have it."

"It's true, mister, he's a real baron," Oska whispered to me. "He forges certificates of destitution and false membership cards. Even the seals look real. If you want a residence card, he's your man. His prices are fine. Except the cost for forms, it's a ruble and a half per page. For permanent documents, three rubles."

"Permanent?"

"Yes, a landed gentry's passport or a retirement certificate. He'll write it up with ranks and medals."

"A baron... a colonel..," I mumbled in thought.

"But the Colonel is real, and not just some junior colonel. She lives with him. The place is in her name."

Here, the Colonel interrupted him, and, sprinkling her words with broken French, recounted how, as a teenager, she had been given in marriage to an old man, a garrison colonel, and how she escaped abroad with her neighbor-accomplice, how he abandoned her in Paris, and how she returned home and ended up right here in Bezymyanka.

"Well, you vulture, if you're going to wag your tongue, go get us some beer," the dealer yelled, not even looking around.

---

2. A formal way to say "if you please," (literally: "I pray you").

Kabak, by Andrei Ryabushkin (1891).

"I'm going, you loser. Why are you yelling? This is hard work!"

"Turkey! No luck... Huh? Which? No, you listen. I'm putting it on the six. On P. I've got half on P. Points in advance. Got it. I'm showing the card. Lost. I put it on same spot and lost. I put on another and lost. In a row! In a row!"

"That means you lost?"

"Dope! If only I had gotten that last card. I got a spade. I watched the cards, and, wham, I lost. Would you loan me more... until we meet again?! That card..."

Again I gave him 20 kopeks.

"*Oll-rayt!*[3] This is refined language. Until we meet again." The Colonel poured beer into four glasses, and for me into a glass mug with a German silver lid decorated with an eagle. The Baron tore himself away from the cards for a moment, and with a raised glass, loudly and clearly toasted:

"To our ladies' health! Hur-rah!"

"Why aren't you drinking? Get started!" said the Colonel.

"I don't drink beer," I answered curtly.

At this point, the game ended. The dealer, putting the cards and the money in his pocket and turning up the flame in the lamp, stood up. "Gang, until tomorrow! All of you get out." The players, accustomed to obeying him, jumped-up and left silently. Only the Baron stayed, still eager. The dealer threw 20 kopeks at him. "Listen, get out of here! I'm sick of you. Asking for cards with no ante. You've got a kopek's worth of ammunition but a ruble's worth of ambition. Get out of here before you go too far." The dealer took the Baron by the shoulders, and in a flash put him out the

---

3. The Baron uses an English exclamation, "All right!" (Ол-райт!).

door, which he immediately locked with a hook. The Baron did not even have time to run his mouth. Only Oska, the pickpocket in the Hungarian cloak, the drunken female Colonel, and the dealer were left. He sat down with us. From the next room, card players could be heard. The Colonel poured refills, and pushed my untouched glass over to me:

"Have some, don't insult us."

"But I'm not alone, am I? That young man isn't drinking."

"The brat? He can't," said Oska.

"The doctor told him he can't," the Colonel reassured me.

"You, boss, why aren't you drinking? That's not the way it's done here. Please drink!" said the bearded dealer and reached out to toast with me.

I refused.

"This is an insult. You're disgusted by us. That's not the way it's done here. Drink! Well? Don't act like it's a sin, drink!"

"No!"

"No, eh? Oska, pour it down his gub."

The dealer jumped up, grabbed my forehead with one hand and my chin with the other to force open my mouth. Oska stood with the mug, prepared to pour the beer into my mouth. This was the decisive moment. I grabbed a set of brass knuckles from my pocket and jabbed the dealer right in the teeth. Howling, he crumpled to the floor.

"What's going on in there?" a voice rang out from behind me, and a man in a black frock coat came through the door. Behind him, two others stood at the threshold. The man in the suit turned to me and we both froze with surprise. "Is that you?" the man in the frock coat shouted, and in one motion knocked aside the dealer, who had jumped up from the floor, his beard covered in blood, and leapt to attack me. He fell again. Before me, confused and surprised, stood the "racing fan" who had given me a ride home from the track. All the others turned to stone.

He grabbed the mug from Oska's hands and splashed the beer out onto the floor.

"Get out," he ordered the Colonel, who was trembling in fear. "Vladimir Alexeyevich, how did you end up here? Let's go stop by my room."

"You can go to hell. I'm heading home."

I put on my cap and moved toward the door. The dealer lay on his gut on the floor, moaning and spitting out teeth.

"No, no, I'll show you out!"

He jumped up behind me, took my elbow, helped me up the damaged stone stairs, and mumbled excuses. I stubbornly kept silent. I thought to myself, "ends in the water, Larepland with *malinka*, the German, the lid with a bird..." The "racing fan" continued to offer apologies and added, "After all, in the end I did save you from Samson. He could have crippled you."

"I saved myself when I didn't drink the *malinka*."

"How do you know?" he shot back looking surprised, then added in another tone, "What kind of *malinka*?"

"The kind you poured out of the mug. It doesn't make any difference."

"You... you..." His teeth banged together and he could not get a word out.

"I know everything, but I also know how to keep quiet."

"I see, sir. That's why I wanted you to drop by my room. It has a private doorway. Some friends got together to play some cards. After all, I don't even live here."

"I saw... Goliath... the scorekeeper... and I recognized it all."

"Yes, he sat next to you... Krechinsky went back and forth. The Heron was there too, Vatoshnik, then..."

"Vatoshnik? Timoshka Vatoshnik? But he's a detective!"

"To some, he's a detective, to us he's a good friend! Again, we ask your kind forgiveness."

"Remember: I know everything, but I'll never give you up. It's as if nothing happened. Goodbye!" I shouted to him from a cab.

Whenever I ran across him, the "racing fan" tried not to be seen. Once he caught me alone in a side alley and in a shaky voice whispered, "You promised, Vladimir Alexeyevich, but look what you wrote in the newspaper? Good thing no one paid any attention: it's over for now. But even so it's all obvious. Everyone knows Fenka is the Colonel, and you called the Baron by his first name and patronymic, and simply gave him a different surname. The police know everything about him, he's even registered to live in Moscow. The main thing is that the Baron..."

"Calm down, I won't write any more."

I had, in truth, published a short story, "In the Dead of Night," that described what I saw in the slum, the card game, and the visitor poisoned with *malinka* whom they had taken for dead and dragged away to throw into the sewer. I simply renamed Kolosov Alley as Bezimyanka.[4] I described the details of the situation and participants. Baron Dorghauzen, Otto Karlovich, was his real name.

There was an epilogue: When the Neglinka sewer was cleaned, bones were found that resembled human remains.

---

4. *Bezimyanka* in Russian means "no name."

DRAMATISTS FROM DOG HALL

EVERYTHING IS IN THE DETAILS – like a hole in a pocket. During the time that I'm now writing about, I had a conversation:

"Persian daisies![1] Oh no, you're not joking. If there were no such thing, I would not be the same person, and my patron would not be a member of the Society of Dramatic Writers, and I would not have received thousands in author's honorariums, and the Dog's Hall... Do you know what the Dog's Hall is?"

"No."

"A famous reporter and you don't know Dog's Hall?!"

This conversation took place on the steps of a horse-drawn "imperial" from Petrovsky Park to Strastnoy Monastery.[2] The man next to me, in a clean suit, a hat, and a wool scarf tied "as the devil may care," was greying at the temples and had an actor's clean-shaven face. When I climbed the stairs and stepped out into the upper passenger area, he greeted me by name, shifted over on his seat, and suggested I join him. He was smoking an enormous, cheap cigar. His first words were:

"Savings. Down in the main car the fare is five kopeks, but up here, outside in the fresh air, it's three kopeks. However, I don't ride up here in the so-called 'imperial' section for the savings, but because of these," and pointed a smoldering cigar at me. "These are the only cigars that I smoke. Three rubles for a train car full, a ruble and a half per heap, their smoke can kill lice, yes sir, a genuine 'imperial,' because you can only smoke them when you ride in the imperial section of the car. Would you like to become an imperialist?"

That is, he offered me a cigar.

---

1. Persian daisies were used, in powdered form, against lice.
2. Imperials were doubled-decked, horse-drawn streetcars.

"I don't smoke." As evidence, I showed him my snuff box, and offered a pinch.

"No, thank you kindly. I'd still be sneezing when I got home."

And then he threw out the line about Persian daisies. He tossed the stogie onto the forehead of a cop standing on the road, took a fresh cigar from his pocket, lit it, and introduced himself.

"I am Glazov, the playwright. You, of course, I know."

"What plays have you written?"

"Me? Well…" and he listed around 10 works, which, judging by the titles, came from the pen of a certain well-known director, famed for rewriting foreign plays. I knew the man, and thought that he had written them.

"Hey, you're listing plays belonging to…" and I mentioned the name.

"Yes, he has the rights, but I'm the author. I did 17 plays for him in the last year, and was paid 334 rubles. He squeezes me for every kopek. He is considered a playwright, though he spells like a dog.

"In the old days, backstage at the theater, they gave scissors to barbers who cut the hair of the poor while they learned the trade. Today, you make some money, win an award, and you're considered a real talent, chair the Society of Dramatic Writers. The catalog lists over 100 plays in his name translated from French, English, Spanish, Polish, Hungarian, Italian and others. But it's all a scam."[3]

A horse-drawn "imperial."

"How is that?"

"Well, here's how. About two years ago I wrote a comedy. I sent it here and there but no one would take it. I went to see him at the theater. I didn't catch him. I went to his home. He received me in a luxurious office. He sat self-importantly, stretched out on an armchair, next to a writing table."

"I proposed: 'I wrote a play but no one will take it because I'm an unknown. Agree to put your name up next to mine, and I will give you half the fee.'

"He took the play, started to read, and gave me a cigar and a newspaper.

" 'You have talent and understand the stage, but putting your name next to mine is just so awkward. Besides, the play does not fit our theater.'

" 'A pity.'

" 'You, of course, need money, yes?'

3. Glazov is alluding to the fundamental dishonesty of the underlying process, not any one language.

" 'Frankly, I'm broke.'

" 'Well then, rewrite this play for me.'

"He gave me a French play, translated by someone not entirely unknown, from Kharkov. I looked through the new, three-act play fresh from the censor's office.

" 'What should I rewrite? After all, it's just been translated.'

" 'Well, it's simple: you need to do it in such a way that the play remains just the same but so that the author and the translator can't recognize it. I would do it myself but I don't have the time. As soon as you get this done, I'll give you another.'

"At first, and for some time, I failed to understand what exactly he wanted, but he began to explain rewriting with examples, so that I understood what was needed.

" 'Well sir, get the play to me in a week. A week, that's just for starters; later, you'll have to get plays sewn-up in two days.'

"I brought the play back in a week. He praised me, and gave me money and another play. From there, it went on and on: two days for a three-act farce and 25 rubles. The play is his, the signature is his, but the work is totally mine."

I was interested, but understood exactly nothing. The car stopped at Strastnoy Boulevard, and, exiting the Imperial, Glazov suggested we sit for a while on the boulevard near the Pushkin monument. He was in the middle of a fascinating tale. I listened with interest.

"How and what did you rewrite? Where did the director find so many plays to rewrite?" I asked.

"He's a director, after all. They send him plays to put on in his theater and he turns to me right away. I would go to see him secretly in his office. The doors open a bit, I hear familiar voices in his sitting room, co-workers from the stage, and I stand like a thief. The doors to the office are locked. He hands me a play, fresh from the mail, and says, 'Have it done by Friday. On Saturday I have to send it back. You can't hold on to it for more than two days.'"

"Once, a letter was left in a play I had gotten from him: he had written to the letter's author that the play could not be presented for reasons beyond his control. Why put on someone else's play when you have your own?! Within two days, I gave this play a new face, and it was put on within a month. But the farce, along with the letter I found, was sent to the author on the same day that I gave them back."

Glazov got carried away: "How many plays I rewrote for him! How simple! You take a brand new play, read it, and the first thing you do is give it a fitting title. For example, if the author called his play, *In the Hands*, I might call it *Up a Sleeve*, or if the author's surname is Fisher I might call it *On a Fishing Trip*. After you change the title, you start on the characters. Give them the first names that pop into your head, as long as they don't sound French. Make the lesser characters your own: make an Italian a Greek, and an Englishman an American, a butler a maid, and just so the play is completely impossible to recognize, include a machine-gun or a parrot. When a parrot or a machine-gun is on stage, narration can come from the wings. Well, sir, once you are done with the characters, change the props and scenery. Make the phrasing your own and rearrange events. Write an effective ending. Replace some of the original salt with a bit of spice, and the play is done."

The tone of his voice immediately dropped, "I steal from talented authors! I only resorted to this after I was evicted from my apartment... and then I got used to it. I did it to eat, but he puts his name on plays and gets the laurels and the wealth. He's shoveling in the royalties, goes to the track... and me? The expenses are all mine, I get 25 rubles per play and pay five out immediately for copying. I treat the hangovers of these half-dressed scribes, and pour them tea. Until their hangovers are gone their hands can't stop shaking."

He told me much more, and made me give my word to visit him. "It's my wife and I, the two of us. She's a former actress from the provinces, an *ingénue*. I'm free tomorrow, no orders yet. So come by tomorrow around one."

"I give my word."

The next day I went down to Glazov's apartment on the basement floor of a building next to the Moldavia on Zhivoderkaya Street. In the dim entryway, where the doors of two apartments opened, three pitiful men stood, clothed in rags. A fourth, in just a starched shirt and a vest, sprinkled the vagrants with powder from a box. It smelled familiar.

"Hello, Glazov!" I yelled from the stairs.

"Oh, is that you Vladimir Alekseyevich? Just a moment, I'll just sprinkle these devils." He threw handfuls of powder in the three wretches' collars, shirts, and even under their waistbands. The unfortunates shook themselves out, giggled from the feeling of the powder, and sneezed.

"Wait for a second until they crawl out of here. Now we can go. If you please!"

He opened the door in front of me into a relatively clean apartment.

"What was all that about?" I ask.

"My transcribers arrived," Glazov answered seriously. "They just delivered a rush order."

"So what's going on?"

"I sprinkle them with Persian daisies. Without that, it's impossible. Excuse me, I've got to change." He threw on a jacket.

"Ellen! My friend is here to see me. A writer. Fix us a bite to eat. But come here."

"*Mille pardons*. I'm still not dressed." A young woman came out of the bedroom in curlers with traces of makeup and powder on a tired face.

"My wife... Stasova-Sarayskaya. An *ingénue*."

"Oh, George. He can't get by without his silly jokes." She smiled at me. "Excuse our mess. George deals with those derelicts, the scribes. They sit and scratch, and we spend 40 kopeks a day on Persian daisies. But, without it, they'd make this place such a zoo that you'd have to run out. They're from Dog's Hall."

Glazov interrupts. "Yes. Persian daisies are a great thing. Thought this up myself. Now I sprinkle it all over, in beards, on heads, and in underwear for those who have it. Then you make them stand for half an hour in the hall, and everything is fine. They can write, they don't scratch, and the room stays clean.

"So you're saying that without Persian daisies you couldn't finish a play?"

"Wouldn't happen. After all, I can't let them in the apartment without it. They're a literate bunch and they know the stage. Some of them are former actors. And we can put a play together in two days. One, two, three and the pot is boiling."

"Ellen, you serve our guest breakfast, and I'll get busy on the play. Please excuse me; I have to turn this in tomorrow morning. Visit for a while with my wife."

We went into a room adjoining the bedroom. A bottle of vodka stood on the table, along with some meat fried on a kerosene stove. Outside, a wet, penetrating December cold prevailed. Snow melted, there were puddles. Moscow's vile streets couldn't be navigated, neither on a sleigh nor wheels.

It was just the same on Zhivoderkaya Street, at John de Gabrielle's Dog Hall. Filled with a mix of people such as drivers, gypsies, and waiters, the street was extremely noisy day and night. When all of the "establishments serving beverages" closed, and a willing man had nowhere to get the water of life, he would come to this street and satisfy his desire in the Peter Pitt Tavern. Such was the name of a wine bar owned by Ivan Gavrilov, but called by its regulars Dog's Hall, a part of Peter Pitt's Tavern.

In the words of John DeGabrielle himself, he worked two schedules: from seven in the morning to 11 at night for drinking, and from 11 at night until seven in the morning for curing hangovers. At night, at 11, the doors to the bar were locked; however, a room in the basement was opened. Two enormous trunks stood there, one with full bottles, one with half-full bottles. A *babushka* sold them to go and for drinking in Dog's Hall. They sold carry-out through a slot. The customer would knock, put money in silently, and silently get a bottle. The slot was called a *shlanboy*.[4] There were many *shlanboys* just like it in Moscow: in Grachyovka, on Khitrovka, and in the outlying areas.

If you needed to get vodka at night, you walked straight up to a cop, asked where to get it, and he'd point out a building. "Go through the gates, there's the *shlanboy*, a red curtain. You go in, the slot opens, later, you'll give me 20 kopeks or a swig from the bottle."

Returning home somewhere around two in the morning from Lesser Gruzinskaya Street, I tripped and slid along the pitted sidewalks of Zhivoderkaya Street.

---

4. See footnote page 44.

Near one of the few lights on this gypsy street someone called out my name, and in a moment in front of me loomed a ragged, unshaven man with an actor's face. He had a familiar look, but I couldn't place him.

He told me his name.

"I made a mistake, brother, and started drinking. It's my second year at Dog's Hall. I gave up the stage and now rewrite plays."

I remembered him as a young man, a talented new actor, and it was painful to see this hollow wretch: swollen, shaking, eyes tearing, jaws chattering.

"Some vodka would be nice," he said to me, tentatively.

"Yes, well, it's late. Otherwise, I'd buy."

"Oh no, what are you saying?! Come with me, right next door."

He took me by the sleeve and hurriedly marched me down the icy sidewalk. On the corner of the alley stood a two-story wooden building and next to it, through a gate and lit by a lamp, was an old wing with a custom green sign, "Wine Bar."

We stopped by the gate.

The actor knocked.

"Who is it now?" croaked out from the yard.

"Open sesame," my companion answered.

"Who?" the yard croaked louder.

"*Shlanboy.*"

The gate opened at this magic word, a stench wafted from the yard, and we walked past a watchman in a sheepskin coat wielding an enormous wooden baton. We stepped onto the wing's porch and found ourselves at an entrance.

"Hold onto me or you might fall," my companion warned. Our roles had switched: now, I held *his* hand. He opened the door. It smelled of body heat, the horrible, stinking body heat of a living slum. It is a picture worth describing: a small room, a dirty table with empty bottles lit by a crude lamp; on the left, an enormous Russian stove (the room had been built beneath the kitchen), and on the floor in a heap slept more than 10 people of both genders, mixed together so closely there was nowhere to put down a foot to get over to the table.

"Here we are, home," said my companion, bursting out in a wild voice. "Wake up you corpses, rise from the grave! We brought vodka!" The heap of rags started rustling; unhappy voices complained. He repeated, "We brought vodka!" He climbed up on the oven. "Woman, vodka!"

"He got it for you, demons of the darkest night, may you never find peace..."

"Arkashka, is that you?" came a voice. People got up from the floor, wiped their eyes, and mumbled, "Where's the vodka?"

"Give me water, devils! My throat is parched," moaned a half-dressed woman, deathly pale, with uncombed hair and a bruised forehead.

"Arkashka, whom did you bring? Karas?"

"What difference does it make, woman? Vodka!"

A dirty, wrinkled old woman crawled down off the stove. A ragged actor carefully struggled with a pince-nez with only one lens. The other lens was broken, so he closed the eye on that side. "Also an artist and author," Arkashka commented.

I looked around the room. Above the table, in the corner, was a crude caricature depicting a man who, judging by his face, had loved much, and had suffered much from love. Under the picture was a caption: "Dog's Hall at John DeGabrielle's." Dramatists and actors lived here, working for their illiterate bosses.

MERCHANTS

IN WELL-MAINTAINED CITIES, SIDEWALKS RUN on both sides of the street. Sometimes, in especially crowded places, concrete or asphalt crosswalks are laid across the pavement for the comfort of pedestrians. In Moscow, Greater Dmitrovka Street is crossed by a nice walk of granite blocks. No one ever crosses here because there is no reason: there are no side streets nearby. This granite crosswalk begins near the entrance of a large mansion with mirrored windows. Right here, around midnight, on both sides of the granite diagonal, Greater Dmitrovka was always the noisiest street.

In 1883, the Korsh Theater opened in Bogoslovsky (Petrovsky) Alley. At nine in the evening, drivers, without passengers, started arriving here from all over the city, formed a line on both sides of the alley, and those who failed to find a spot stretched out down the street to the right, since the left side was full of single-horse carriages and pairs who had paid the city large fees for their spots. "Johnnies," yellow-eyed cab drivers from the lower classes, and "*kashniks*," those who had come to the city for the winter only, paid off the street cops.

Guards and janitors maintained order, and walked up to every arriving driver, who placed in their hands a 20-kopek coin set aside earlier. A city cop would self-importantly stroll down the middle of the street and count harnesses to track the split. Occasionally he would walk up to drivers and shake their hands: there was nothing to be gotten from those who had just paid for a space. Perhaps someone would treat him to a cigarette.

There were few passersby to or from the theater during these hours. More often, poorly dressed students ran by, returning to a dormitory in the rear courtyard of a nearby merchant's mansion. Drivers stood about in groups near their sleighs, smoked, gossiped, sipped warm, honeyed drinks, and sometimes a bit of vodka, which was poured by the honey drink vendor with the cop's tacit permission.

At the start of the evening, a few sanitation tankers, hitched to pairs of horses and allowed to work only at night, pulled into the mansion's courtyard. These "night

Korsh Theater.

Merchants' Club.

perfumers," nicknamed for a well-known perfume company, opened waste pits, emptied their contents with long-handled buckets, and carted it off to the dump. Work continued. Students squeezed through the rows of buckets surrounding the dormitory's entrance. Suddenly, the drivers started moving and lined up along the sidewalk in expectant poses.

"Korsh is done!"

Happy and excited, theatergoers poured out of an alley.

The drivers attacked:

"Where to? Sir, come with Ivan!"

"Just a ruble. Where to?"

The drivers shouted at the top of their lungs, pushing and shoving one another, blocking the road.

"Where to? Where to?" hangs in the air.

A street cop walked by, giving the impression of no lesser rank than an army commander, and shouted now and again.

At this moment, the mansion's gates open and a pair of horses with a tanker... "Where are you going? Get back!" a thunderous exclamation from the cop rose above the noise. "What are you looking at, dog face! Can't you see that people haven't left?"

The watchman, sitting by the gates, reinforced this with a forceful gesture right in the driver's face. "Take off, devil."

The pair of horses was backed-up, with some effort, into the courtyard, and the gates were closed. But the stink had already poisoned the complaining public. The taxis left. People walked off. Private carriages drove up to the lights, shining like apples at the entrance to the Merchants' Club, and customers, after feasting, rushed to restaurants on the edge of the city to "take the air."

The Merchants' Club was located in a spacious building that belonged, at the time of Catherine the Great, to Field Marshall and Commandant of Moscow, Count Saltykov. After Napoleon's march it went to the landed gentry family of Myatlev. The Moscow Merchant's Club leased the place in the forties from this same family. At that time, Greater Dmitrovka Street was filled with gentry. The Dolgorukys, the Golitsyns, the Urusovs, the Gorchakovs, the Saltykovs, the Shakovskys, the Shcherbatovs, the Myatlevs. Only later did such mansions pass into merchants' hands. At the turn of the century, the gentry's coats of arms disappeared from the façades, and signs belonging to the new owners appeared: Solodovnikovs, Golofteyevs, Tsyplakovs, Shelaputs, Khludovs, Obidins, Lyapins.

In the old days, Dmitrovka was still known as Klubnaya Street – three clubs were located there: the English Club in Muravyov's building, Dvoryansky's became the Philanthropical Society, the Prikazchy Club moved into Muravyov's, and the Merchants' Club moved to Myatlev's. Grand chambers were occupied by merchants and the lordly ambience was replaced by mercantile ways, just as the extravagant French menu was replaced by traditional Russian food. Sturgeon soup, two-foot sturgeons, pickled white sturgeon,

An *izvozchik* (cabbie) naps between fares.

"banquet veal," turkey white as cream, raised on walnuts; white fish filets; liver; pork with horseradish; pork with whole grains. Pork for the "second" lunches at the Merchants' Club was bought at great expense from Testov's, the same that was sold in the well-known tavern. He fattened pigs at his dacha in special feeding pens where their legs were trapped by a grate: "to keep them fat," Ivan Yakovlevich explained. Fish and chicken came from Yaroslavsky's Rostov, and the "banquet" veal from Troitsy, where calves were fed with whole milk. All of this was sold in enormous quantities at the second lunches, crowded and noisy.

Aside from wine, a sea of which was poured, especially champagne, the Merchants' Club was praised for Moscow's best *kvas*[1] and fruit drinks. The secret was known only to one elderly leader of the club, Nikolai Agafonovich. At his appearance in the reception room, where, after coffee and liqueurs, merchants digested their Lucullan meals, voices instantly called out, "Nikolai Agafonovich!" Each demanded his favorite beverage. Some liked aromatic tea: black elderberry smells of buds, as if you were laying under a shrub in the spring; some preferred cherry – the color of a ruby, the taste of ripe cherries; some liked raspberry; others liked sweet white *kvas*, and still others sour *shchi* – a carbonated beverage, so it had to be kept in champagne magnums. Wine bottles would explode. "Sour *shchi* tickles your nose, but its kick will knock you over," 350-pound Lenochka would say while drinking it mixed with an equal amount of frozen champagne. Lenochka invented the 12-layer casserole. Each layer had its own filling: meat, various types of fish, fresh mushrooms, chicken, and all kinds of game. This casserole was prepared only at the Merchants' Club and at Testov's, and had to be ordered a day ahead.

Stepan Ryabov's orchestra played during luncheons. Choirs sang, sometimes Gypsies, sometimes Hungarians, but most often Russians from the restaurant Yar. This last choir was especially beloved and its owner, Anna Zakharovna, was respected by the partying merchants because she knew how to entertain them, which singer to recommend to whom. Singers fulfilled the boss's every order, because their contracts were under her complete control. Only a few of the choir's leading performers such as, for example, the throaty singer Polya, and the Adonis, Alexander Nikolaev, were considered untouchable, and could choose whom to love. The others were Anna Zakharovna's slaves. Less frequently, Fyodor Sokolov's Gypsy choir was invited from Yar and Christopher from Strelny, because the Gypsies were not quite so easy to keep happy. Money can't buy a Gypsy. The merchants did not like Hungarians either. "How will I speak with her, baby talk?"

After lunch, while the gourmets digested, players sat down to cards, and music fans from the club listened to singers, or bargained with Anna Zakharovna. When the choir left, they rushed over to Yar: in the evening, a cabstand was right outside the Merchants' Club. "Abducting talent" from the club was prohibited, and singers could leave with their admirers only from Yar.

During the season, at night, the street was filled on both sides with carriages. To the right of the entrance, as far as Glinishchevsky Alley, the merchants' personal carriages were parked, waiting, not infrequently, until morning for owners sitting in the club. To the left, as far as Kozitsky Alley, were, first, single drivers, then, behind them, bells jingling, stood pairs of horses, harnessed to three-seat sleighs decorated

---

1. Made from rye bread, *kvas* is a lightly fermented drink (0.5-1.0% alcohol) whose color depends on the darkness of the loaves used. It is popular even today across the former Soviet Union and Eastern and Central Europe.

with tin. In the middle, a trotter stood in a type of harness used near the Don River, so that if it turned its muzzle to the left, it was guided to the ground by a hoop.

The drivers knew their club-going grey-hairs, and the grey-hairs knew their drivers. They walked right up, climbed in, and left. Occasionally, swift *troikas* were called to the club from Yechkin or Ukharsky, and, bells ringing, they would take a happy group beyond the gate on the trail of the choir, which had left on long-distance pairs.

Carousing merchants sped over the potholes of Tverskoy Boulevard, sometimes singing. Silent and self-important drivers, horses trotting, caught up with the cabs and *troikas*. "Hey, hey, you're being robbed," the drivers used their favorite exclamation, a leftover from the days of highway robbery that sounded fierce on sleepy Tverskoy, where there not only were no robbers, but no pedestrians after dark.

Slightly drunk fans, "clubbies," hurried to Yar after lunch, and card players went to the game rooms, but at the "glutton" table in the brightly lit dining room, gourmets continued their meeting after resting on the comfortable sofas and chairs in the reception hall, imagining and roundly discussing various exotic dishes for dinner. A chef in starched whites and a toque issued a running commentary and, not uncommonly, with one word, eliminated "culinary fantasies," while ignoring a group of Moscow's well-known merchants sitting at the table. But, if there were a guest of honor, then the chef only silently expressed surprise, and would not offer his own opinions. Once, at a table of regulars, a guest appeared that not even the chef critiqued, but only feigned enthusiasm and jotted down the guest's words. He ordered meals that could make the gourmets open wide and feast until morning. He was a lawyer, still young, but a solidly built man, weighing no less than anyone at the table. It was no accident that he collected printed and handwritten manuscripts for a culinary library. There was a poem about him going around:

I saw the glutton's library
He gobbles delicious recipes
From the Caucasus to Izhory
Gathered 100 years of them.

Second lunches were especially crowded. Here, the rich merchants lost interest, instead roughing it in their warehouses or offices, sending out to taverns like Arsentych, or to "appetizer row" for hot ham, sturgeon with horseradish and red vinegar, or they would simply get appetizers and fried *pirozhki* from vendors working the city streets and trade warehouses on Ilyinka and Nikolskaya Streets. "Steam-ing *pirozh-ki!*" Other days of the week they lunched on Taganka Street or at home near the Moscow River, where their spouses waited behind a samovar and served lunch, however meager, however humble, and always greasy – a characteristic of traditional cooking. Wives preferred not to add anything new to menus created many years earlier.

On Tuesdays, the merchants went to the club to stuff themselves. In the seventies and eighties, "Khludov's table" enjoyed an especially fine reputation. Here, the most powerful merchants presided, including the owner of an enormous library, Arkady Ivanovich Khludov, his brother, his nephew, and his son Mikhail, who was a Moscow legend.

IN *BURNING HEART*, DEPICTING KHLYNOV the merchant, A.N. Ostrovsky had in mind Khludov, who was much admired for his success at the end of the previous century. *Entertainment*, a fashionable, illustrated magazine of the time, published on its front cover for an entire year an illustration of a drunken merchant. All Moscow knew that it was Misha Khludov, the son of the millionaire-industrialist Alexei Khludov, to whom was dedicated a page in the *Brockhaus Enzyklopadie*[2] as the founder of the famous Khludovskaya Library of Ancient Manuscripts and Books, which had been cataloged by well-known scholars.

This library was bequeathed to a museum. Old man Khludov, until he turned completely grey, spent his evenings like a young man, and ate Lucullan meals every day at the Merchants' Club, until, in 1882, he died before his time on the way from home to the club. He usually wore high boots, a long black frock coat, and always a top hat. When, at nine in the evening, Khludov's carriage, as usual, wheeled up to the club and the doorman opened the carriage door, Khludov lay on the pillows in his top hat showing no sign of life. His estate went to his children. Misha continued to burn through life. His brother Gerasim was his complete opposite, a boring drudge who lived unnoticed, but continued the firm's brilliant business.

Misha was a living legend. He was his father's favorite, a loner and strongman, a passionate hunter and adventure seeker. As early as the sixties, he went off to Central Asia to the recently founded city of Verny[3] to look for markets, and got caught up there, spending time hunting tigers. At this time, he published in the *Russian Gazette* a series of most interesting letters about this then-unknown region. There, he befriended General M.G. Chernyayev.

Khludov was always accompanied by a huge tiger, which he had trained like a dog. Soldiers were amazed at the "civilian with a tiger," loved him for his boldness and mad courage, and for wasting huge amounts of money buying them drinks and helping anyone that asked. That's what eyewitnesses said about him. Later, Khludov appeared in Moscow and reveled without bound.

---

2. A German-language encyclopedia published by Brockhaus widely referenced in Russia. The first edition appeared in 1796-1808.
3. Verny: Founded onsite of Russian fort in 1854. In 1921, the new city was renamed Alma-Ata (now Almaty). Today it is the largest city in Kazakhstan; and its capital until 1997.

At this time, he married a furniture dealer's daughter, whom he met through his sister. His sister lived with his father in a home
purchased for her on Tverskoy Boulevard.
After the wedding, he continued his life unchanged, except he hosted feasts more often
at Khludovsky Court, which he always attended in costume, sometimes from the Caucasus, sometimes from Bukhara, sometimes
as a half-dressed Roman gladiator with a tiger
skin on his back, which looked good on him
thanks to a miraculous figure and muscles so
fit they drove the Moscow ladies wild. Once,
he was colored black and came to the dinner as

Mikhail Khludov, a Moscow legend.

a Negro. The tigress was always with him, on a leash, gentle, and lived into old age
like a house dog.

In 1875, the events in the Balkan commenced.[4] Herzegovina revolted. Chernyayev conducted a secret correspondence with the Serbian government, which invited
him to become commander-in-chief. The correspondence, of course, was read by
the Third Department, and Chernayev was put under surveillance.[5] In Petersburg,
he was refused a foreign passport. Chernyayev then went to Moscow, to Khludov,
who arranged at the Governor-General's chancellery for foreign passports for himself and Chernyayev. Without a word to anyone, they left Moscow together on a
swift *troika*. The order to refuse Chernyayev exit from Russia had not yet made it to
the border. In a word, in July 1876, Chernyayev was in Belgrade and was the commander-in-chief of the Serbian army. Misha Khludov was inseparable from him.

An acquaintance of mine, a participant in the war, described the following scene:

"I arrived in Deligrad with a report for Chernyayev. I was led to the commander-in-chief's tent. A hulking redhead in a red tunic with an enlisted man's St. George
pin and a Serbian decoration for bravery exited the tent holding a bottle of wine and
a tea glass.

" 'You here for Chernyayev? For Misha?' he asked me. I responded affirmatively.

" 'Well it's all the same, he's Misha, I'm Misha. Here, have a drink.'

"He poured a glass of wine. I declined.

" 'You don't drink? That means you're a fool.' He tossed back the wine.

---

4. In July 1875, Herzegovina rose up against the Ottoman Empire. By August, the revolt had spread into Bosnia. The
   uprising was supported by nationalist volunteers from Serbia.
5. The Third Section of His Imperial Majesty's Own Chancellery was the Imperial regime's secret police. Created by Tsar
   Nicolas I following the Decembrist Revolt in 1825, it included only 16 investigators. Disbanded in 1880, it was replaced
   by the Okhrana.

"Then, Chernyayev glanced out of the tent and shouted: 'Mishka, get to sleep!'

" 'Yes, Your Excellency.' After saluting, glass in hand, he disappeared into the next tent."

Khludov returned to Moscow, and married a second time, again to a woman from an untitled family, since he liked neither merchants nor nobles. He loved his wife very much, but drank according to his old habits and hosted his usual feasts. To this day in Moscow there are people alive who remember dinner on the 17th of September, his wife's first name day after the wedding. All of the city's government and business elite were there. Before the meal, guests were invited into a room to view the gift which the husband had given his young wife. An enormous box, perhaps six feet long, was carried in, and workers opened it. Khludov, axe in hand, worked with them. They knocked off the lid, turned it upside down, and lifted. Out fell an enormous crocodile.

I saw Misha Khludov for the final time in 1855 in the Manezh at the Dog Show.[6] An enormous crowd surrounded an iron cage. In the cage, on a stool, in a coat and top hat sat Misha Khludov drinking cognac from a silver goblet. A tigress sat by his feet, beat its tail against the iron bars, and put its head on Khludov's knee. This was his last tigress, recently imported from Central Asia, but already trained. Not long after, Khludov died in an insane asylum. Mashka, the tigress, was taken to a zoo, where she was caged and died of consumption.

THESE WERE ALL PEOPLE WHO ate through an enormous amount of money. But there were some fans of the second lunches who, due to frugality, attended no more than monthly. One of the Firsanovs was this sort. Because he was a miser, he was called "eggshell omelet." He was a millionaire, a timber trader, a major wholesaler, and, to a rare degree, a skinflint. He had no living children and his millions were inherited by distant relatives whom, while alive, he did not want to know. He spent all day in his office, a small hut at the lumberyard, in an out-of-the-way spot not far from the railroad loading station. Here he met with wealthy men as well as those in need, counted his bonds for enormous sums at high interest rates, and did this with ease, but in small things he was unbelievably cheap.

In a thoughtful moment, he once said: "Money means suffering, not life. I woke one night and started reviewing accounts. I had spent 100 thousand rubles that day. A few tens of thousands here and there, you don't worry – you know they were used for deals, no regrets. But little things! Here's what bothers me. The deliveryman brought some supplies from my estate: oil, oats, and flour. You take it from him and, like a statue, he stands there and looks you in the eye. He expects a tip, you see. It's

---

6. Moscow's famous Manezh was built from 1817 to 1825 as an indoor training ground for horse parades (from the French, *manege*) and the site of an officer training school. Since 1867, it has been an exhibition hall and, during the Soviet era, an art museum. It is the setting for several scenes in this volume.

their custom! Well, you take a wallet out of your pocket, grab a 20-kopek coin thinking to give it to him, and then it flashes in your head: I'm paying him a salary after all, why should I give him more than that? Again I think: that's the way it's done. With an aching heart you give it, and then at night you get up and think, those 20 kopeks were lost for nothing. I thought it out and decided to give the delivery man three kopeks and say, "Here are three kopeks, add two of your own, go to the tavern, order some tea, and drink it any way you like, as much as you want."

In 1905, expropriators showed up at Firsanov's business.[7] Ordering workers to put their "hands up," they went up to "himself" in his office, put a revolver to his temple, and demanded, "Unlock the safe!" He described the situation: "I'm opening the safe and my hands are shaking, and I'm not even worried about the money: I'm afraid that they'll shoot. I opened it. They took a little more than ten thousand rubles; they frisked me, took my gold watch and chain, and ordered us not to leave the office for a quarter of an hour. When they left, I started laughing about how I had swindled them: while they were groping in my pockets, I held in my fist 10 gold rubles that I had snatched from the table. They did not think to open my fist. That's how I tricked them! Hee-hee-hee!" and he shook with quiet laughter.

As was common among merchants, he was sometimes made the target of jokes. He never took offense at anyone. A person with the same last name and a large red moustache like a cobbler's brush did not have the same inclination. No one called him by his family name, but simply Pasha Red-stash, to which he willingly answered. Pasha considered himself a gourmet, although he didn't know the difference between a fish and a bird. Once, some diners made mean-spirited fun of him, and he did not come to the second lunches for maybe two years, but they finally changed his mind, and he again started to frequent the lunches. The past was forgotten. Suddenly, it surfaced completely unexpectedly, and the group was forever deprived of Pasha's company. Among the diners this time was the entrepreneur F.A. Korsh,[8] a frequent visitor at the club; he sat directly across from Pasha Red-stash.

"Pavel Nikolayevich, how is it I haven't seen you at my theater?"

"I'm sorry, Fyodor Adamych, I go rarely. However, for this Sunday, I ordered a box for the boys. What are you presenting?"

"Sunday? *Marriage.*"

"Wha-at?"

"*Marriage*, by Gogol."

"Why are you putting on that filth?" F.A. Korsh hadn't even succeeded in widening his eyes when the entire table shook from laughter.

---

7. Sometimes they requisitioned goods for state purposes. Often, they were robbers.
8. This is Fyodor Adamovich Korsh, owner of the Korsh Theater (1852-1923).

"You're all degenerates, that's what! Bastard!" Pasha Red-stash yelled, jumped up from the table, and left the club.

The laughter continued, and during a break they told the astonished F.A. Korsh why Pasha Red-stash had left. Two years earlier, at dinner, while everyone was ordering, Pasha decided to show off his gourmet taste. "I would like a snipe," he said to the chef who had been summoned to take orders.

"Snipe? Do you know what a snipe is?" someone asked.

"Of course I know. It's a small bird, with wings, like a grouse, but large legs and a long bill."

The chef wanted to object that snipe can't be had during the winter, but a jolly Korolyev winked at the chef and followed him out. Dinner continued.

Finally, in a covered ceramic dish, the snipe was served.

"Where is its bill?" Pasha asked, placing a small bird with long legs on the plate.

"In the winter, the snipe's head is removed. As a diner you may not know this," Korolyev explained.

"Ah!"

He began to eat and sliced a leg.

"Why is the leg sewn on with thread? And the other one too?" Pasha asked the waiter.

The waiter started to laugh but hid it with a napkin. All looked-on in confusion until Korolyev explained seriously, "Because I ordered a chicken leg to be sewn onto a grouse." The next day, word of this got around the city, and by the day after Red-stash's nickname had become none other than "Chicken Leg." Once, friends dragged him to the Maly Theater to a performance of *Marriage*, where he heard the line, "You have a chicken leg!" and he jumped up and ran. When a monument to Gogol was erected, Pasha crudely complained: "To him! What a joker!"

Still another amazing person went to the "second lunches," Ivan Savelyev. He carried himself proudly, despite an ill-fitting frock coat and cheap boots. He owned a bakery on Pokrovka Street where, as he put it, things were done under "martial law." He called himself a field marshal, his son, who ran a second bakery, was called a commandant, pie makers and roll makers were guards and the bread bakers were the troops. He never simply punished mistakes, but organized a formal court martial. A table was covered with a green cloth, bread and a silver salt service were set, and kitchen benches were brought for the accused. Punishments varied: hard labor in exile meant cleaning the outhouses and trash bins, exile meant demotion from the first bakery to the second. Arrest signified a monetary fine, stripping of rights meant a salary reduction, and the death penalty, dismissal. All of the older workers had nicknames from military heroes or government leaders:

Skobelev, Gurko, Radetsky, Alexander the Great, etc.[9] They answered only to these nicknames, and their own names were forgotten. The pay book recorded:

Alexander the Great – pretzel maker, 6 rubles
Gurko – roll maker, 6 rubles
Napoleon – water carrier, 4 rubles

Long-time customers also called the workers by these names. Note that all of these "heroes" worked with pride, and thereby justified their honorable nicknames. Gourmets gladly invited Ivan Savelyev to their tables when he made a rare appearance at the club, because it was always a joy to dine with him. Entertainment! He was even able to amuse the always-serious Lyapin brothers, who never missed a single lunch. They were nicknamed "The Inseparables." They had still one other moniker, "Even and Odd," but that had been largely forgotten, recalled only by those who had known them as young men. They came to the club for lunch and left after dinner. They did not play cards, but sat all evening in the club, drank, ate, conversed with acquaintances, or went to the reading room. Note that it was always fairly empty, even though the club had an excellent library and subscribed to all the Russian-language magazines, as well as many from abroad.

The Lyapin brothers were older men, roughly the same age. The elder, Mikhail Illiodorovich, was hugely obese, sedentary, with a yellowish face, on top of which, in the words of Arkashka Schastlivtsev, "instead of hair 'some kind of feathers' grew." The younger brother, Nikolai, was energetic, bearded, and Mikhail's complete opposite. The bachelors lived together in a mansion with a winter garden. The Lyapins had substantial financial resources and spent their money on philanthropy. Their story was legendary, and merchants who knew them since their youth recited it to everyone they met, and not without cause. The Lyapins were born peasants, perhaps in Tambov, perhaps Saratov. As a young man, Mikhail Illiodorovich had worked for a wholesaler, driving herds to Moscow. Somehow, in Morshchansk, during one of his trips, he got acquainted with *Kastraty*, who convinced him to join their sect, proposing in exchange to pay him handsomely.[10] They convinced him to have the operation, but they did only half the job, and after handing over part of the promised money, they decided to wait a year to complete the procedure and pay the

---

9. Mikhail Dmitriyevich Skobelev (1843-1882), a highly-decorated general during Russia's wars in Central Asia and especially the 1877-78 Russo-Turkish War. Iosif Vladimirovich Gurko (1828-1901), a Russian Field Marshall known for his victories over Turkey in 1877-1878. Fyodor Fyodorovich Radetsky (1820-1890) a Russian infantry general who earned numerous awards and appointments thanks to his leadership in military victories stretching from 1843-1878.

10. *Kastraty* or, more properly, *skoptsy* believed there was only one truly effective means of battling the weakness of male flesh. They were outlawed both in Tsarist Russia and the Soviet Union. In 1929, as part of a widespread anti-religious campaign, a group of sect members was put on trial.

Textile factory owned by Morozov and Sons, one of the richest merchant families at the turn of the century.

balance. But Lyapin grew wealthy with the money he had been paid and declined the operation and the rest of the money.

Mikhail Illiodorovich grew obese and sickly because he overate. There was a snowless winter in the middle of the eighties. During Shrovetide,[11] when everyone in Moscow usually used sleighs, there was such a strong thaw that the streets were bare and, instead of sleighs, carriages and carts rumbled with their iron-covered wheels along the thawing stones – rubber tires were at that time unknown. Friday and Saturday of Shrovetide the entire street around the Merchants' Club and the Lyapin's mansion was carefully covered by a thick layer of hay. Under the hay nothing was visible, not even the granite crosswalk that, for their comfort alone, the Lyapins had built stretching from their mansion's entrance to the Merchants' Club.

At their entrance, after rustling through the hay, a carriage stopped. The younger Lyapin got out and helped the famous Professor Zakharin. After walking through a series of luxurious rooms, he climbed a narrow wooden staircase to the second floor, and arrived in a small, low-ceilinged bedroom. It smelled of furniture oil and turpentine. In the corner, on a comforter, on a large feather bed with a mahogany frame, the elder Lyapin reclined, breathing with difficulty. The doctor looked at

---

11. The days right before Ash Wednesday and the start of Lent. In much of Europe, there are celebrations involving pancakes (or other traditional foods and feasting) on the Tuesday immediately before Ash Wednesday. In the United States, this is known as "Fat Tuesday," the start of Mardi Gras.

him angrily. The younger brother told the doctor about the second lunches, and that the patient had gorged on *bliny*, maybe 20 of them, before lunch.

"What is this?" shouted the doctor, poking the wall above the bed with his finger.

"He's just a small boy, sir," said the trusted servant Mikhalych, sitting close on the sick bed.

"You live like swine. You crawled into this pit, while the rooms below are empty. Move the bed to a room with light. To the reception room! Into one of the great rooms!"

The doctor took his pulse, examined his tongue, prescribed a powerful sedative, grumbled a bit more, and announced, "Tomorrow you can get up!" He took 500 rubles for the consultation and left. The next day, toward evening, all the hay had been removed, but the brothers did not carry out Zakharin's instructions: they did not move their bedrooms. They each looked in a separate mirror, fastened to the wall outside a window in such a way that each reflected its own side of the street. They reported to one another:

"Firefighters went down Stoleshnikov Street."

"A university student walked up to the entrance."

Mornings, Nikolai went off to Ilyinka Street to the office for their large textile business, and the elder sat all day at the window in a comfortable leather chair, looked at the mirror, and waited for visitors, whom the doorman would let up to him directly, unannounced. Mikhail Illiodorovich always spoke with callers himself. Mostly, they were university students asking for a place in the Lyapin's dormitory. The doorman knew whom to admit, all the more so since anyone approaching the door was earlier visible through the mirror. A poorly dressed youth might enter the room.

"I would like to stay at your..."

"Well, that's a possibility. Who might you be?"

If a university student, Lyapin would ask him his department, and would himself name the chairman, and if the youth was a student at the art school, he would ask in what specialty, still life, portraiture... and also would talk about the instructors and, at that, refer to each by first name and patronymic.

"So, sir! Seems you want to live here?"

He would open the Residents' Register, look at the notations for the dormitory, and if there was a vacancy, give him a residence certificate.

"Go with this paper to the dormitory, ask for Mikhaylich the head man, and get settled."

LYAPINITES

IN THE COURTYARD OF THE Lyapins' enormous property, behind the mansion, stood a large stone building, which at one time served as a storehouse, but at the end of the seventies was reconstructed as living space. A free dormitory was opened for university students and students at the Academy for Painting and Sculpture. Students would move in and stay until they had finished their studies, and sometimes remained after finishing, living at Lyapins' until they found a position.

In general, few students had sufficient funds – most were destitute. University students and those studying at the art school were sharply divided into the wealthy and the rootless poor. These two groups, different both in essence and appearance, kept as far apart as possible. The poor students had no connections, nowhere to go, and, for that matter, nothing to wear. They found shelter in corners and rooms, and gathered for companionship in the cheapest places. Their favorite tavern was located not far from the university, in a one story building on the corner of Ulansky Alley and Sretensky Boulevard. Or they went to Kolokol on Sretenka Street, where church painters gathered. Students lived collectively: if one had a ruble, he'd treat the rest.

Many students envied the Lyapinites. Only the lucky ones ended up there. The dormitory was always full, and had an endless waiting list. Many Lyapinites became well-known doctors, lawyers, and artists. P.I. Postnikov, the famous surgeon, lived there for a time; Korin, the artist, stayed there until he was appointed a professor at the Academy; Pyrin and the Petroviches lived there too. The Lyapins' dormitory saved many from poverty and death. There were also "lifetime Lyapinites." Three artists, L., B., and Kh., lived in Lyapins' for 10 or 15 years and stayed long after they left the academy. They had grown accustomed to it, and lazy. They managed in various ways: they drew for Sukharev, and painted houses when they were sober. The

Lyapins knew this but did not drive them out. They let them stay, for otherwise the artists would perish in Khitrovka. For many students, Lyapins' was a real piece of good luck. Not infrequently, homeless students spent nights on the street.

IN THE EIGHTIES, 1884 IT would seem, Doctor Vladimirov, a seminarian from Galicia, graduated from Moscow University. While in his fourth year, a half-starved Vladimirov found himself without an apartment, and for about two weeks in May spent his nights wandering Tverskoy Boulevard from the Pushkin monument to the Nikitin Gate. Around midnight, the Chief of Police would leave his office and head across the boulevard to see a well-known, beautiful dressmaker. In the morning, around 4 or 5 o'clock, Kovloz would return home along this same path. Vladimirov, like the rest of the homeless spending the night on Tverskoy Boulevard, knew the secret of Kozlov's journeys. The pale youth in a broad-brimmed hat, then a fashion among students (you only see such hats now as props for robbers in the theater), caught Kozlov's attention. They happened to run into each other that morning and Kozlov, primly adjusting his military-style moustache, asked, "Young man, why do I see you wandering up and down the boulevard every night?" "Because not everyone has the good fortune to stray *across* the boulevard every night."

LYAPINS' WAS DIRTY, BUT THERE was no boss. Every room had four beds, tables with drawers, and stools. Rooming was free, but they took money for board. A cafeteria was on the bottom floor, where a two-course lunch with meat cost 15 kopeks. Once a day, free tea and bread were served. The cafeteria was also used as a club where "rebellious" speeches were made, and songs were sung, and where revolutionary proclamations were read openly (detectives never entered and there were no provocateurs or informers). As soon as a suspicious face appeared, the Lyapinites would sense it, surround him, and conduct an interrogation Lyapin style; this dampened the investigators' enthusiasm. Nonetheless, there were raids of Lyapins' and, not infrequently, young men were arrested. The gendarmes tried to do this, for fear of conflict, not in the building itself, but on the street where they could catch students alone. At times of student unrest, meetings took place here. For decades, Lyapins' helped young men seeking an education. Only one case is known where the brothers refused to accept a student from the Academy of Painting – they were always especially well disposed toward painters.

At one of the student exhibits at the Academy of Painting, a work, *Dead Lake*, impressed everyone. It was an excellent piece, and terrifying: a rocky desert, bloodied by the rays of a setting sun, and, in the center, a lake the color of dried blood. Its painter was an awkward, poorly dressed man, already old, unattractive, with an angry cast to his eyes, and a messy cap of hair that had never seen a brush. This was the student Zhukov. He had gone to Lyapin to ask for a place in the dormitory, but his appearance and a bitterly impudent interview made such an impression on the brothers that they decided to refuse him a spot. He left, and met a driver on the street who came from the same village where he had worked as a scribe for the local government before art school. The driver worked for some princess, and, after learning that Zhukov had no place to live, took him into his own room off the stable.

Zhukov also had done an allegorical painting, *After the Flood*, for which the professors' council awarded him first prize of 50 rubles, but the money was not paid, because Zhukov was only auditing the course. Prizes were paid only to those who were enrolled. At the time, he was taking a class with Professor Savitsky, who described him as "the pearl of the school"! But the school's pearl perished. When he moved from the stable into a room in the main residence, a servant took to mocking him and he often heard the frightful word "freeloader." One cursed day, the servant, going in to tidy his room, saw human legs sticking out of the fireplace. In the fire lay the unfortunate artist's charred torso. The school's director, Prince Lvov, donated 100 rubles for Zhukov's burial, which his fellow students arranged at the Danilov Cemetery.[1] His closer friends – and he had few – said that he had left behind a lengthy poem dedicated to a girl whom he had never met, but secretly loved. They said he was troubled by his unattractive appearance and was painfully vain. After all, it was thought, if the school had given him the 50 rubles, he would have been a master, an original artist. This is what Savitsky and his students had expected, believing in Zhukov's talent.

Many talented people died from poverty. Such was Volguzhev's fate. He was a metalworker, then a student at the school, a participant in major exhibitions, and a resident at Lyapins'. His Volga landscapes were excellent. He died from consumption when he fell ill and had no money for medicine. He was also a proud man, stubborn.

Once, before finishing their studies, a few of the students, the best landscapers, were invited by Moscow's Governor-General, Prince Sergei Alexandrovich, to his estate outside Moscow, Ilyinskoye, for the summer, to relax and draw *études*. Volguzhev was among them. At the Christmas student exhibit, Sergei Alexandrovich, who invariably attended these events, stood in front of the piece that Volguzhev had painted at the estate and showered it with praise. He inquired about a price. Volguzhev was called over. In a ragged suit coat, like most students of the time, he walked up to the Governor-General, who was two heads taller, and literally buttonholed him, horrifying the entire administration.

"What's the price for this painting? I like it. I'd like to acquire it," said Sergei Alexandrovich.

---

1. The Danilov Cemetery is one of several established by Catherine II during the plague of 1771. Before the revolution, it chiefly served merchants and tradesmen. The Danilov Monastery was closed in 1918. The cemetery was destroyed in 1931.

"500 rubles," Volguzhev responded sharply.

"That's too expensive."

"Well, if it's too expensive you don't have to buy it. I won't sell for less!" Volguzhev let the button dangle and left.

The price was unheard of, and, moreover, based on the exhibition commission's appraisal, it had been listed at 100 rubles. This was pointed out to Volguzhev.

"I know. For anyone else it would have been 100 rubles, but for him, 500. Since he's so very important. I can be self-important too. Who are you to me?"

A PORTRAIT OF A WOMAN painted by a student, B.A. Serov, was shown at an exhibit. Serov lived at Lyapins'. This portrait, a young maiden in a white dress on a white background, made an impression, and one young woman wanted to meet the artist. She was introduced to him, a real "Lyapins' Lyapinite." But this proud young woman paid no attention to his suit, and asked him to paint her portrait. The next day, in his only suit jacket, he showed up at a luxurious apartment across from the Governor-General's, and began to paint two portraits at the same time, one of her and one of her daughter. Taciturn, and at first embarrassed by the situation, the artist finally gathered his courage, and began to converse. The lady asked him all about the artists' life, and expressed a desire to organize an evening for them.

"Invite your fellow art students here, but tell me what and how to serve them."

"Vodka, white fish, cucumbers, salami, and if you please, beer would be nice. Tea is not necessary. How many to invite? Is five too many?"

"Oh, what are you thinking! Invite as many as you'd like. The more the better."

"I might be able to get as many as 30!"

"Well, we'll happily prepare for 30."

On the appointed day, at seven in the evening, a loud group of 30 arrived from Lyapins'. The doorman was horrified and would admit none of them. The lady of the house appeared and ordered the prince's doorman, in a luxurious uniform, to remove and hang up all sorts of coats and cloaks that the vestibule had never before so much as glimpsed. All that remained empty was the spot for galoshes.

The group crossed the rugs, entered the luxurious dining room, and immediately sat down around an enormous table set with all kinds of appetizers, wine, beer, and vodka. The hostess and two of her lady friends took places at the end of the table. Planning ahead, the party's organizer had seated between the ladies two specially chosen non-Lyapinites, artist-dandies, quite handsome, rooted in high society, who were acquainted with the hostess and her lady friends. No other outsiders were there. The hostess's husband was home, an old general, who would have entered, and he looked in and bowed, but no one even noticed him, so he stole away, carefully leaving the door cracked.

With every glass, the company became livelier, clinked glasses, drank, poured for one another, raised a ruckus, and one Lyapinite, completely drunk, even began "toasting the host's parents."[2] More sober friends convinced him to leave, the doorman helped him on with his coat, and Atamonych went off to Lyapins', which luckily was close by. Another six artists were "tactfully" led out the same way by their friends, and when everything had been eaten and drunk, the guests slowly began to leave.

The participants long remembered that little feast.

THE "LYAPINS" ALSO HAD THEIR own entertainment. The Korsh Theater sent them free gallery tickets five times a week, and the Salamonsky Circus, every day except Saturday, when the box office was packed, sent 20 free passes, which Mikhalych the administrator distributed to the students, demanding, for some reason, one kopek for each. The students paid willingly, but where these kopeks went, no one knew.

Aside from this, there were no pleasures for Lyapins' students, if you don't count free entry to art exhibits. The Lyapinites also were entertained during the student uprisings, almost always being at the forefront of the movement. Once, more than half of the Lyapinites spent the night at a transfer prison.

---

2. A tradition with a defined sequence of toasts that honors relatives and friends.

PAINTERS' WEDNESDAYS

BEHIND NARYSHKIN SQUARE, ON THE corner of Lesser Dmitrovka, across from the Strastnoy Monastery, in an old, grand home, was the Art Lovers' Society, which organized fashionable Periodic Exhibitions. There, the best paintings won cash prizes and sold wonderfully. During the winter season, the society organized Fridays at which, in the evening, artists gathered. A natural scene was set, and "letting their hair down" in public, the artists drew, quiet and focused, while sipping tea and tossing around an occasional word. Someone might play piano while one of the guests, a singer, crooned, or someone read poetry. Evenings ended with a humble bite to eat.

Only leading artists attended these events: the Makovskys, Polenov, Sorokin, Nevrev, and members of the Society – rich donors like P.M. Tretyakov, Sveshnikov, and Kumanin. Young artists had no access to the participants, and therefore Fridays were tedious and boring – there was a reason they were called "prison Fridays."

The art lover K.S. Shilovsky was almost always there, as was Loshivsky, later an actor at the Maly Theater, full of life, talented, and educated. He was bored at these meetings and once invited a Friday member to visit him on a Saturday. So the artists started to gather at his house in Pimenovsky Alley. They drew, spent the evening at tea arguing happily, listened to music, read, and sang: many young people attended as well. All this was followed by dinner. V.E. Shmarovin, an artist and a collector, attended these Saturdays. At one of the student exhibitions he was the first to "discover" Levitan[1] and bought one of his smaller *études*. This was the first piece Levitan sold, and it was the start of their friendship. Shmarovin often befriended half-starving young students from the Academy of Art, bought their work, and invited some to his home for evenings that were also attended by well-known artists.

---

1. See note, page 53.

At one of Shilovsky's Saturdays, Shmarovin invited Levitan and all the guests to his place on the following Wednesday, and thus, slowly, people stopped coming and the Fridays died-off. Shilovsky's Saturdays, which had so entertained the artists at first, also failed to catch on. The hospitable Shilovsky, down to his last rubles in his small, beautifully decorated apartment, offered his guests wine with dinner. The painters grew embarrassed at eating and drinking on someone else's account, especially in such elegance. But Shmarovin's Wednesdays were democratic. As a member of the Wednesday group, the artists felt at home, but like guests too. They drank and ate on their own funds, and the host, "Uncle Volodya," was, so to say, only an organizer and executive-director.

At Wednesdays all the painters did watercolors the entire evening; Levitan – landscapes, Dik de Lonlay, the military painter and Frenchman – martial scenes; Klodt – caricature; Shesterkin – still life; Vogatov, Yaguzhinsky, etc. – everyone did as they liked. The price that an artist wanted for his watercolor was placed on the work, from one to five rubles. These paintings were left there for "public examination," and before dinner a lottery was held, 20 kopeks per ticket. Whoever purchased a ticket, and some relatively better-off guests might buy 10 or 20, everyone was ecstatic to win a Levitan for 20 kopeks. Leftover paintings were sold in the shops Datsiaro and Avantso. From the lottery receipts the artists were immediately paid the price of their work and the rest went toward a humble dinner. Moreover, on the tables lay folders with watercolors that guests eagerly bought. Wednesday visitors understood that they neither ate nor drank for free.

Saturdays and Wednesdays were attended by almost the same group of people. At Saturdays they ate and drank to the sound of a tambourine, and at Wednesdays they drank from the Cup of the Great Eagle to the sound of the hymn *Wednesday*, consisting of one line, "Not a bad try," to the music "Ta-ra-ra-boom-biya." At one of these Wednesdays, in 1886, K.S. Shilovsky arrived at the height of the friendly conversation and said to V.E. Shmarovin, "The eagle and the tambourine should be together, let them be here with you, on Wednesdays. Saturdays ceased and Wednesdays endured. The honored Cup of the Great Eagle was carried on Shilovsky's tambourine to every new member of Wednesdays, and was drained to the tune of "Not a bad try," and the tambourine. This was an initiation ceremony. In the same way, the Eagle was given to honored guests or any member of Wednesdays who distinguished themselves by a fine speech, telling remark, or a well-executed drawing or caricature. Wednesdays became a happy tradition. They met, drew, drank and sang until morning. In the art world around this time, the Society for Art and Literature was founded, many of whose members belonged to the Wednesday group.

In 1888, the Society for Art and Literature organized a glittering ball at the Philanthropic Society, with exact reproductions of historical costumes, decorations, scenery, and theatrical make-up, all done exclusively by Wednesday members.

I. Levitan, Goloushev, Bogatov, Yaguzhinsky and many others worked ceaselessly. The ball succeeded – and Wednesdays grew stronger.

In 1894, at an enormous table where Wednesdays artists painted watercolors, V.E. Shmarovin set out a sheet of paper, and in an ornate hand scrawled at the top, First Wednesday of 1894. It was filled immediately with drawings and was the first recorded "attendance" at a "Wednesday." Every Wednesday from that time forward they took "attendance." Major names sparkled under drawings of contemporary life. Aside from artists, poets wrote poems. M.A. Lokhvitskaya, E.A. Bulanin, V.Y. Bryusov each wrote a few lines for the record. This took place at a new location, a mansion on Greater Molchanovka, where for Wednesdays 100 or more participants and guests gathered. And that, in Savelevsky Alley, was only the beginning of Wednesdays.

At the request of the Wednesday guests, V.E. Shmarovin stood up to speak. "Well, here, my friends, thank you for coming! Without you something was missing." Or to warm guests up from the cold he would usually greet a new arrival. He was surrounded by familiar people. When receiving, V.E. Shmarovin sometimes stood in front of the new arrivals: in one hand he would have a silver flask dating from before the time of Peter, in the other hand a glass from the days of Catherine the Great.

The largest group of guests arrived sometime around 10. An older, friendly woman helped people with their coats. Uncle Volodya came out and shared kisses. He opened the door to the colonnaded hall, draped with paintings. The middle of the table was brightly lit by a shaded kerosene lamp, and maybe 10 artists were seated, one drawing, another filling out the "attendance record." The guests circled the table examining the work. Impromptu, someone would sit down at the piano. This "someone" was invariably a well-known figure from the world of music: either Lentovsky or Asperger would pick up a cello, and work would proceed in a still merrier fashion, accompanied by music. Newcomers did not say hello, or interrupt, but would go on farther, either into the reception hall, or to the right, into an office decorated with paintings and baubles. Here, seated on soft furniture, guests would converse. A tambourine, guitars, and balalaikas lay there. Across the hall was the dining room, where a samovar steamed, and the hostess offered tea with cookies and fruit preserves. Farther on was a room from which carried the notes of a harp – this was the host's daughter, playing music with her girlfriends. Later, she played in a quartet with some well-known musicians in the grand hall of the Molchanovsky mansion.

There was also a room known as the "Dead Man's Room." This was a most cheerful place, lit by a red ceiling lamp. Along the walls were items unearthed from ancient grave sites, a whole cabinet of antique earrings and rings, weapons dating from the Stone Age, lances, helmets, and clubs. There were wide Turkish divans, and in front of them small tables with matches and ashtrays, and a water pipe for its devotees. They would sit, laugh, and talk endlessly. Someone would strum a balalaika, others would snooze. It was called "Dead Man's Room" because, by morning, those who drank too much or had to travel too far to get home were sleeping on its divans.

At midnight, the sound of a tambourine rang out in Uncle Volodya's hands. This was the first signal. The artists would finish their work. In 10 minutes, the tambourine would sound again. Brushes and paper were put away; paintings, still damp, were placed on the piano. Everyone at the table stood, and in the hall dinner was served.

Appetizers, listed on a menu, were served on a stack of dishes, many decorated by the artists. Salami: soft, hard, regular, turtle, bear's ear with fat, sautéed walrus tusk, dog's delight pilgrim's heels... Vodkas: firewater, kicker, knock-down, herbal, and others... Cocktails: a mess, stewed slowly, decadent water, fruit juices, auction water, poison for mosquitoes and roaches... Wines from Wednesday's own vineyard on the shores of the Everyday Ocean, rose with raisin puree for the ladies. The dinner menu: 1) miracle fish, 2) Turkey, flesh on the bone, 3) experimental fish with pureed whale fin sauce, 4) Cheeses; brie, Darya, Marya, Tambourine, 5) Desert; frozen "not a bad try."

On the table stood antique vodka decanters with official seals, and small glasses with and without handles: all of this was collected over the decades by V.E. Shmarovin at Sukharevka Market. A small beer keg was placed in the center of the table, and in front of it sat Uncle Volodya himself, standing watch for Wednesday, who poured beer from a pitcher. They drank. They ate. Uncle Volodya got up and signaled with the tambourine. Everyone grew quiet. "Dear friends, you have speeches to make." Without warning, he would point to someone, and that person had to speak. The painter Sintsov was at the piano, prepared to conclude the speeches with the anthem. Someone would be speaking well and the table would yell, "Eagle!" The cup would be emptied to the anthem of "Not a bad try."

Morning. Light squeezes through the blinds. Those with families, and the ladies, are gone. The keg is long empty. Snoring can be heard from the Dead Man's Room. One of the artists draws a still life in bright colors: the table with dirty dishes, the empty Eagle stands out amidst abandoned wine glasses, the keg with an open tap, Uncle Volodya nods, elbows on the table. A Wednesdays poet scribbles on a used menu:

Yes, the hour of parting is nigh,
the day is now colored white.
The keg empty but upright,
The "Eagle" stands drained and dry...

1922. WEDNESDAYS STILL MET, NO longer on Greater Molchanovka Street, but on Greater Nikitskaya Street, in S.N. Lentovsky's apartment, irregularly. From time to time, Uncle Volodya sent invitations ending as follows: "on February 22, Wednesday, there will be a Wednesday tea party. There are the following rules: 1) samovar and tea supplied by Wednesday, 2) sugar and other edibles to be brought by guests at their own expense, quantity and assortment according to their own taste."

NOVICE ARTISTS

IN OLD MOSCOW, THERE WERE few genuine art lovers willing to take personal responsibility for the fate of young artists. They limited their support to purchasing
paintings for both their galleries and for "bragging rights," while bargaining over
every kopek. One genuine patron, similar in this regard to P.M. Tretyakov and K.T.
Soldatenkov, was S.I. Mamontov,[2] himself a painter, entertaining and wise. A circle
of people gathered around him, some of whom were already well known, as well as
those who had shown from a young age that they would become important artists,
which later turned out to be true.

The poor, the proud, and the unsuccessful sometimes treated donors with suspi-
cion. "They got close to Mamontov and got their collars starched," poor artists said
of those who became part of Mamontov's circle.

It was difficult to knock the poverty out of people. Most were children of poor
parents, peasants and the petty bourgeoisie, and they went to the Art Academy
thanks only to a passionate attraction to art. Many talented people, finishing school
half-starved, had to find another occupation. Many of them became church painters, working on murals. S.I. Gribkov[3] was one of these, as was Bazhenov, both prize
winners at graduation, the hope of the academy. There were many like them.

After graduation, Gribkov for many years had a painting studio and decorated
churches; nonetheless, he doggedly participated in exhibitions. He was friendly with
the talented artists of his time. By origin petty bourgeois, from Kasimov, and poor, at
graduation he received a prize for his painting *Argument Between Ivan Ivanovich and*

---

2. Savva Ivanovich Mamontov (1841-1918), a wealthy industrialist who made his fortune in railways and industry. His
famous artists circle was centered in Abramtsevo, north of Moscow.
3. Sergei Ivanovic Gribkov (1822-1893), a realist painter, teacher and icon painter.

Ivan Nikiforevich.[4] Later he was awarded a prize from the Society for Art and Historical Paintings. His spacious church painting studio was in a building he bought
near Kaluga Gate. It was large, two-storied, and occupied by poor folk, laundresses
and tradesmen who never paid rent. He not only did not demand payment, but he
renovated the apartments, and his students painted the walls and finished the trim.
In his large studio there was a place for everyone. Artists from the provinces would
show up and live there, contributing nothing of course, while drinking and eating
and looking for work. If a painter lost his job, he would come by and stay there until
he could find a job.

Gribkov never had fewer than six boys as students. They kept house, ran errands,
ground colors, and painted roofs, but every evening they were given a still life painting exercise under Gribkov's guidance. More than a few good artists came from
among S.I. Gribkov's students. From time to time he entertained them, organizing
holiday parties where vodka and beer were not allowed, but only tea, cookies, nuts
and dancing accompanied by guitar and song. At these events he sat in a chair late
into the night, happily watching the youngsters enjoy themselves. Sometimes at
these parties he sat with his friends and other artists, who often came by: Nevrev,
Shmelkov, Pukirev, and others.[5]

The well-known artist A.K. Savrasov would stay with him for months at a time.[6]
In later years, when Savrasov had surrendered entirely to alcohol, he sometimes
came to Gribkov's studio in rags. Students joyously greeted the famous painter and
took him straight into Gribkov's office. The friends would embrace, and then Gribkov would send Savrasov with one or another of the students to the *banya* near
Krimsky Bridge, from which he would return with his hair cut, dressed in Gribkov's
underwear and clothes, and start sobering-up. These were happy days for Gribkov.
Savrasov would stay for a month, another, and again disappear, sheltering in the
slums, doing drawings on demand in taverns for the buffet manager in exchange for
vodka and food.

Gribkov helped everyone, but when he died his friends had to pay for his burial:
not a kopek was to be found in his home. While alive, Gribkov never forgot his
friends. When the famous Pukirev was paralyzed and lived in a rundown apartment
on an alley off Prechistenka Street, Gribkov sent him a student with 50 rubles every
month. He always spoke ecstatically about Pukirev: "This is a Dubrovsky after all,
Pushkin's Dubrovsky![7] Only he was never a robber, otherwise his entire life was
just like Dubrovsky's. He was a handsome man, powerful, and talented, but just the

4. A story by Nikolai Gogol, *The Tale of How Ivan Ivanovich Quarreled with Ivan Nikiforovich.*
5. Vasily Vladimirovich Pukirev (1832-1890), famous for the painting *Unequal Marriage.*
6. Alexei Konstantinovich Savrasov (1830-1897), best know for his painting *The Rooks have Landed.*
7. *Dubrovsky* is an unfinished novel written by Alexander Pushkin in 1831 and not published until 1841, after his death.
   The title character's land was confiscated by the state. He gathered a band of outlaw serfs and stole from the rich to
   give to the poor. Theater, film, and television versions of the popular story have been produced.

Alexei Savrasov (right) and his famous painting, *The Rooks Have Landed*.
Right inset, Savrasov late in life, ravaged by alcoholism.

same fate!" A companion and friend of Pukirev from their youth, Gribkov knew the story behind the painting *Unequal Marriage*, and the tragedy of the artist's life. The old and proud clerk in the painting was a real person. The bride next to him was a portrait of Pukirev's fianceé, and the man standing with crossed arms, as if alive, was Pukirev himself.

N.I. Strunnikov also started his art career with Gribkov, becoming one of his students at the age of 14. Just like all the others, he was "on the run," painted, ground colors, washed brushes, and in the evenings learned to draw. Once, Gribkov sent the young Strunnikov to an antique shop by the Kaluga Gate to restore an antique painting. At that hour, P.M. Tretyakov[8] also was on his way there to buy Tropin's portrait of Archimandrite Feofanov. Catching sight of Tretyakov, the dealer rushed to help him with his coat and boots. When they entered the shop, he grabbed Strunnikov, who was working on the painting, and forced him to bow down to the floor. "On your knees and bow down. Do you know who this is?" Strunnikov pushed back in confusion, but Tretyakov freed him, put out his hand, and said, "Hello, young painter!" Tretyakov bought Tropin's portrait right away for 400 rubles. When he was gone, the dealer rushed around the room and started whimpering, "Ahh, he underpaid, he underpaid."

---

8. Pavel Mikhailovich Tretyakov (1832-1898), a famous industrialist and patron of the arts. His private collection formed the first holdings of Moscow's famed Tretyakov Gallery.

Strunnikov, a peasant's son, came to the city without a kopek in his pocket: it was not easy to survive. After his time with Gribkov, he enrolled in the Academy of Art and restored paintings for Brokar, the well-known Moscow perfumer and owner of a large gallery. Brokar gave Strunnikov nothing for his labor, paid 50 rubles for him to the Academy, and kept him "ready for anything." They let him share half a cot with a worker in the warehouse. They slept and ate together with the kitchen servant. Strunnikov worked a year and then went to Brokar and said, "I'm leaving." Brokar silently took 25 rubles from his pocket, but Strunnikov refused them. "Take them back." Brokar added 50 rubles. Strunnikov took the money, soundlessly turned, and left.

Life was not easy for these novice artists, with no family, village, acquaintances, or savings. "People in starched collars," as they said at the time, found it easier to start down this path. Such people cultivated the acquaintances needed for support, and for this you had to be refined and well educated. The Zhukovs, Volguzhevs, and others like them, their names were legion, had neither. In childhood, they had nowhere to be refined, the Academy of Art gave no formal education, and its general education courses were weak. The students themselves looked at education as a trifle. They were convinced that a painter needed only a brush; education was secondary. This mistaken view became firmly rooted, and there were almost no educated artists. They could copy nature miraculously, make life-like portraits, and that was fine. The knowledge needed for polite behavior, in even the least significant manner, was nowhere to be had. They were completely suspicious of all polite society, "starched collars," and education too. Could painters worry about education or science when they had no apartment, no clothes, when their toes stuck out of their boots, and their pants were such a mess that they had to keep their backs to the wall? Could an artist wear such an outfit to a wealthy home to paint a portrait, even if he could paint better than another? Were not these the conditions that led to the death of Zhukov and Volguzhev? There were hundreds just like them who perished without money or support.

Only a few succeeded in fighting for a place in life. It was I. Levitan's good fortune, from his youngest days, to fall into Anton Chekhov's circle. Levitan was poor, but made an effort to dress politely to be included in Chekov's circle, which was also poor, but talented and happy. Further, through acquaintances, the wealthy, elderly Morozova supported the talented youth, though she had never even seen his face. She supplied him with a comfortable, splendidly-furnished home, where he painted his best pieces. A.M. Korin made his way into society, but did not survive long.[9] Life at Lyapins' had ruined his health. They loved him at the Academy as a former

---

9. Alexei Mikhailovich Korin (1865-1923), a member of the Itinerant school.

Lyapinite who had fought his way out of the same circumstances. They loved him dearly. They bowed before the Coryphaeus.

They loved A.S. Stepanov[10] as they loved Korin. Stepanov's studio at the Academy of Art was in a wing to the right of the Yushkov Alley gate. It was an enormous, messy room. Cold. The stove smokes. In the middle of the room, on a perch, an animal stands: a goat, a sheep, a dog, a rooster, or maybe a fox. Quickly but calmly, it sits and looks around; then, it decides it wants to lie down. A student rushes over from his easel, pokes its leg or muzzle with a stick, threatens it gently, and it resumes its pose. All around, students paint. In their midst, Stepanov himself comments and instructs.

Student exhibitions took place once a year, from 25 December to 7 January. They started in the seventies, but became especially popular at the beginning of the eighties, when names like Levitan, Arkhipov, the Korovin brothers, Svyatoslavsky, Aladzhalov, Miloradovich, Matveyev, Lebedev, and Nikolai Chekhov (the writer's brother) had already made their mark. The exhibits featured the students' summer works. In the spring, when lessons at the Academy of Art were finished, students each went their own way and painted *études* and portraits for this exhibition. Only those who really and truly had no place to go stayed in Moscow. They went to Moscow's outskirts to paint *études* and give drawing lessons, hiring themselves out to churches to paint their walls. This was the most profitable activity, and in the course of the summer break students often earned enough to survive the entire winter. Students with money went to the Crimea, the Caucasus, and some went abroad, but there were too few of these. Those who could not scrape together any savings during the summer could only hope to sell some of their paintings.

Student exhibitions were popular, they were well attended, written about, and Moscow loved them. Gallery owners, such as Soldatenkov, as well as anonymous Muscovites, acquired inexpensive paintings, sometimes by future well-known figures, which became enormously valuable. This was a sport: predicting a celebrity painter was the same as winning 200 thousand rubles. There was one year (1897 it seems) when all of Moscow's best paintings were bought by "foreigners": Provais, Gutkheil, Knop, Katois, Brokar, Hopper, Moritz, Schmidt. After the exhibit, the lucky ones who had succeeded in selling their paintings, and received money, bought new clothes, paid up the owners of their apartments, but first settled accounts with Moiseyeva.

In the courtyard of the Academy of Art, for many years, in the same wing as Volnukhin's sculpture studio, there was a small cafeteria that took up two vaulted rooms. In each stood clean, simple wooden tables piled with sliced black bread. Diners sat on benches. The cafeteria was open every day except Sunday, from one

---

10. Alexei Stepanovich Stepanov (1858-1923), a brilliant realist painter, perhaps best known for *The Cranes are Flying*.

to three, and was always full. Wearing no coats or jackets, straight from class, students would run over as quickly as they could, take a plate and a metal spoon, and go straight to the burning stove, where the half-blind old woman Moiseyeva and her daughter served hot food. A student would sit down at the table with a hot meal, go back for the second course, and only then pay the old woman and leave. Sometimes, if he had no money, he would ask her to wait, and Moiseyeva trusted everyone. "You really must bring it... in case I forget," she would say.

Lunch, with two courses and soup, with a piece of beef, cost 17 kopeks, and, without the beef, 11 kopeks. The second course was sometimes ground meat patties, sometimes kasha, or a potato dish, and sometimes a full portion of cranberry drink and a glass of milk. At the time, cranberries cost three kopeks a pound, and milk cost two kopeks for a glass. There was no cashier and no tickets. There were only a few who might try to cheat Moiseyeva. Everyone paid cash. They might borrow 11 kopeks from someone and pay. After exhibitions, everyone settled accounts without fail.

There were cases where a well-dressed man would show up at Moiseyeva's and push money on her.

"Why are you doing this, dear?"

"I owe you, Moiseyeva, take it!"

"Who might you be?" She would look with half-blind eyes carefully into his face.

Her daughter would recognize the man sooner than she and call out his name. Or sometimes he would.

"Oh you dear man. Is that you, Sanka? I would not have recognized you... Look at what a fine man you are! But why are you giving me so much?"

"Take it, take it, Moiseyeva. I had my share of free lunches from you."

"Well then, thank you, you dear."

TRUBNAYA SQUARE

… Nobles rode, cigarettes in teeth.
Local cops prowled the street...

Such was the caption under a caricature in the magazine *Iskra* in the beginning of the sixties of the last century. A *troika* was depicted in the middle of the street. In the sled, four dandies smoked cigarettes, and two city horses stood. These caricatures in a satirical magazine were a response to a street smoking ban. The guilty were taken to police stations, "without regard to rank or title," as mandated by the chief of police in a decree published in newspapers. This decree led to not a few scenes in the street, and not a few fires: smokers threw away their cigarettes in fear, without aiming.

In those years, cigarettes had only just started to replace snuff, which remained in fashion for some time. Snuff is convenient! You can use it anywhere, and not spoil the air at home. Most importantly, it's cheap and strong! Slight acquaintances might meet in the street, tip their caps, and if they wanted to prolong the conversation, they would take out their snuff boxes.

"Indulge me and try some."

"Nice. But mine..."

He taps it on the lid, opens it...

"Yours is better. Mine is mint from Kostroma. Tobacco with strong enough flavor that you'll rip your eyes out."

"Take for example His Excellency Prince Urusov – I supply his oats – he treated me from an engraved gold snuffbox to some Khra… Khra… that's it… Khrappe."

"Rappe. From Paris. I'm familiar with it."

"Well then. It's aromatic but not overwhelming."

"I didn't like it. So I said, 'Your Excellency, don't condemn… don't miss the chance at my…' Well, you see, here's my very own snuffbox, Annie With a Tail, a monkey, and I handed it to him. The Prince packed both nostrils, rolled his eyes, and put in more. How he sneezed! While he was sneezing, and in between sneezes, he asked, "What kind of tobacco is that? Aglish?"[1] So I said to him, "Your Khrappe is French, but mine is homegrown, Butatre." I explained that I bought it at a stand on Nikitsky Boulevard. The Prince gave up his Khrappe, switched to "my blend" and became the first customer at my stand. He came by himself in the mornings on his way to work. Then I moved the stand out onto the corner.

Various tobaccos were offered for sale: from Yaroslavl, Dunayev and Vakhrameyev; from Kostroma, Chumakov; from Vladimir, Golovkhin; Voroshatin, Bobkov, Aromatic, Suvorov, Rose, Zelenchuk, Mint. Tobaccos in "packages with tax stamps" came in many different names, but in the end, in Moscow, most people used either "homegrown," or "home blend." They ground the raw leaves, and each person added aromas to their own taste. Every tobacco lover kept his recipe a secret, allegedly handed down from his forefathers. The best tobacco that had become fashionable was named Rose. It was made by a chorister who lived in the courtyard of the Troitsy-Listy Church and died an old man of more than 100 years. This tobacco was sold through a small window in one of the tiny stands, settled deep into the earth under the church walls on Sretenka Street. After his death, a few bottles of the tobacco were left as well as the recipe, which was so unique that it must be given in its entirety:

Buy four feet of aspen firewood, burn it, and sift the ashes through a small net into a vessel set aside for the purpose.

Take leaf tobacco, 10 pounds of dry leaf, dry it a bit. Take a simple sack, a so-called *kolomensky* sack. Put some tobacco in the sack and grind until it is difficult to make the particles any smaller, and the volume is about half a glass. When all the tobacco has been ground, sift it through the finest filter. Then take all of the tobacco and sift it again, taking the bits that are too large and grinding and sifting them again. Also, sift the ash a second time.

Mix the tobacco and ash as follows: pour two glasses of tobacco and one of ash into the sack. Moisten the glass that holds the ingredients with water, not immediately, and just a bit at a time. Then, grind the mix again. Repeat this process until all the tobacco is used up, storing the finished product in one place.

Add the scent as follows: take a quarter of a pound of concentrated pine oil, two small spoons of rose oil and rose water warmed together, but not too hot; add this mixture with care to the tobacco and ash and stir everything.

When all of the tobacco has been stirred in with the mixture, sprinkle it with one small spoon of rose oil and mix it by hand. Then, put it into bottles, seal them with corks and put them on the oven for 5 or 6 days, and then for a night in the oven, but they must be placed in a horizontal position. The tobacco is done.

LONG BEFORE HERMITAGE WAS CONSTRUCTED, on the corner between Grachyovka and Tsvetnoy Boulevard, there stood – as it stands now – the three-story Vnukov Building, with a wide façade looking out on Trubnaya Square. Today, it is lower because it has settled deeply into the earth. But long before the restaurant Hermitage, it was home to the wild Crimea tavern. During the winter, *troikas* and cabs always waited there. When it rained, part of Trubnaya Square was an impassable swamp, water flowed down Neglinnaya Street, but it never reached Tsvetnoy Boulevard or the Vnukov Building.

The licentious Crimea occupied two floors. The third floor of this second-rank tavern was occupied by gamblers, card sharps, con men and all sorts of scam artists, all relatively well dressed. Singers comforted the audience. The mezzanine was decorated in bright colors, crudely, but with pretensions to *chic*. In the hall, there were an orchestra stand and places for Gypsy and Russian choirs. During intermission, customer requests, whatever pleased the crowd, were played on a thunderous organ: operatic arias were followed by chamber music, or a hymn might give way to the widely-loved *Luchinushka*.[2]

Merchants and other provincial travelers, after enjoying a good time, would relax here. Under the mezzanine, the lower floor was filled with commercial spaces, and beneath that, still further underground, below the entire building between Grachyovka and Tsvetnoy Boulevard, ran an enormous basement, the entire space completely filled by a single tavern. It was a most forsaken, dangerous place, where the criminal world came from the Grachyovka slum, the alleys of Tsvetnoy Boulevard, and some even came over from Shipov's Fortress itself after especially successful jobs, betraying their own usual dives, The Polish Tavern on the Yauza, and Hard Time on Khitrovka, which seemed a boarding house for highborn maidens in comparison to Hell.

---

2. A version by Nadezhda Vasilevna Plevitskaya (1879-1940) who emigrated with her husband after the revolution is available [http://bit.ly/luchinushka]. Pining for Russia, her husband worked for the Russian Secret Police to try and earn his way home. He allegedly took part in a kidnapping attempt made on a White Army general. He ran, she was arrested. She died in a French prison in 1940.

For many years, within sight of the famous Hermitage, the well lubricated and loud Crimea trumpeted away while Hell[3] maintained an evil silence, and not a single sound made it from the cellar to the street. As late as the seventies and eighties, it was just as bad as earlier, and perhaps even worse, because 20 more years

The Hermitage Restaurant, Trubnaya Square.

of filth had permeated the floor and walls, and gas lamps had stained black right through the ceiling, which had settled noticeably, and cracked, especially in the underground passage from the enormous public room stretching from the entrance on Tsvetnoy Boulevard to the exit to Grachyovka.

The entrance and exit were unique. Don't look for an entrance, or even a porch. Just don't. A man sits on a bench on Tsvetnoy Boulevard and looks at the street and the enormous Vnukov Building. He sees five people walking down the sidewalk near the building, when suddenly – no one! Where did they go? He looks – the sidewalk is empty. Again, no one knows from where, a drunken crowd appears, makes a racket, pushes and shoves... and disappears again. A guard marches along in a hurry... and also falls through the earth, but in five minutes grows up out of the earth again, and walks along the sidewalk with a bottle of vodka in one hand and a package in the other.

The curious fellow gets up from the bench, walks up to the building and the secret is revealed: in the wall, below the sidewalk, is a staircase leading to a wide door. A woman with a bloody face, cursing non-stop, runs out, right toward the man. A bum appears right behind her, knocks her to the sidewalk, and dealing her deadly blows, repeats "We live like we live!" Two more gallop out, flog the bum, and lead the woman back down the stairs. The beaten bum gingerly makes an effort to stand, and crawls across the street on all fours, moaning and cursing, collapsing on the grass in the middle of the boulevard.

From the open door, together with a stinking stream of cheap tobacco smoke and the smell of drinking and every kind of human funk, came a deafening mix of the most incompatible sounds. Through a general rumble cut the high notes of a lead singer and his second, the animal roar of a choir of drunken voices, and above that could be heard the ring of breaking glass, a wild feminine shriek, and many voices swearing. Basses boomed off the arched ceiling and covered the roar until the

---

3. Not to be confused with the student housing building of the same nickname, see page 237.

shrieking second singer cut through both. And you couldn't muffle a violin's sour notes. The noise combined with warm vapor and the smell of leaking gas could stop your breathing within a minute.

Hundreds of people sit at rows of tables along the walls and in the middle of the enormous hall. A curious person walks quietly along the floor, soft from dirt and dust, past the enormous stove, where they were frying and boiling, to what passed for a buffet, where bottles of strong drink were displayed: acorn, pear, various sweet wines, and rum. A half a bottle, spewing flies, does not prevent him from mixing half rum, half tea to make "punch," the favorite drink of "greenies," or *boldokhs*, which is what they called returnees from Siberia or escapees from prison.

All drank for hours, roared, sang, and cursed. Only the left corner behind the buffet was quiet, where games of strap and *naperstok* were played. No one ever beat the card sharps, but nonetheless, being dutiful drunks, they played. Everything was simple. For example, the goal of *naperstok* was to guess under which of three shells a ball of bread was hidden. In plain sight, the scammer put the ball under a shell, but it actually stuck to his fingernail: there was nothing under the shells. The game of strap was also simple. A narrow leather strap was rolled up a few times to make a circle, and a player, before the belt was released, had to guess where the center would be; that is, they place their finger, or a tack, so it would be in the center of the newly formed circle when the strap unwound, in a loop. But the belt is wound in such a way that no loop could form.

Playing these primitive games, gamblers lost everything: money, stolen goods, a coat – still warm, just snatched from someone on Tsvetnoy Boulevard. Thieving tailors hung out near the players and bought up all kinds of trifles; anything valuable or large went to Satan himself. That's what they called the owner, although no one ever saw his face. The buffet manager and two big bouncers managed everything. They, too, were fences. They swam to the surface when things got really loud and struck indiscriminately, right and left, and the regulars always came to help. The *boldokhs* were friendly with them, as with people they needed, people with whom they "did deals" to unload stolen goods, offered shelter when it was dangerous to spend the night in flophouses or in their hideouts. No police ever even glanced in this direction, except for maybe city cops from the nearby guardhouse, and then with only the best of intentions – getting a bottle of vodka. Even then they never went farther than the main room, which was only the front half of Hell.

The other part of the tavern was called Purgatory, and access was only granted, so to say, to "decorated *boldokhs*" known to the buffet manager and the bouncers, who, much like grandees, were "allowed to drive into the courtyard." So, it was that these decorated *boldokhs*, who were "allowed to drive into the courtyard," as well as Ivans from Shipovsky Fortress, Volga, Dry Ravine, and Khitrovka, had two entrances, one public door from the boulevard, and the other from Grachyovka. This second entrance was used most often when bundles had to be brought in quietly – which could not be done if you needed to carry them through a crowded tavern. Purgatory took up just the same amount of space as the basement, and consisted of corridors that had rooms along each side: the small rooms were known as Hell's Forges, and the two larger rooms, The Devil's Mills. Here, card sharps from Grachyovka dealt "bank," the only game recognized by the Ivans and *boldokhs*, in which they lost their swag, sometimes countless thousands.

It was always quiet in this half of the tavern. The bouncers did not tolerate drunks, and everyone feared even a single word or a silent gesture from them. The Devil's Mills ground around the clock when the business was worth it. The smaller rooms had their own functions: at times they were the location for "splitting the loot," that is the division and sale of goods stolen by the participants, at times they were used for fulfilling orders for forged passports or other false documents drafted by various specialists. A few rooms were furnished as bedrooms (a two-person bed with a hay mattress, again only for honored guests and their "kittens"). Sometimes, disheveled students dropped in, sang *Dubinushka* in the great room, and made a racket, taking advantage of the respect afforded them by vagrants and even the bouncers, who gave them private rooms when they could not find a spot in the hall.

That's the way it was in the sixties and seventies in Hell; earlier, it had been simpler. Purgatory and The Devil's Mills allowed couples entry from the street. All guests who wanted privacy could simply go to the rooms from the hall. Sometimes, in the seventies, honored guests would stop by Hell – actors from the People's Theater and the Artists' Circle, to study character types. Also, there were Kireyev, Poltavtsev, and Vasya Vasiliyev. At the time, the police did not even glance in there, and still later, when police detectives came into existence, no searches were conducted. They would have led nowhere anyway. There were passages under the building, left over after work on the water pipes at the time of Catherine the Great. At the end of the last century, during construction of the sewers, they ran into one of these passages under the gates of this building at a time when Hell was gone, and only some basement establishments were left (one of them contained sleeping quarters for tavern workers lit even during the day by kerosene lamps).

Hell was tied to the April 4, 1866, assassination attempt on Alexander II (1818-1881). Meetings took place there to work out a plan for the attack. In Moscow, in 1863, a circle of youths was formed to battle the government. These were students from the university and the Agricultural Academy. In 1865, when the number of participants grew, the circle assumed the title "The Organization." The circle's organizer and leading spirit was a student named Ishutin, who led the group headquartered in the home of the petty bourgeois Ipatov on Greater Spassky Alley, off Karetny Row. Taking the name of the building, they were called Ipatovists. Here, unknown to other members of the Organization, the idea of regicide was hatched.

The Ipatovists chose the most convenient spot for their conspiratorial meetings – Hell, where no one stopped them from gathering in the hidden Devil's Mills. Adopting their hideout's name, Ishutin's followers called their group Hell. Aside from Hell, they also met on Greater Bronnaya Street in the tumble-down Chebyshev building, where Ishutin outfitted a modest bookbinding studio, also dubbed Hell, where members of the group who called themselves "dead men walking," that is, fated to die, were headquartered. Among them was Karakozov, who unsuccessfully fired at the tsar.[4] The mass arrests that followed the attempt terrorized Moscow. Nine Hellists were exiled to hard labor (Karakozov was hanged). In Moscow, everyone was so frightened that no one even dared hiccup about Karakozov's crime. Thus, everything was forgotten.

Even in the last century, Hell's connection to the trial was talked about, but writing about it, of course, was forbidden. Only in private conversations did the veteran writers N.N. Zlatovratsky, N.V. Uspensky, A.M. Dmitriyev, and Peter Kicheyev recall Hell and Chebyshy. Certain of the *Russian Gazette's* older employees also knew the details. This group included one of Hell's main participants, who had been at the meetings of the "dead men walking" at both Hell and Chebyshy. This was N.F. Nikolayev, a member of the first group convicted at the Karakozov trial, and sentenced to 12 years of hard labor in exile. As early as the eighties, he turned up in Moscow and became an employee of *Russian Gazette*, as a translator. He also wrote for *Russian Thought*. It was too risky for him to live in Moscow, so he stayed in small, nearby cities, but often visited Moscow, where he overnighted with friends. In the newsroom, aside from those closest to him, few knew his past. He shared his memories with friends. This last of the Karakozovites failed by just a bit to live until the Karakozov Exhibition in Moscow in 1926.

The first half of the sixties was a wild dawn for Moscow. After emancipation, aspiring landowners from quiet corners of Russia struggled to get to Moscow to earn money for land buy-out payments.[5] Shop owners who sold "luxury and fashion," and the best taverns, grew wealthy; but the latter, in the end, did not satisfy the extravagant tastes of gentlemen who had been abroad. Live fish and lightly steamed caviar did not impress them. Distinguished grandees gave feasts in their mansions, ordering for lunch Strasbourg *pate*, oysters, crab, lobster, and wine imported for crazy sums. It was considered especially *chic* when lunch was prepared by Olivier, a French chef still well known at the time for his invention of the "Salad Olivier,"

---

4. Dmitri Vladimirovich Karakozov (1840-1866) was the first Russian revolutionary to make an attempt on a tsar's life, when he shot at Alexander II and missed in April 1866. Nikolai Ishutin, Karakozov's cousin, who had been a lecturer at Moscow University, had his death sentence for the attempt commuted to exile for life. He perished in 1879 after suffering from mental illness.

5. The Emancipation Manifesto of 1861, instituted by Alexander II, liquidated serfdom in the Russian Empire.

Trubnaya Square, 1884.

without which lunch was not lunch, and whose secret he never revealed. As hard as gourmets tried, it never came out right: the same salad, yes, but not *that* salad.

On Trubnaya Square, near a newsstand, two fans of its bergamot-scented tobacco often met, Olivier and one of the Pegov brothers, who every day left his expensive home in Gnezdnikovsky Alley for his favorite bergamot tobacco, and always bought a kopek's worth, so it would be fresh. That was where he and Olivier came to an agreement, and Pegov bought all of Popov's enormous empty lot, almost four acres. Olivier's Hermitage appeared, wiping out a guard house and Afonkin's tavern. In a place where the croaking of frogs at night used to sound out from a swamp, and the cries of mugged tavern regulars were heard, now shone a temple of gluttony's windows, in front of which, day and night, expensive gentry carriages parked, sometimes accompanied by liveried lackeys.

Olivier did everything in the French manner to please his demanding clients. Only one Russian custom remained – there were no waiters in starched uniforms. Moscow regulars provided service, sparkling in shirts of bright white Dutch linen and silk waistbands.

Hermitage enjoyed an immediate, unprecedented success. The gentry just about poured into the new French restaurant, where, in addition to the public spaces and private dining rooms, there was a columned hall where one could order the same lunches that Olivier prepared in mansions for grandees. Delicacies were ordered from abroad for these luncheons, and the best wines; for example, a cognac with the Trianon seal certified to be from the palace cellars of Louis XVI.[6]

Pampered diners pounced on fine cuisine without any idea how to spend their money. Three Frenchmen managed the whole affair: general supervision – Olivier; for select guests – Marius; in the kitchen, a Parisian celebrity – Chef Dugas. This initial, elegant period for Hermitage lasted until the beginning of the 1890s, when the old nobility was pushed aside by upstarts from the government and merchant worlds. At first, they dined in separate rooms. Later, the sated nobility began to disappear. The first to appear in the main dining room were Moscow's foreign merchants – the Knops, the Bogaus, Hoppers, and Marks. They came directly from the office, prim and formal, and each group took its own table. Right behind them came the Russian merchant class, only recently having exchanged traditional coats and boots for luxurious tuxedos. Now they were seated in the main dining room of the Hermitage with representatives of foreign firms.

Olivier did not bother with merchants. Marius, who had preached to beaming gourmets, waited on the merchants, but spoke with them in an offhand and even patronizing manner. When Russian merchants became customers, Chef Dugas stopped creating new dishes and left for France. But even then business went brilliantly. On the square in front of Hermitage, grand carriages were replaced by cabs with uncomfortable sleighs harnessed to trembling, cheap nags. Cabs also waited on Strastnaya Square and near the hotels Dresden, Slavyansky Bazaar, Greater Moscow, and Prague. But the best were at Hermitage, and paid the city up to 500 rubles per year for the right to stand there. Outfitted in baggy shirts of expensive fabric, belted with custom silk waistbands, cab drivers proudly watched the public walking by and spoke only with "shining personages" exiting the restaurant.

"Yrr-sellence!"[7]

"Yrr-sellence!"

For a Muscovite to be awarded this princely title, he had only to walk up to a cab driver, sit proudly in the cab on its soft tires, and shout commandingly, "To Yar!" Immediately, he was treated as "Yrr-sellence!"

Floppy shirts appeared on drivers after the long forgotten time when an angry noble beat his serf coachman with his fists and kicked him in the spine. In such an instance, a floppy shirt, stuffed with cotton to the point of non-recognition, saved the driver from eternity and kept him whole. Now, just like livery drivers use the forgotten title Lord, cab drivers are never without a floppy shirt and use the forgotten title, Yrr-sellence!

---

6. The restaurant was located at what is now Neglinnaya Street 29/14. Today, the building is occupied by the theater, School for Contemporary Plays.

7. "Your Excellency" when fully articulated (in Russian: "Вась-сиясь!" short for "Ваше сиятельство!")

Everyone enjoyed being Yrr-sellences! An especially large number of them appeared in Moscow after the war with Japan.[8] They were purchasing agents for the army and their protectors – quartermasters. Sales clerks at Yeliseyev's had spotted their growth, and at Hermitage they already were Yrr-sellences! Before the war with Japan, there was a fat headquarters captain, promoted by the cab drivers from Strastnoy Boulevard to "colonel." He was subsequently awarded the title of Yrr-sellence! by the cabbies from Hermitage, even though his epaulettes still had the four stars and single stripe of a headquarters captain. Earlier, the headquarters captain had walked or perhaps dragged himself home from the horse track in a five-kopek carriage. Later, he was appointed to a Commission, and began to free wealthy people from the need for long journeys to the front, and in some cases from a soldier's cloak entirely. Even his clerk, a half-literate conscript, could afford a *dacha* love nest near Moscow.

"Yrr-sellence! Come with Ivan!" "Yrr-sellence!, come with Fyodor!" drivers would greet them near the entrance to Hermitage. Skinny little junior officers in outmoded cloaks went to the races, pooled their bets, put it up against the house, and had to walk home from the track after losing their last red ruble. They bargained at Hunter's Row for fruit or sausage – but suddenly – war with Japan! They came alive! They started going to Yeliseyev's to buy salami, apples, and then caviar, marmalade, and Port No. 137.[9] At Yeliseyev's, sharp-eyed sales clerks noticed how their quartermaster-protectors filled out, softened, and multiplied. They began to arrive in coaches, later in cabs, and still later in their own carriages.

"Eh... Eh..."

"Ah?"

"Send me everything on this list... then add whatever you consider necessary... and the bill…" he would say in a deep bass, trying to make an impression.

Then he would go to Hermitage, where a spot had been saved for him, and 10 just like him, as regulars, both officers and civilians, all Yrr-sellences! But Hermitage and the drivers also put many of them "out on the street!" Born nobles dined at Hermitage, but it was difficult for up-and-comers to hold on to such a spot. Wartime income disappeared, but noble ways were unchanged.

To enjoy Hermitage and its delicacies, and then rush in a cab to Yar to dine with Gypsies, Hungarians, and Anna Zakharovna's choir girls, even those wearing clothes, something like three thousand soldiers had to go half-dressed: substandard fabrics, black bread, and poorly-fitted shirts. If Yrr-sellence! purchased headwear, maybe two thousand winter hats had fur an inch too short, and old, and in place of a cotton lining soldiers had to make their own. If he worked in boot supply: for one

---

8. The Russo-Japanese War (February 1904 - September 1905) was set off by clashing ambitions for control over Korea and Manchuria. Russia wanted a warm-water port on the Pacific Ocean, but was defeated.

9. Yeliseyev's is treated in detail in the chapter starting on page 250.

cab ride, 10 soldiers on the march would rub their feet raw and fight rheumatism the rest of their lives. Soldiers *did* march half-dressed, in stinking, moldy winter coats at the same time that supply officers, Yrr-sellences! and dolled-up women, "impressed with themselves," made the rounds of the Yars. At the expense of the soldiers' winter coats, they bought sable stoles and sealskin jackets. The lordly quartermaster Yrr-sellences! ate imported delicacies while the army's flour had maggots.

Time passed. Yrr-sellences! in greatcoats started to disappear. From a titled Yrr-sellence!, a headquarters captain was demoted to simply "Sir." Not just the cab drivers, but the "yellow-eyed" coachmen, and even the "winter" drivers[10] with their old nags, stopped considering them Sirs. Hermitage, as well as many of their drinking buddies, had "put them out on the street." Cab drivers knew the whole story about every Hermitage regular. Cabbies did not trust Yrr-sellences!, and preferred celebrating merchants. As a sign of respect, the cabbies referred to each of them by first name and patronymic.

Hermitage became the property of a trade syndicate. New directors replaced Olivier and Marius: Polikarpov was the decorator, Mochalov managed the seafood, Dmitriev ran the buffet, and Yudin did the purchasing. Clever men, just what was needed for a new clientele. First, they renovated Hermitage, making it even more luxurious. Separately, but in the same building, they installed a luxurious *banya*. They also constructed a new building with meeting rooms. Hermitage was expanded with a glass-encased gallery and a summer garden with a separate entrance and luxurious private dining rooms, walkways, and a small, sweet-smelling garden.

Hermitage became enormously profitable – drunkenness and debauchery were unleashed. Moscow's "name" merchants and lesser-known, well-to-do guests went directly to private dining rooms, where they immediately disrobed . Fine-grain caviar was served in silver buckets. Accompanied by cries of delight, two-foot sturgeons were brought in and killed at the table. But, despite it all, they still ate asparagus with their knives and sliced their artichokes. Special acclaim was accorded the Red Room, where Moscow's "fast livers" ate the clown Tahiti's trained pig.

Dinners, where Moscow's revelers gathered after a show, were especially well regarded. The room was filled with capes, tuxedos, greatcoats, and women in low-cut dresses sparkling with diamonds. An orchestra accompanied choirs, there was a river of champagne, and the rooms overflowed with people. Everywhere, room numbers for parties were exchanged eagerly. Rooms cost from 5 to 25 rubles for a few hours. Everyone came! Everything was secret. The police did not interfere, especially since they might bump into their bosses!

10. Elsewhere in the text called a *kashnik*, a seasonal winter driver.

Hermitage's white hall of columns was luxurious. Here, anniversaries were celebrated. In 1899, during the Pushkin festival,[11] they held a Pushkin lunch attended by all of the day's famous writers. The richest merchant weddings with hundreds of guests were held here. Diners with filthy hands ate from Saxon services: there were Rouen duck copied from the French, red partridges from Switzerland, and salted fish from the Mediterranean. Apples *Calville*, each with a coat of arms, sold for five rubles apiece. Guests from near the Moscow River hid apples and pears in their back pockets to spirit off to Taganka, to their old-fashioned homes, reeking of wood oil and spoiled cabbage. Expatriates rented the white room often for honoring well-known arrivals from their homelands. Foreigners also celebrated New Year's and German Shrovetide. Ryabov, Moscow's best orchestra, played all the hall's events.

In 1917, Hermitage closed. Some small circles met in the rooms, but even they emptied. Hermitage was depressed, not a soul around: people were even afraid to walk by. Later, there were crowds around Hermitage. Enormous lines formed near the entrances. Dozens of handcarts belonging to customers waited. Lucky ones received an ARA package, which filled all of the halls, offices, and service space in Hermitage.[12]

NEP arrived.[13] Hermitage once again glowed with nighttime lights. Tattered coachmen crowded around, trading places with ragged cab drivers, but all riding on the same black market tires. Autos arrived and departed, moving drunkenly. A former manager of Hermitage had revived a pale version of the once-stylish restaurant. Names of dishes again appeared on table cards: cutlets *Pompadour*, Marie Louise, Ballarua, Salad *Olivier*. Meat cutlets were unchewable, and prepared with castor oil. The Salad Olivier was made from leftovers, which was entirely acceptable to the NEP-man visitors.

In the cloak room: sealskin coats, beaver collars, and sable coats. In the great room, the same chandeliers shined, the same white table linens and dishware were used. On the wall across from the buffet table M.P. Sadovsky's autograph remained intact. Here, he breakfasted, made fun of "fast-livers," and watched people go by. Instead of white-shirted waiters, servants in stained jackets brought the food and ran up when called, shining through their pants, tattered like lace. Customers looked a bit askance at visitors in leather coats.

A loud group concludes lunch with champagne. They get up, make a commotion, some dandy with a gut in a tuxedo rants. Powdered, with lip color, a lady lights a cigarette and blows smoke into the face and wine glass of a man in a frock coat. He

---

11. The poet Alexander Pushkin was born in 1799, so in 1899 a huge centenary festival was held. Many leading writers refused to take part in it, however, calling it a vulgarization of the great writer.

12. American Relief Administration: a relief mission to post-revolutionary Russia led by a young Herbert Hoover to fight a famine in 1921.

13. NEP, or New Economic Policy, was a short-term attempt by the Bolsheviks to take a breather from early excesses that had destroyed the economy's ability to produce sufficient goods and services.

finds the entire situation a bit awkward, apparently, but he is the center of attention. The fat dandy's expressive gestures are directed at him. From the other side, close by, a quick moving man flashes some papers. The man in the middle waves his hand and does not look at them, but the man with the papers tries and tries...

This is a scene straight out of the play *Inflatable Pastry*, which ran with success at the Theater of the Revolution. Everything lifelike. Semyon Rak gesticulates in just the same way, Rita Kern, a made-up dancer, behaves just as rudely. Nearby, the uncomfortable bank director Ilya Kromyslov waits for Miron Zont, requesting a subsidy for his journal... And further, clerks, secretaries, directors, merchants from Obrydlov, and the same Semyon Rak, self-satisfied, starting to grow fat. At other tables, it's just the same.

A year later, the Moscow City Council replaced Hermitage with the Peasants' Club.

MOSCOW'S UNDERBELLY

HUNTER'S ROW WAS MOSCOW'S UNDERBELLY. It was built with a number of old buildings along one side, and on the other a long, one-story building with one roof, despite the fact that it belonged to dozens of owners. Only two of these buildings were residential: the building where the Continental Hotel operated and the Yegorov tavern next to it, famous for its *bliny*. All the rest were shops, all the way to Tverskoy Boulevard.

Yegorova's tavern at one time belonged to Voronin, and its sign depicted a crow with *bliny* in its bill.[1] All of the shops on Hunter's Row sold meat or fish, and beneath them were root cellars. The shops' back doors opened onto a huge courtyard, Monetny,[2] as it had been called since ancient times. On it were also one story meat, fish, and egg shops, and, in the middle, the two-story tavern Monetny. In the rear part of the courtyard was a row of small barns with cellars and storerooms that seethed with hordes of rats.

Hunter's Row received its name back in the days when it was permitted to sell game brought here by hunters from the Moscow region. In front of the shops, in the courtyard along the wide sidewalk, stood portable booths. Vendors milled around with baskets and sacks filled with every kind of foodstuff. Hunters walked by, with ducks, grouse and rabbits hanging all about them. From women's baskets swung chicken heads. There were chicks. Piglets, in sacks, screamed. Traders, taking a piglet out to show a customer, would invariably lift it above their heads, holding its bound rear legs. On the street, in front of the booths, wandered pie sellers, and vendors selling *bliny* and hot cereal cooked in Lenten, vegetable oil. Sellers poured,

---

1. In Russian, the word for crow is *vorona*.
2. Literally, "Monetary," signifying that the State Mint (the "New Red Mint") was located nearby. Constructed by Peter the Great in 1697, it lies just off Red Square, behind the newly rebuilt Kazan Cathedral.

for a penny per glass, hot *shiten*, a favorite honey drink that warmed coachmen and sales clerks freezing in the cold shops. In the summer, the *shiten* sellers were replaced by *kvas* sellers, and the favorite was pear *kvas*, made with stewed pears, which lay cooked, in pyramids, on the counters. *Kvas* was scooped from buckets with mugs.

Meat and fish shops had two departments. In the first department, meats of various types lay on the counter – game, chicken, geese, turkeys, spotted piglets for baking and, in ice water, clear skinned piglets for the stovetop. Sheep carcasses and milk-fed veal swung on hooks along the walls. The entire ceiling was hung with hams of every possible size, prepared in all possible ways: smoked, cooked, dried. In the second department, gloomy, lit only by the door into the courtyard, hung dozens of carcasses. There were cellars under all of the shops.

Hunter's Row was especially busy before major holidays. Stylish merchants' wives with expensive horses and carriages pulled right up to the shops. Clerks carried out baskets and crates with goods and put them in the sleighs. It was not unusual for a ham to stick out of a basket next to the sable coat of a millionaire merchant's wife. Across from the bear counters might lay, in all its beauty, a huge sturgeon.

The cellars gave off a stench, but first-class goods lay on the counters. In the fish department, they had the best fish, and in the meat department, chickens, geese, turkeys, and piglets. Near the counters, managers in long, stained aprons and caps bustled, praised the goods, and lied ceaselessly. On their belts hung an assortment of knives, which were only washed at day's end. Here, cleanliness was not in style.

The most important customers were chefs from the best taverns and restaurants, next came chefs for nobles and merchants, then housekeepers for merchants, and finally cooks. All of these crowded in together, bargained, and quarreled over kopeks. A Hunter's Row trader would serve a customer while keeping in mind his singular slogan: "Don't scam, can't sell."

The poor shopped in the booths and from street vendors' trays, loaded with the worst cuts of meat: hips, tripe, and cheap ram-mutton. They could not afford the best shops' goods, which were, as Gogol said, "for those who were better scrubbed." But both the sellers in the shops and the street vendors promised the same things and shortchanged everyone, rich and poor alike. This was an old custom of the traders on Hunter's Row, consistent with their trusted slogan "Don't scam, can't sell."

Hunter's Row is the best example of the level of 1880s sanitary inspection procedures. Inspections began with the meat shops and Monetny Courtyard.

Concerning the shops, they seemed tidy from the outside, but the parts not visible to customers were horrid. All of the so-called "booths" are used as henhouses, where live birds are kept and slaughtered. Starting with the stairs leading into the booths, the floors and cages are maintained carelessly, droppings are not removed, congealed blood is everywhere and permeates the booths' walls, which are not-painted with an

Along Hunter's Row. Below, left, a fish seller; below, right a *kvas* merchant.

oil-based product, which would be consistent with sanitary norms. Strewn in the corners on the floor are rubbish, feathers, mats, and brushes; the chopping blocks for butchering meat are in poor condition and maintained carelessly; carcasses are hung on rusty iron hooks; shop workers are dressed in stained clothing and filthy aprons; dirty knives hang from the butchers' belts in filthy, bloody sheaths, which appear never to have been cleaned. In barns attached to some of the booths stand tubs used to soak hides taken from slaughtered animals. They give off an unbearable stench.

After inspecting the shops, the commission visited Monetny Courtyard. In its center was a trash pit, jammed with a pile of decaying animal and plant refuse, as well as a few wooden tubs that served as a wastewater pit, intended for disposal of all of Hunter's Row's dirty water and sludge. Almost level with the top of the pit, stinking filth stood in the tubs in a thick mass, in which could be seen internal organs suspended in blood. All this filth was poured, with no permit, into a city sewer pipe and flowed unfiltered into the Moscow River.

The filth of the rear courtyard "defied description." Almost half of it was officially occupied by a slaughterhouse for cattle located in a large, two-story stone barn. The interior of the slaughterhouse was disgusting. The asphalt floor was coated with a thick layer of congealed blood, which also permeated the bare walls. The establishment had a fairly spacious killing floor, in which cattle were slaughtered for all of Hunter's Row, and it gave off a stink that, to an unaccustomed person, was unbearable. This building had a small section that smelled even worse, where a guard in charge of cleaning the slaughterhouse, Mokeyev, lived. The courtyard area was covered by a thick layer of blood and shreds of innards congealed between the stones. Next to the wall were piles of steaming manure, kidneys, and other rotting refuse. The courtyard was surrounded by cellars and locked sheds on abandoned construction sites.

> After protracted demands for a key, the door to the butcher Ivan Kuzmich Leonov's barn was opened. Out of the barn and across the yard, a red liquid had seeped from a pile of a few hundred rotting hides. The next storehouse was used for dressing slaughtered cattle belonging to the Andreyev brothers, and was almost worse than the first. It contained salted beef filled with worms, etc. When they opened the door, a swarm of rats scurried out of boxes of rotten meat, trundled off, and disappeared beneath the floor. It was like that everywhere...

This inspection report made history. It was read aloud at a city council meeting and elicited lively debate, which, like always, would have ended in nothing if not for the sincere, yet simple, Zhadayev. The debate over, a semi-literate craftsman – a box maker, small, shaggy, in dirty underwear and scuffed boots – asked to speak: his ringing, sharp tenor followed the testimony of Doctor Popandopodo, who had sketched out the horrors of Hunter's Row. Miasmas, bacilli, bacteria, unsanitary conditions, ammonia: all adorned the doctor's presentation.

"T-rrrrr-uuuu - th! What Vasily Konstantinovich says is the truth! We supply Hunter's Row with crates, so we've seen our fill... What kind of miasmas they have there, and in what numbers! You look in a barrel and can see them swarming in a swarm. They crawl all over the salt beef... And as far as bacteria go, they brush up against your legs, red, with tails... they rub up against you and you have to take care not to step on them."

There was Homeric laughter. Zhadayev's eyes flashed, and his voice rose above the roar.

"What are you braying about? You think I'm lying? Huuuge, with tails, and red. Huuuge! Bump right up against your legs!"

He spread his hands apart about two feet.

Zhadayev's speech ended up in the newspapers, and gave Moscow a laugh. Then the cleansing of Hunter's Row was undertaken. First, it was ordered that all the shops get cats. But most already had one. This had been a sport – raising the fattest cat. Sated, enormous cats sat on the counters, and the rats paid them little attention. Cats were removed from the booths all around the courtyard after the night when rats devoured one.

They were helpless with the rats until one of the locals, Grachyov, found, finally, a way to exterminate these predators. And this succeeded only thanks to Zhadayev. The editor of the magazine *Nature and Hunting*, L.P. Sabaneyev, after reading a notice about Zhadayev, met with Grachyov, chuckled about "bacteria with tails," and presented him with a fox terrier puppy. They named him Boy and settled him in a shop. They fed him meat until he was full. Grachyov's neighbors walked by and made fun. The rats ran in herds. Boy grew up and grew strong. One morning, they opened the shop and found two dead rats. Boy stood near them, his stub of a tail wagging. The next day, a rat *troika*, the following day five, and then there were no more rats in the shop – he had killed them all.

Next, Boy cleared out Grachyov's warehouse. Neighbors appealed to Grachyov and Boy went on tour, killing rats. Following Grachyov's example, other traders got fox terriers to protect their top-grade food inventories, which accumulated in large amounts, especially around the holidays, when wealthy Muscovites threw money at gifts and gluttony.

After the October Revolution, the booths on Hunter's Row were razed, and replaced by the 11-story Moscow Hotel. All that remained of Hunter's Row were two ancient buildings on the opposite side of the square. These two buildings had stood for hundreds of years covered with grime and filth until a "Commission on Old Moscow" noticed them, and the State Science Directorate's Museum Department undertook their restoration. They demolished all the sheds and storehouses, and cleaned the dirt from the building originally constructed by Golitsyn, where, earlier, chickens were slaughtered and there had been a warehouse for all kinds of junk. After knocking plaster off the walls, they found stripes, trim, and other ornamentation artfully designed in brick. When they removed from the cellar stinking barrels filled with herring, and demolished the space where the herring were smoked, they found, under the floor, white marble rooms. No Muscovite even suspected that the white marble walls contained a smokehouse.

Vasily Golitsyn, a favorite of Peter's sister, Tsarina Sofia,[3] was considered by some the most learned man of his day. He built these chambers in 1686 to receive foreign

---

3. Tsarina Sofia, Peter the Great's sister, ruled Russia as regent for seven years while Peter and his mentally incompetent half-brother Ivan shared the throne. In 1689, Peter married and asserted his right to the throne, and eventually banished Sofia for life to Moscow's Novodevichy Monastery.

Hunter's Row, 1914. After the revolution, the booths were torn down.

aristocrats, who considered it their responsibility to visit what was then written about abroad as the "eighth wonder" of the world. Next door to Golitsyn's building, an equally spacious area belonged to Golitsyn's sworn enemy, *boyar* Troyekurov,[4] the commander of the *streltsy*. "The *boyar* opined it a most great misfortune and appeared much angered" that "Vaska Golitsyn" owned such chambers!

At this time, Peter I had just ordered his favorite, Troyekurov, to manage the construction of the Sukharev Tower.[5] In addition to the tower, Troyekurov started to construct a building, next to Golitsyn's, to "rub his nose in it." The materials were right at hand – from the Sukharev Tower. Peter learned about it, and accused Troyekurov of embezzlement; nonetheless, in 1691, Troyekurov's two-story building appeared next to Golitsyn's. Later, Troyekurov added a third floor with arched vaults eight feet high, the like of which which had never been built before and haven't been since.

Due to the intrigues of his enemies, including Troyekurov, Vasily Golitsyn was exiled and his property confiscated. Peter I gave his building to the Georgian Tsarevich, whose descendants no longer lived in the house when it was leased out as a commercial property. In 1871, it was sold to a merchant. The building had become a slum. The same thing happened with Troyekurov's building. The Troyekurov family line died out in the first half of the eighteenth century, and the building went

---

4. Ivan Borisovich Troyekurov (1633-1703), a powerful *boyar* under Peter I and the last head of the Streltsy.
5. Peter ordered the tower built in 1692 to commemorate the victory over his sister Sophia. It was named after L.P. Sukharev, who commanded the *streltsy* in 1689 and helped Peter escape for a time to the St. Sergius Monastery.

to the gentry family Sokovin, then to the Saltykovs, then to the Yurevs, and finally in 1817 was bought by the Moscow Petty Bourgeois Society, which used it in a bourgeois manner: they leased it as the Hotel London, which soon became the dirtiest coachmen's tavern, serving until the October Revolution as a hideout for card sharps, muggers, speculators, and all sorts of criminals. During the same period, also from jealousy and to rub Vaska Golitsyn's and the embezzler Troyekurov's noses in it, Prince Gagarin built his own palace on Tverskoy Boulevard. He was a bigger embezzler than Troyekurov, as is claimed in a song:

Oh you son of a bitch, Gagarin.
You're a stray dog playing baron.
Drooling cur, you bolted our bread,
stole our pay and instead,
dishonestly lied and misled.
Built a great big mansion, on
Tverskaya, a grand new home.
Past Neglinka you now roam,
Beneath a glazed glass ceiling.
The Moscow River – you don't own –
feeds your fountain's deep new dish,
Grandly stocked-up with live fish…

It is not clear whether Matvei Gagarin ever succeeded in "wiping" Golitsyn's and Troyekurov's "noses in it," but it is quite certain that Peter I cut off his head.

The restored Golitsyn and Troyekurov buildings are reminders of Hunter's Row, and the only ones left if you do not count Peter Kirillov. This product of Hunter's Row is sometimes referred to when something is sold dishonestly: "Don't send me Peter Kirillich!" Peter Kirillov, because of whom stamps had been introduced for payment in taverns, was a real person who made a permanent mark not only in Moscow but in the provinces. Even in distant Siberia, traders would complain: "You sent me Peter Kirillich!"

Peter Kirillov was born in the forties in a village of the former Ulitsky Region. As a 10-year-old, he was brought to Moscow and contracted to train as a waiter at Yegorov's tavern. After getting a good long look at Hunter's Row and its traders who shortchanged customers, fixed scales, and swindled, Peter neatly applied their business methods to his own profession. At the time, food orders were discussed with the guest and agreed upon, and money received from the guest was then taken by the waiter directly to the buffet. They paid, got change, and carried it back on a dish directly to the guest. If a guest left a tip, it was turned in on account at the buffet to be divided later. It seemed impossible to steal anything, but Peter outwitted everyone. He hid money in his sleeve, and stuck it in a couch where a friendly co-worker would sit, take the money, carry it off, count it, and later, at home, settle accounts with Peter. Many knew about this, but no one could catch him. He was really very skilled. A guest might give him 100 rubles to change. He did it in a flash, counted it out in plain sight of the guest, who put it in his pocket, and the deal was done. But another guest might begin to recount it:

"What did you bring me? A fiver is missing, 95 in all."

Peter Kirillov acts surprised. He counts it again himself, puts the money on the table, and puts a salt shaker or a plate on top.

"You're right, this is short a fiver. I'll run and see if I left it on the buffet." He returns in a minute, beaming, and throws down a five. You were right. I left it on the buffet..."

The guest is satisfied, and Peter Kirillich twice as much. While he was counting, he palmed a red, 10-ruble note and added back just a five.

If a guest was a little tipsy he would be treated as follows: if he drank, let's say, three shots of vodka and ate three *pirozhki*, it meant that for three shots and three *pirozhki* he should pay the buffet 60 kopeks. The guest sat, his nose pecking down toward the table:

"How much do I owe?"

"From Yrr-sellence!... well, let's see," Peter Kirillov bends his fingers counting. "Per glass three glasses, for twenty kopeks three twenties; thirty, three *pirozhki* for twenty each thirty; three shots, thirty. You didn't order cigarettes? Two rubles, thirty."[6]

"How much?"

"Two rubles, thirty."

"Why that much?"

"Well... why, sir? You had vodka, ate *pirozhki*, smoked cigarettes, you did not ask for cigars." He bends his fingers: "per shot, three shots; for twenty kopeks, three twenties; thirty, three *pirozhki*, thirty. For twenty, three twenties per shot, three shots; and three *pirozhki*, thirty. Cigarettes, no cigars ordered. Two rubles, thirty."

The guest, not understanding a thing, throws down three rubles. Sometimes, confused, he does not even take his change.

Everyone knew that Peter Kirillich was shortchanging customers, but no one could understand how exactly. His fellow waiters rejoiced: "There's a fine waiter!" They tried to copy him, but not everyone could. When "stamps" were introduced as payment in taverns, Peter Kirillich quit and retired to a richly-furnished home on the Volga, out past Uglich.[7] His neighbors said that when he shopped in Uglich

---

6. The point here is that Peter spews indecipherable gibberish at drunken guests.
7. A town located in the Yaroslavl region, roughly 100 miles from Moscow.

and merchants used an abacus, he would grow angry and say, "Don't pull a Peter Kirillich on me, of all people!"

Peter Kirillich also bequeathed his co-workers a special method for cutting fish pies. The Yegorev tavern, aside from *bliny*, was known for its fish pies. They were round, stuffed dough, the size of a dinner plate, with a thick filling made from ground fish, and an open center, topped by a slice of sturgeon garnished with lemon peel. Sauce was included for free. Dexterous Peter Kirillich was the first to figure out how to slice such a pie "artfully." Fork in one hand, a knife in the other; a few waves of the hand, and in a blink the pie was sliced into 10 extremely thin slices, running out from the central piece of lemon peel to the thick, ruddy edges of the pastry, and retaining its form. This popular method spread across Moscow, but there were few who could slice a pie as "artfully" as Peter Kirillich, perhaps only Testov's Kuzma and Ivan Semyonich. They were artists!

Yegorov's tavern was right out of the Old Testament, one of a kind. The owner, an Old Believer, forbid smoking. "So the place doesn't smell like a dirty shack." The lowest floor of the tavern, Nizok, had an enormous oven. Here, they served customers *bliny* straight from the pan. *Bliny* were prepared in plain sight, non-stop, from morning until night. They were thick and ruddy, with various fillings, Yegorov *bliny*. In this hall, guests sat in winter coats and ate their *bliny* quickly, filled with roe, or sturgeon with horseradish and red wine vinegar. In the hall on the second floor – for the "well-scrubbed" public – with decorated walls, there was a sturgeon tank. Wealthy lovers of Russian cuisine stuffed themselves with herring and other fish dishes. *Bliny* were free.

Across from the gates to Hunter's Row, off Tverskoy Boulevard, stretched narrow Loskutny Alley, turning into Obzhorny, which curved to the Manezh and Mokhovaya Street. The lower floors of these shabby buildings were occupied largely by small vendors who offered, for three kopeks, a mug of *shchi* made from spoiled cabbage, without meat; for five kopeks, green-grey noodle soup made with flax or hemp oil, and fried or boiled potatoes. Gluttons' Row, from daybreak until midnight, was full of working people: those who were half-starved ate at holes-in-the-wall, while those closer to starvation ate right on the street, from meat vendors using clay hearths. None of the products eaten at Gluttons' Row could be sold in the shops or even the booths of Hunter's Row. Goods sold to the poor, lightly spoiled, were said to be "the rats' loss."

Before holidays, Hunter's Row delivered to Moscow's Skvoznik-Dmukhanovsky Monastery loads of edible bribes, and also gave "crackers" in an envelope.[8] At Gluttons' Row only desk cops took "crackers," posted cops and those in the guardhouse

---

8. The word "crackers" was slang for cash.

were satisfied by "nature" – appetizers for vodka. "Well, boss, cut through the throat and grab a bit of lung…"

During the War with Japan, the majority of taverns came to be called restaurants, and even ancient Testov's tavern changed its sign to Testov's Restaurant. (The entrance to the courtyard was from the direction of Tverskoy Boulevard, across from Obzhorny Alley.) All that remained of Testov's tavern was two or three rooms of antique furniture. You would not recognize any of the rest. Even the walls were new. Old-time Moscow gourmets stopped going to Testov's. Travelling merchants, who had not been in Moscow for several years, did not recognize the tavern. First of all, there was a decadent painting on the mirrored window in the vestibule. In the great room, there was modernist furniture on which a 300-pound merchant would be afraid to sit. New arrivals walked into the second, low-ceilinged hall, filled with wide oak chairs. They took their favorite table, to which they had become accustomed, arranging themselves on divans. Here it's the Testov way, like it was before! Two waiters approached at the table. The same white shirts and green waistbands, but they did not have the traditional billfolds for cash and stamps in their waistbands.

"What happened to your stamps? Where is your wallet?"

"We don't accept payment in stamps. Now we use coupons."

"Where is Kuzma? Where is Ivan Semyonich?"

The waiter hesitates: he can see these are important guests.

"Retired, sir. Off to the country for his old age, to a village."

"Are you from Uglich?"

"No, we're from near Moscow. Not many from Yaroslavl left"

"Why are you standing there like a stump? Why aren't you waiting on your guests? Well, when Kuzma Yegorich was here…"

"That's not our concern sir. We have a *meer-dottle…*"

The maître d'hôtel approached in a tuxedo and a white tie, presented a menu card, and belted-out by heart: "Filet of Partridge, Chauffeur with sauce *Provençale*, Beef Roast, Filet Portuguese, Pudding Diplomat, and, completely unexpectedly, Shashlyk *á la* Caucasus with English Mutton."

He also presented a card with a list of Caucasian dishes with the note: *Shashlyk* Cook Georgy Slukhanov, nephew of Prince Argutinsky-Dolgorukov.

The men listened to everything and read the card.

"What a famous tavern this was," sighed the enormous, grey-haired, old man.

"It's a restaurant now, not a tavern," the maître d' proudly declared.

"You say restaurant! But we came here to have Testov's famous roast suckling pig, eat pickled cabbage and brains, enjoy some Achuyevsky roe, and munch on some sturgeon, and here you have… well, we were bored sick of eggs out on the steppe!"

Music trumpeted in the large hall filled with people.

"Where is your famous music machine?[9] Where is it? It played *Luchinushka*... opera..."

"It's over there, but we don't use it: many guests take offence at the machine, say it is old junk. We now have a Romanian orchestra." At that, the maître d'hôtel turned and hurried off to another table.

The fish pie was served.

"Can this really be fish pie? More like a boot than fish pie! Fish pie is round. Well now, how will you slice it?"

"Today, guests slice it themselves," the old man told his neighbor. "You can't blame the tavern: its business is to sell, which means that the public itself changed and does not want player pianos, salted fish, or fish pie. Let them have their Romanians, their turtle soup recipes, and filet *Bordelais*. Merchants go after customers. When Yegorov was here, smoking was not allowed, and now the smoke reaches the ceiling, so smoke as much as you like. That's because in the past, in Moscow, we had the *narod*, but now we have 'the public.' "[10]

---

9. Perhaps a player piano.

10. Without implying too much depth of thought, it seems clear that the speaker expresses regret over the shift he perceives from "the people" (*narod*) whose actions were based on traditional values, to "the public" whose behavior is primarily motivated by self-interest, money, and the market.

LUBYANKA

IN THE 1890S, NEWLY-FLUSH INSURANCE societies, their coffers bursting with cash, found it profitable to invest some of this enormous capital in real estate. They started buying land and building in Moscow to generate rental income. That's how, on Lubyanskaya Square, between Greater and Lesser Lubyanka Streets, a huge building was constructed. It belonged to the All-Russia Insurance Society and was built on property owned by N.S. Mosolov. In the eighties, Mosolov, a wealthy landowner, academic, well-known engraver, and collector of rare prints, rented at this location a building whose bottom floor housed the Warsaw Insurance Society. The other wing was leased by the photographer Mebius. Mosolov lived alone in an enormous apartment, but kept a servant from among his former serfs. He usually spent half the year abroad, and the rest in Moscow, receiving almost no one. Occasionally, he would go out accompanied by his driver, a former serf whose name no one knew, but whom everyone called Noodle. Across from Mosolov's, on Lubyanskaya Square, was a stand for rental carriages. When Mosolov sold his building to the All-Russia Insurance Society, he gave his carriage and horses to Noodle, who then joined the stand. Excellent equipment gave him the chance to do well: riding with Noodle was considered *chic*.

Mosolov died in 1914. He donated his valuable collection of prints and plates, both his own work and that of artists from abroad, to a museum. Old-time Muscovites remember this Turgenev-like[1] figure, but only rarely did he consider someone worthy of a visit. He spent entire days alone at home, working. Sometimes he

---

1. Ivan Turgenev, the author, was known for being particularly tall and broad-shouldered. His best-known work, the novel *Fathers and Sons*, was published in 1862.

The building of the
All-Russia Insurance
Society, later renovated
into the Lubyanka
headquarters of the NKVD.

relaxed with a long cherry-stemmed pipe. He would stand by a window looking out into the courtyard where, since the eighties, Generalov's grocery had been.

The grocery had a meat department. To reduce the cost of making sausage and salami, the owner, when the time was right, would buy up large loads of kidneys. They would fester in barrels giving off a horrible stench. In the yard, they kept a terribly nasty dog, a German shepherd that despised the police. All it needed was to catch sight of a street cop and it would attack. It would also tear apart any dog that ran into the yard.

Gusenkov's tavern was located in the neighboring wing of Mosolov's building, and on the second and third floors there were furnished rooms. On the second floor, there were around 20 rooms, and on the upper floor a few less. I was in them for the first time in 1881, visiting the actor A.D. Kazakov.

"Here, we're all from Tambov!" Mosolov said. Originally a Tambov landowner himself, Mosolov leased the whole building to another Tambov businessman, to be rented out as rooms. That man died at the end of the eighties, but his heir honored the agreement. The rooms were all monthly rentals, leased in a standing arrangement by their residents. Among these, until they died off, were Tambov landowners (including Mosolov himself) who had come to Moscow in the seventies to finish their days on the remnants of payments received for emancipation.

They had to be creative decorators! The building had narrow little corridors, like tunnels, with the characteristic smell of a hotel room. Servants, with silent steps, ran constantly back and forth with badly polished and unscrubbed samovars enveloped in clouds of steam. Wearing quiet, soft shoes at the owner's instruction, one could still sense in their servile economy of motion a vestige of the typical, morally and physically corrupt, yet able and loyal serfs that had belonged to the former land-owning gentry. In reality, in 1881, these types still existed, former serfs brought in from Tambov estates. In those years, the residents of the furnished apartments were from estates on the steppe, landowners slowing dying off in an urban setting. In a few years they were gone, first the servants, former serfs, and then the former landowners. Yazikov, a Tambov horse breeder, held on longer than others, expiring in his room at an advanced old age, surrounded by his beloved dogs and two cleaning "girls" – also elderly – loyal to their boss. A retired cavalry colonel lived there too, laying for entire days on a divan with a pipe, sending letters imploring his old friends, who from time to time paid for his apartment. Mosolov helped some residents, elderly Tambov landowners who had no resources.

Little by little, in place of the disappearing landowners, the rooms were leased by new residents, and always for the long term. For many years, the writer S.N. Filippov and Doctor Dobrov lived here. Moscow's actors lived here, calm people of modest means who loved comfort and quiet. Kazakov lived here with his friend Oznobishin, the Tambov landowner, a cousin of Ilya Oznobishin, a dramatic writer and excellent amateur actor, who took a room during his winter trips to Moscow.

Each suite consisted of three, high-ceilinged rooms with tall windows looking onto the square. On the floor was a large, soft rug with a Persian design, a type woven at the time by peasant craftsmen. All the furniture was mahogany with bronze, including a glass-fronted rococo cabinet, a table, with a cabinet at each end with drawers both large and small, and in front of them a Voltaire-style armchair. In a case between the windows were valuable jeweled baubles and an enormous English clock with bass chimes. On the walls, on top, were portraits of ancestors, and under them watercolors of hunting scenes and photographs. Everything was framed in mahogany. On the mantel there were expensive bronze candelabras with candles ,and between them a clock, made from a combination of china and bronze.

In the bedroom there was an enormous bed, also made of mahogany, and above it a rug with a hunting horn, daggers, and portraits of Borzoi dogs. On the other side, there was a Turkish divan; above it hung an oil portrait of a strikingly beautiful Amazon, and, again, photographs and engravings. Next to a portrait of Alexander II wearing a casual grey outfit, with a dog at his feet, were photographs of Herzen and Ogaryov, and, on the other side, Princess Dagmar with a dog in her hands, and Garibaldi in a round little cap. This was all that remained of an enormous and grand estate and it continued to decorate the existence of the solitary old noble, at one time glowing with life, now in Moscow to spend, in this suite, his final years.

The actors Kireyev and Dalmatov came as guests to Kazakov, and one of the literary types. The old man was bored all alone. He asked: "You know what? Have you ever seen man-servant theater?"

"We don't understand."

"We… you will see!"

He called. A servant came in who was fairly rough around the edges, but extremely self-possessed, with grey sideburns and a completely bald head. Tall, good posture, a noble appearance.

"Would you like a samovar, Alexander Dmitriyevich?"

"Yes, if you will. I'm very bored…"

"Well, it's that time of day, sir, everyone is out… In the whole corridor only Yazikov is home, sir. Some went to the park; some are sitting out on the boulevard… They'll be back in time for bed, but the sun hasn't even set."

The old man stood with his arms on the back of the chair, and apparently was happy to chat. "Nikanor Markelych! I have a request for you… My friends here are actors. Play for us the old noble. Is our Grigori here?"

"He's in his nook making cigarettes for Suite No. 8."

"Call him and do the skit… we'll each chip in a ruble."

"Please, sir, what are you saying? I'd be happy to do it for nothing."

"We're dying of boredom, entertain us…"

"I'll run and get Grisha."

He took the large armchair, moved it to the corner opposite the window, said "At once!" and disappeared. Kazakov gave one answer to our questions: "You'll see. For now, let's each put up a ruble."

In a few minutes there was a light knock on the door, and a proud noble entered wearing a feathered cap and a Turkish robe with red ties. Not paying us any attention, he walked through as if there were no one in the room, sat down in the armchair, and drummed his fingers on its arm. Then, he closed his eyes as if sleeping. In the small entrance someone coughed. The noble opened his eyes, yawned widely, and clapped his hands.

"Vanka, a pipe!"

In a flash, a greying man with clipped sideburns ran in, one foot bare and the other shod, holding a pipe with a long cherry stem. He gave the noble the pipe, got down on one knee, struck a match on his pants, lit a scrap of paper, and held it to the pipe.

The noble smoked and stretched.

"Where's Proshka, that bastard?"

"Demons cart water for that guy…"

"Ahhh!" the noble let out a cloud of smoke and fell to thinking.

"Vanka my boy! Fetch half a bottle of vodka, *allez*!"

"Where should I get it, boss?"

"Oh you Tartar! Take it from the stash!"

"How the hell do you know where you even put it?"

"What kind of champagne do we have?"

"The kind they lock gates against."

"What did you say? I don't hear well!"

"What I said was… the horse loved it."

"Vanka, my boy, you're an experienced old chap, might you have a fiancé for me to think about?"

"Yes, the best in the world, so beautiful that half a sack of turds follows her around. As soon as one declares his intentions, he's gone, disappears. She limps on one leg, has one crossed-eye, looks just a little bit like a horse, but on the other hand… she's r-r-r-r-r-iiiiich!"

"Well, that's no tragedy, give her here… What kind of dowry?"

"A large estate, you can't see the end of it, a palace in the middle, two suits of armor, storehouses full of nice stuff, goods from across the seas, what all isn't in there… food supplies you could never finish: 40 barrels of salted frogs, 40 bales of dry roaches, cattle, a rooster and hens, bronze tableware – everything from a cross to buttons. And what a mug! But from the road you can't even hear her."

"Vanka, my boy! What do they write from my village? Do my serfs live well?"

"They write that they are barely breathing, but live enriched by their passion. They dig for gold with a spade, for filth with their tongues, and no one has a shirt or pants."

"Here, the mailman brought a letter…"

"Where is he, the old devil?"

"He's on the other side, cooking hot pitch for his Master."

The servant took a paper out of his shirt and gave it to the noble.

"Oh, you son of a bitch! Why didn't you present this letter to your master on a silver platter?"

"Well, our silver is all tarnished. I would have presented it on a gold platter, but everyone is out."

The noble read the letter aloud, "Father most noble, sick foal, Mikhail Petrovich died, they tore off your noble skin and sold it for proceed money, bought a sturdy animal for Your Kindness at the fair, a pig breed, Your Kindness was pleased."[2]

"Vanka! You cow! This letter is an antique."

"We smoked half – it was a long one."

"Back then, I had a coat of arms in the courtyard, a blue shield on a gold field…"

"Today, boss, your future amounts to this," and, after sticking his thumb between his index and middle finger, the servant gave his boss the *kukish*.[3]

He turned to us, "The show is over. The boss and I have nothing else." The guests started clapping and the ecstatic Kireyev jumped up and began to shake the actors' hands. We forced them to accept the money. The man who played Vanka told us that this "show" was quite old. Before emancipation, it entertained the serfs,

---

2. Broken grammar and outdated language of uneducated peasants.
3. A rude hand gesture.

Lubyanskaya Square.

who risked a whipping or forced service as a soldier just to watch. Old man Kazakov confirmed that the man was an actor before emancipation, something he tried to hide.

Next to Mosolov's building, on land belonging to the Consistory,[4] was a working men's tavern, Uglich. The tavern served coachmen, although it did not have a court-yard, where horses were typically fed and watered while their owners drank tea. But at that time in Moscow there was a "simplification" introduced by Vlasov, the Chief of Police in the first half of the nineties. Before Vlasov, Lubyanskaya Square called itself a carriage yard: between Mosolov's and the fountain was a carriage stand, be-tween the fountain and Shipov's, a stand for carting loads, and along the entire sidewalk from Myasnitskaya Street to Lubyanskaya Street was a cab line crowding near the horses. In those days, drivers were not required to sit on benches. Horses stood with feedbags on, unbridled, feeding. On the street, along the sidewalk, were uneaten hay and splashes of filth.

The horses ate unwatched, flocks of pigeons and sparrows flitted between their legs, and in the tavern drivers sipped tea. A driver, leaving the tavern, would scoop water from the base of the fountain with a dirty bucket and treat his horse while

4. An administrative department of the Russian Orthodox Church.

a line of water carts with barrels circled the fountain. They rolled up with eight barrels at a time, parked around the fountain, and with bucket-shaped scoops on long handles took water from the fountain and filled the barrels. The entire square hummed with profanity from morning until late at night.

Next to Uglich, on the corner of Myasnitskaya Street, were the Myasnitskaya furnished rooms, rented by traveling merchants and salesmen carrying samples of their goods. The building where they stayed was built by Malyushin on land leased from the consistory.

Consistory! This word is now incomprehensible to most readers. The devil fell into a trap and yelled out in fear, "Is this the Consistory?" That was the folk saying about this institution. It was a church directorate consist-ing of high-ranking spiritual leaders – a council of petty bureaucrats headed by a secre-tary, its most powerful figure. The secretary was everything. The bureaucrats received a tiny salary and lived entirely on bribes. This was practiced openly. Rural priests carted loads of bribes, flour and live-

Consistory on Myasnitskaya Street.

stock, to the bureaucrats' apartments. Muscovites paid with cash. Deacons, nuns, church workers, and graduates from the church academy or seminary, who received employment, also paid bribes.

The Consistory controlled a large stretch of land on Myasnitskaya Street, from Furakovsky Alley to Lubyanskaya Square. It was headquartered in a two-story build-ing resembling a barracks, and had a large garden. Later, the building was razed and rebuilt, but in the new building they continued to accept bribes the old-fashioned way. Church leaders worshiped here, trials were held, and divorces were finalized. Divorces included enormous bribes and mercenary witnesses, needed to establish the infidelity of one or the other spouse, a requirement for divorce under the old law. They testified to the court, grey-haired archbishops, about the smallest details of the physical betrayal, which they allegedly witnessed. The court was not only in-terested in evidence that a traitor to marital fidelity was caught in bed; details were required that no third party could have ever glimpsed, but the witnesses "saw" and testified with feeling. The judges smacked their lips and "judged."

The Holy Synod outranked the Consistory. It was located in Petersburg, in a building under arches, similar to another arched building occupied by the Senate.

A joke was made about this. "The blind Holy Synod and thieving Senate both live thanks to bribes."[5]

Between the Consistory and the furnished rooms on Myasnitskaya Street, there was an extremely old three-story building where government clerks lived. At one time, this was a house of horrors. I saved some notes written by an eyewitness:

> I needed to visit a clerk who lived there. The apartment was on the lowest floor of the old, three-story building, in low-ceilinged, communal rooms. It gave an awful impression, despite the completely unremarkable domestic situation; a pair of canaries even chirped to one another in a deep nook near the small window. The walls and ceiling were unbelievably massive. Thick, rusty iron hooks with enormous iron rings stuck out of the ceiling and walls in the dining room.

> Seated at tea, I looked with surprise at the ceilings, hooks and rings. "What kind of strange building is this?" I asked the clerk.

> "It's a curiosity of sorts. Here, for example, we are sitting in the very room where 100 years ago Stepan Ivanovich Sheshkovsky, the head of the Secret Chancellery,[6] tortured arrestees. The hooks above us are restraints for hanging torture victims. And this little cabinet is no more and no less than a lockbox. We removed and replaced its iron door with a wooden one, and now, as you see, it contains homemade beverages, which we'll taste in a bit. But in Sheshkovsky's time they put criminals' valuables in here; you see, it's only two feet deep, five feet wide, and a bit more than five feet tall. Beneath us, and also underneath the archive next door, are basements with torture chambers and horrible fixtures, where even now the iron rings for chaining prisoners are intact. Over there, it's even more frightening. Still another lockbox remains intact with an iron door."

That basement was full of all kinds of junk. In further conversation, the clerk said,

> "I've lived here for 40 years and still run across people who remember Sheshkovsky and his assistants, Cheredin, Agapych, and others, some who even knew Vanka Kain himself. The son of the building's senior watchman, who lived here as a teenager, remembers better than others, and told me about some of the horrors of living here."

---

5. This is wordplay. *Podarok* means gift. In the instrumental form it becomes *podarkami*: "by means of gifts." A building's arch is *ark* and "under" is *pod*, a preposition that requires the instrumental case, thus *pod arkami* means "beneath the arches."
6. Peter the Great created the Secret Chancellery in 1718 and it was liquidated after his death in 1762 (only to be superceded by Catherine II's Secret Expedition), both were charged with carrying out internal investigations and judgments particularly against any and all threats to the crown.

"In his day, torture had become less frequent. As soon as Paul I was coronated, he freed all those who had been imprisoned by Catherine II and her predecessors.[7] When they were led out into the courtyard, they no longer resembled human beings: some screamed, some flew into a frenzy, and some dropped dead. In the yard, their chains were removed and they left, each to their own destination, the majority to a home for the insane. Later, during the reign of Alexander I,[8] the restraints and torture stands were removed and the prisons cleaned. Cheredin still managed everything. He even lived here, in my day. He told me how Pugachyov was tortured in front of him – my father also remembered this.[9] He also saw Saltychikha here in this very room where we are now sitting. Later they took her from here to the Ivanovsky Monastery, to a cell where she lived for 30 years until her death. I myself saw her at Ivanovsky Monastery. She was kept at the time in an underground cell. She stood looking out through a window grate, shrieking, cursing, and spitting. She was never let out, and they served her food through one single window. At the time, I was around eight years old. I went to the monastery with my mother and remember everything well."

Since that note, more than 20 years had passed when, at the turn of the century, I was returning home from a lengthy journey. Coming from Kursk Railroad Station on Myasnitskaya Street, I was surprised to see that the building had vanished. Only a pile of stones and rubble remained. Masons were demolishing the foundation. I jumped from the carriage and walked right up. Apparently, a new building was planned. "They just started demolishing the underground chambers," the foreman said. "I've seen it," I responded. "No, you saw the prison. We already demolished that, but underneath was still another space, the scariest. In one of its chambers, potatoes and firewood lay on the floor, and the other was filled with corpses. We didn't know it was there. We broke through and ran into an oak door sheathed with iron. We knocked it down and found a human skeleton. When they broke in the door you could hear the chains rattle. They buried the bones. The police came and took away the chains and shackles."

We crawled through a break in the wall and went down four stairs onto a stone floor; there, the underground murk fought light coming from a hole in the ceiling at the other end of the chamber. Breathing was difficult. My guide took a candle stub from his pocket and lit it: there were shackles, rings, hooks. Further on, it was brighter. We snuffed out the candle. "This is where the skeleton in chains hung." There was a blackened oak door, sheathed with iron, dotted with mold, a small

---

7. Paul I (1754-1801) was coronated in 1796 and assassinated only a few years later, following a number of controversial policy decisions.
8. Alexander I (1775-1825).
9. Yemelyan Ivanovich Pugachyov (1742-1745), a pretender to the Russian throne, led a Cossack rebellion during the reign of Catherine II. Saltychikha was Darya Nikolayevna Saltykova (1730-1801), a landed gentry who was found to be a sadistic serial murderer of her serfs. She was convicted and sentenced to life in a monastery prison.

window, and behind it a short stone lockbox, just like the one that held drinks in the old man's apartment, only with some sort of depression, like a narrow niche. On further inspection, we saw other niches in the walls.

"I'll come by tomorrow with a photographer. We must document this and publish it in a magazine."

"Please, come. Let it be known how they tortured people. Come."

I went out on the street and had just decided to get a cab, when I saw a colleague from the magazine business, the illustrator N.A. Bogatov.

I stopped him. "Nikolai Alekseyevich, do you have a pencil?"

"Of course. I never take a step without a pencil and a sketch book."

I told him briefly about what I had seen and in a few minutes we were in the cellar. Bogatov and I spent around three hours there while he completed an excellent sketch; moreover, the foreman gave us the exact measurements of the chamber. The horrid enclosure where the skeleton was found was a little over two meters high and two meters wide. Its depth at the niche was less than a meter. Why they had made it we couldn't even guess.

The building was demolished and replaced.

In 1923-1924, on the spot where the Myasnitsky furnished apartments had been located, new commercial space was built. Underneath the apartments were deep cellars with pipes and posts reminiscent of the neighboring prisons of the Secret Order, to which they probably belonged.[10] Now they are filled in, but before the revolution they were used by the merchant Chichkin for storing dairy products.

On the other side of Myasnitskaya Street, on Lubyanka Drive, was the Romeyko property. Arsentych, a tavern that faced the drive, was in the building. It had a rear façade that looked out on a huge courtyard stretching almost all the way to Zlatoustensky Alley. The yard was covered with retail shops where seasonal goods were traded: cucumbers and greens in the spring, berries in summer, fruits, mainly apples, in the fall, and year round, crabs delivered in enormous wooden baskets from the Oka River and the Volga, but mainly from the Don. This business was essentially for certain customers – food booths and street vendors. At the start of the nineties, this enormous trade ceased. Romeyko's property was bought by the wealthy Siberian N.D. Stakheyev. In place of the demolished tavern, he constructed a large building, which he later lost at cards.

Behind Shipovsky Fortress was an enormous empty lot, where, during the winter, frozen meat, fish, and poultry were sold from carts, and at other times of the year vegetables, livestock, and fruits. Street vendors, mostly from Tver,[11] bought their goods here and patrolled all of Moscow, right out to the edge of town, carrying

10. Secret Order (Тайный приказ). Formed around 1653 by Tsar Alexei Mikhailovich (father to Peter the Great), it was perhaps Russia's first secret service, subordinated only to the tsar.
11. Roughly 200 miles to the northeast of Moscow on the M10 highway.

on their heads 10-pound boxes, delivering them to their regular customers. From them you could buy a large sturgeon or, for five kopeks, a treat for your cat. House-keepers especially valued deliverymen in the spring and fall, when the streets were impassable from muck, or in the deep cold of winter. There were few good shops in Moscow and it was a long way to the markets.

Once, back in the days of serfdom, on Lubyanskaya Square, a carnival arrived in town with a small menagerie and an enormous elephant, their main attraction. The elephant went on a rampage, tore the logs attached to his chains right from the wall, and swept through the troupe, trumpeting triumphantly and striking terror into the crowds surrounding the square. The elephant, enraged by the crowd's screams, tried to escape its chains, but the logs that shackled him got stuck in debris. The elephant broke one of the logs and rushed the crowd, but by this time the police had brought in a squad of soldiers. With a few volleys, they killed the giant. The Polytechnical Museum now stands on this spot.[12]

The Polytechnical Museum soon after its construction.

12. In a dark twist of history, the headquarters of the All-Russia Insurance Company, built in 1898 atop the horrific prisons and torture chambers of the Secret Chancellery and Secret Expedition, was nationalized in 1919 by the Bolsheviks and transformed into the headquarters for the Cheka. Needless to say, the Soviet secret police (through its successive acronym-changes) exceeded its predecessor by many orders of magnitude in the orchestration of terror from this central Moscow location.

UNDER THE WATCHTOWER

FOR 150 YEARS THE BUILDING that now houses the Moscow City Council has stood on Tverskaya Street. Count Chernyshev, Moscow's Governor-General, built it in 1871 based on plans by the famous architect Kazakov.[1] From that time, uninterrupted until the 1917 revolution, it was the Governor-General's building. Its façade looks out onto Soviet Square, which earlier was called Skobelevskaya Square, and before that Tverskaya Square. Ceremonial receptions were held in this building as well as glittering balls, which, in the eighties, Prince V.A. Dolgorukov, who ruled the capital like a patriarch, especially enjoyed. All of Moscow came to these events, held in the building's luxurious halls. There were high society ladies sprinkled with diamonds, brilliant military uniforms, the boots of millionaires from near the Moscow River, and the long frock coat of Kashin the Money Lender. Fences and owners of the worst criminal slums attended these balls, disguised in the uniforms of charitable organizations. Admission was given to anyone who donated money. Many of these men even obtained ranks and decorations to hide their criminal deeds, making them appear untouchable to the police.

On the day of the ball, Vanka Kulakov (a pseudonym) rides up to the entrance of the Governor-General's palace in the white trousers and tailored "charitable" uniform jacket of a "reserve general." He walks into the entrance hall, drops a sable outer coat into the doorman's arms, and, after saluting the duty officer with the noble pride of a three-star general, goes up the stairs surrounded by a crowd of ladies and honored guests. The guard, a former cavalry officer, is required to treat him, after taking his elbow, as a guest of the Governor General and an officer of an

---

1. Matvei Fyodorovich Kazakov (1738-1812), one of Russia's most influential neoclassical architects. His works included the original Moscow University and several royal palaces.

The Moscow Governor-General's Building.

acclaimed charitable organization enjoying protection from the highest level. Well, after such an introduction, how could you fill out an arrest protocol for the owner of the criminal hideout Exile, a tavern near the Khitrov market?

It was here at these balls that necessary connections were made and various little deals were put together. The good-spirited "boss of the capital," as they called Dolgorukov at the time, sprinkled beautiful ladies with pleasantries, while a wall of government bureaucrats surrounded him, screening him from what he wasn't supposed to see.

The Prince, an old bachelor, lived like a tsar, and loved presiding over all kinds of ceremonies. On designated days he received visitors and petitioners, who, of course, were filtered by his office. Bureaucrats informed the Prince ahead of time of who had come, and why, and characterized in their own way the personalities of the petitioners. People known to the Prince had access to him in his office, where he listened to them alone, and later gave the bureaucrats orders on how to proceed. The Prince quickly forgot everything, and his commands were not always executed.

One could recount many anecdotes about Dolgorukov's time as Moscow's Prince, but I will limit myself to only one, related, essentially, to the Governor-General's building, since the goal of my notes is to reminisce primarily about Moscow's buildings and neighborhoods. At the end of the seventies, a gang known as Deuce of Hearts was working in Moscow. They were brilliant con artists who later were all convicted by a regional court and sentenced to exile, except the leader, Ataman[2]

---

2. In the Russian Empire, *ataman* was the official title of the Cossack military's top leaders. It was appropriated by criminal gangs as a title for their own leaders.

Shpeier, who disappeared to parts unknown for the rest of his life. Most interesting was the judge's final statement: when the verdict was read, a respectable old man with the look of a professor left the courtroom, got in a taxi, called over a city cop, gave him an envelope addressed to the presiding judge, and rode off. The envelope contained Shpeier's business card, and written on it in pencil, "Thank you for today's show. I am very satisfied. Shpeier."

Prince Vladimir Dolgorukov

This was the same Shpeier who, disguised as a wealthy landowner, had gotten into the ball to see Dolgorukov. At their first acquaintance, he charmed the old man with pleasantries, and then called on him on receiving day, in his office, and at once asked for permission to show the Governor-General's building to an acquaintance, an English lord visiting Moscow. The Prince assented, and on the next day Shpeier brought the lord, showed him, accompanied by an on-duty clerk, the entire building, the courtyard, and even the stables and the horses. The clerk was a silent presence since he understood no English.

About two days later, while Dolgorukov was still away, a baggage cart stopped near the building's entrance loaded with trunks and suitcases, and right behind it, in a carriage, the lord had arrived with his English secretary. He gave orders to carry his things directly to the prince's office. I don't know all of the details of this scandal, there are different versions. The only certainty is that the affair concluded with a secret dismissal from the Governor-General's chancellery.

The Englishman made a scene and insisted that he owned the building, that he had purchased it from the owner, Shpeier, for 100 thousand rubles with all its furnishings, and that he had arrived to live there. As proof, he presented a notarized title, proving that the money had been paid in full. This scam by Shpeier never went to court, it was kept quiet, and any settlement with the Englishman was not disclosed. Later, it was learned that a fake notary's office had been built for one day on Second Yamskaya Street – the same place where the sale of the building took place. Only then did the hunt for the Deuce of Hearts gang begin. Shpeier was simply never found. All of Moscow kept quiet about it, and only a short story writer, Pastukhov, knew the truth. Dolgorukov made him swear that he would never as much as hiccup about the affair.

Many years later, Pastukhov, in confidence, while we were fishing, told me about this oath, and then confirmed that the card player N.V. Popov, well-known in his day, and friendly with almost all of the members of the Deuce of Hearts gang, had revealed a series of details unknown to Pastukhov himself. I learned that Shpeier was the second ranking player in the scam, and that the top man was a certain disgraced count, who, not on account of this affair, but for a series of other scams, had previously been exiled to Siberia.

Dolgorukov did not take bribes. He did not need them. An old bachelor who had gone through an enormous estate and several inheritances, he was not a Bacchanalian, never played cards, but loved to give balls. He did not know how to count money and had never even held it in his hands. In official business, his right hand man was the head of the Secret Department in the Governor-General's Chancellery, P.M. Khotinsky, who was a permanent fixture in Moscow. Through him, an intelligent and moneyed individual could get anything done. The Prince's other hand was a man who was even closer to him, his irreplaceable butler, Grigory Ivanovich Veltishchev, a small figure with a big moustache. He kept all of the Prince's expenses and accounts.

"Grigory, do we have everything ready for the New Year's Ball?"

"Not yet, Your Excellency. The money still hasn't been sent. For now, we need to find perhaps 20 thousand rubles. I think we can put it on the engraver's account. He lives across the way, his relatives are in town, and he's preoccupied."

"I don't understand anything. Bring more fresh flowers!"

"Another thing, Lazar Solomonovich Polyakov is also requesting..."

"Well, yes, he's an excellent fellow. Tell Pavel Mikhailovich that I commanded..."

At the New Year's ball, with his spouse on his arm, Polyakov the banker, dressed in white pants and the uniform of a reserve general of a charitable organization, proudly addressed the room. A joke about him was making the rounds: "Well do you really want to work your tongue that hard? Lazar Solomonovich, Lazar Solomonovich! Address him – simply – as "Your Excellency!"

Today, in front of the windows of the Moscow City Council is Soviet Square. Behind the square, enlivened during the day by groups of strolling children, is the Institute of Marx, Engels, and Lenin. Across from its reception hall's window, at the other end of the square, where now there is a small park, was the Tverskaya Precinct's watchtower. It was an unnerving place. All day long, starting in early morning, there was rumbling on the cobbles. Carriage drivers passed with torturous screeches; wrecking crews thundered; workers' carts scraped; all to build this square, a most lively place connecting two areas of the city through Stoleshnikov Alley.

At the end of the last century in Moscow, no one had the slightest understanding of the rules of the road: neither the right lane nor the left was commonly accepted for travel: everyone did as they pleased, ran into one another, or flipped over. A ceaseless din rang out around the clock. This was for the ear. Eyes could not have been happy with the view from the parade windows at the Governor-General's palace: at times, drunks and rowdies were led off under guard, at times corpses taken from the streets were dragged off to a holding room at the precinct. Not always the best for the sense of smell, either.

Moscow Firefighters.

On moonlit nights, according to the guidelines of the City Council's calendar, even if the moon was not visible, street lights all over Moscow were not lit. In the darkness, a stinking, nocturnal convoy would drag along: 15 water tanks, each hitched to a pair of banged-up, balding nags. On the cart, between the horses and the tanks, a rope seat was hung on which napped the "jeweler," as the state sanitary inspector was called in Moscow. The convoy would bump along the street, splashing its contents onto the cobbles, rumbling down the whole block. After midnight, a similar convoy, barely moving, dragged up Tverskaya Street past the palace. The convoy stretched out. The last tanks, hitched to chronically limping horses, were falling behind. One inspector was asleep. The other was eating a large roll that he held between two fingers.

"Ding... Ding," a signal rings out from the watchtower, and the guard uses a pulley to raise two torches up a tall pole.

"How many?" the head of the fire watch hollers from below.

"Three, near the university," responds the firefighter from above, pointing to the fire.

Three meant that the fire had burned through to the exterior.

The fire convoy, like a rabid dog, tears out right behind the signalman, who holds aloft a torch, sowing sparks. The horses, beastly, sturdy giants from Voronezh, are white, dappled with red. The stones in the street shake, windowpanes tinkle, and building walls quake. A cart with firefighting tools streaks across the square along Tverskaya Street and Hunter's Row, tipping a water tank, and flies on. The tank is above the wheels. A "jeweler" struggles in a puddle of spilled water. He stands with one arm raised, worried mostly about his roll. These rolls are their special treat: they are convenient, since it's not easy to hold food with dirty hands. Firefighters rush up Tverskaya, and the tanks stretch out up the hill to the gate. Flying straight at them are nighttime revelers, finished canoodling with perfumed ladies at Yar, a restaurant in Petrovsky Park. With a yell, they slice through the square on *troikas*, pairs, and cabs rushing along Tverskaya Street or down along Stoleshnikov Alley to Petrovka. In this chaotic location lived Moscow's Governor-General!

Along Tverskaya Street on a hot summer day, a cab moves slowly with its cover up despite the fine weather: six legs stick out the windows, four in boots with spurs, and two in shoes with laces untied, attracting the attention of passersby. It is standard practice to transport political prisoners under guard to the Tverskoy precinct. The carriage turns into the square, into the courtyard of the Tverskoy precinct, and stops alongside a dirty two-story building, on whose ground floor is located a firehouse. The upper floor has a secret prison with cells for political and other important prisoners. The carriage stops. Two gendarmes and a "political" get out, hunched over. They take him off to one of the cells where small windows look straight out onto the Governor-General's building. From the outside, nothing is visible through them. On top of the window's iron grate stretches a piece of insulated wire, grown over with dust. They called this prison the "flea bag."

The main building, colonnaded and with a beautiful façade, had a brig in the center of its ground floor. The brig's door was between two columns and facing a parade ground, with a fence marked in prison colors, black and white stripes. Near the guardhouse, painted the same colors and hung with a bell, stood a guard who nervously glanced in all directions as if to deny entry to a walking or riding general, at whose appearance it was required to "summon the guard." When a General came into view on Tverskya Street, or Stoleshnikov Alley, or coming from the hotel Dresden,[3] or from the entrance to the Governor-General's building, the guard struck the bell twice and the entire detail, 20 men led by an officer and a drummer, came leaping down the steps, rushed into formation next to the guardhouse, and to the beat of a drum shifted their weapons to the "on guard" position.

How many dozens of times was it necessary for them to trot out to salute generals?! Weren't the ones who cut through the square to Tverskaya Street enough?! Many generals waved their hand from a distance as if to say, "no need to call out the guard," but there were generals who loved it, especially recently promoted officers,

---

3. Located on this same square, at a right angle to the Governor-General's building, the Dresden was one of the capital's most prestigious and well-appointed hotels. The writers Turgenev, Nekrasov, Ostrovsky and Chekhov all stayed there, often for long periods, as did the composer Schumann and the painter Surikov.

Heading out.

The Watchtower.

who would take pleasure in walking by the brig an extra time just to touch the brim of their hat for the assembled guards.

Thus it was every day from sunrise to sunset. There is a special military ceremony, performed by the guard on the parade ground mornings and evenings. For a quarter of an hour before the appointed time, a bugler would play *Summons to Dawn*. After the quarter of an hour, the guard assembled near the booth, and to the beat of a drum performed the ceremony. After the evening ceremony and before the morning session, the generals were denied their ceremonial salutes. The soldiers slept in the guardhouse, changing watch every hour to guard the arrestees from two posts: one under the windows of the "fleabag," and the other under the brig's windows, which looked out onto a yard where arrested officers were held in separate cells. Aside from the "fleabag" in the yard, next to the morgue, there was an isolation cell where they brought inebriates and rowdies.

The enormous firefighting yard was filled with piles of manure shoveled every day from the stables. From under the dung, especially after rains, dark stinking rivulets flowed across the entire yard, under the locked gates to the alley, and down the street to Petrovka. Next to the gates stood a short, stone, windowless building with a door looking out into the yard. This was the morgue. They called it a "chapel." It was rarely empty. Now and again, corpses from the street, or crime victims were delivered here. They were sent for autopsy in the anatomy lab, or by court order were released to relatives for burial. The homeless and those without identification were prayed over right there and sent in long open carts, in plain wooden coffins, to the cemetery.

The duty room was on the right side of the bottom floor, sharing a wall with the brig. On the other side was the police doctor's apartment. Above the precinct was the captain's apartment and above the guardhouse, brig, and doctor's apartment was a barracks for the firefighters, dirty and airless. The firefighters, on two cramped and stuffy floors, were jammed like sardines in a barrel, and slept side by side on cots. All around, on ropes, hung clothes soaked at fires. Half the company, on duty, never undressed and slept right there in their clothes and boots.

After spotting a fire from the tower, the watchman pulled the signal bell's cord. Firefighters often ran out in damp clothes. Past the Governor-General's house a firefighting convoy would rumble: on fours – the pikes, on a *troika* – a firefighting apparatus, and on pairs, a column of water tankers. A herald on horseback rushed ahead with a flaming torch, fiercely sounding a bronze trumpet. Day and night the square rumbled and hummed.

The square's secret cells held, in another time, interesting people. In 1877, the "Shlisselburger," Nikolai Alexandrovich Morozov, was detained here.[4] Writing with a matchstick on the smoke-covered wall, he finished his first poem, which started his literary career:

All around an impenetrable murk,
the ravine on the steppe is cloaked
and dark and hot in the remote desert.
No life, no light there.

Later, this couplet was joined by others. In its initial form, this poem was published in 1878 in the magazine *Forward*, and was included in the first edition of the book *Starlight Songs*, for which, in 1912, N.A. Morozov was convicted and imprisoned in Dvinskaya Fortress. In a revised form, this poem was later published with the title Prisoner of Shlisselburg.[5] In 1862, this same corner cell held Peter Grigorevich Zaichnevsky, known for the case of Young Russia, whose proclamation horrified the government at the time.[6] Even earlier, in 1854, not in the "fleabag," but in the brig's officer cells, A.V. Sukhovo-Kobylin, accused of killing Dimanche, a French woman, was held. He wrote his first play here, *Krechinsky's Wedding*, which has not left the stage since.[7]

---

4. Morozov, a revolutionary, spent 25 years in prison. After the October Revolution he showed little interest in politics and concentrated on a scientific career.

5. Prisoner of Shlisselburg: Until 1612 known as Oreshek, this ancient Russian fortress on the Neva River near Petersburg served military purposes for centuries. In the beginning of the eighteenth century it became a political prison. By the beginning of the nineteenth century it was thought that it had lost its military value; nonetheless, it played a role in the 500-day failed Nazi siege of Leningrad.

6. Peter Zaichnevsky (1842-1896) was an unrepentant revolutionary. Arrested in 1861 for forming a discussion circle, he refused to renounce his ideas and was given a sentence of over two years hard labor in Siberia. In prison, he wrote a manifesto, *Young Russia*, that called for a Jacobin-Republican revolution. Allowed to return to European Russia in 1869, he again in 1888 was arrested for setting up revolutionary circles in Oryol and Kursk. He spent the next seven years in Siberia and died while returning from exile.

7. Today generally considered innocent, Sukhovo-Kobylin fought the charges and won, allegedly thanks only to large bribes. Based on these experiences he wrote three satirical plays about crime and corruption in the court system: *Krechinsky's Wedding* (written while he was under arrest), *The Trial*, and *Tarelkin's Death*.

The revolution replaced the prison, the brig, the morgue, and the police precinct, and moved the Tverskoy firefighting team to another location that still allowed them to celebrate, in 1923, a century of continuous operation under the watchtower. One hundred years of humble, risk-filled work by several generations was plainly visible to all of Moscow. Even today, many Muscovites remember the impressive firefighting feats of these brave men, as well as the Khodynskoye catastrophe at the tsar's coronation in 1896, during floods, and finally, in 1920 at the artillery warehouse fire.

Count F.V. Rostopchin founded Moscow's fire department.[8] Earlier, it had been a random collection of firefighting tools tossed down around the city. Independent, amateur volunteers kept watch and were responsible for ringing the local church's alarm bell and responding to fires, some with pikes, some with buckets. The fire chief would eventually arrive.

In 1823, the Fire Department became a municipal institution. Fire precincts were established and numbered in each of the city's administrative divisions. Gradually, tools, equipment, and horses were supplied. It was not until 1908 that the first firefighting automobile appeared in the fire department depot on Prechistenka Street. This was a small car with a folding ladder affixed to its top for rescuing people on upper floors, but no higher than the third. The first to rush to a fire in this car were the fire chief, his deputy, a medic, and a few brave, axe-wielding firefighters. The car rushed right past firefighting convoys harnessed to excellent horses.

Until there were telephones, firefighters were constantly on watch in the tower. At that time, there were no skyscrapers, and all of Moscow was visible from the tower as if on the palm of your hand. In the tower, under signal balloons, a guard patrolled day and night. It was difficult for this "highly positioned" person in storms and bad weather, especially in the winter frost, and in summers it was even harder: the sun would bake him, and fires were more frequent than in the winter. "Be careful, don't even yawn." The guard would walk around the tower and "eye the area."

Brave, strong, a simple heart,
Untouched by the storm of daily life,
Busy with the biggest problem,
Keeping watch in the tower.

Out of nowhere a cloud of smoke, a flash of flame, the guard briskly pulls the alarm cord, and the signal bell rings on the post in the middle of the courtyard. At the time, electric alarms did not exist. Firefighters run out, dressing on the way in

---

8. Gilyarovsky relies on his readers' knowledge of history for a bit of sarcastic humor. Count Fyodor Vasilyevich Rostopchin (1763-1826) was Moscow's Governor-General during the French invasion and eventually confessed to ordering the fires that destroyed the city. He was disgraced in 1815.

damp clothes. A herald in a helmet, holding a trumpet, appears on a splendid stallion. The fire chief rides out, and raising his head shouts:

"Where? Which?"

"On Hunter's Row! Three-alarms," responds the guard from above.

He is already raising two balloons on the tower's mast, the signal for the Tverskoy precinct; other signals included: City center – one balloon, Pyatnitskaya precinct – four balloons, Myasnitsky – three balloons, and the rest, one precinct a balloon and a cross, another – two balloons and a cross, signals the part of the city that had the fire. And then, in a desperate voice, a guard would yell from above, "Five alarm on Ilyinka! Five!" Joining the signal balloon signifying the City center, a red flag is raised on the other side of the mast, an all-precinct alarm. The fire is not under control. Fire convoys rumble along the cobbled street on steel wheels, shaking the windows. Cabinets with dishware shimmy across the floor, and people run to the windows or out into the street to look at the watchtower.

At night, torches were raised instead of balloons: one balloon was the equivalent of one white torch, a cross equaled one red torch. If the red torch was to one side, in the same place as during the day, it meant a general alarm to all precincts. A Three Alarm meant three precincts were out, a Five meant all precincts were out. If, from above, they yelled, "First!" that meant an enclosed fire: smoke was visible but no flame. At that point, a mounted firefighter on a monstrous horse would speed to the location identified by the watchman to check the location of the fire and trumpet. People dash off in all directions, but a firefighter, with the brave heart of a hero, rushes ahead and trumpets.

A maid, pointing to the window, says with envy to a cook, "Look, it's your..." In those long ago times firefighters, same as Nikolayev soldiers, still were required to perform 25 years of mandatory service. They were almost all bachelors, but had "dependable" sweethearts – cooks. When they were not fighting fires, the men went to see their sweethearts, whom they visited in the kitchen. House owners looked at them not as a simpleton, but as a dependable man. So, when cooks were hired, it was formally agreed with the housekeeper that a "stallion" would be visiting. Housekeepers assented to the practice, and in merchant homes it was even encouraged. Why not encourage it when the folk saying in those times went: "Every merchant's wife has a husband – by law, an officer – for her feelings, and a coachman – for pleasure." Why shouldn't a cook have a stallion-firefighter?

Every firefighter was a hero. He spent his entire life at war, every moment at risk. At that time, particularly so: go ahead and climb up on a roof in winter, on bare ice with water streaming out of your tattered hose, when the thick cloth of your jacket and pants (even dry they won't burn) stiffens into casts, and enormous, awkward boots, with iron nails for strength, become cast iron. A frozen figure in icy boots clambers up the slippery steps of the staircase to a blazing rooftop and executes the most head-splitting acrobatics; sometimes curling-up on the edge of a cornice to avoid the flames, and sometimes waiting for the rescue ladder with half of his body pressing to the wall and the other half hanging over an abyss. Axe bearers, who wear their helmets backwards while tearing sheet metal off roofs, constantly risk falling into the fiery rubble through columns of black smoke. Right behind the fire chief, a hose-man crawls into the unknown, and risking suffocation or a kerosene explosion, searches for the fire and sprays. The job is difficult in winter, but unbearable in summer, when fires are frequent. I remember one unusually dry summer in the mid-eighties when there were 14 fires, two of which summoned all districts. One day, the Zarya and Rogozhskaya post offices were both burning at the same time, and all around them were smaller fires.

In the last century, one of Moscow's newspapers printed a poem:

Firefighter

Blazing, burning, sparking nigh,
Tongues of fire way too near.
Still, our colors, I hold up-high.
Firefighting perils I do not fear,

Except long long weeks without shut-eye,
Standing, watching, night and day.
Crack, a rotten wood-step now lies,
Bent and twisted, giving way.

Belching black smoke, whirling sparks nigh,
A cornice provides safe haven.
Day and night, I tirelessly fight,
Always working, fires happen.

Agile, bold, and brave, we try,
Dictates our brotherhood's law.
Even when wet coats freeze dry,
Icy hair stalks stand like straw.

Spray the water straight and true, you
Pound a hole right through the wall.
Pass up hoses, frozen stiff too.
Brave fire, sparks, and flames and all.

Way up lofty rooftop towers,
 I'm at home in a firefight
I don't fear red hot spark showers,
 I'm at war my whole life.

In our time, there are no fire horses, automobiles replaced them. But in the old days firefighters were proud of their horses. In the sixties, the Chief of Police, the veteran cavalry officer Ogaryov, a ballet enthusiast, a passionate fan of firefighting, and a horseman, organized a special supply of horses for the fire teams. These fire horses were Moscow's best. You couldn't help but stare at them. Ogaryov himself travelled twice a year to Voronezh and Tambov horse farms, selected animals, brought them to Moscow, and distributed them among the 17 precincts, personally looking after their care. He would arrive at a precinct without warning, walk to the stable, take a handkerchief from his pocket, and evaluate the horses' grooming.

Moscow was indebted to Ogaryov for the practice of dividing horses into color groups: each precinct had its own "jersey," and Muscovites could tell from a distance which team was rushing to a fire. The Tverskaya team – yellow piebalds, Rogozhskaya – black piebalds, Khamovnicheskaya – straw with black stripes and large, messy black manes, Sretenskaya – straw with white tails and manes, Pyatnitskaya – black with white stockings and a spot on their heads, Gorodskaya – white with no marks, Yakimanskaya – grey with spots, Taganskaya – white with black manes and tails, Arbatskaya – light red with black manes and tails, Sushevskaya – bright gold, Myasnitskaya – red, and Lefortovskaya – red with white spots.[9] They were all draft animals, beautiful and strong. How the firefighters loved their horses! What pride they took!

THE FIRE CHIEF BESPALOV, A former executive officer of the 1st Don Calvary, spent his whole life in the stables. He was there all day, and nights too. After his death, his son inherited the position of Tverskoy Fire Chief, still a young man, just as bold, born and raised in the stable. He died at his post: during a fire he panicked, fell three floors, and perished. Korolyev, Yushin, Simonov, Alekseyev, Koryto, and Vyshnevsky served for decades as fire chiefs, always at the scene, always, like every firefighter, a hair's breadth from death.

In the old days, in addition to battling flames, firefighters were dispatched everywhere, from dragging suffocating workers out of deep pits, or pulling people poisoned by gas out of cellars, to performing sanitation duties. This was all done without any safety measures. When the widely-regretted Khodynskoye Field

---

9. In British English, piebald refers to a horse with large white (unpigmented) areas and black patches. The common North American term is pinto. Specialists argue over all sorts of sub-classifications.

catastrophe occurred,[10] at dawn, while cries of those crushed still rang out, firefighters from all of Moscow's precincts arrived on carts, rescued survivors, and transported them to hospitals. Later, they removed mutilated corpses, furiously rushing carts with the deceased to the cemetery so they could return faster, and take more, and again more...

Firefighters had still one more responsibility. Not all of them, that is, but only the Sushchevsky Precinct, where they burned books banned by the censor.

"What's that smoke above Sushchevsky Precinct? There's no fire is there?"

"Don't worry, it's nothing, they're burning *Russian Thought*."

There, in the rear storage building, stood an enormous oven with an iron grate, similar to the cage (now located at the Museum of the Revolution) in which they transported Pugachyov to his execution. When needed, they dragged it out of the barn into the yard, poured kerosene over books and papers, and burned them in front of the bosses.

What didn't the bosses force the firefighters to do, treating their men like serfs?! They used them for personal chores, and even rented them out. In the seventies, Chief of Police Arapov allowed his friends, entrepreneurs from nightclub theaters, to use the firefighters as staff. In Petrovsky Park at this time, there were two theaters: the enormous wooden Petrovsky, a former state theater, where at times, with Arapov's permission, A. A. Rasskazov's troupe played on holidays, and the German Club's summer theater at the other end of the park, near the Kirgov cottages.

One Sunday, Rasskazov was presenting *Uncle Tom's Cabin*, and in the garden at the German Club there was a melodrama with devils. Near the Petrovsky Theater, firefighters equipped with pikes stood guard alongside the harnessed, bright gold stallions of the Sushchevsky Precinct. Next to the German Club were four piebald horses from the Tverskaya Precinct.

Eight o'clock. The audience gathers. Actors are costumed. Firefighters in the Petrovsky Theater sit in the rear courtyard wearing striped jackets, made-up as Negroes: their faces, necks and arms blackened like boots. The orchestra had begun the overture when a rider on horseback rushed up from the German Club and went straight to Koryto, the commanding officer of the Sushchevsky Precinct, who, as a member of the leadership, sat in helmet and uniform by the theater's entrance. The rider shoved a paper into his hands, the same that he had given to the commanding officer of the Tverskaya Precinct. Koryto jumped up and called to the firefighters: "Boys! A general alarm! A fire on Nikolsky! Get moving in whatever you have on! Step lively!"

---

10. A panic ensued during Moscow's May 1896 coronation celebration for Nicholas II, when rumors spread among half a million attendees at the Khodynskoye Field ("Khodynka") festivities that there would not be enough beer, pretzels and commemorative cups. Some 1389 people died.

The Tverskaya Precinct was soon rushing along the park's paths and further down Petrovsky Highway amid clouds of dust. A firefighter with a shining helmet rushed ahead, all in red, with red arms and a red tail, riding an enormous, frenzied, piebald stallion. Behind him were carts with red devils and pikes. The audience rushing out into the park trails still had not come to its senses when it saw a black devil with a flaming torch riding off on a golden stallion, and behind him long carts with black devils in bronze helmets. Black devils scared the people even more. Crashing noise, flame, smoke.

One after another, devil trains rumbled furiously up Tverskaya Street past the Governor-General's building and the Tverskaya Precinct, which displayed a red flag, a general alarm to all precincts. Trailing the firefighters, standing on the seat with one hand holding the driver's shoulder, Colonel Arapov feverishly sped up Tverskaya, but couldn't catch the firefighters. At Ilyinka Street, red and black devils had already climbed across the roof through grey smoke and tongues of flame.

The next day, all Moscow talked only about the devil train. After a few days, the Fire Chief, Colonel Potekhin, received an order concluding with the words, "and, in the strictest terms, I forbid using firefighters in theaters and other inappropriate locations. Colonel Arapov."

Today, firefighting in Moscow is much improved, its employees are educated, professional, and supplied with everything they need. Discipline is exemplary, with the same old courage and boldness, but conscious, armed with technical preparation, physical training, and science. The dispatch speed for a fire is now measured in seconds. In a clean barracks on the second floor, men on duty are dressed and ready. There is a large opening in the barracks floor, through which can be seen thick, smoothly-polished firepoles. When an alarm bell rings, the men rush to the firepoles, hug them, slide down to the lower floor, and in a few seconds all are at their assigned places in the truck: helmeted, they don their protective clothing on the move, flying down the street.

A bunch of street urchins yell, "Firemen in trucks! Firemen in trucks!"[11] I heard this word for the first time in my life at the end of the first year of the imperialist war, when refugees from Poland increased the number of our building's residents, especially in the side wings.[12] For me, an old Muscovite and, most importantly, a veteran firefighter, this word resonated. Moscow, when admiring its famed fire convoys – first on beautiful horses chosen for their colors, and later on silent trucks, bronze helmets gleaming – had always said with pride, "Firefighters!" Now, they were being called "firemen," a petty, squalid, insulting word. It calls to mind a small, regional city, the type where the whole town has three leaky fire barrels, one and a half pikes, a rusty pump with a hose leaking like a fountain, its wheels grinding up

---

11. The new word being used is a diminutive, пожарники, whereas previously firemen were пожарные.
12. Gilyarovsky refers here to World War I.

a step in an unwashed alley's sucking mud, with maybe 10 invalid firemen dragging behind.

In Moscow, long ago, the word "fireman" was in widespread use, but had an entirely different meaning: it signified a particular type of poor person that appeared in Moscow for the winter season, together with their masters, owners of rich estates. The landowners came to the city to live on income from their estates, and their serfs to get money, part of which was to pay *obrok*,[13] part of it went into their masters' pockets. This was done under the pretext of collecting money for places that had "burned down." Fire victims, real and fake, came to Moscow as families, on foot, and by other means. Women with children arrived in sleighs to solicit donations of money and clothing, presenting a certificate with an official seal confirming that the bearer of the document was collecting donations to help burned-out towns and villages. Some of them bought special-made sleighs with charred frames, proving that they had only just barely torn it from the fire. Muscovites made fun of the "burnt frames," but gave anyway. When a sleigh stopped at the gates of some home in a quiet alley, the kids would run in and report, "Mama, the fire victims are here."

Two places supplied "fire victims" for all of Moscow. These were the regions of Bogorodsky and Vereysky. The former were known as "geese" and the latter as "shuvaliki." Bogorodsky's geese were especially well known. If you ride through their town, you would see that the windows in the houses were shuttered with no trace of a fire – this meant that the "fire victims" had left as a family to ply their trade. Count Shuvalov,[14] who in the time of serfdom owned huge estates in the Vereysky region, was the first to allow peasants to go to Moscow to collect for "burned-out" homes, because they paid an increased *obrok*. This was very profitable to the landowner.

When such "fire victims" were arrested and asked:

"Where are you from?"

"We are *shuvaliki*," the arrestees would answer.

There were, of course, people who had suffered from real fires, with authentic certificates from their local government, and sometimes their local police, but in police records these were called "burn-out victims," and the fakers were called "fire victims." That's where the insulting word for old-time firefighters came from: "fire victims."

---

13. *Obrok*: payments in cash or kind from serfs to masters.
14. Count Peter Ivanovich Shuvalov (1711-1762); hence, *shuvaliki*.

BAKERS AND BARBERS

ON TVERSKAYA STREET, ACROSS FROM Leontevsky Alley, towers a building once owned by the baker Filippov. He rebuilt it at the end of the century out of a long, two-storied structure that belonged to his father, who had been popular in Moscow thanks to his pastries and rolls. Filippov the elder was so popular that the well-known poet Shumacher marked his passing with a four-line poem known by all of Moscow.

Yesterday, a bright burning flame flickered off,
Moscow's most popular, master roll maker.
Roach-Raisin eater, Prince Ivan Filippov,
Even the insects mourn this famous old baker.

Filippov's bakery was always full of customers. In its far corner, gathered around hot metal counters, a crowd always stood, munching on Filippov's famous *pirozhki* stuffed with meat, eggs, rice, mushrooms, *tvorog*, raisins, and jam.[1] His customers ranged from young people still in school to old government clerks in cloaks, from stylish ladies to poorly dressed working women. Made with good oil and fresh meat, the five-kopek *pirozhok* was so big that two of them made a filling breakfast. Ivan Filippov, the bakery's founder, still made them himself, and was praised far beyond Moscow for his bread and rolls, but most of all for his excellent black bread. The counters and shelves on the left side of the bakery, which had its own entrance, were always surrounded by crowds buying loaves of black bread. "Black bread is the worker's favorite food," said Ivan Filippov.

---

1. *Tvorog:* a sometimes-sweetened, thick dairy product that is similar to a cross between cottage cheese and cream cheese.

"Why is only your bread so good?" he was asked.

"Because bread likes to be crafted. Baking is baking, but all the strength is in the flour. I buy no prepared flour. I buy select grains harvested locally. I have my own people at the mills to avoid contaminants or dust. After all, there are different types of rye grain, you need to pick. I get more and more from Tambov, near Kozlov, and the best flour comes from the Rominskaya Mill."

Filippov always ended his speeches with his favorite folk saying, "It's very simple!" Black bread, pastry, and rolls were sent every day to Petersburg to the tsar's court. They tried to bake locally, but things did not work, and old man Filippov maintained that in Petersburg such rolls couldn't be made. Why? "It's very simple! Water from the Neva is no good."

There were no railroads then, but in the winter, convoys with his cookies, pastries, and rolls went as far as Siberia. They used a special method to freeze them when they were hot, fresh from the oven, transported them 1,000 *versts*,[2] and thawed them right before eating, also using a special method, in cold towels. Aromatic, hot rolls were brought to the table, somewhere in Barnaul or Irkutsk, fresh from the oven.

Moscow enjoyed pastries and rolls of every type. Then came an innovation that customers shopped for in droves, rolls with raisins.

"How did you think that up?"

"It's very simple!" said the old man.

This really did happen simply. In those days, Moscow's all-powerful dictator was Governor-General Zakrevsky, before whom all bowed and scraped. Every morning he was served tea with Filippov's hot rolls.

"Wha-aat kind of filth is this! Bring me Filippov the baker!" the Governor-General burst out one morning at tea.

Servants, not understanding the problem, dragged a frightened Filippov to their boss.

"Th-This is what?" he asked, and shoved toward Filippov a roll with a roasted cockroach sticking out.

"Th-this is what! Ah?"

"It's really very simple, Your Excellency," the old man said, turning the bun.

"Wha-at? Wha-at? Siiiimple?"

"It's a raisin, sir!"

Filippov ate the piece with the roach.

"You're lying, you bastard! How can a roll have raisins? Get out!"

Filippov ran to the bakery, grabbed a bag of raisins, and poured it into the roll dough, to the bakers' great horror. In an hour, Filippov treated Zakrevsky to a roll with raisins, and in a day there was no stopping the customers.

---

2. A *verst* is approximately 3,500 feet or 1.067 kilometers.

When recalling the roll with raisins, Filippov said, "It's very simple! If you grasp this principle, everything comes out fine. Take even the candy that they call a "Landrin." Who is Landrin? What is a *monpan*? We learned long ago from the French how to make them.[3] All the candy shops sold them in little paper wrappers. Then, Landrin comes along, with a foreign-sounding name, which is vital for sales, and everything turned out very simply."

At Grigory Efimovich Yeliseyev's candy shop, an assistant named Fedya worked with the *monpans*. Every morning he prepared a tray. He did this in a special way, each was half white, half red, and striped. Aside from him, no one else could do it, or the wrappers. After one name day, possibly hung over, he jumped up to bring his work to Yeliseyev. Fedya saw the tray covered with finished candies. He grabbed it, and ran out, not wanting to be late. He brought the tray in. Yeliseyev unwrapped it and shouted at him:

"What did you bring? What?"

Fedya realized that he had forgotten to wrap the candies, grabbed the tray, and ran out. Tired, he sat down on the curb near a womans' *gymnasium*. Students ran up; one, another...

"How much are the candies?"

He did not understand.

"Will you take two kopeks each? Give me five."

She gave him a 20 kopek coin.

Another student was behind her.

Fedya took the money and realized that he was earning a profit. Students continued to approach, bought out the tray, and said, "Come here tomorrow at noon for our break. What's your name?

"Fedya, family name Landrin."

He counted the money. It was more profitable than selling to Yeliseyev, and the cost of the wrappers diminished the profits. The next day he brought candy to the *gymnasium*.

"Landrin is here!"

He began to sell, at first on the sidewalks, then moved to various spots, and later even opened a factory. They started to call the candy a "Landrin" – the word seemed French. A Landrin is a Landrin. And he's just a simple guy from Novgorod whose family name came from the Landra River, near his ancestral village.

It's really very simple. He didn't miss his chance. Say it, "cock-roach."

Filippov was a principled man and did not take advantage of every situation where he could make money. He had his own sense of honor. Whereas some bakers did not

---

3. *Monpan* does not appear in French dictionaries. Many hand-made candies were given unique names and wrappers, so one theory suggests that the original word cited by Filippov, *monpans*, could have been an unconscious corruption of *ma pensée*, French for "my thought."

Lubyanskaya Square billboards. One for Landrin is located top center.

consider it a sin to profit through deception, Filippov acted otherwise. Bakers made
big money before holidays, when they sold older goods for full price to charities as
alms for prisoners. From ancient times it was a custom on major holidays – Christmas, a christening, Easter, *Maslennitsa*, and also on the "day of remembrance for the
departed," and on "parents' Saturdays" – to send alms to prisoners, or, as they said
back then, "the unfortunate."

In this regard, Moscow made an especially good showing. Bakeries received orders for 1,000, 2,000 and sometimes more rolls and pastries, delivered on holiday
eves and divided among the arrestees. Moreover, no one forgot about the soldiers
quartered in Moscow. Guard duty was considered a difficult and risky assignment,
but before major holidays soldiers volunteered. For them, some who had never seen
a piece of white bread, these were holidays. When the donations were plentiful, they
even brought bread back to the barracks and shared it with their mates.

The primary donors were merchants, who thought saving their souls required
donating food to "unfortunates," who would pray for the donors. They fervently
believed that prisoners' prayers reached their goal faster. This was demonstrated
even more clearly by Old Believers,[4] who, in their tradition, were required to render
assistance to all of the Antichrist's victims, such as "outcasts in prison." The main

---

4. Old Believers separated from Russian Orthodoxy in 1666 in protest over reforms made by Patriarch Nikon. Old Believers
continue the liturgical practices and other rituals of the pre-reform church.

destination for alms was the central prison, Butyrskaya Prison Fortress.[5] From all across Russia, arrestees arrived there after being sentenced to exile; from there, before the Moscow-Nizhgorodskaya Railroad was built, they left on foot for Siberia, on the Vladimirka Road. In those days, before 1870, the view of Vladimirka was terrifying.

> *…Over there, clouds of*
> *Dust. Ever closer… tromping steps,*
> *Rhythmic clinking of rusty chains,*
> *Creaking axles, bayonets.*
> *Closer. Louder. In the sun*
> *Gleaming guns. The escorts wait.*
> *Further, long lines of exiled men,*
> *Greyish clothes. A stranger's hate,*
> *Your foe, while unknown and friend,*
> *All glum, shuffle, all in queues,*
> *Exiles share a painful burden,*
> *Iron bars connect the crews…*

Vladimirka begins out past Rogozhskaya Sloboda, whose inhabitants for generations watched horrible columns of prisoners shuffle past their homes a few times per year. The children spotted them first, and then the grey-haired old men and women. They always saw the same scene and sounds: moaning, clanking chains. Of course, they gave what they could, trying to give the alms personally. Sometimes the donors themselves delivered the goods to the prisons, or a single poor person would wait with a pair of rolls or a home-baked roll on the Garden Ring Road, part of the route followed by the transport party. Breaking through the cordon and pushing into the hands of arrestees their hard-earned bread, they sometimes were rewarded by a soldier's fist. The movement of these groups was horrifying. Along the sidewalk on the entire Ring Road and all the streets on the route, an armed cordon of guards kept watch. The group would walk in

Butryskaya Prison

---

5. In one of those "stranger than fiction" post-Soviet moments, "Butyrka," has its own web site that provides a map for visitors (along with some nice historical background), while, Google Earth, perhaps in the same way that it puts clouds over certain military objects, has the prison confusingly labeled, thus impossible to find. Go to the prison web site to get the map: butyrka-sizo.ru

irons, crawling, clinking and clanking. At times 1,000 or more prisoners moved from the transport prison along the Garden Road, then up Taganka and Rogozhska-ya.[6] At the head of the group, exiles rattled in shackles, hand and foot, revealing now and again the shaved half of their heads. They had to beat back guards from alms thrown to them. Endless rows went by in grey coats with yellow diamonds on their backs, and letters in the same yellow cloth above the diamond: "S.K.," "which meant "exiled to hard labor." The people translated it in their own way: "strong labor."

A heavy wagon carrying unfortunates sentenced to corporal punishment squeezed through the cordon, kicking dust up onto rooftops and fences. Next came the exiles to hard labor, then, in shackles, walked exiles to Siberia, joined together in small groups by iron bars. Behind them were vagrants without papers, transfers, those arrested for living in Moscow without registration, and those being sent back to whence they came. Behind them was a baggage column, also carting the sick, and women with children, who elicited special sympathy. While the group moved, street traffic halted. They avoided Taganka, traipsed past the gate, and there, beyond the gate, on Vladimirka Road, thousands of people arrived with goods. They waited. These were Muscovites, peasants from the surrounding countryside, and specula-tors with empty bags from the edges of Moscow and from the bazaars.

Ahead of the group, a platoon of soldiers arrived, and cleared people from the Vladimirovka Road and a big field next to it on both sides. This was the end-point of the first stage. Here, the final roll call and inspection of the group were conduct-ed, and arrestees accepted and divided donations, which they immediately sold to profiteers, who filled their bags with rolls and bread, paying cash, which was highly prized by arrestees. Vodka was even more valued, and profiteers supplied the group.

Then came the heart-rending moment for leave-taking. There were tears, scenes. By that time, many of the arrestees were a bit drunk, and there was horseplay and fistfights. Finally, the escort managed to quiet the group, get it in formation, and set off on Vladimirovka on the long journey. For this, it sometimes was necessary to summon a reinforced squad of troops, and blacksmiths to add shackles to trouble-makers. Mainly, it was not the exiles – they were experienced arrestees – who drank too much and made trouble; it was the transfers, considered "hooligans."

When the Nizhegorodskaya Railroad was completed, Vladimirka ceased being a dry River Styx. Charons with bayonets no longer drove sinners across to hell. In place of a road worn into the earth to the sound of chains:[7]

---

6. Taganskaya Square on the Ring Road; Subsequent construction seems to have replaced some or all of Rogozhskaya Street with Nizhegorodskaya Street. The railroad mentioned here is still in place. The M7 highway now lies on much of the Vladimirka right of way.
7. The full version of this poem, titled "Vladimirka – The Great Road," approximately four times the number of lines in this selection, can be found in Russian in, Vladimir Gilyarovsky, *Sobranie Sochinenii*, Moscow: Byk, 2010.

'tween darkening in a light mist
fields, by horse and plow neatly tilled,
the road stretches, straight, a ribbon,
and greener than green, an emerald.
But all it passes, now so different.
Just roadside birch, planted doubles,
stood and heard and watched the wailing,
stood and saw the tears and troubles,
and stayed unchanged.
Yet how wondrous…
in splendid spring raiment, so bold,
all the flora 'round them! No rain
could help these shoots, so lush, take hold.
It was sweat and tears, that poured and drained,
formed a river in days of old.
Now free and wild, not hoed or trained.
All is in bloom, in numbers untold,
Flowers now, where bitter tears rolled,
when huge dust clouds billowed and fell,
a prison carriage thundered, yet strolled,
down Vladimirka, milestoned hell.

Vladimirka was closed and the site beyond the gate, where the first stage formed and donations were divided, was destroyed.

It was forbidden to accept donations near train stations; they could be brought to the transfer prison before the group's departure and handed over, not personally to the arrestees, but through the bosses. This was especially disturbing for Old Believers from Rogozhskaya Sloboda[8]: "How will the unfortunates know who gave it to them? Whom will they pray for?" Donors from Rogozhskaya outright refused to bring their donations to the transfer prison, and preferred the two closest jails: the Rogozhskaya and Lefortovo police precincts. On designated days, they buried the two precincts with donations. The rest of Moscow continued to send donations, as always, to all the prisons. Scam artists sniffed this out and took advantage. Before major holidays, to the great surprise of the bosses, Lefortovo and Rogozhskaya Precincts overflowed with arrestees, and all over Moscow there were fistfights and arguments. Moreover, for lack of registration papers, an unbelievable number of

8. Historically, a *sloboda* was a "free settlement" on the outskirts of a city or town, a place where immigrants would settle. The word derives from the word for "freedom," свобода. Initially settlers of *sloboda* were freed from certain taxes and levies for various reasons. Freedom from taxes was an incentive for colonization. By the middle of the eighteenth century, *slobodas* were abolished and they became ordinary villages, towns or suburbs or larger cities. The word has persisted in many town names.

vagrants said that they resided in Lefortovo or Rogozhskaya, where they were transported to establish their identities. In addition to the prisoners, they took delivery of entire cartloads of donations, which were distributed immediately to the arrestees, who traded them for vodka.

After the holidays, all of these criminals turned out to be petty thieves or runaways from Moscow landowners or tradesmen who, when their identities were established, were allowed to go home. They left after getting through the holiday with a full stomach at the expense of "do-gooders" who expected fervent prayers for their souls from "unfortunates" who had been snared by the "anti-Christ's slaves."

Bakeries and bread shops made money on donations. Only old man Filippov, who saved his enormous business by eating a cockroach and calling it a raisin, was in this case an honest man. First, on these orders he never sent second-day products to the arrestees, but always fresh rolls and pastries; second, he always kept a separate account for goods sold for a profit from donations, and this amount he personally brought to the prison and donated for improving the diet of sick arrestees. He did this all "very simply," not for the sake of either awards or medals, or for lapel badges from charitable organizations.

Many years later, Filippov's son, continuing his father's business, constructed on the site of his two-story building the large building that stands there now. He decorated it in a foreign manner, creating the once famous Filippov Coffee Shop, with mirrored windows, marble tables, and servants in tuxedos. Despite its appearance, this Paris-style establishment became known as "the louse exchange." Just like old times, a crowd always stood near its ovens with hot *pirozhki*. But there was a completely different clientele in the coffee shop: the people of "the louse exchange." There were regulars. Few knew them, but they knew everyone, although they customarily never gave the appearance that they knew one another.

Seated close together, they would toss words back and forth; one might approach an occupied table and ask permission, as if from strangers, to sit down. Their favorite spot was furthest from the window, as close as possible to the darkest corner. These people were the scam artists, second-hand goods dealers, suborners of theft, organizers of shady deals, and agents of the gambling houses who lured to their dens inexperienced risk seekers,

Filippov's Bakery.

cheaters from the clubs, and card players. These last, after sleepless nights spent in the slums and clubs, rose at midday, and went to Filippov's to drink tea and devise a plan for that night. Detectives who occasionally stopped by the coffee shop called them "gamers."

On days that the horses were running, about two hours before post time, the coffee shop overflowed with people of varied caliber holding race cards. Here, there were merchants, clerks, and wealthy young people, all habitual gamblers. They came to meet "gamers" and "beetles" – regulars at horse tracks – to get tips. "Beetles" connected them with card sharps, starting recruitment for the gambling houses. An hour before the start of the race, the coffee shop emptied. Everyone left for the track except random people who had wandered in. "Gamers" did not come back: after the track, their path led to clubs or gambling houses. "Gamers" later became a common word characterizing a layer of society, a guild, giving one, so to say, the right to live in Moscow. Now and then the police, when making arrests, had to be satisfied with answers to the question of occupation by one word: "gamer." Here is a word-for-word conversation at a precinct during the interrogation of a typical sharp:

"Your occupation?"

"Gamer."

"I don't understand. I'm asking how you acquire the means for existence?"

"I'm a gamer! I learned handicapping at the Imperial horse societies. I play with cards that are, as you know, printed by the Imperial Reform School... I play games sanctioned by the government."

Released, he went straight to Filippov's for his morning coffee. But not everyone could get into the coffee shop. Two signs brightened its walls, "No dogs" and "No enlisted men." I remember one case. One day, not long before the war with Japan, a student from the military medical school, whose epaulettes could be confused with an officer's, sat by a window with a street trader. Further on, near the other window, engrossed in a magazine, sat an older man. He was dressed in a waterproof cape buttoned at the collar. A young Hussar officer came in with a saber and a lady on his arm who wore a hat almost the size of an airplane. After throwing his coat to the doorman, the officer looked, but found no seats: all the tables were occupied. His eyes fell upon the young soldier, and he went right over and stood before him. The young soldier sprang up in front of a superior, and the officer's lady, feeling completely within her rights, took his place.

"Endeavor to leave this coffee shop, can't you see what is written?" the young officer commanded pompously, pointing to the sign. But he had not even lowered his finger when a voice rang out: "Junior Flag Officer, come over here, if you please!" People looked up. In place of the humble old man in a cape, sat the majestic General Dragomilov, a professor at the military academy. The Junior Flag Officer abandoned his lady and stood to attention in front of the General. "Endeavor to leave this coffee shop. You should have taken a place only with my permission. I allowed the enlisted man to sit. Go!" The embarrassed Junior Flag Officer took his saber and hurried out. The young soldier resumed his place by the enormous mirrored window.

About two years later, on 25 September 1905, to be exact, the coffee shop's mirrored window flew to shards. What happened here that day shocked Moscow. This was the workers' first revolutionary act, as well as the first armed shoot-out in the capital's center, and right near the Governor-General's residence at that. In the middle of September 1905, Moscow was nervous. There were strikes. Workers' demands became ever more resolute. On Saturday 24 September, a deputation of workers appeared at Filippov's and declared that, starting Sunday, they had decided to strike.

Around nine in the morning, as always on a holiday, workers stood in small groups near the factory gates. All was quiet. Then, near 11, completely by surprise, a squad of city police with sabers drawn entered the coffee shop through the parade staircase from Glinishchevsky Alley. They quickly ran through the accounting office to the service entrance and appeared in the courtyard. The workers cried: "Police!" A scuffle ensued. Bottles and bricks were thrown from the factory. The police were driven off.

Everything quieted down. Then a police chief appeared near the building, accompanied by gendarmes and Cossacks, who hurried to Glinishchevsky Alley and, completely by surprise, fired two volleys at the five-story building's upper floors, which looked out on the alley and were filled with private apartments. The factory building was located inside the courtyard, so there was not much cover for the police. Bricks were being thrown from the factory's windows, and the police even reported gunshots.

Glass flew. Plaster dust fell. Peaceful tenants scrambled in horror. The police chief led a squad of soldiers into the coffee shop and commandeered axes and sledge-hammers to break apart the barricades (there were none). Then, the chief assembled the soldiers in the courtyard, and ordered them to call to the workers and warn them that if they did not come out he would open fire. Police and soldiers were sent around to all the workshops, they took lunch-goers from cafeterias, and sleeping people out of bed. They drove workers, young boys, janitors, and street sweepers into the courtyard. The police doubted the older servants' assertion that everyone had left, and ordered a volley at the seventh floor of the factory. About 200 workers were led out, surrounded by a convoy of guards, and brought to Gnezdnikovsky Alley, where the secret police office and the courtyard gates of its chief were located.

Around four o'clock, three teenage workers accompanied by police appeared at Filippov's office, wounded, with bandaged heads. Later, more and more workers started to arrive and said that they had been taken to the secret police's chief's court-yard and beaten. Some of the wounded were sent in first aid carts to hospitals.

Frightened by this unprecedented event, Muscovites crowded onto the corner of Leontevsky Alley, cordoned off from Tverskoy Boulevard by a chain of police. On the corner, across from Filippov's bakery, on the porch steps leading to the locked door of Leon Embo's former barber shop, stood a group of curious onlookers who had no place to go. There was a crush of people in the alley and on Tverskoy Boulevard, including police and troops. On the top step, next to the door, unwillingly, a handsome, brown haired man with a large greying moustache attracted attention. This was Jules. Looking at him brought to mind lines from Nekrasov's poem, "Russian Women":[9]

> *Oh, people yawned, and people yakked,*
> *perhaps one hundredth knew the facts,*
> *of what he really did…*
> *Sly smirk inside, at rubes he squinted,*
> *Soothed nerves, and doubts dismissed.*
> *A Frenchman's guile, bred, storm-tested.*
> *A Moscow stylist.*

Jules, a Parisian who remembered the battle of the Paris Commune, worked as a senior barber for Leon Embo, the "court" hair stylist for V.A. Dolgorukov.[10] Leon Embo was a short Frenchman with a fluffy, well-groomed moustache, always extravagantly attired according to the latest Paris fashion. He stretched the Prince's wrinkles daily, brushed the wig on his completely bald head, and, pasting hair to hair, groomed the rejuvenated, old man's moustache. During appointments, he comforted the Prince and chattered ceaselessly about everything. He reported all the capital's gossip, and at the same time expedited various large business deals. This is how he became an influential man in Moscow. Through him, you could achieve much with the all-powerful master of the capital, who loved his barber. During Embo's trips abroad, either Orlov or Rozanov took his place. They also enjoyed the old Prince's goodwill and never missed an opportunity to help themselves. Their barbershop was across the street from the home of the Governor-General, underneath

---

9. *Russian Women* tells the true story of two princesses, Yekaterina Trubetskaya and Maria Volkonskaya, who followed their husbands, participants in the failed Decembrist revolt of 1825, to exile in Siberia. Nekrasov's most important poem was *Who's Happy in Russia?* (1873-1876) which tells the story of seven peasants who traveled about, asking various elements of the rural population if they were happy, to which the answer was never a simple "yes."

10. Paris Commune: a city council (French, *commune*) that ruled Paris from late March to late May 1871 and is widely considered an important episode in the history or workers' revolutions. It issued a number of extreme decrees and was brutally suppressed.

the Dresden hotel, and among the barbers were Frenchmen, then fashionable in Moscow.

Frenchmen owned half of the best barbershops in the capital. Their shops became trade schools. Since ancient times in Russia, Western culture has found a foothold only on the surface, such as through barbers and fashionable tailors. When a Frenchy from Bordeaux is working on some Lenka or Seryonka from Taganka Street, he prances around just so, and, again, just so, bends forward, waves discreetly, and commands:

"Ah'zeez'an! Zee-zahz!"[11]

While a dexterous assistant is fussing with hot scissors, Lenka and Seryonka, drenched in *eau de cologne* and hair cream, pick their noses. In one voice, they request:

"Style it so that when Daddy's not around I look like that French singer, but when he's here I can make it look Russian."

Here, hairstylists acquired the boss's habits, hairstyles, and learned a refined tone, to help attract brides-to-be from down by the Moscow River or flatter singers from Yar. Prize-winning first class hair salons had the look of the finest French establishments. Everything was done as it was abroad, using the best hair care products. Their perfume selection was from London and Paris. Stylish magazines, specially-delivered from Paris, decorated the waiting rooms. In the ladies' section were great hairstylists, creative professionals, *cognoscenti* of style, psychology, and conversation.

In the *boudoirs* of fashionable ladies – merchant's wives reclaiming their youth, and millionaire brides – hairstylists were entrusted with all of their secrets, which they knew how to keep. They were also friends with the house servant – she tossed him gossip about her bosses. They knew all their clients' latest news and private details, and how to calculate what one could say to whom, whom to associate with and how to behave. They were very observant, even sharp-witted. One of them, like all the rest, after beginning his career wrangling scissors, sent his diary to a publisher. It had truly unique pearls: he mispronounced *boudoir* as "blew dare." In the word "bride," he always wrote the first two letters separately. When these errors were pointed out to him, he would maintain: "It will be more realistic."

This diary, which had been thrown into the editors' wastebasket, described the first "electric" ball in Moscow. This occurred in the mid-eighties. The first electric light was installed in the merchant home of a young widow-millionaire, and the first ball with electric light was scheduled there. The luxurious palace, with a multitude of rooms and all sorts of cozy nooks, shone with multicolored light. Only the

---

11. "Assistant! Scissors!"

ballroom was lit by bright white light. All of Moscow's fast-livers gathered, from the gentry to the merchants.

The diary's author was at the ball, of course, with his friends, the servants. They put on their makeup in the hostess's "blew dare," preparing for the new light. It was marvelous, even though Moscow's fashion conscious young ladies, in diamonds, under the new light in the ballroom looked like badly painted puppets. They were accustomed to gaslight and lamps. The hostess, a beauty, was the only one with life-like face color. They danced until dinner, which the famous Marius from Hermitage prepared with his own hands. In the lily-white light of the dining room, paneled in oak, all faces seemed lifeless, and the guests tried to artificially induce rosy cheeks with copious rounds of expensive wines. Despite what had happened, the dinner was happy, loud, boozy... when, without warning, the lights went out. After about 10 minutes, everything lit up again. Scandal! Some guests had crawled underneath the table, some were crawling out from underneath. They were lit up in all types of poses. And the ladies! The author of the diary told me that he still cuts the hair of a woman who, even at the time of the ball, was not young. "Now an old woman, I give her a trim every Sunday, each time in her "blue door." She laughs and talks about that evening. "Yes, it really is time to forget," I said to her once in passing. "Oh, what are you saying?" she replied. "Discussing something enjoyable is always a pleasure!"

Stylish hair salons sparkled with Paris *chic* in the sixties, when, after the fall of serfdom, landowners burned right through the fees received for land and souls. Moscow went totally *chic*, and in crawled hairdressing-Frenchmen from Paris, and right behind them were Gallicized Russians. One barber, Elizar Baranov on Yamskaya Street, was slow to take down his sign: "Barber: Leeches, bloodletting, haircuts, shaves. Baranov." He also had grown a goat-like beard. Motioning to an assistant he might scream: "Assistant! Scissors! Move it devil!" All tastes were satisfied.

Long before this time, the first to shine was the Parisian hairdresser Givartovsky on Mokhovaya Street. After him came Glazov on Prechistenka, who quickly grew wealthy from gentry clients in his area of Moscow. He earned enough to buy dozens of buildings, which is why there is an alley named Glazovsky. Agapov on Gazetny Alley next to the Uspensky Church was considered the best of all. There was no one like him, either before or since. Near his home, in the glory days of the ballroom, you could not ride through the alley: carriages were parked in two rows, and two mounted gendarmes maintained order and managed the drivers. Agapov stuck in the throat of every Frenchman: he had nine of the best first class stylists visiting 15-20 homes every day. Agapov's clients were exclusively from the born gentry, princes, and counts.

In the sixties, they wore their hair on their shoulders with woven ponytails and braids, "presentations" based on hanging hair. The dawn of hair salons came in the eighties, when styles using artificial hair worn forward became popular. Later came "transformationals," with hair hanging down around the entire head, all done using the best, natural human hair. At that time, Russian hair was commonly used because it held color better. The most expensive hair was French. They spared no expense. To acquire hair, "cutters" travelled to villages and bought tresses for ribbons, kerchiefs, beads, rings, earrings, and other one-kopek junk.

Cuts came in various styles, the most fashionable: "Catherine II" and "Louis XV" and "XVI." After the assassination of Alexander II, starting in March of 1881, all the Moscow gentry wore mourning dress for a year, and hair stylists did no work for them. Only merchants' wives, not required to keep the mourning tradition, had expensive haircuts. The mourning period hurt expensive hair stylists. Starting in 1885, French masters started, for good, to look for Russian cutters. Teodor, for example, had become popular and had expanded his business greatly.

No matter how brilliant the French, the Russian hair stylists Agapov and Andreyev (the latter starting in 1880), were artists of their trade and took first place. Andreyev even received, in Paris, the title of *Professeur de Coiffure*, and a number of awards and honorary diplomas. In Gazetny Alley, the hair stylist Bazil was widely acclaimed. Everyone thought that he was French, but he was really the honored Muscovite, Vasily Ivanovich Yakovlev.

Fashionable hair stylists at the time made good money: there were no taxes. "They cut and shave and line their pockets," was the saying at the time about French hairstylists. Artemev put an end to that, opening a spacious men's salon on Strastny Boulevard and advertising, "Shave, 10 kopeks with *eau de cologne* and hair cream. Our stylists do not accept tips." The public crowded into his shop, where he also opened a "leech department."

Before Artemev, there was only one "leech depot" in Moscow, which for more than half a century had been located in a small grey building snug up against the wall of the Strastnoy Monastery.[12] In the window, to distract fidgety children, they had large aquariums with leeches of various sizes. The leeches were sourced somewhere in the south, and were purchased at the "depot" by hospitals, medical assistants, and struggling barbers from the far edges of the city, where even hair cutters still applied leeches. The "depot" belonged to Molodtsov, from whose family came the well-known tenor of the sixties and seventies, P.A. Molodtsov, the best Torop of his time.[13] He successfully debuted at the Bolshoi Theater in this role, but left after quarreling with the managers. He went to the provinces, where he enjoyed enormous success.

"Oh why, why did you, Petrushka, leave the imperial theaters, and Moscow too, for Tambov?" friends asked him.

---

12. This amazing cultural treasure, built in 1654, was destroyed in 1937 as part of a modernization program on Tverskaya Street.

13. *Torop* – a young townsman, a tenor role in *Askold's Grave*, an opera by Alexei Verstovsky (1799-1862).

"Because of the leeches," he answered.

There were great women's' hairstylists, but no less great were the masters working on men. Lipuntsov on Greater Nikitskaya Street was widely praised for his great skill at trimming mustaches, and after him Lyagin, and later, still very young, and even better, Nikolai Andreyevich. Lyagin always visited older actors, and Dalmatov called him, "my friend."

In 1879, in Penza, a boy, little Mitya, was a student of Shishkov, the theatrical hair stylist. He was a favorite of the Penza entrepreneur V.P. Dalmatov, who allowed him alone to touch his hair and taught him makeup art. Once, V.P Dalmatov, at a benefit he produced, put on *Notes of a Madman*, and ordered Mitya to make a bald wig. He got a wet bull's bladder and started to put it on Dalmatov's fluffy hair. The actors ran to the dressing room when they heard Dalmatov scream. "You are a great actor Vasily Panteleymonovich, but allow me to be an *artiste* in my own trade," the brazen youngster justified himself, sticking his chin out. "Just try it on!" V.P. Dalmatov finally consented, and after a few minutes the bull's bladder was fitted, in places with lubrication. The actor's eyes shone with pleasure: a completely bald skull in combination with his black eyes and expressive makeup made a powerful impression.

THE 80-YEAR-OLD MAN IS STILL working in Moscow, clean-shaven and spry. "I saw everything, grief and glory, but I always worked, and I work even now, as my strength permits," he tells his clients.

I'm a serf from the Kaluga region. When they freed us in 1861, I left for Moscow – there was nothing to eat at home. I ended up with a watchman from my hometown, who sent me to the barber Artemov on Sretenka in the Malyushin building. I slept on the floor, dressed in a small, torn winter coat, with a log for a pillow. It was cold in the shop in winter. People from Sukharevka came in for haircuts. At five, the housekeeper woke me to fetch water, or sent me to Sukharevka, or Trubnaya Square. In winter, I went with a water barrel on a sleigh and in summer with buckets on a yoke. Shoes – the boss's old, worn-out boots. You put out the samovar, cleaned the boss's boots. From the well in the courtyard next door, you got water to clean the dishes.

They woke the masters at seven for tea. Both were cranky. The boss had tuberculosis. They beat you with whatever was at hand, and for everything. Nothing was ever right. They tied me to a bench and beat me bloody. Once, after a beating, I was in the hospital for two months with an infected spine. Once, in the winter, they threw me out onto the street and locked the door. I was in the hospital for three months with a fever.

At 10, we sat down to work. We made wigs, weaving single hairs: our daily quota was three parts of 30 rows. Once I fell asleep while working, tore through a section, and was cruelly beaten. We had one stylist who would hit me when he was drunk. Once, carrying a note from the master, I led him down the block to the precinct house, where, because of the note, he was beaten. At that time, the laws were such that beatings were done by the police according to the master's instructions. I did nine years with this master, received certification as a junior stylist, and then went under contract to Agapov for six years to become a stylist. I then opened my own shop, and later in Paris received the title of *Professeur*.

This was Ivan Andreyevich Andreyev. In 1888 and 1900, he took part in French hairstyling competitions in Paris. He received a number of awards and honorary diplomas, and the title of Distinguished Professor of the Art of Hairstyling. In 1910, he published a book with hundreds of illustrations immortalizing hairstyles of the previous 50 years.

TWO CIRCLES

THE MOSCOW ART CIRCLE WAS founded in the 1860s and disbanded at the start of the 1880s. The Circle took up the entire mezzanine floor of the former Golitsyn Palace, purchased in the 1840s by the merchant Bronnikov. The Circle occupied a series of halls and guest rooms, which formed a circle with enormous windows on one side on Greater Dmitrovka Street and on the other on Theater Square. The windows of the white Golitsyn hall faced Hunter's Row. The other side of the building, at that time, was occupied by a stage and hall that had been rebuilt after a fire at the start of the century.

A circle of luxurious, interconnected halls and guest rooms included a few small, windowless service rooms that formed an island, and were well hidden behind walls that curved around a circular foyer. Its white walls, soft furniture and cozy nooks made it a favorite spot for people to relax. During Lent, this foyer overflowed with a colorful group of provincial actors who arrived to contract with entrepreneurs for the upcoming season. Leading "personalities," badly dressed minor actors, and male and female singers strolled along the shining parquet floor, dressed in handmade costumes. They blended into a crowd that included the leading lights from Moscow and provincial stages, as well as producers in gold chains and gloves, there to assemble troupes for touring cities and towns. Here, too, there were shaggy, tragic actors with thunderous voices. There were comedians whose work seemed effortless, but who actually were highly rehearsed. There were "Arkashas" in women's Russian national costume and boots without soles, "lost" on journeys "from Vologda to Kerch and from Kerch to Vologda."[1] Everyone was loud, hummed, kissed, hugged, argued and talked. The grand did not behave self-importantly, the humble did not bow and

---

1. Comic effect: the distance between the cities is nearly 800 miles.

Theater Square, taken from near the front of the Bolshoi Theater.

scrape. Everyone was relaxed: Hamlet and a gravedigger, Piccolo and Achilles, Mary Stewart and the carpenter Poshlepkin. They reminisced about seasons past in Pinsk, Minsk, Khvalinsk, and Irkutsk. All actors and actresses had complimentary entrance into the Circle, which for them was a necessity: it was the only place to meet with producers.

From year to year, actors stayed at favorite hotels and clean, furnished apartments, whose owners were forewarned by post, although in those days it was unnecessary. There were enough vacant rooms everywhere, especially in large hotels such as Chelyshy. Today the Hotel Metropole, with its multi-colored frescoes and *Princess Grace* by Vrubel who, along with the architect Shektel, assisted S.I. Mamontov, towers over the former location of Chelyshy. At the end of the last century, Chelyshev's huge old building, with a multitude of rooms at all prices, overflowed during Lent with actors who had travelled to Moscow. At Chelyshy, celebrities stayed in mezzanine rooms with enormous windows, rugs, and heavy drapes, and the brotherhood of average actors stayed on the upper stories – with a separate entrance from the square – where the narrow, curved, and dark corridors were saturated with the smells of kerosene and cooking. In the second half of Lent many moved out of the mezzanine to the upper floors – it was cheaper.

A second actors' haven was found in the rooms of the Golyashkin, later Faltsvein's, on the corner of Tverskoy Boulevard and Gazetny Alley. Not far from them, along Gazetny and Dolgorukovsky Alleys, were the Prince, Caucasus, and others. Today, the buildings are no longer there; the central telegraph building stands in their place. A no less popular place was Chernyshy, in the Osufelsky Building, across from

Brusovsky Alley. There were other actors' rooms on Greater Dmitrovka, Petrovka Street, and relatively dirty ones near the Kitai City baths, on Neglinnaya Street. The least expensive were the furnished rooms of Semyonovka on Sretensky Boulevard, where in 1896 the huge headquarters for the All-Russia Insurance Society was built. Guests with dogs were allowed to stay in Semyonovka. During Lent, old comediennes from the provinces were its primary customers.

Starting with Chelyshy and ending with Semyonovka, for the first week of Lent the actors lived happily. They had vodka, beer, samovars, and loud conversations. Conversations led to poetry reading. Rooms gradually freed up: someone left for the provinces after finding a position, someone moved in with a friend in another room. Kerosene stoves started to be used: some who earlier ate in the restaurant started to cook at home, especially men with families.

A kerosene stove more than once decided a person's fate. Let's say Actress A had a kerosene stove. Actor B, from the next room, had made it this far eating lunch in the restaurant. An accidental conversation in the corridor, permission to grill some meat on the stove... One, two... "I also intend to buy a kerosene stove! After all, they're very convenient," said Actor B. "Why should you do that, when I have one?!" Actress A responded. A few days went by. "Well why pay for a room for nothing? Bring the stove to my room. I have more space." Thus a happy marriage was made on "economic" grounds.

Actors could also meet with producers in theater restaurants: Shcherbaky on the corner of Kuznetsky Alley and Petrovka Street, Livorno in Kuznetsky Alley, and Velde behind the Bolshoi Theater. But for actresses, except for Kruzhka, there was no place else. Here they met with producers, with friends from the stage, and they

The Hotel Metropole, early in the twentieth century.

could get theater passes and meet playwrights: Ostrovsky, Chayev, Potekhin, Yurev, and also many other writers whom they knew only by their works. Here they could meet famous actors from the capital: Samarin, Shumsky, Sadovsky, Lensky, Muzil, Gorbunov, Kireyev. Provincial actors also had a chance to debut in plays performed at the Circle's stage – the only place where performances were permitted during Lent. The Circle cleverly got around the law forbidding performances during Lent, on the eve of holidays, and on Saturdays. The Circle performed, even in Lent and on Saturdays, with the permission of Governor-General Prince Dolgorukov, who considered Moscow a separate principality, not subordinate to Petersburg. Although works were presented in their entirety, the Prince's one requirement was that play bills had to be titled: "Scenes from the Tragedy *Macbeth*," "Scenes from the Comedy *Inspector General*," or "Scenes from the Operetta *Elena Prekrasnaya*."

The Literary-Artistic Circle was founded in a German restaurant, Alpine Rose, on Sofia Street, and it happened almost by accident. Entrance to the restaurant was restricted: it had a carpeted stairway decorated with tropical plants and doormen at its foot. Coming here from their offices to breakfast were, primarily, Moscow's Germans. After performances, actors from the Bolshoi and Maly Theaters also gathered here, with seating in two modest rooms. In one of them, the singer A.I. Bartsal presided, and in the other the writer-critic and theater historian V.A. Mikhailovsky. Both were former regulars at the defunct Artistic Circle.

Once, in memory of an institution that had united the artistic world, V.A. Mikhailovsky proposed to organize occasional dinners, and to begin the gatherings on the following Saturday in the Moscow Grand Hotel. This was agreed unanimously, and about 20 artists attended with their families. They spent the time happily, sang and danced to a piano. They re-enlisted immediately for the next week, and so many showed up that they needed to rent a larger hall in the same hotel. All of the brightest lights of the Bolshoi and Maly Theaters came for this evening: writers and musicians. M.N. Yermolova[2] recited poems, Khokhlov[3] sang, Brandukov[4] the cellist played. The program proved to be rich.

In the spring of 1898, in the restaurant Hermitage, a founding meeting was held and a charter was drafted. In October 1899, on the hundredth anniversary of the birth of Pushkin,[5] the Literary-Artistic Circle opened in the home of Countess Ignatyeva on Vozhdivenskaya Street. There were luxurious reception halls, soft furniture, separate tables, nooks with trellises, fireplaces, rugs, and a concert piano. It was comfortable and private. It was the intimacy of the circle that was most attractive.

---

2. Maria Nikolayevna Yermolova (1853-1928), one of the most talented actresses in the history of the Maly Theater. Stanislavsky said she was the greatest actor he had ever seen.
3. Pavel Akinfiyevich Khokhlov (1854-1919), a leading soloist at the Bolshoi and Mariinsky Theaters.
4. Anatoly Andreyevich Brandukov (1858-1930).
5. Not his exact birthday, of course. Pushkin was born May 26, 1799, old style, June 6 new style.

Members came here to relax, gather strength and inspiration, exchange impressions, and experience joyous moments listening to and evaluating artists in an atmosphere unlike any club. Inspired by the general mood, or electrified by the previous act, one of those present would get up and perform a monologue or recite poetry standing at their table, or if they were a singer or musician step up to the piano. Shalyapin, still young, shy and humble, would move carefully through the tables, his velvety young bass booming:[6]

People perish for metal...

Next, Sobinov's soft tenor charmed the room. After him others stood, the greats of that time. The notes of well-known musicians of the day were heard... Skryabin, Igumnov, Koreshchenko.[7] A wit once said Koroshchenko's music could kill puppies all the way out in the courtyard, but this did not diminish popular enthusiasm for the young composer-pianist.

The number of visitors grew and grew and so did the club's membership. This was the one club at the time where ladies could be members. From the flood of guests and new members, it became crowded in Ignatyev's halls. They found a new location, on Myasnitskaya Street, a beautiful building on the corner of Furkasovsky Alley. Back in the time of Peter I it belonged to the Kasimovsky Tsarevich, then Dolgorukov, who died in Berezov in exile in 1734, then Chertokov, who donated his famous library to the city, and in the end the merchant's wife Obidina bought it from Prince Gagarin, Chertokov's heir, and rented it to the Circle.

It was an expensive location, but the number of members grew not by the day but by the hour. To become an acting member, a new term appeared: "community helper," that guaranteed selection. Candidate members were selected simply, without any kind of ranking. But membership dues turned out to be weak. They had to organize a card game, with a forbidden "iron cage."[8] Members of a hunting club, also members here, organized a high stakes game at the club, and the table stakes of players sitting "behind bars" filled the till. Stakes were: at 2 o'clock in the morning, 30 kopeks; 2:30, 90 kopeks, that is twice the current base plus the original base; 3:00, 2 rubles 10 kopeks; 3:30, 4 rubles 50 kopeks; 4:00, 9 rubles 30 kopeks; 5:00, 18 rubles 60 kopeks; then, the Circle closed at 6:00 in the morning and the players were supposed to leave the premises. Not infrequently, however, the game continued through the following day and again into the evening.

---

6. Fyodor Shalyapin (1873-1938) was a Russian opera singer with a deep bass voice who enjoyed a successful international career. His name is sometimes transliterated in the French style as Chaliapin.

7. Alexander Nikolayevich Skryabin (1872-1915), a towering figure in music as both a pianist and composer. Konstantin Nikolayevich Igumnov (1873-1948), a pianist. Arseny Nikoleyevich Koreshchenko (1870-1921) was a composer and teacher. The puppies quote has been attributed to the composer Taneyev.

8. A style of play, not a literal cage.

Two Circles

The game was forbidden, the police watched the club, and there were cases when they wrote up a violation and the "cage" was closed. Next, concerns were raised about a permit; articles were even published in defense of the club's games. Heart-wrenching letters were submitted to the Governor-General arguing that gambling was not harmful, and practically charity. They would start again and play until a new warrant was received.

The place became crowded and the card rooms were too visible to the public. At this time, Yeliseyev, in his "Temple of Bacchus,"[9] set aside a luxurious space with paneled ceilings and rented it to the Circle. There were comfortable, private rooms for "cages," and rooms for executive meetings, concerts, and festivities.

The Circle became the most fashionable bourgeois club, and the Yeliseyev's location again grew crowded. A plan was developed to set aside an old, noble mansion on Greater Dmitrovka Street. In the mezzanine, there was an enormous, two-chandeliered hall for meetings, anniversaries, shows, ceremonial lunches, dinners and after hours "discussions." When this room cleared, around two in the morning, the chairs in front of the stage were removed, 10 round tables were rolled in for "cages," and gambling began in full, with players coming in from various dining rooms, guest rooms, and special card rooms. When the hall was occupied, games were played in other locations. There were all kinds of rooms on the three floors! A spare dining room, the marbled dining room, the mirror room, the upper Great Hall, the upper Reception Hall, the lower Reception Room, the Reading Room, the Library (one must note its excellence), and a Portrait Room, which was the director's. The Billiard Room was downstairs, and when that became crowded, in the left wing of the building a special room was set aside, the "gambling" room. The summer dining space was in a small, shaded garden with an enormous chestnut tree and climbing flowers, among which were positioned small conversation nooks, lit with electricity for dinners with cheerful groups. The entire length of the garden was fronted by a wide balcony, built against the club building. Here, each group had its favorite table.

There was hardly any other place in the capital that had such a quiet and cozy corner in the fresh air, surrounded by greenery and sweet smelling flowers, although the quiet and the aroma were sometimes disturbed by a disorderly neighbor, the yard and building of the Tverskoy police precinct. It was separated from the garden by a low wall. Higher than the ancient walnut stood the fire department's watchtower, from which the guard occasionally issued fire alarms, followed by the noise and rumbling of a departing fire team. More frequently, the uncensored cursing of drunks locked up to sleep it off could be heard, and likewise the wails and wild cries of stubborn rowdies fighting off a police assault on their freedom. Sometimes the sweet aroma of flowers was overpowered by the stench of manure piles outside the

---

9. Yeliseyev's is described in great detail in the chapter beginning on page 251.

stable, the stink of firefighters' garments drying, and the smell from the morgue's open window. It almost always had corpses tagged "lawful claimant(s) unknown," meaning crime victims taken from the streets pending autopsy. The morgue stood next to the garden wall, but it had become so familiar that no one noticed it.

Once, at the Club's table of "community helpers," one of them, selecting a wine from the list, stopped at the portrait of Pushkin on the label, and with concern remarked:

"What does Pushkin have to do with this? This is a profanation!"

"Pushkin is always relevant. He was a great prophet. Remember his words relating to me and to you and to many sitting here. Wasn't it about us that he said,

"On the rubble of monarchy
"They'll write our names."

A giddy neighbor added:

"Well they'll either write our names there or they won't, but *here's* where Pushkin was right:

"Let at grave's edge,
"The young play at life."

He pointed with one hand at the morgue, and with his other, at the next table, filled with card-players arguing loudly. That conversation took place in August 1917, when such clubs truly were at "grave's edge." A month later, the Circle was closed forever.

When a new gambling location became available, a large two-chandeliered hall, dinners were moved there from the upper dining rooms when the hall had an evening free from meetings. Groups had dinner there, and each had a favorite table. A long table with 20 place settings enjoyed special significance. This was called the "beer table," since beer was the favorite beverage of those who sat there. A small keg of beer was placed on it. In addition, the table had two other nicknames: "professor" and "director." The table's regulars showed up after 10 o'clock and were seated for appetizers. Some had dinner, others played small stakes games of *vint* or *preferance*,[10] still others lost money in "the cage," and with their losses covered the Circle's enormous expenses.

In 1905, when the pre-revolutionary temperature began to rise quickly, this was reflected in the Circle more brightly than anywhere else. From the stage, things began to be said out loud when there previously had been silence. Freedom of action

10. *Vint* is a card game similar to bridge or whist. *Preferance* is from Eastern Europe and is played with a 32-card deck.

and speech were tolerated. Everything was allowed, or better said, nothing was forbidden. With the onset of reaction, the stage went silent, and the decay process strengthened. The government feared only revolutionaries, and encouraged all the rest: card sharps' dens, private clubs, debauchery, masquerades, and degenerate literature were allowed, as long as they didn't smell of politics. Gambling was allowed in all the old clubs. The English Club stood alone, unchanged, but even there gambling flourished as before. The authorities had not managed to stick their noses in there, nor had women.

In the Merchants' Club two-foot sturgeons were devoured at lunch. On Hunter's Row, scantily-clad women "ate delicacies," and played at masquerade, but were not allowed in the card rooms. At the German Club, they held masquerades, and girls would lure drunks from the boulevards, and cardsharps would take their money in gambling rooms. There was an enormous two-chandeliered room. There were 10 round tables, 10-12 players sat at each, ringed with bystanders making side bets against the house. The most varied audience. At the "ruble" tables a noisy crowd, arguments.

"You took a ruble from here!"

"No, you grabbed it from me."

"Officer?!"

"Who stole it? Did he steal it from you or did you take it?"

At the "gold" tables, where the ante was no less than five rubles, the audience was more "serious" and played for "paper." And with a "bullet" of 25 rubles, they were quite "reliable."

Ladies wearing diamonds tossed down packets of credits from golden purses. Quickly, their cavaliers would sit down, participating in the game from the side, or impatiently waiting until their ladies lost in order to take them away to a club. Many such ladies in diamonds appeared at the Circle after the war with Japan. They were called "quartermasters' ladies." They threw away thousands of rubles. One blonde woman, whom everyone called "Countess," played at all the clubs. She was covered with diamonds. But she quickly lost everything: first the diamonds disappeared, and then she disappeared. Later, she could be seen on the sidewalk outside the Sandunovskiye Baths.

The highest stakes table, where the lowest ante was 100 rubles, was located in a room either on an upper or a lower floor. Sometimes, in this room, aside from the 100-ruble "cage," they played baccarat. Once, the baccarat game reached a level never seen. There were bets of five and ten thousand. Two eastern men, handsome but with brutish faces, ran this game wearing suits of expensive fabric, and gold belts with long knives sparkling with large precious stones. Whoever signed the guest register for them on the first day was unknown, but the amount they gambled made such an impression that in the following days these two brother-princes, the

Shakhovs, were gladly admitted to the club. They kept a responsible bank in bacca-rat, guaranteeing their bets with packs of new, large denomination credits for tens of thousands. "Servants" never left their sides.

Players waited impatiently every day for the princes: without them, the games just did not seem to flow well. When they appeared, the table perked-up. For a week they came every day, lost more than 100 thousand rubles, as they say, without blinking an eye, but one evening simply did not appear (it had already been decided to promote them to candidate members of the Circle).

"Where are the Asiatics?" worried the players.

"There's no reason to wait. You won't see them again," declared a newspaper reporter entering the room.

Silent surprise.

"My editorial office was informed today that they have been arrested. I con-firmed the news: neither of these men is a prince, they are leaders of a gang of bandits, and the money that they gambled they brought from their last robbery in Turkestan. They attacked the postal service. Their gang ambushed a convoy, then stabbed and killed postal workers, and stole valuables along with three hundred thousand rubles in uncirculated notes that were being transported to the treasury. They both have been sent to Tashkent, where a scaffold is waiting."

PEOPLE MAY ASK: "WHY DOES the author portray only the clubs' bad side, and not describe its useful social and educational activities?" The author answers confidently, "Because my readers are more interested in the side of life that was secret even during the clubs' existence, hiding the true financial support for clubs' 'community activities.'" As for the latter, so much was written at the time, and probably remains to be written in the memoirs of contemporaries, who only knew the official story: celebrities attending executive meetings, symphonic evenings, literary discussions, writers' anniversaries, and famous artists. It is in that context that the Literary-Ar-tistic Circle, which had approximately 700 members and 54,875 attendees per year, will be remembered. Issues of the *News of the Circle*, printed on thick paper with Pushkin's portrait as a watermark, can still be found. Unfortunately, they have not a word about the club's daily activities, or the gambling on which it lived and feasted.

THE HUNTING CLUB

THE MALKIYEL BUILDING, HOME OF the Brenko Theater, was bequeathed to the millionaire Spiridonov, who rented it to the Hunting Club. This club was born in a small ground floor tavern on Neglinnaya Street next to Trubnaya Square, where on Sundays there was a dog market and bird bazaar.[1] The tavern was even called Dog Market. Hunters and bird lovers filled Trubnaya Square, where there were baskets with chickens, doves, turkeys and geese. There were cages hung on stands, holding all kinds of songbirds. They also sold bird food, fish keeping supplies, aquariums with cheap goldfish, and all sorts of pigeons. The dog market took up a large corner. Every type of dog was there. Borzois, and mixed breeds, hunting dogs of all breeds, mutts, and bulldogs. Sellers offered all types of long-haired and short-haired dogs. Dog thieves worked here.

Near each breed of dog stood its enthusiasts. Long-haired bologneses stood next to hairless miniature borzois shaking like aspen leaves. Dandies moved through, the ladies' yes-men, looking for a gift for their lady's heart. Near the setters, hunting dogs rested and paced. There were solid members of high society, armed hunters. Near the courtyard were the mutts and all kinds of trash on leashes, without collars, sold to caretakers and homeowners from the outskirts of town looking for a chained guard dog.

Vagrants, who had only just caught a dog, dragged it to the market. There were certain specialists among them. Every Sunday for almost two years, a hooligan brought here on a leash a beautiful, gentle red dog named Caesar that belonged to a cleaning woman who lived in a tavern's coach yard in Stoleshnikov Alley. And he sold it. Every Monday the dog, after chewing through his leash, would be back

---

1. Chekhov has an amusing short story, "The Bird Market," which can be found in many anthologies.

The Bird Market on Trubnaya Square, early 1900s.

at home, waiting for the following Sunday. It happened that sometimes the dog was recognized by merchants, but there was no way to prove it, and Caesar would be sold again.

Borzoi enthusiasts were a colorful group, surrounding a collection of the dogs: hunters, trackers, and purebred runners. These men arrived in carriages and carts with money belts, with hunting horns across their shoulders, or with flasks and brightly decorated hats. A glance was enough to know that any one of them could easily stop a horse at full gallop, leap from their saddle onto a she-wolf slowed by a speeding dog, fall upon her, grab her by the ears with iron hands and press her to the ground, holding on until she gave up.

They examined the dogs and argued. Not just anyone could understand their conversation: the words would gush and the most familiar might be "scissors." [2] This, as it turns out, refers to a *borzoi's* muzzle.

There were old men here with grey mustaches and expensive, unbuttoned coats, under which were money belts. These were *borzoi* fans, Muscovites, who in winter lived in the capital and in summer at their estates; every year there were fewer of them. Dog hunting, which had flourished in the days of serfdom, was disappearing. Here and there they still kept kennels, but on a smaller scale. In the winter, hunters came to Moscow from everywhere for a dog exhibition on Trubnaya Square. This

---

2. Here Gilyarovsky lists a series of incomprehensible and out of context words: "*Pazonki*, black meat, *vyzhlets*, *pereyarok*, scissors, profit, *otryzh*."

Yar restaurant, 1911-12.

was a meeting place for provincials and Muscovites. From the market, they went to the Hermitage to have lunch and end their day, or, more exactly, to end their night at Yar with Gypsy choirs, "following the example of their fathers."

Armed hunter-Muscovites went as a group to the tavern Dog Market, known to all hunters by this name, although officially it was named after its owner. Dog Market was not on the square itself but close to it on Neglinnaya Street, and was considered to be on Trubnaya Square. It was a grimy basement tavern. It had what was known as the clean room, where the hunters sat on Sundays. On this day, each group had its own table waiting.

Hound and gun hunters, after examining the smallest details and analyzing down to the bones every dog worthy of attention, went off to their dive, and with a glass of vodka opened the conversation "about hunting." Now and then dog traders came into the tavern with puppies strapped to their bellies and in baskets (they did not let dealers with large dogs into the tavern) and the exams would start, and sometimes dogs were bought.

Crooked Alexander Ignatyev, a dealer and a known dog thief, offered a yellow spotted pointer for sale and said convincingly, "From Lansky himself on Tverskoy Boulevard. Born yesterday," he held up the puppy by its nape. "His mother won a gold medal last year at the dog show in the Manezh. Dyanka. Remember?" Alexander Mikhailovich Lomovsky, a general, the most respected figure among Moscow's hunters, gently fingered the pup's tail and formed a hook with his hand.

"That's nothing, Alexander Mikhailych. This kind of tail is desirable." Lomosky again silently made a hook with his hand.

"Please, Alexander Mikhailych, this cannot be. His mother is Dyanka, a cousin, after all..."

"In a word, 'first cousin to the sire, which is bad for breeding,' and which you, undoubtedly, know," remarked the editor of the magazine *Nature and Hunting*, L.P. Sabaneyev. He spoke directly to the seller, "Leave, Sasha, don't get greedy. Did you find someone to scam! If you ever bring a dog to Alexander Mikhailych, remember the tail. Understand? Remember the tail."

The seller left in confusion, remarking:

"Well, you can kill me, but I saw no crook in that tail. If Alexander Mikhailych hadn't pointed out the tiniest kink... Well, how could that even be? After all, he is Dyanka's pup... cousin to the dog..."

A third person in the conversation, Nikolai Mikhailovich Levchayev, a city engineer, well known for the reconstruction of the pipes holding the underground Neglinka River, at the same time, paying attention to no one, was making an appetizer for his vodka, a "Levchayevsky" salad, which would make your eyes crawl out onto your forehead.[3]

The most respected Moscow hunters walked up to the table, sat down, and conversations sometimes continued until late at night. On one of these Sundays, it was agreed that a Hunter's Club should be founded. The next day, Sabeyev wrote its by-laws, which were signed by influential people, headed by Lomovsky. In a month, it was approved by the minister.

Almost all Moscow hunters, people of means, became club members, and this quickly became fashionable. It began with hunting conversations, organizing exhibitions, family evenings, hunters' lunches, and dinners on Saturdays with the ladies, and Gypsy, Russian, and girl choirs. But there was immediately a problem. Expenses exceeded revenues. One billiards session and one small stakes commercial card game among old-time hunters were not enough. Table stakes, not kopeks, had become the primary revenue for clubs in general. They needed gambling. M.L. Lazarev came to help, a former secretary of the Equestrian Society, and a passionate gambler. Lazarev took to the task feverishly, and in the first month the club's till began to swell. But primarily, it was the club on Tverskoy, in the building where Brenko's Pushkin Theater had been located, that began to make money. That's how the gambling started.

On the third floor of this building, under the ballroom and dining room, there was a secret room that people in the know could reach by a stairway and some confusing, narrow corridors. Only members of the club were allowed: big time gamblers. Games started after midnight, and table stakes by five o'clock in the morning rose as high as 38,000 rubles. They started gambling so late to keep the stakes high:

---

3. The expression "eyes crawl out on your forehead" (глаза на лоб лезли) suggests that something will be tasty.

there were fewer conversations, fewer curiosity seekers, and fewer small stakes players. For big time gamblers, competing for thousands, the table stakes were nothing.

In one of these rooms there were four round tables, each seating 12 players. There were "ruble" and "gold" tables, and next door, in exactly the same type of room, stood a long table covered with green felt for baccarat, and two round 100-ruble tables for "cage" play, where an ante of less than 100 rubles was not accepted. Here, games started no earlier than two o'clock, and there were cases when gamblers sat in the room until the club opened the next day, at seven in the evening, and after resting there on the soft furniture, continued the game.

The club reached its full flower in Count Sheremetev's building on Vozdvizhenka Street, where the city services office had long been located. When the department moved to a new address on Voskresenskaya Square, the old building was taken by the Russian Hunting Club, which luxuriously renovated the grand chambers that had been desecrated by the bureaucrats. Masquerades with prizes were organized, as were luncheons, exhibits, and Saturday dinners, attended by dissolute bourgeois of both genders. No other club could compete with the Russian Hunting Club's new venue; later, the Circle became a worthy competitor in gambling entertainment.

The hour was late. Fifteen or so people sat or stood at a long table. A baccarat game was on. A brilliant dark haired fellow kept bank in the middle of the table, methodically moving chips along the green cloth, with a slightly trembling, jewelry-free hand, holding a reference card. Now and then, he picked up a cigarette and smoked without hurrying, trying to appear cold-blooded. From time to time, he blinked his eyes somewhat oddly, but his handsome face was motionless, like a mask. In front of him lay packs of hundreds, about five thousand, and across from him sat an assistant with piles of smaller credits and also a pile of hundreds.

His assistant, prematurely bald, a colorless young man in a tuxedo, was the unlucky product of a once-wealthy merchant family. He worked as a croupier, paying when his bank lost, and accepting winnings. After every payout he ever so accurately organized the credits, sorting them. Around them sat the usual punters, baccarat fans. A man with dark red hair, who had the best looking beard in Moscow, was at the table, which distracted the ladies. This cost these Moscow merchants' wives a great deal of money. In front of him was a mound of scattered hundreds, partially covered by a gold snuff box with a large, sparkling French N on its lid. He had paid an outrageous sum for this snuff box in Paris, as it had belonged to Napoleon. Because of the snuff box, the owner said, Napoleon had lost at Waterloo. Busy sniffing tobacco, he had misheard an adjutant's report, confused the direction of attack, and moved the cavalry to a crossroads and the infantry through a ravine. "A sniff of tobacco overturned the world!" he said, concluding his tale and showing the item to his friends, removing from an envelope the official certificate of authenticity attesting that the box had belonged to Napoleon.

Without counting, he threw stacks of money, and with a steady hand took his winnings, ignoring losses. It was obvious that all of this either bored him, or his thoughts were far away. Perhaps he was recalling an unbearded, young gambler, or maybe he had a premonition of hungry times on the Riviera and in Monaco. Next to him, just as calmly losing and winning pots, smiling as widely as his round, rosy face would allow, twirling his moustache, there sat a wealthy, well-built young man from the Volga. He played like a child, distracted by whatever toy caught his attention at that moment, rejoiced and thought of nothing. Near him was a tall young man with a longish face and the mannerisms of an Englishman. He resembled a statue. Not a muscle in his face moved; on it was written the cold concentration of a man occupied with serious business. Only his hands betrayed him. To an experienced eye, it was clear that he was living out a tragedy: losing frightened him. He kept his face in check, but his hands trembled uncontrollably.

At the other end of the table sat a well-groomed, balding "gentleman" handicapper with an English hat, who was a devotee of "cards, women, and horses," and preoccupied with the game. He paid attention, following every card, watching every throw of the dice, even when they were sitting in the box next to the banker. Sometimes he placed small and, unpredictably, large bets, and almost always won.

The banker winked and nervously shuffled the deck, glancing down. He waited for a diamond. He wouldn't start any sooner. This millionaire was a most honorable player, but he was nervous and superstitious. His nervousness was betrayed by blinking, and sometimes his cheek twitched, revealing the highest anxiety.

The club moved to the Sheremetev building after a late-night fire in the Spiridonov building. Everyone had left the lower floors. Only upstairs, in the secret room, was there still a "cage" of 10 high stakes players at the table. Noise from the lower floors did not reach here, so the fire horn was not audible through the thick walls. The club's service people left at the first sign of smoke. A young hooligan-card player ran in for the players on the upper floor, and behind him a lackey, both with frightened faces, cracked open the door, shouted "Fire!" and got out.

But no one paid them any attention. The late night players, as always, were sharply focused. A high stakes game was underway. Alexander Stepanovich Sarkizov (Sarkushka), a wealthy man and able player, cold-blooded and practical, was cleaning up. He won hand after hand, and raked in gold and credits.

"It smells like smoke. Can you smell it?" The tobacco seller raised his head, sniffed the air, and started to worry, blinking his eyes out of habit.

"That's the smell of your cigarettes," joked Sarkushka and revealed a nine.

There was a rumble of steps out in the corridor. The doorman, a firefighter, and smoke rushed into the room.

"Be gone you devils! You'll burn!"

"There's a way out through the corridor!" shouted the doorman.

A few jumped up in fear, understanding nothing; others kept playing. Sarkushka again showed a nine, and while raking in money shouted to the firefighter, "Vut you care! Let zee bahnk sveep up."

"Well, it's your coats that are on fire," the doorman said, justifying himself.

Sarkushka jammed the money in his various pockets, grabbed a box of cards from the table, and with a laugh flung it into the corner. Through thick smoke, the players barely made it to the entrance stairs, which still had not caught fire, and descended to the coat room, where anxious doormen awaited them. Participants of that awful night loved to retell the details of the fire. Sarkushka took offense, "Vutt mess! Zay got in zee vay of my vinning!"

In the grand hall of the former Sheremetev Palace on Vozdvizhenka Street, where the club had masquerades, large luncheons, family dinners, and Saturday events with girl choirs, they built a stage. Amateurs, who later founded the Moscow Artistic Theater, used it. They put on shows, while the audience, purely from the clubs, preferred masquerades and comedy dinners, and more than anything enjoyed *Sunken Bell*,[4] and especially its long haired forest spirit, who leaped across rocks and hollows, and a frightening water spirit in the form of an enormous frog, that splashed in the river shouting, "Bre-ke-ke-keks!"

General Mikhail Skobelev

The troupe was experienced and excellent. It commanded a select repertoire. Much was written about all of this – just as masquerades were written about in newspapers and the names of valuable prizes for best costumes were publicized on play bills. One of the most coveted prizes was received by a handsome Moscow man who appeared in a black cloak, top hat, and with a bright blue beard combed, *á la* Skobelev,[5] in two directions. This costume stood out among the others, including merchants' costumes adorned with precious stones. "Prince Raoul Bluebeard" won a gold cigar worth 500 rubles.

---

4. A 1900 opera by Alexei Davidov, based on an 1896 German play of the same name by Gerhart Hauptmann.
5. Mikhail Dmitriyevich Skobelev (see footnote, page 121), was a highly-decorated general. A monument and square were dedicated to him directly opposite the Moscow Governor General's residence, but razed for political reasons after the October Revolution. Skobelev wore his beard split down the middle and combed to the sides (see photo, above).

LIONS AT THE GATES

THE ENGLISH CLUB REMINDS US of that long-gone day when "fire rumbled and roared across all Moscow," when only one magnificent palace remained whole along all of flaming Tverskaya Street, along which the remains of Napoleon's army advanced. The palace stood in an ancient park on a few acres between Tverskaya Street and the Kozim Swamp. The park ended at three deep ponds, now recalled only by a street sign: "Three Pond Alley."

This palace was built in the mid-1700s by the poet M.M. Kheraskov,[1] and in the time of Catherine the Great secret meetings were held here of the first Moscow Mason's circle: including, Kheraskov, Cherkassky, Turgenev, N.V. Karamzin, Engalychev, Kutuzov, and "brother Kinovion," N.I. Novikov's Rosicrucian name.[2] In 1792, he was arrested, along with other members of the circle and many Masons.

After 1812, Kheraskov's palace became the property of Count Razumovsky, who added two side wings, making his beautiful building on Tverskaya Street more grandiose. The palace itself, with its luxurious halls, where between marble columns the flower of the most enlightened people in Russia at the time gathered, remained completely untouchable. In 1831, the English Club settled there.

Leo Tolstoy in *War and Peace* describes a luncheon where the English Club in 1806 honored Prince Bagration,[3] recently arrived in Moscow: "...The majority of

---

1. Mikhail Matveyevich Kheraskov (1733-1807) was the son of a Romanian noble who settled in Ukraine. Mikhail was educated abroad and appointed a dean at Moscow University at age 30. Catherine the Great considered him Russia's most important living poet.
2. Rosicrucians: a philosophical society based on alleged ancient secrets, said to have been founded in late medieval Germany by C. Rosenkreuz.
3. Peter Ivanovich Bagration (1765-1812) general and hero of the Russian army, he entered the service in 1782 as a sergeant and had a brilliant career. He commanded the left wing at the Battle of Borodino and died shortly thereafter of his wounds.

Mikhail Kheraskov

One of the lions atop the English Club Gates, 1904.

those present were older, proud people with wide, self-confident faces, thick fingers, and decisive gestures and voices." It was these same people who moved to the Tverskaya Street location, where, at the gates, to this day, slumber their contemporaries – stone lions with enormous gaping jaws, like nobles petrified while alive and digesting a Lucullan lunch. The lions look disinterestedly at the noisy, happy crowds of tourists streaming to the Museum of the Revolution, and at automobiles flying by on Tverskaya. They appear just as disinterested now as they did 100 years ago looking at Razumovsky's crest, at the gold-spangled greatcoats of club members on parade days, or at the *troikas* hauling drunken revelers, rushing through the night to the Gypsies. On winter nights, with the same disinterest, the lions watched coachmen out on the broad club courtyard warming themselves around fires. Dressed in velvet hats and baggy shirts sewn from expensive fabric, the drivers did not know where they would end up the next day: home or with a new boss? Would the new boss send him somewhere to an estate in "a village, the backwoods, or to Saratov," and sprinkle his family around other regions?

The fate of the serfs was decided every night in the club's Hell Room, a gambling spot where the lives of people and estates hung on one card, on one point, and sometimes even on an adroit dealer, able with a quick hand "to right the mistakes of fortune," as Fyodor Tolstoy put it. An "American," a regular of the Hell Room, he was the one about whom Griboyedov wrote:

Night time robber, duelist,
Exiled to Kamchatka, returned an Aleut,
Firm handshake, unclean hands…

Apparently the "American" was proud of these lines, and Konstantin Aksakov himself, at a lunch at the club, said they were written about him. Zagoretsky also gave him much credit. Pushkin immortalized the "American" as, in the words of Zaretsky, "Ataman of the card gang."[4] The Famusovs, Skalozubovs, Zagoretskys, Repitilovs, Turgoukhovskys, and Chatskys all frequented this club.

Neither Pushkin nor Griboyedov wrote exact portraits: creating artistic images, they used them as raw material taken from daily life. Griboyedov, in *Woe from Wit*,[5] sketched the Moscow of his day in a few types, some of them taken from everyday life at the English Club. Herzen, in *My Past and Thoughts*, wrote that the English Club was less English than anything else. "In it, dog-men shout against emancipation and blow-hards make noises about the natural and inalienable rights of the gentry."

This, the most beautiful building on Tverskaya Street, was hidden by a row of poorly built shops. The October Revolution swept away the shops, built in the first decades of the twentieth century, and before our eyes appeared a rose-colored palace with white, well-formed, decorated columns. On the façade, the white crest of the republic replaced Count Razumovsky's gilded crest. Today, in this palace – now the Museum of the Revolution – anyone can follow the triumphant progress of the Russian Revolution from the Decembrists to Lenin. As an introduction to the history of the Great Revolution, as a bloody glint of dawn, shining from the depths of the tyrannical past, for those entering the Museum. On the floor of the vestibule, is the figure of Stepa Razin and his followers, the work of the sculptor Konenkov. Just above them is a canvas by the artist Gorelov:

From the Don, these river boats swooped through,
churned this watery, wide blue-azure.
Stepan, his courageous and daring crew,
leads from the front, to hunt for treasure…

This recalls Razin's first appearance "along the Mother Volga." And here is his end: an enormous painting by Pchyolin, *The Execution of Stepa Razin*. Imagine Moscow, Red Square full of people, *boyars*, *streltsy*, and an executioner. Razin stands on

---

4. Fyodor "the American" Tolstoy was indeed a colorful character. For more on his life, see *Russian Life*, September/October 2006 (republished in *The Best of Russian Life*, vol .2).
5. *Woe from Wit*, Griboyedov's classic comedy in verse that satirized high society in Moscow after Napoleon.

a scaffold with a raised hand threatening, bids farewell to the life of a rebel, and weighs the future:

At the fall of a man's severed head,
you think, that's the end, his demise —
But from every last drop of scarlet,
a new, courageous, fighter will rise.

You go up a flight of stairs to reach the Museum's door. The first room, the former reception room, is now called, "Pugachyov's Time," a term first used in print by Pushkin.[6] Just outside this room, the Museum starts with a large bust of the first Russian revolutionary, Radishchev.[7]

In the former English Club's reception room stands a narrow iron cage. They brought Yemelyan [Pugachyov] in it from the Urals to Moscow, and set it out in the squares and in the bazaars of cities along the way "to show and to frighten" the large crowds who had so recently followed him. They brought him in this cage to Bolotnaya Square for execution on 16 January 1775. One hundred years ago, in the very place where the cage now stands, stood the embarrassed author of *History of the Pugachyov Rebellion*, the great Pushkin. And in the place where now hang the chains that held Pugachyov to the prison walls, there hung a "blackboard," on which they wrote the names of those excluded from the club for failure to pay bills, and to whom entrance was denied until the debts were paid. This space was known as the "judgment room."

Imagination suggests an image: a sad and gloomy poet walked out of the club and went home. He headed to the Nikitsky Gate at the Goncharov Building, then went along Tverskaya Street to Strastnaya Square. He stopped on Tverskaya in the place where a monument to him now stands, assumed the very same pose, took off his hat, revealing a sunburned head. Summer. Moscow was empty. Everyone was at their country estates. His apartment was empty and he had nowhere to go. He saw the club, the "lions at the gates," and behind them the brightly lit halls, soft rugs, wine, cards, and his beloved "conversation." His friends were there, Chaadayev, Nashchokin, Rayevsky. But the poet walked alone down the street. After returning to his empty room, he wrote on 27 August 1833 to his wife, "Tell Vyazemsky that his mother-in-law died. Prince Peter Dolgorukov, who received an inheritance, has not yet wasted it at the English Club, which local society greatly regrets. I have not been to the Club, and I'm practically excluded because I forgot to renew my membership.

---

6. *Pugachyovshchina*. Russians add the suffix "*shchina*" to words to create an event or period of time with negative connotations. This Pugachyov construction is said to have been used first by Pushkin.
7. Alexander Nikolayevich Radishchev (1749 -1802) was a social critic and writer jailed and exiled to Siberia in the days of Catherine the Great for his depiction of Russian reality in *Journey from St. Petersburg to Moscow* (1790).

I will have to pay a fine of 300 rubles, but I'd be prepared to sell the entire English Club for 200 rubles." As a direct consequence, Pugachyov helped him pay the club, and he again began to visit. In a letter to P.V. Nashchokin, A.S. Pushkin wrote on 20 January 1835, "Pugachyov has become a kind and honest payer of the debt... Emelka Pugachyov provides support. He brought me enough money to pay, but ever since I've been living in debt, almost two years, I have no savings left and everything goes for payments."

Both Pushkin and Griboyedov knew the club well. In *Woe from Wit*, Griboyedov's Moscow and many of its types are drawn from members of the English Club. Once I found in excerpts from the club's *Old Folks Magazine* a description of a situation "accurately remembered": "In 1815, a candidate member, Mr. Chatsky, proposed by member Sibilev, was not elected. They voted a second time and he was not elected." They voted at the English Club. What an event! All of noble Moscow talked about it. Who was Chatsky and why wasn't he elected? But I would like to propose that there is something in common with *Woe from Wit*. At the least, the surname Chatsky is really Chatsky. But there's a question: why would they not elect to the club a candidate, that is, a person who had been coming to the club for nearly a year before the ballot? More to the point, what views, inappropriate for that time, did Chatsky express in his "rambling"?

The speeches and monologues that we read in *Woe from Wit*, of course, with freedom of speech in "ramblings," could be expressed by a candidate member, but when voting it was impossible for them to elect him as a member, and they probably were happy to get rid of such a "Jacobin." Famusov of course would not elect Chatsky. These, of course, are my own suppositions, but I am convinced that the Chatsky not elected in 1815 and Griboyedov's Chatsky from the play, finished in 1822, undoubtedly have something in common. In any case, the writer for some reason remembered the rare surname.

"Public meeting of the probe into the chambers of the English Club." Perhaps Pushkin is alluding here to political discussions in the English Club. P.Y. Chaadayev was too close to him, spending every evening in the English Club.[8] He was a bachelor, not a card player, who attracted in "ramblings" a circle of people who boldly discussed the politics of the day and club affairs. Some of Chaadayev's actions Pushkin later ascribed to Onegin in the description of his bachelor life and living situation.

Reading through this immortal comedy today, I am again convinced that the Chatsky on the ballot is *the* Chatsky. Would Famusov, "the Anglish Club's true son, to the day he's done," have tolerated Chatsky? And almost all of them were Famusovs. How could they manipulate the vote? Start rumors that he's crazy! Repetilov's entire monologue is a portrait of the English Club's members.

---

8. Peter Yakovlevich Chaadayev (1794-1856) a Russian philosopher who's *Philosophical Letters* were written and published in French due to their critical political content.

Chatsky: "Tea at the club?"
Repetilov: "At the English Club! We have a society and secret meetings on Thursdays.
    It's a Secret Pact."
Chatsky: "At the club?"
Repetilov: "Exactly. We make noise, brother, noise."

The English Club could find no reason to exclude even Chaadayev, who had been declared mentally incompetent because of his essays. In *My Past and Thoughts*, Herzen called Chaadayev a "cataract in the English Club's eye." Nonetheless, the situation ended well, and Chaadayev, from his youth to his death, on 14 April 1856, was a member. Tradition holds that Chaadayev read, in the club's "discussion room," Lermontov's poem upon the death of Pushkin. He read while the "pitiable descendants of founders glorified for their depravity" listened.

Chaadayev mentioned the English Club twice in his letters. In a letter to A.S. Pushkin in 1831: "I sometimes spend time at – can you guess where? The English Club! You told me that you had to spend some time there; I would meet you there, in this beautiful building, among these Greek columns, in the shade of excellent trees..." Later, nearing the end of his life, Chaadayev, apparently needing money, wrote and requested his cousin Shcherbatov: "to cover all current debts at the club. I am limited to 50 rubles, which sum your cousin spent long ago." Two days before his death, Chaadayev, still at the English Club, rejoiced at the end of the war. At this time, in the "talking room," he boldly discussed political questions, and spoke about the war and serfdom.

Even Nicholas I listened closely to meetings in the "discussion room" and, not without apprehension, asked those close to him, "What do they say about this at the English Club?" Here, even in the most terrible times under Nicholas I, they spoke freely, even about the Decembrists. In that same issue of *Old Folks Magazine*, on 24 September, they wrote:

Alexey Gerasimov Sokolov, a waiter at the club, arrived one morning to tidy the room. On a table, he found a printed letter addressed: "To Ivan Petrovich Bibikov, Gendarme Colonel. I ask the senior member to give this to him." Club elders, when presented with the letter, planned to invite Mr. Bibikov and burn the letter in his presence. But, if Bibikov expressed a desire to keep it, inasmuch as it belonged to him, they planned to give him a fake. Bibikov did not want the letter, and it was burned in the presence of the elders.

In Semennikov's book, *Book Publishing Activity of N.I. Novikov*, (Gosizdat, 1921), among the numerous publications mentioned, one book comes to mind. The author was V.V. Chichagov. This name reminded me of a great deal. In the last century, in the eighties, I associated with people who remembered tales told by an old Mason, a former English Club member, who talked a lot about the building, originally owned by the poet M.M. Kheraskov. It was built in the second half of the eighteenth century by the poet, together with his brother Brigadier General A.M. Kheraskov. The poet Kheraskov lived here with his family until his death. While M.M. Kheraskov was alive, there was only one section of the building, the middle palace, with columns and wings. The façade with columns and gates with the lions was constructed after 1812 by Razumovsky, to whom the Kheraskovs sold the estate following the poet's death in 1807. During the fire of 1812,[9] it was untouched, probably thanks only to the thick growth in the park. If one went up in the building's attic, decorative molding from the former outside walls was visible on the walls of the main section.

In the first half of the last century, a "discussion club" that the tsar monitored carefully met in the chambers of Razumovsky's palace. For 100 years, in the poet Kheraskov's home, Masonic speeches rang out, ending with arrests. After Chaadayev's death in 1856, the "discussion room"[10] became a "coffee room," where bold speeches were replaced by the recitation of articles from *Moscow Gazette* to over-fed gourmets and losers at cards, all relaxing in soft chairs.

L.N. Tolstoy, who visited the club in the 1860s, called it, in *Anna Karenina*, a "Cathedral of Uselessness." He also recalls the "discussion room," but it was no longer similar to the one in Pushkin's time. In *Anna Karenina*, Prince Gagarin, leading Levin into the room, called it the "intellectual room." There, three gentlemen were discussing the latest political news. He describes in another place the impression the Club made on the Decembrist Volkonsky, in the sixties, when he returned from hard labor exile in Siberia:

> He walked through the chambers, with little old men at tables playing *Yeralash*, then turned into the "infernal room," where the well-known "Puchin" began his move against "the group." He stood for a few minutes next to a billiard table, where, grabbing at the edge, a proud, little old man lined up a shot, and just barely hit his ball. After glancing into the library, where a spectacled general read carefully, holding the newspaper at a distance, and a young guest trying not to make noise looked through, one after another, all the magazines, he went into the room where intelligent people gathered for conversation.

---

9. The fire that raged through the city just as Napoleon and his troops occupied it in September 1812. The best historical evidence has it that fires were set on the orders of Count Rostopchin. An estimated three-quarters of the city was decimated by fire and explosions.
10. The **горовирльная**, so perhaps more literally the "talking" room.

The English Club, circa 1900-04.

One of the peculiarities of the "discussion room" was that its visitors, when they chose to, knew about everything that was being done in the world, no matter how secretly it happened.

In *War and Peace*, a luxurious ball is described that was given by Moscow for Bagration in the English Club. That's all there is in literature about this 100-year-old refuge for Moscow's gentry. There's nothing remarkable. Could a mere mortal, a simple journalist, be admitted? No and no! If, a few times in the last and current centuries, I got into the club, then it was not as a journalist, but because I belonged to hunting and sporting societies that had dual membership with the English Club.

By then, the building belonged not to Razumovsky but Shablykin. Striking luxury and deathly quiet ruled, except in the "infernal room" where a game of chance was simmering along on cash money. At the beginning of this century, rich merchants appeared among the Club's members, and wherever there's a merchant, money goes on the table. A humble, low-stakes, quiet, and wordless game of cards was taking place. Little old men played at their decades-old places. Four stearate candles stood on each table, at the corners, and it was so quiet that the flames never wavered. From time to time, a player, with a hand, would summon a servant who, like a shadow, appeared before his boss without a sound, no one knew from where. The pair would gesture silently in a way known only to them. The servant, the same age as his boss, would disappear, and in a moment a service cart would appear next to the card tables.

The "portrait" room was called by the members, in jest, the "children's' room." It was called this not to make fun of the old men who met there, but because such low-stakes games were played there, and the players, like smart little kids, were as silent as the portraits on the walls. And if anyone raised their tone even a bit in an argument over cards, astonished voices rang out, a command was given, and everything quieted.

Access to the "portrait room" was through the entry hall, which, for practical purposes was where the club started. The entrance hall was an enormous room with a table in the middle, on which, on appointed days, ballot boxes were placed and every new arrival who was a club member, before they went on to the next rooms, were required to place balls in the box, witnessed by the on-duty elder. These were voting days for electing full members.

Along the walls of the entrance hall stood surprisingly comfortable, soft divans where, after lunch, club members and guests digested their food in clouds of smoke from aromatic cigars and, in the old days, Zhukovsky tobacco in pipes with foot-long cherry wood stems, which lackeys tended. Old men especially loved to sit on the divans and in chairs in the entrance hall and observe passersby, or to nap sweetly. I still remember an old man who completely resembled Prince Tugoukhovsky out of *Woe from Wit*. They would lead him – wearing soft slippers or cloth boots, and a scarf around his neck – into the entrance hall or the "coffee room," and sit him down in his chair. Each person had a favorite chair, which in his presence, no one else dared occupy. "Gennady Vasilevich's chair." The old man sat, looked around, tried to listen at first, but then quietly fell asleep. An old lackey, who served here during the time of serfdom, knowing the old boss's habits, placed a serving table before him at the appointed hour with a service and a steaming silver bowl, then carefully woke him, glancing at the clock:

"Your Excellency!"

The clock chimed 9:00 o'clock.

"Your Excellency! *Kasha* is served."

"Ehh? Nine already? I hear!"

He enjoyed the *kasha* and was led out to his carriage.

To the right of the entrance hall was the door to the "fruit room," where tables with fruits and candies stood. After the "fruit room" there was a large dining room. The left door out of the entrance hall led to the "portrait room" described above. In one of my early visits to the club, I went to the reading room, and the "discussion room" along the way, and caught a glimpse of an old military man and two civilians sitting on a divan in the corner. In front of them stood an enormous man, full of energy, with a greying, leonine mane, wearing a black suit, and now and then adjusting his slipping *pince nez*. He cursed up and down "the noble scum" sent around the country under guard to manage the regions. This was the famous winemaker Lev

Golitsyn,[11] a brilliant graduate of Moscow University, a favorite of professor Nikita Krylov, a well-known conversationalist, a passionate orator, always loudly proclaiming that he had "not been shamed by any ranks or orders."

The seated military man was A.A. Pushkin, son of the poet. The second fellow, fat, with greying sideburns, was Governor V.S. Perfilev, probably a model for "the American" in *Anna Karenina*, who was married to Tolstoy's daughter. Lev Golitsyn was less than beloved at the English Club for his sharp and uncensored language, by the standards of that time (the beginning of the eighties). But Lev Golitsyn feared no one. He always wore, winter and summer, a broad beaver hat; and his enormous figure attracted attention on the streets. Coachmen called him the "wild noble." Tatars on his estate in the Caucasus nicknamed him "Aslan Deli" – Crazy Leo.

He threw money away right and left, and never refused anyone anything, especially students. On Tverskoy Boulevard, on the corner of Chernyshevsky Alley, next to the Governor-General's home, he had a small shop, New World, selling wine from his Crimean vineyards. He retailed pure, natural wine for 25 kopeks per bottle. "I want a working man, a tradesman, or an average sales clerk to drink good wine!" he declared.

At the end of the 1890s, there was a political demonstration during which shots were fired from the Governor-General's residence and gendarmes swung clubs to disperse a crowd of students and workers. At the first hint of a demonstration, all the shops, of course, were closed tightly. I saw a few men fall. The crowd rushed to Strastnoy Boulevard. I saw how, in the open doors of Golitsyn's shop, there appeared, in a suit and with a messy mane of grey, the owner's enormous figure. He shouted at the police and demanded that they carry the wounded to him for bandaging. In a minute, his shop was full of refuge seekers. The wounded were bandaged in the back room by Golitsyn's daughter and wife, and he himself uncorked bottle after bottle of expensive wine and treated everyone. When the police knocked on the door, he locked the shop with a key and

Prince Lev Golitsyn, circa 1915.

shouted. "Today's my name day. These are my guests." Using the service door, he later let everyone out for whom it would have been dangerous to fall into the hands of the police.

The next day, in the English Club's "discussion room," he complained about the authorities' actions. Of course, such a member of the English Club was no kindred spirit of the Secret State Advisors, but he was listened to in the "discussion room."

11. Prince Lev Sergeyevich Golitsyn (1845-1915) – founder of the winemaking and champagne industry in the Crimea.

Once, Lev Golitsyn, in a thunderous voice, waving his hands, and constantly adjusting his *pince nez*, just as heatedly argued for banning vodka, so that people would drink only pure grape wines: "We are rich, our south was created for viniculture!" A handsome, tall, blond man with a pointed mustache tried to object. This was V.I. Martynov, a respected official from a certain governmental organization. Martynov was the son of Lermontov's murderer.[12] In front of him stood an old man with white puffy hair and a beard. He shared his memories with his neighbors. Names were heard: Lermontov, Pushkin, Gogol. This was A.A. Stakhovich, the well-known horse breeder and author of interesting memoirs, an admirer of Pushkin's, and a friend of Gogol's. At his estate, Palne, near Yelts, he built a monument to Pushkin: a bust on a granite pedestal.

Other types also spent time at the club. In the beginning of the eighties, the bald head of Moscow's Vice-Governor, a jolly man, I.I. Krasovsky, gleamed. A four-line poem was written about him, perhaps by Shumacher:

Beauty of the Moscow inspectorate
and the whole region there.
Ivan Ivanovich Krasovsky,
Where, oh where, is your hair?

Moscow's Chief of Police, A.A. Kozlov, who never missed a single significant fire, was a member of the English Club. According to a long-standing custom, all visitors to the English Club were informed about all fires: a special servant went to the halls, rang a bell, and in a quiet, refined voice announced:

"In the City district, five-alarm fire, on Ilinka Street."

"In Rogozhskaya, Durny Alley, a three-alarm fire."

At the first appearance of a messenger, A.A. Kozlov would jump up, whether it was time for lunch or dinner, and rush off on a fleet pair of horses, changing on the fly into his waterproof coat and donning a helmet kept in the carriage. He would return from the fire to the club to finish his lunch or dinner. P.I. Bartenev, publisher of *Russian Archive*, and K.K. Tarnovsky, the playwright, sometimes met there.

Past the "talking room" was a large guest room; in it, as in the "portrait room," card tables were filled with high stakes players in commercial games. Tens of thousands of rubles met their fate in games of *Pulki* and Robber. Beyond the large guest room was a "gallery," a long room, an entryway to the billiard room and the reading room, and also with an exit to the garden.

The billiard room maintained its traditional character, described by L.N. Tolstoy. Even at my last visit to the club in 1912, I saw the Chinese billiard table, a memorial

---

12. Mikhail Yuriyevich Lermontov (1814-1841) – a gifted poet and writer (*A Hero for our Times*) who perished at a young age in a duel.

to Tolstoy. On this table, in 1862, Lev Nikolayevich lost 1,000 rubles to an officer passing through town, and suffered an awkward moment: he had no money to pay, and the club rules were strict – he might even end up on the "blackboard." How this might have ended is unknown, but M.N. Katkov, an editor of *Russian Messenger* and *Moscow Gazette*, was in the club at the time, heard about the problem, and handed Tolstoy a loan of 1,000 rubles. In the next book published by *Russian Messenger*, Tolstoy's short story *Cossacks* appeared.

In the left corner of the entry "gallery" was a small door to the "infernal room" and the "elders' room," where urgent meetings of the elders took place in the event of any sort of argument or misunderstanding among the club's guests or members. Here they held court and punished offenders, whose names were displayed on the "blackboard." Next to the "elders' room" was an internal corridor and a room that the servants called the "worry room,"[13] and the members called the "lackey room." Here gamblers' lackeys, in livery, who had sat at the table in the "infernal room" through the night, waited and napped on their bosses' winter coats, piled on the wooden benches. This "worry room" for travelling lackeys, who came here in days gone by on the footholds of carriages and sleighs, was for them a club. Here, the lackeys talked, gossiped, and shared every last bit of dirt from under their masters' fingernails.

Past the "gallery" and the billiard room was an additional reading room, put in by Razumovsky after 1812. Construction of the room was managed by Gilardi.[14] You enter and find not one person from the usual crowd. You sit down in a soft chair. Not a sound. Only the old clock ticks. Green cloths on a red table with newspapers and magazines, rarely touched, set out in an astonishingly neat order. Silently and proudly marble columns support decorated arches, crafted by artisans in Kheraskov's time. Golden lettering on leather bindings shines through bookshelves' mirrored windows. The room's windows are curtained. Only through the semi-circular window tops, uncurtained, does the dark sky peek.

Marvelous columns with molded cornices transition to graceful arches reminiscent of the Masons' secret huddles. According to longstanding tradition, Kheraskov's office had been here. Through the gloom, ornamentation stands out in relief like the heads of knights. The upper semicircle of the window is lit by the moon, peeking out from behind clouds, but again it goes dark. The clock chimes midnight. At the twelfth strike of the old clock another starts ringing in the next room, and at the next twelfth strike, in a further room, the rich, deep bass sounds of an antique English clock recall conversations in Sevastopol, and, perhaps Pushkin's epigrams for the tsar and Lermontov's passionate lines about Pushkin's death.

13. The word used was ажидация – a creative conflation of агитация (agitation) and ожидание (waiting).
14. Dominico Gilardi (1745-1845), a Swiss architect working in Moscow who was instrumental in the post 1812 reconstruction.

Days of ceremonial luncheons showed the Cathedral of Uselessness in a bright light. At six in the morning on such holidays of gluttony, the English Club was full. Old men, youths, military greatcoats, capes. They stand in groups, walk and talk, packed tightly in the "discussion room" closest to the large reception hall. The doors into the large reception hall are bolted: an enormous meal is being laid out there with drinks and appetizers.

"One must track the seasons," droned the senior member of the executive department, P.I. Shablykin, a celebrated gourmet, who had eaten through all his money. "One must track the seasons so that everything happens in its own time; when to eat Flensburg oysters, when from Ostand, and when from the Crimea; when to get Atlantic salmon and when to get Pacific salmon. You can't serve March whitefish with fresh cucumbers in August!"

Everything that P.I. Shablykin served was in season. He missed nothing. And when, as it happened, toward New Year's, they delivered fish and fine-grained, red caviar from the Urals, it was sampled at the English Club first. Juices also varied by season: birch buds, black whortleberry, grasses, leaves – and various sparkling waters – a club secret.

The clocks in the halls, one after another, ring six o'clock. The doors to the large reception hall open, voices hush, and shuffling and the ringing of spurs can be heard. Crowds surround the appetizers. They drink "with whitefish," "with beluga caviar," "with sweetbreads on toast," etc. They drink and eat appetizers for exactly one hour. Then, from the reading rooms, the first strike of a clock is heard – seven o'clock – and a servant's rich baritone voice rises above the clink of glasses and the clank of knives: "Dinner is served!"

A brilliant crowd of about 200 men moves through the "talking room," "the children's room," and the "fruit room," into the large dining room, divided from the club by the entrance hall. They take places according to their preferences.

For the choirs, there was orchestral music. Below the orchestra there was a choir stage – they were Gypsy, or Hungarian, or Russian, or from Yar. The dining room stage was the only place where women were allowed, and then only in a choir. No woman was ever allowed in the club itself, in accordance with a rule established at its founding. Men even washed the floors.

Performers took their places. The eldest Gypsy, Fyodor Sokolov, stroked his grey moustache, and with sparkling eyes lightly tapped a foot, struck a guitar string – and the Gypsy choir sang. On the left, near tables set with steaming pans, frozen like statues, in white uniforms and starched white hats, with silver serving spoons in their hands, stood the servers of the Cathedral of Uselessness. The Meeting Hall in the Museum of the Revolution now occupies that space.

Even this club went bankrupt. The majority of the gentry lost their luxurious estates. The club's business affairs started to weaken; instead of 600 members, just

200 remained. When, bit by bit, merchants were allowed to become members, it became more crowded at the club, especially in the card rooms, since only the English Club had the right to allow gambling, which at that time was strictly forbidden in other Moscow clubs, where games went on in secret. At the English Club, where the Governor-General was a respected elder, and the Chief of Police was a full member, the police did not even dare show their noses.

After the 1905 revolution, when they started to gamble freely at all of the clubs, the English Club's business affairs again weakened; it became necessary to find ways to make money. They elected for this purpose a special commission. Its members decided to make use of the empty courtyard along the Tverskaya Street side, and replace the decorative fence and the historic lions with a row of commercial buildings. A few members of the commission were upset at the blow to the courtyard's beauty and the death of a tradition. They submitted a dissenting opinion, in which, among other things, they wrote that "the club is not fit to partake in risky enterprises that in no way conform to its traditions," and ended with the proposal "not to change the look of the building to avoid winding up as a tenant in the merchants' courtyard."

The number of new members grew, and the English Club's wonderful façade, the historic home of the poet Kheraskov, the Razumovsky Palace, ended up in the merchants' courtyard, and the lions were thrown in the cellar. The club's business affairs grew worse and worse, its membership changed character, and Saturday luncheons – the parade luncheons had already stopped – grew boring and less popular. Luncheons were set for 10-15 people. The final parade luncheon, where the club had really shined, was in 1913 on the Romanovs' 300th anniversary.

Half of the club was turned into a hospital. The club kept the entrance area, the reception hall, the "portrait room," the "coffee room," the large guest hall, the reading room, and the dining room. All the rooms looking out on Tverskaya Street became part of the hospital. Renovation was done. For gambling, the "infernal room" was replaced by the large guest hall, where they played baccarat; "cage" play was conducted at tables placed in the middle of the room; in the "children's' room," as in the past, small-stakes games were played. In this way, the club stretched out its existence to the beginning of 1918, when it was seized for use by the government.

One of the first orders issued by a Commission on Preservation of Monuments of Art and Antiquities, part of the People's Commissariat for Education, was to demolish the row of commercial enterprises along the front of the building. The Revolution unveiled the wonderful façade behind the iron gate. The lions were once again placed at the gate. A museum of Old Moscow was organized in the halls of the former English Club. On 12 November 1922, in the restored halls of the former English Club, the opening ceremony for an exhibit, "Red Moscow," also marked the establishment of the Museum of the Revolution. This first exhibition was the beginning of the Museum of the Revolution in the former Cathedral of Uselessness.

The exhibition opened at 6 o'clock on 12 November. Electricity glowed brightly in the former English Club's cold, long-unheated, grand halls. Red flags decorated the antique stairway's cold marble. From the "portrait room" could be heard voices, shuffling of feet, and the ringing of spurs. It was the very same "portrait room," only different subjects. On the walls were the fighters of the October Revolution in Moscow.

The room was overflowing with People's Commissars, various institutional representatives, and people from workers' organizations, as well as all their coats, jackets, leather outerwear, and military cloaks. For the first time in 100 years the hall had women among its guests of honor. People gathered near the corners and the windows. Each found a suitable spot, depending on their mood. The walls were hung with weapons, surrounding photographs of Moscow's final battles. These were collected from participants by the People's Commissariats. People recognized one another in the action photographs. They talked...

Fighters remember days gone by
and battles they fought together.

STUDENTS

BEFORE THE REACTION OF THE 1880s, Moscow lived its life, and the university lived another life entirely.[1] Students, for the most part, since the 1860s, had come largely from the provincial poor, and their parents occupied the lowest ranks of society. These students had nothing in common with those from Moscow, and they lived in the "Latin Quarter," between the two Bronnaya Streets and Palashevsky Alley, where wooden structures with tiny apartments crowded unwashed streets.[2]

In addition, two abandoned, imposing buildings owned by the noble Chebyshevs, with wings on Kozikh and Greater Bronnaya Streets, were almost entirely filled with students. Residents called the first building "Fort Chebyshev," or "Chebyshy," and the second was called "Hell." This was a holdover from Nechayev's day.[3] At the end of the sixties, this was the headquarters for the Nechayev students, and even earlier for Karakozov's followers, members of the Hell circle. Typically, four people lived in each little one-room, student apartment in the Latin Quarter. They had four shabby beds, four chairs, a table, and a bookshelf.

Students dressed in whatever they could, and frequently four roommates owned two pairs of boots and two pairs of pants, which meant taking turns: one day, two go to lecture and the others stay home. The next day, the other two went. They ate in cafeterias or had simpler fare at home. Instead of tea, they had chicory, which cost three kopeks for a round tin containing three-quarters of a pound, and lasted the

---

1. Moscow State University's main campus is today located approximately five miles southwest of the city center, and on the opposite side of the Moscow River, probably with good reason, as this chapter suggests. The University's School of Journalism occupies the old university campus downtown, across the street from the Manezh and steps from the Kremlin.
2. This area is about a mile from the campus.
3. Sergei Gennadiyevich Nechayev (1847-1882) was a Nihilist revolutionary known for espousing violence. See page 146 for more on the Hell circle.

four about 10 days. At the beginning of the school year, on the gates of each building, hung slips of paper advertising apartment rentals. Starting in mid-July, the slips
would slowly disappear.

In the 1870s, students did not yet have a uniform, but they followed fashion, and
you could always tell students both by their manners and their attire. The majority
of the most radical were dressed in the style of the 1860s: long hair, a hat tilted down
toward the eyes, with a wide brim and sometimes – the height of luxury – a caftan
and glasses, which gave young people a scholarly look and heft. That is how students
dressed before the 1880s, a time of reaction.

After ascending the throne, Alexander III implemented harsh rules.[4] They even
touched the university. The 1884 university charter destroyed the professoriate's
autonomy and doubled lecture fees. To deprive poor students of a higher education
and add a new expense, the students were required to wear a uniform: an outer coat,
a suit with crested buttons, and blue-collared capes.

The charter clamped down on the students for good. Petitions circulated and
meetings were held, but none of this ever went beyond the walls of the university.
Moscow Bulletin, the government newspaper, supporting the reaction, loosed on the
students a series of articles in defense of the new charter. The students' first steps
onto the streets were elicited by this newspaper.

Greater Dmitrovka Street begins at Hunter's Row and ends at the spot on Strastnoy Boulevard known as Naryshkin Square. Only the third building on Greater
Dmitrovka that had not been acquired for commercial purposes, it is last on the
right side of the street and faces the boulevard. Talyzin constructed the building at
the end of the eighteenth century, and in 1818 his widow sold the building to Moscow University. For exactly 100 years, from 1818 until 1918, the university press was
located there and printed *Moscow Bulletin*.

The building was never renovated nor even painted outside. This was, without
doubt, the dirtiest-looking building in Moscow, with broken stucco, mold, windows
that had never been washed, and an interior coated with smoke. The enormous press
was lit by kerosene lanterns, so its ceilings and walls were black, and the typesetters
arriving for the night shift, even if they were blond, worked with dark hair because
of the lantern ash. The press's windows looked out on Dmitrovka and the mansion
where the editorial board and the managing editor's apartment were located.

After agreeing on a "cat concert" to punish *Moscow Bulletin* for its articles, a crowd
of students surprised the police when they appeared on Naryshkin Square in front
of the press's windows. A howl went up, squeals, shouts, and cussing. Spoiled food,
such as soft cucumbers and rotten eggs, flew at the windows. The police arrived. A
division of gendarmes galloped in from the neighboring barracks to disperse the

---

4. Alexander III ruled from 1881-1894.

The "new" university building, 1890-1900.

demonstration. Immediately, stones flew at the windows, and glass smashed. On the boulevard, mounted gendarmes raced after students. On one side of the street, they used batons, and on the other, rocks and sticks. Horses without riders charged up the boulevard and nearby streets overflowed with the curious. The battle raged full strength: Cossacks were summoned to reinforce the police. They surrounded the crowd, and marched them to Butyrskaya Prison. Lyapinka, the dormitory described above for students at the Academy of Art, had completely spilled onto the boulevard.

When the crowd of students was surrounded on the boulevard, some bystanders were caught up by chance. They too were led from Strastnoy Boulevard to Butyrskaya Prison. At the head of the procession, a huge merchant in a mangy fur coat with no shirt or hat attracted attention. This was the stevedore-construction worker Gromov. All of Moscow knew him for his *bogatyr* figure. His shoulders were above the heads in any crowd. He fell into the crush completely by accident, after exiting a tavern. A mounted gendarme struck him in the face with a baton. The giant tore the gendarme from his mount and tossed him in the snow. "His Worthiness" was marched to jail. His servant, standing on the sidewalk among the curious, recognized Gromov:

"Sidor Martynych, what's wrong?" he shouted.

"Agapych, run home and tell them that the stew-dance and I had a rye-valation!" Gromov bellowed with all his strength.

Students in Moscow, circa 1905.

Revolution... Revolution... the word resonated in the crowd and flew off across Moscow. But it was a long way to the Revolution! This event, and a series of subsequent protests, were all disorganized sparks of expression that never went beyond the university's walls. They were supressed by arrests and exile, about which the majority of Muscovites knew nothing, since newspaper coverage was strictly forbidden. In 1887, when the university charter was amended to limit enrollment, and inspectors and university detectives drove the students beyond their breaking point, there were major street demonstrations. Firearms were used. But even this went unnoticed by most of the public.

Each year, students took to the streets with greater frequency. But the police were on guard. As soon as gatherings began near the university, police started maneuvers. They would surround the alleys leading onto Greater Nikitinskaya Street and block off Mokhovaya Street, near Hunter's Row, and Vozhdvizhenka with a cordon of city police and gendarmes. Then, the Manezh doors would be opened and they would drag in students and anyone else that happened to be within reach.

The brightest point in the last century was a university action after which more than 150 students were sent off to the army. Ensuing protests demanded abolition of "temporary rules" by which the government conscripted students. This measure, linked with the students' restiveness, elicited protest from the entire intelligentsia, as well as complete sympathy among broad layers of the population. But in print no facts or opinions were allowed: people discussed the situation quietly. At the time, illegal poems were passed from hand to hand. Here is one of them.

Seek out!
"Seek out the rational, beneficent, timeless"[5]
Seek out the students on planet Earth's streets.
Encourage the weakest everywhere to profess
All of their heartrending grief.
Let noble sentiments swell to no less
Than tears, a cleansing immersion.
Freedom of expression will then
Open up Rus's vision.
Let everyone know that vulgar old ways are
Gaining ascendance once more
Dissemblers soon claiming the day
Wage, against enlightenment, war.
Know, torture chambers are unchanged,
Old masters at their places,
Loose their wild, furious rage,
Upon our most talented faces.
Our wide open steppe is free and windblown
Russia is broad and menacing
New seeds will grow – everywhere sown
Germs of bright new thinking.
Those who long and stubbornly doubted
Truth found in free expression
Soon will understand, they miscounted,
And drove out their very own sons.
Crowds you dispersed; but did you scare all men
Watching your deeds, vile and base?
Success seals your damnation,
Monument to your disgrace.

As it happened, students forced into the army and sent off to Russia's various cities, were welcomed warmly everywhere. They spoke publicly wherever they went, whereas they had previously kept quiet. This revolutionized even the deep, distant provinces. Another poem, "The Gossip and the Chief of Police," describing the pacification of student unrest in Moscow, failed to make it into print, but was distributed by hand.

---

5. Gilyarovsky notes that the author borrowed this line from Nikolai Alexeyevich Nekrasov (1821-1877), a Russian poet, writer, critic and publisher. His poems about Russian peasants were acclaimed by the intelligentsia.

I witnessed terrible street scenes
My poor old head spins even now
from wild students' vented spleens
and the hum in the streets of old Moscow,
crowds hastened to chase after crowds
Whistlers... Chanters... Whippers... Howls
Soldiers all round, Cossacks stand proud,
Blue uniformed gendarmes cower.
No matter what street, just the same stew
Folks everywhere, cops everywhere
Kids, thrown in the Manezh, out of view,
roar like a wild river in there.
Behind the students, they threw in
the Manezh people scared silly.
Those who shouted and those who didn't
Swept off the street, willy-nilly.
Off to the Manezh!
An urgent mission,
For the soldiers there's no easy win,
Catch them! Hold them!
A cook walking,
Holding a perch for his kitchen
The brave troops no doubt are itching
A move, another, they set the hook!
Clubs fly and bayonets swish,
The Manezh quickly accepts the cook
As well as his frozen fish...

They really did drag a cook off to the Manezh once when a crowd of students had poured out of the university onto Mokhovaya Street. The students saw, flying toward them on a pair of horses harnessed to a high-backed sled, the Chief of Police himself. In the crowd of students, gathered in the middle of the street, he had to rein back and ride quietly. "I'm asking you to disperse!" the General shouted, standing up in the sleigh. In response there was some noise, and then behind the sled an explosion of laughter and shouts:

"Down with autocracy!" and again laughter and shouts.

"Down with autocracy! Down!"

The frenzied Chief of Police scrabbled up onto the gates of the Manezh and pointed at the cook with the fish, who was grabbing him by the sleeve and howling:

"Your Grace, let me go! My fish will spoil..."

The cook thrust the thawing fish at the General. Near the entrance, accompanied by laughter from the crowd, city police removed from the rear of the Chief's sleigh a banner with a slogan in colorful lettering: "Down with autocracy!" While his sled was not moving, students had attached a banner rushed out by Lyapins' painters for display around the city: "Down with autocracy!" This slogan later became a threat, but at that time was still fresh.

At Moscow University, "Tatyana's Day," 12 January by the old calendar, was a student holiday. Moscow's streets were never as noisy as this day.[6] Crowds of students strolled Moscow's streets singing late into the night. Three or four students would pile into a cab meant for one, howling. All the day's songs intentionally played on the words: "bedroom" and "Tatyana."[7] This was a carefree, noisy holiday. The police, insofar as they had goals and orders from above, arrested no students. There were also orders to keep rank insignia out of sight. At that time, the students' favorite song was *Dubinushka*.

Moscow University teachers, circa 1913.

On the morning of 12 January, the capital's supreme authorities attended a university ceremony. Poor students filled three-quarters of the room. Excused from class, they wore scuffed boots, small capes with collars, once blue, now a faded white. But in their midst flashed well-groomed dandies – with fine collars atop magnificent greatcoats tailored from expensive fabric, with white silk lining and fashionable golden details. These were the children of the wealthy.

After the ceremony, the students poured down Greater Nikitskaya, and in crowds, singing *Gaudeamus igitur*,[8] they moved to the Nikitsky Gates and up Tverskoy Boulevard to their favorite beer halls. But these were only the poor students; the white linings, after donning their "Nicholas" cloaks with beaver collars, left on expensive horses for their parents' wealthy homes. After "reloading" in bars, crowds of

---

6. St. Tatyana was a third century Christian martyr in Rome. St. Tatyana's name day, January 12, was the same as Empress Elizabeth's, who on that day in 1755 endorsed the university's creation. The Russian Orthodox Church declared Tatyana the patron saint of students, and a St. Tatyana Church was built on campus.

7. In their songs, the semi-rhyme for "bedroom" and the Saint's name – *spalnya* and Tatyana –.were used to great effect.

8. *Gaudeamus igitur*, said to have been a beer-drinking song in ancient Rome, is now sung at university graduations, mostly in Europe. There are many versions, several poking fun at administration and faculty.

students went singing down the boulevards to Trubnaya Square, but *Gaudeamus* was replaced by *Dubinushka*. A few white linings had rejoined the group, not wanting to fall behind their fellows; they had thrown down their luxurious clothes at home, put on old coats, and followed down the boulevards. In front of the *Moscow Bulletin* all stood and chanted:

In parks we hacked
switches for nobles backs....

Singing, the crowds headed off to the luxurious Hermitage, with its mirrors and statues, traipsing in boots up its white marble stairs. The restaurant was prepared for the event by removing its plush, expensive rugs. Starting in the 1870s, the Hermitage's owner, Olivier the Frenchman, let the students use his restaurant to celebrate Tatyana's Day. Traditionally, on the eve of the 12th, the Hermitage's enormous dining room was transformed. Expensive silk furniture disappeared, the floor was thickly coated with sawdust, sturdy wooden chairs were brought in, as well as serving tables and simple stools. In the buffet and kitchen there was only cold food, vodka, beer and inexpensive wine. This was a people's holiday in the bourgeois Palace of Gluttony.

On that holiday, even during the fiercest reaction, this was the one hall in Russia that allowed bold speech. Hermitage was in the hands of students and their guests: favorite professors, writers, and lawyers. They sang, they talked and shouted, they spilled beer and vodka on the floor, and the room was filled with smoke. They hoisted professors on tables. Orators spoke one after another. Even today, there are people who remember the Tatyana's Day at Hermitage, when, after his speech, V.A. Goltsev was "rocked" so strongly on a tabletop that his suit jacket split in half; when, following Goltsev, they just as enthusiastically honored A.I. Chuprov, who broke his glasses when he was thrown in the air and smashed into the ceiling. Right after Chuprov, a wild-haired student in a red shirt and a reddish hat jumped on the table, and roared above the noise in an improbable bass, emphasizing his O's, like a seminar speaker:

"Co - omrades! Co - omrades!"

"Down! Down in front!" the students shouted, carried away by their favorite professors' speeches.

"Co - omrades!" the bass stubbornly rumbled.

"Do - o - own!" the room mocked, and those closest tried to tear him off the table.

But the bass, with effort, rose above the noise, "Yes, down!" he rumbled, raising his arms in threat, and those closest fell silent. "Down with autocracy," he thundered and leapt off into the crowd. Something unprecedented had just happened. In a moment, the students again were "rocking" and the room thundered with shouting. But later, on the streets, students interrupted their singing all night long to shout, "Down with autocracy!" This slogan became the battle cry at all student actions. In 1905, it sounded like a special threat at Moscow University, when students and workers sat together in the university's auditoriums in their first joint meetings. Here, the slogan rang in speeches and shone on banners, and only disappeared when autocracy was gone. Inside the walls of Moscow University, this battle slogan was not an empty threat: the first barricades in the center of the capital appeared spontaneously on the 15th of October 1905, inside the walls and courtyards of this oldest institution of higher learning.

NARYSHKIN SQUARE

NARYSHKIN SQUARE, THE FINEST OF Moscow's shaded boulevard parks, was built in the middle of the last century. Today, it sits between the inner and outer lanes of Strastnoy Boulevard. In the past, there was only one lane, the inner, and where the square is now there was a spacious garden owned by Prince Gagarin. The garden, since 1838, had been the site of the former Catherine Hospital. In 1926, when they were building the lane across from the hospital building, 100-year-old stumps, still whole, stuck out of the soil. They were reburied and the street was built right over them. This garden was linked to Putinkovsky Drive, in those times, by the dirty Sennaya Street, along which stretched a row of buildings from the Catherine Hospital to Lesser Dmitrovka. At the other end, next to Strastnoy Monastery, was S.P. Naryshkin's large building. In the sixties, Naryshkin bought Sennaya Square, built a park on it, and donated it to the city, which then named it Naryshkin Square.

Next to the Catherine Hospital stood a wonderful, antique mansion. Until just before the October Revolution, it belonged to Count Volkonsky, who inherited it in the fifties from Prince Meshchersky. Speaking of this building, one is reminded that two doors down stood a mansion with a romantic history. Earlier, it belonged to Captain Krechetnikov, and was bought from him in 1849 by the Titular Advisor A.V. Sukhovo-Kobylin. This Titular Advisor was none other than the playwright and author of *Krechinsky's Garden*, Alexander Vasilevich Sukhovo-Kobylin, who lived here until 1859. One of Prince Volkonsky's relatives, Count Shuvalov, a powerful grandee who had been paralyzed, lived in the building for many years. He was often called in his wheelchair to Naryshkin Square.

After Shuvalov's death, at the end of the 1890s, Volkonsky rented his building to Zavyalov the candy maker. A sign was installed on the stately building: "For Rent: Weddings, Balls, and Wakes." Thus, until 1917, did this building serve, passing

Catherine Hospital on Strastnoy Boulevard.

from hand to hand, from a candy maker to a candy maker, from Zavyalov to Burdin, to Feoktistov and others. Sometimes, lights would shine in the windows all night, and the premises hummed with music from weddings and merchants' balls, attracting the public from the boulevards to its windows. At other times, the bass of deacons singing *Eternal Memory* drifted out. Huge merchant weddings were held here, with magnificent carriages parked near the building. There were modest weddings too, with carriages rented from theaters, on whose benches actors from the imperial theater usually were carried to shows and rehearsals. Sometimes, the bottom would fall out of these carriages, and someone who had just been riding would find himself running down the street calling for assistance. This was not especially dangerous because the sickly horses barely moved. There was a case just like this in the 1880s on Petrovka Street that ended with a ticket from the police.

On the days of wedding celebrations, a golden, glass covered wedding carriage, in which the groom and bride went from the church to the wedding feast, was hitched to a pair of massive horses in white rigging, under a blue silk net, if the bride was a blonde, and under a rose silk net if the bride was a brunette. The groom wore a suit jacket with a white tie and the bride, all in white, with a tiara of orange flowers and a veil, was in full view of passersby.

Caterers prepared feasts for any price: choices included cold and hot dishes, civil generals and military generals, and with "cavalry" and "without cavalry." Military men with wide rows of service medals on their chests, sometimes with a ribbon across the shoulder, were highly prized and showed up for rich merchants, but not, of course, for the "biggest names," who had their own palaces and "their own" generals. Servants were priced according to how impressive they appeared. There were some with combed grey sideburns that one might mistake for government ministers. A stained, secondhand cape might give them up. Waiters were hired largely depending on their appearance. They also served wines "to the public."

"Fetch the wines from Depre: Cognac No. 184, Port wines No. 211 and No, 113, with the rose label... You know?" ordered a one-time merchant, who had cribbed names of fashionable wines from taverns.

"Yes, sir... but for this price I can only get half bottles."

"Well, alright, if it's halves, it's halves. Put the bottles with eagle labels on the head table, and the crow labels in the back."

Merchants were smooth, and caterers even smoother... "Eagle" and "crow," and both from Depre.

Peter Smirnov, the vodka maker, had two customers, Karzin and Bogatyrev. They left him and opened their own wine cellar on Zlatoustensky Alley, and started to pour their own wines – swill, of course. Their wines went nowhere. The firm was about to go up in flames, but, luckily, a vagrant happened to come in and propose a joint project. When he showed his passport, the partners were ecstatic: the passport was for landowner Caesar Depre. Port wines 211 and 113, Cognac 184, Cognac "fine champagne" 195, both the rose and the white labels were copied exactly from Depre. Who's going to notice that it's C. Depre not K. Depre? Who will notice that K. Depre has an eagle on the label and C. Depre has a crow without a crown? You won't see the difference at a glance. At balls and weddings and memorial luncheons, where the people were "grey," wines with the crow were appropriate. This continued for some time, but finished in court. It was revealed that C. Depre, the associate of the firm with this name, was a real person and his passport was genuine.[1]

At a wedding reception, guests coming from the ceremony arrived first. They entered in pairs: fat merchants' wives in silk, together with their husbands in coats with tails. Some were decorated with medals "For Steadfastness." There were young men with ladies on their arms. All waited in rows along the wall. When everything was set, the master of ceremonies arrived in livery with a wand-like scepter, and following him, on the arm of the groom, was the bride with her bouquet. They stopped in front of the guests, and right behind them, couples entered: first the parents of the groom, who stood to his right. Then, the parents of the bride approached him, and stopped next to the bride, first kissing their young ones and then each other.

Waiters served champagne in delicate flutes: Roederer or Clicquot for honored guests and Laninskoye for the simpler guests.[2] Congratulations and toasts. The

---

1. This history is ironic indeed, given that, just over 100 years later, the Smirnov name would be embroiled in a similar dispute over who had a right to use that name on their vodka.

2. Honored guests were served the foreign labels.

Depre wine cellar, Moscow, circa 1900.

sound of a glass breaking on the floor occasionally rang out, and was considered a good omen. An orchestra played quietly. After congratulations, everyone took their places around the table. Tea was served. Then some of the guests went into the next room to play cards. They gambled, both high and low stakes. Others surrounded the buffet. Then dancing started, and wedding celebrations. When all had danced until they were tired, they went to the wedding luncheon, which immediately became loud, because the buffet did its job. The wedding general gave a congratulatory speech, and then there were toasts and speeches, each trying to outdo the other. Young people, nobles and officers, threw bread balls back and forth across the table, and then everyone joined in, and heads of lettuce flew, bread crusts, and, occasionally, a red crab that had garnished the sturgeon. After the "young" guests left, whatever was left was imbibed, and the card players, settled in at their game, sometimes played until the next day.

On the edge of the city, in rainy weather, especially in the fall, unwashed alleys resembled squishy swamps, covered with puddles. One had to know how to maneuver, know the deep spots. A special trade thrived. Boys "kept watch." They were thieves. If an expensive carriage came by, this spot was trouble.

Once, a glass-windowed wedding carriage, with bride and groom, was riding through an alley in Khapilovka. This place was widely known to harbor pirates. The "young couple" was visiting a rich but stingy relative who lived on the alley. They impressed the local population with their innovative carriage and an expensive pair of horses under a blue silk net. The pirates' eyes immediately lit up at the booty.

"Whose spot are they going through, boys?"

"Here, to the left. More to the left!"

They led the carriage to a deep rut covered with water: instantly, the horse was immersed up to its belly, and the carriage was on its side. People ran up, bargaining started, and the "young couple" paid 50 rubles to have the carriage unloaded, and 10 rubles each to be hand-carried to the uncle's home. Now there are asphalt roads there, and, as concerns wedding carriages, probably not even a memory remains.

At memorial luncheons in the cold winter, the caterer did not heat the building. "People will warm up; by the second course everyone will be hot," he said, soothing the guests.

"But my legs are freezing!"

"Well, don't take off your boots. Hey, doorman, bring boots for Their Honors."

The fat caterer, Feoktistov, suggested the same thing when I was removing my coat in the frozen anteroom.

The memorial lunch consisted of rice pudding with raisins, and *bliny* with fresh caviar by the spoonful, served on plates by lackeys. At the table, along with the scraping of knives, there was a constant tapping. If you closed your eyes, you could imagine that you were sitting in a stable with a wooden floor. The noise was the guests warming their feet. The sole heir, to whom the deceased left a considerable inheritance, sat in the place of honor, across from representatives of the church, and constantly poured vodka and wine for the "Holy Fathers." He, too, tapped his feet to keep warm.

"At the right time, and in such a low temperature, wine is useful for the body," an enormous deacon loudly thundered before every glass of vodka, which he splashed into his enormous glass. "Well look, our dear little departed, adored raspberries. Let us remember the soul of the departed with some raspberry juice. Father Nikodim, if you please, let us be as one," and the heir dragged over the old man, a friend of the deceased. "No, I prefer Cahors.[3] I'm no lover of raspberry juice. Cahors is better, it gives you strength and helps you relax. I'm for Cahors."

"But look here, I'm for raspberry..."

When a cloud of steam rose above the diners, and the tapping had ceased, almond *kisel* was served along with almond milk.[4] The clinking of glasses cut through the thick din of 300 voices, occasionally drowned out by deafening laughter. Then, there was a beastly roar. This was the deacon standing, stretching, and coughing. They adjusted their seats, silence reigned, and the deacon intoned:

"Eternal memory... E-E-ter-nal Me- em -o -o ry!"

Enormous panes of glass shook in their window frames, and glass ornaments on a princely, antique lantern tinkled. The memorial luncheon had ended.

---

3. A French wine, it was introduced to Russians at the table of Peter the Great, who soon moved from importing to domestic production of a fortified sweet wine. It was used as a sacramental wine by the Orthodox Church. Today, French Cahors is a dry wine, unlike products still bottled under various names in the former Soviet Union.

4. From a Slavic root meaning sour. *Kisel* is often described as a cold broth or drink, usually made from fruit and thickened, often sour.

THE STORY OF TWO BUILDINGS

THE MERCHANTS' CLUB HAD A shaded garden where, in the summer, members ate lunch and dinner, played cards, or clinked champagne glasses, all on a wide terrace where they could greet the rising sun. The garden looked out on Kozitsky Alley, which earlier had been called Uspensky, but from the time that Catherine II's State-Secretary Kozitsky built a palace on Tverskoy Boulevard for his beautiful wife, the Siberian gold industrialist E.I. Kozitskaya, the alley has borne her name. In those days it was one of the biggest and best in Moscow, with a façade that looked out on Tverskoy Boulevard. Built in the classical style, it had a crest above the door and two stylish balconies. After Kozitskaya's death, the building passed to her daughter, Princess A.G. Beloselskaya-Belozerskaya. The historic Moscow salon of Beloselsky-Belozersky's daughter – Zinaida Volkonskaya – was in the building. Here, in the 1820s, representatives of the day's art and literature gathered. On a visit to Moscow, Pushkin called on Zinaida Volkonskaya, and dedicated to her a well-known poem![1]

> In the middle of hectic Moscow,
> At crowded games of cards,
> Where prayers are babbled nonsense
> You love Apollo's games.
> Tsaritsa of the muses and of beauty,
> With a gentle hand you hold
> the magic wand of inspiration,

---

1. This fragment was written in 1927. In a letter to frequent correspondent P.A. Vyazemsky in January 1829, Pushkin notes with private satisfaction that he had of late been "taking a break from Zinaida's cursed luncheons."

above a thoughtful brow,
twice crowned with laurels,
while the genius waits enflamed.
Don't reject humble tribute
From the bard, your captive.
Hear my voice and smile,
As a traveler in Catalan
Hears a gypsy woman's tune.

One of Volkonskaya's guests, the poet A.N. Muravyov, accidentally damaged a decorative statue of Apollo. Embarrassed, and hoping to defuse an awkward situation, Muravyov wrote a 4-line poem, which moved Pushkin to the following improvisation:

A sword drawn, an arrow flies.
Writhing, the Python died;
Your face shines victorious,
Apollo of the Belvedere![2]
Who spoke for the python,
Who broke your statue here?
You, Apollo's rival,
Mitrofan of Belvedere.

In Zinaida Volkonskaya's salon, the Decembrists' spirit lingered.[3] Down the steps of the residence's white marble staircase, all Moscow accompanied Princess Maria Volkonskaya, wife of a Decembrist exiled to hard labor, when she left in the winter for a place where:

Work boiled with sounds of chains
With song – work above the abyss!
Clattered on miners' mighty chests
A poker and iron hammer.

---

2. Apollo Belvedere or Apollo of the Belvedere, also called the Pythian Apollo is a marble sculpture lost in antiquity but rediscovered in Italy during the Renaissance. Pope Julius II owned the statue before assuming the papacy. He installed it in 1511 at the Vatican's Belvedere Palace.

3. The Decembrist uprising occurred on December 26, 1825, in Senate Square in Petersburg, when approximately 3,000 army officers and men refused to take the traditional oath of allegiance to Nicholas I, who had stepped forward to assume the throne when his brother Constantine refused. The events had their roots, in part, in a secret society known as the Union of Salvation, whose members held a wide spectrum of beliefs, the most common theme perhaps being the abolition of serfdom.

Relatives, confidantes, and friends gathered to see off Maria Volkonskaya, who stopped here for one day on her way to Siberia. In Nekrasov's poem "Russian Women," Maria Volkonskaya is far away in the snowy tundra. He recalled that unforgettable evening:

I listened to Italian singers here, rather
Well known back in those days.
Co-workers, and friends of my father
were killed in this very place.
Right here my dear friends had gathered,
The place where I myself hastened.
But a group of writers that really mattered
Were bidding me farewell as their friend.
Odoyevsky and Vyazemsky among
them, plus a poet, inspired, the nicest
young man. He courted my cousin; but too young,
was sent to his eternal rest.

And Pushkin was here…

Zinaida Volkonskaya settled permanently in Italy, where the salon of the "Northern Corinna," as they called her there, attracted Rome's highest society. But, in the end, the Catholic hierarchy took everything, and she died in poverty. The Moscow salon ceased meeting after her departure in 1829, and the building went to the Beloselsky-Belozerskys, servants of the tsar's court, until the end of the seventies, when the businessman Malkiyel bought it from the prince.[4] Before that time, it is known only that, at the end of the sixties, the building was occupied by Repman's *pension*, where the children of the wealthy studied. The entire period from Volkonskaya to Repman remains unknown. All that came down to us is a legend, saved by the old neighbors and retired police from the Tverskaya Precinct, who were still alive in the eighties and shared the details.

In the middle of the 1800s, an elderly princess, a relative of the owner, moved into the Beloselsky-Belozersky's palace, and filled half the building with her numerous servants and companions. She locked the public spaces and plunged the palace into silence. Once a week, on Sundays, servants escorted the old woman down the white marble staircase and seated her in a carriage harnessed to six old horses, driven by an old coachman, and on whose footholds stood two tattered lackeys in tailored livery. On the left horse of the first pair rode a stable "boy," about 60 years old.

After she returned from lunch, the gates were locked again for a week. This did not stop the property's groundskeepers from climbing over the fence and

---

4. Zinaida was born a Beloselskaya-Belozerskaya and changed her name when wed.

disappearing for entire nights, for which they were cruelly repaid by the German manager. He whipped them without mercy. At that time, as was the habit in Moscow, the police conducted punishments on Saturdays. The manager gathered the guilty and sent them off to the police precinct with a list of names and instructions on how many times to hit whom. It always concluded with the note, "For each, three rubles are attached for expenses." But punishment did not help, and trips over the fence did not cease. It was too tempting.

On the other side of Tverskaya Street, behind a fence, stood an enormous empty residence, built during the reign of Catherine II by Duke Prozorovsky. In the forties, it fell into the hands of the rich landowner Guryev, who eventually abandoned it. The building stood with windows knocked out and a rotting roof. In the eighties, it housed Brenko's Pushkin Theater.

Later... devils lived there. Rumors stubbornly circulated in Moscow. Nighttime passersby heard howls inside the house, the clanking of rusted iron, and occasionally one of the building's bricks would fly onto the street. Through its broken windows, many saw a white apparition. The devils played, the old princess went to lunch, and the sergeant leading the punishment detail, a soldier from Arakcheyev's unit, got his three-ruble notes, but no one paid any attention to the building where devils lived. "An unclean power has appeared in the Beloselsky building!" A rumor about the apparition started in the courtyard; from the simple folk it jumped over to the noble residents. Disaster at Guryev's foreshadowed the rumor. A zoo owner, Kreitsberg, the well-known naturalist, immortalized in the poetry of P. Weinberg, rented the first floor. The upper floor remained empty, with broken windows and rotted roof. They delivered the beasts and installed the cages. This is where the disaster started among the old noble's companions: "The beasts frightened the unclear power that has moved in here!" Finally, they saw the white apparition, walking on the stairs.

This was reported to the Mistress. The next day, the German manager's *troika* followed the Mistress's six-horse carriage out of the gates. Later, carts stretched along the road to old Kaluga with the servants' possessions and families.[5] The men walked, barefoot and half-dressed. More than half ran off along the way. The Beloselsky palace was empty for good.

Kreitsberg moved into Guryev's, to a room in the menagerie, together with a trained panther. On the very first night the panther was restless. The naturalist woke to the terrifying roar of the beast, which usually slept peacefully. He lit a candle, took a loaded pistol, and went into the menagerie. An apparition in white

---

5. Gilyarovsky may be stretching the truth a little thin here. The *Road to Old Kaluga* is a Russian folk song that refers to the 49th *verst* of the road (a little over 49 kilometers) as a spot haunted by the ghosts of traveling merchants killed by robbers in the nearby woods and ravines. Inside Moscow's outer ring, the Kaluga Highway is now named Profsoyuznaya Street.

moved before him and disappeared, then started to rise up along the stairs to the second floor. Kreitsberg fired a bullet in its tracks, but the shot extinguished his candle and he had to turn back. The next day, on the upper floor, in the run-down rooms, he found a pile of hay and rags, a sleeping place for dozens of people.

The police surrounded the building. Two tramps were arrested in the courtyard, and the sergeant recognized one of them as a "godson," someone whom he had beaten more than once at the request of the Prince's manager. The following night, soldiers and firefighters surrounded the Beloselsky building, and a gang of thieves was arrested in its courtyard while moving out of Guryev's. Even the sheet was found in which a crook had played the "white lady." The arrested included about a dozen who had been recipients of the sergeant's weekly beatings. They confessed that they invented the white apparition to scare off the baron, and most importantly the manager of the beasts, so that the gang could move into the empty Beloselsky palace, since the menagerie made it impossible to remain at their old hideout. The "ghosts" were cruelly flogged at the Tverskaya Precinct, especially the crook who had played the "white lady." Such is the legend about these two buildings.

Right after the menagerie moved out, in the unrestored halls of Guryev's, in the mezzanine, a dancing school opened. There are still Muscovites alive who danced there in the ruined halls, where pigeons and sparrows flew above the dancers, and hay and twigs stuck out of birds' nests on the columns' capitals. Muscovites still feared these buildings for quite some time, and if it was even a little dark out, they would scurry, just in case, to the opposite sidewalk to be farther from the unclean power.

Years passed. In 1878, after the Russo-Turkish war, the millionaire Malkiyel appeared in Moscow. He supplied footwear to the army. He bought and restored both these buildings: Guryev's he named for himself, and remodeled it to suit Brenko's Pushkin Theater. He named the other building after his wife. In the wing that housed Brenko's theater, the journal *Alarm* had its editorial offices. Brenko's theater went bankrupt, Malkiyel went bankrupt, and the building went to creditors. *Alarm* maintained its presence at the location: the editorial office was decorated with portraits of its principal staff writers, including a very young Anton Chekhov, who was depicted by Konstantin Chichagov, and printed in color on a full page in 1886.

After Malkiyel's renovation, Beloselsky's passed through many merchant hands. Malkiyel had completely redone the façade, and the building no longer had the appearance of an old palace. With time, Malkiyel's entire lower floor, with its mirrored windows, was occupied by Korpus the tailor's shop. The mezzanine was filled with apartments for the wealthy. The interior and grand halls were retained. The white marble staircase was kept as well, and the door leading to the parade ground served as a reminder of Maria Volkonskaya's journey.

Yeliseyev's Store.

The building, in turn, was owned by the merchants Nosov, Lanin, Morozov, and, at the end of the nineties, it was acquired by the Petersburg millionaire Yeliseyev, a cologne maker and wine trader, who started his own renovation. The architect hired by Yeliseyev hid the entire building with a plywood fence, which was an innovation in Moscow. It came out looking like a giant wooden box, so smooth that not a crack remained. A year passed, then two, but the smooth wooden fence still surrounded the site. Old-time Muscovites, recalling that at one time devils had lived there and apparitions had been seen, carefully walked over to the other side of the street, all the more so because tall tale after tall tale was told about the secret construction site. Despite the courtyard's guard and a pack of enormous shepherd dogs from the steppe, daredevils snuck in so they could brag about the wonders inside.

"An Indian pagoda."

"A Mauritanian fortress."

"A peasant Temple of Bacchus."

The last turned out to be closest to the truth. The fence finally was removed, the sidewalks were swept, and thousands of lights sparkled through enormous mirrored panes. It *was* a Temple of Bacchus. This name, however, was not official; on the day the fence was removed, a ceremonial blessing and a prayer service were conducted for "Yeliseyev's Store and Cellar for Russian and Imported Wines."

Starting in the morning, a crowd flooded the street, staring at the luxurious "new style" façade, with a doorway on which, in place of a princely crest, there was something out of mythology, some sort of classical figures. On the sidewalk, the crowd greedily peered through the mirrored glass at miraculous displays of goods unknown in Moscow. Imported fruits were piled high; like a heap of cannonballs, there was a towering pyramid of coconuts, each the size of a child's head; unreachable, two-pound bunches of bananas hung; multi-colored marvels of the ocean kingdom lay poured out like a rainbow; denizens of the unknown ocean depths were on display. Electric lights twinkled above rows of wine bottles. The lights reflected off mirrors whose true height was obscured by mist.

Here is how this Temple of Gluttony was described in an unpublished "Poem about Moscow":

On Tverskaya, in the luxurious Yeliseyev palace
Crowds are attracted
By shining displays of salami, cookies, and treats
Rows of ribs, boiled and smoked
Turkeys, geese,
Sausage with garlic with pistachio and pepper
Cheese of all ages – Chester and Swiss
Gooey brie and granite parmesan...
Produce clerk Alexei Ilyich uses fruits
placed in a fragrant pyramid to
Fill baskets, making bright stripes...
Here, everything from select French Calvilles
to pineapples and wondrous Japanese cherries

The store's doors were still locked, although guests had started to gather inside earlier, entering through the yard. Icons delivered for the prayer service were placed in the middle of the store among exotic plants. Finally, toward noon, the police started pushing the crowd back to the other side of the street. A squad of mounted gendarmes rode up, and with their horses blocked traffic for the arrival of the guests of honor.

Exactly at midday, the appointed hour, the store's doors opened, and an enormous doorman appeared near the entrance. Guests started to arrive, shining with medals and ribbons: military leaders, civilian generals in white pants and tricorn, feathered hats, and church leaders in expensive white robes. All had come from an official service at Uspensky Cathedral. Some had stopped at home to change.

Yeliseyev cleverly took advantage of the opening. In the hall, guests were met by a well-built, blond man, Grigori Grigoriyevich Yeliseyev, in an impeccable cape, with an Order of Vladimir on his neck and the French order of Honorary Legionnaire on a shoulder loop. He received this respected decoration for a substantial charitable donation, and was an Honorary Legionnaire thanks to exhibiting, in Paris, French wines from his cellar. Archbishop Parfeni was met by the synod choir in its red camisoles, with wide sleeves, lined up near the icons and church servants with vestments for the priests.

The store's two-toned interior was fantastic to behold. Yeliseyev had merged the ground floor and mezzanine, demolished the halls and reception rooms of Volkonskaya's former salon, and removed the historic white marble staircase to make room for wine. There were impressively carved, gilded decorations on the walls and ceiling. In the back of the room, a dark niche was visible at the top of the wall, a kind of secret box seat. Next to it was a rare English clock, whose enormous golden pendulum appeared motionless and worked soundlessly.

The room hummed like an anthill while preparations were made for the prayer service. The celebrants donned vestments of golden fabric. Quietly, caped and great-coated guests entered. Behind them were late arrivals, the long-tailed suits of Taganka Street's landed gentry.

In the middle of the prayer service, an enormous, powerful figure arrived, at first glance reminiscent of Turgenev, only taller and with a huge mane of greying hair, like a *bogatyr* from ancient tales. His grey suit coat seemed out of place among the greatcoats, but most of the powerful guests turned and bowed in greeting. Because of his nearsightedness, which even a *pince nez* did not help, this guest could see nothing and recognize no one. Near him bustled both Yeliseyev and the black-suited store manager. This was the most valued guest, a leading wine connoisseur, who founded an enormous wine operation and owned the exemplary vineyards known as New World in the Crimea and the Caucasus: Lev Golitsyn.

Breakfast was served in the second section of the room. The tablecloths were white-as-snow, and crystal and silver sparkled, reflecting a myriad of electrical lights, like a waterfall's droplets, frozen in time, filled to overflowing with all the colors of the rainbow. In the middle, among crystal pitchers filled with wines of various colors, tastes, and ages, stood bottles of every conceivable shape – from the simple, wide-necked, clear bottle holding a golden wine, to champagnes from Bourgogne, cubical Madeiras, and unwieldy and primitive bottles of Hungarian wine. In bottles of old Tokay, the effect of time combined with smoky glass to produce a swamp-like tinge.

Everything was brought to the table at the same time, including the cold appetizers. There were delicious soups. Jellies and gelatins trembled. Enormous red crabs and lobsters were hidden in sauces gone cold, like in the clouds, and changed color under the bright lights. A ham dominated the table. It was boiled, covered by a folded piece of skin, and reddened with rosy fat. A Westphalia baked ham, also with a folded piece of skin, contrasted with the soft white tablecloth. Slices as thin as paper were cut in layers with mathematical precision across the entire ham, and the layers were reassembled so that the ham looked whole. Fat Ostend oysters, arranged in a pattern on a layer of snow that covered a platter, seemed alive. Arranged diagonally

Inside Yeliseyev's, upstairs (above), and in the fish, cheese and caviar cellar (below).

across a wide table, spines of whitefish and osetra sturgeon gleamed rose and amber. Small-grained sterlet caviar glistened black in silver buckets, surrounded by a ring of clear ice, while towering in a mound around the rim were dark osetra caviar and an equal amount of large-grained beluga caviar. Aromatic paste caviar, harvested in March by Sakhalin's traders, lay in mounds on silver dishes. Further, dry, bagged caviar – each grain could be cut in half with a thin knife – towered, retaining the form of the bag. The best paste caviar in the world, with a special earthy aroma, stood on plates in enormous lumps.

Rows of tables were arranged in a geometric figure. The service ended. Breakfast started. The archbishop in a black robe and hat sat in the place of honor, facing the clock and the hanging box. All the rest of the guests were seated strictly by rank and social position. Under the box, on a stage, sat an orchestra.

From the church hierarchy, only the archbishop, an old local priest, and a deacon with a rare bass voice stayed for breakfast. It was the bass's responsibility to end the breakfast by singing a blessing. The rest of the church hierarchy, after receiving "crackers" and buckets of treats for their families, left satisfied with their gifts. The archbishop was treated to the most expensive wines, but he only "put them to his lips," while providing a running commentary, however, that would have done honor to the finest gourmet. The archbishop responded to Yeliseyev's zealous hospitality, "Don't ask, I won't do it. Some time, there, after... But now, you yourself can see, it will do no good." The deacon drank as much as he could, pouring an unbelievable amount, glass after glass, from the bottles standing before him. He smacked his lips with delight.

The room grew louder. Quaffing prodigious amounts of expensive wines, the guests went too far. After the toasts, accompanied by soft music from the orchestra, a drunken guest stood up and demanded the floor. Yeliseyev looked, made a nervous gesture, bent down to the Archbishop, and whispered something in his ear. The Archbishop winked to the deacon sitting at the end of the table, who had not taken his eyes from his master. The sound of a knife hitting a plate, the orator calling for attention, still hung in the air when throughout the hall resounded the roar of a lion: this was the deacon coughing to test his voice. Like a mountain, he stood up and his voice boomed across the room, setting to sway the chandeliers' small crystal prisms. "Blessings on this house! Health and prosperity!" and by the time he reached the final "blessing," the audience had grown frightened. The official part of the ceremony was over. The archbishop rose, bowed, and with a gesture suggested that everyone remain seated. The owner escorted him to the exit. Thunderous octaves echoed in a smooth tone near the ceiling, then the curtain to the mysterious box on the wall suddenly opened and, from inside, bright as sunshine, came a lively song:

Horses, troika, fluffy snow,
Frosty night all round...

Spotting in the box a choir of young women in white dresses, the audience forgot the deacon. They wildly applauded Anna Zakharovna, who, small and plump, in a lily dress sparkling with diamonds, bowed from her box, opened her arms, and blew kisses.

The next day, and from then on for many years, until the revolution, Yeliseyev's was crowded with customers and the sidewalks in front were full of hopeless, and at times starving, but curious onlookers in the windows: "They're eating *people*. Well, well!"

Customers did not walk to this store, they rode. At both ends of the building, on both sides of the street, and deep into Gnezdnikovsky Alley, personal rigs were parked: pairs, singles, carts, and larger carriages, one better than the next.[6] A huge doorman with a face like a full moon, dressed in livery with shiny buttons but no crest, accompanied by helpers, carried baskets and packages for ladies dressed in chinchilla and sable, with drivers in beaver hats and luxurious, military Nikolaev cloaks with hoods. With a thunderous voice, the doorman summoned a coachman, loaded the purchases in the carriage, and with his right hand removed the reins from the post on the fly, while holding in his left what he received "for tea."[7]

All the privileged customers knew the store's salesmen, and used the first names and patronymics of the most distinguished. "Ivan Fyodrich, what would you suggest?" Ivan Fyodorovich knew his customers' tastes in both his meat and fish departments. He knew what to suggest: who needed salmon, soft as butter, who needed fresh lobster or a crab, turning red like a monster in the window. He knew who needed caviar, and he remembered that one liked beluga, another sturgeon, and a third a variety from the Black Sea, and salted at that. Ivan Fyodorovich remembered everyone and spoke with every such customer as an equal, working with the tastes of each.

"Over here, Nikolai Semyonich, from Siberia, smoked salmon and marinated, baked trout. Very good. Tried it myself. Yesterday, Count Riboper and Karl Andreyevich came by. Today, they ordered more. Would you like me to wrap some?"

He finished up and hurried over to a tall lady, to whom all bowed.

"May I help you, Olga Osipovna?"

"Here's what you can get me, Ivan Fyodorich, a nice little pound of butter. There's some Finnish butter over there..."

"There is, there is, Olga Osipovna."

"And a little round package of pickled herring. My husband bought some yesterday."

"I know, Madame, Mikhail Provich bought some yesterday."

O.O. Sadovskaya, who came in almost every day, enjoyed a special place of honor as a beloved actress.[8] In general, humbler people hesitated to enter Yeliseyev's golden store. Ladies usually crowded around the fruit display, where the grey, tall, and self-assured purchasing agent Alexei Ilyich was at one counter, and at the other

---

6. The intersection of Greater and Lesser Gnezdnikovsky Alleys is not far off Tverskaya Street, on the opposite side.
7. In Russian, "чаевые," meaning a tip.
8. Olga Osipovna Sadovskaya (1849-1919) – one of the most honored actresses of her day.

stood his assistant, the young and handsome Alexander Ivanovich. They knew all of their customers could pack their purchases so that not a single apple would get a blemish, nor a single bunch of grapes would be damaged.

The store was run by a manager, Sergei Kirillovich, while Yeliseyev came to Moscow only for day trips: he was busy with the construction of an identical Temple of Bacchus in Petersburg, on Nevsky Prospect, where the firm's main store, founded by his father, was located. Arriving in Moscow on one of these trips, he was told that, for three days, a bureaucrat with a badge and a briefcase had been asking to speak with "himself" on important business. He had just appeared again at the store and asked for a meeting. Yeliseyev spoke with the humbly-dressed man in his luxurious office, sitting in an armchair by a writing table. Yeliseyev did not even invite him to sit.

"What would you like?"

"I would like to seal the doors to your store. I could have done that as early as yesterday or the day before, but I did not want to do it without seeing you. I am the newly re-appointed tax officer for this precinct."

Yeliseyev stood, shook his hand, and indicated the middle chair, saying: "Be seated, please."

"If you don't mind, I'd prefer to sit here at the writing table. It will be easier for me to write up a violation."

"What kind of violation?"

"For illegal trade in wine, which, to avoid getting called on the carpet myself, I cannot allow under any circumstances."

Yeliseyev immediately guessed the real issue, and objected:

"The authorities have permitted me a store trading in wine. This, it seems, you should know."

"The authorities licensed you to sell wine, but they missed the fact that an entrance into an establishment selling wine is not allowed within 40 meters of a church. Where are your 40 meters?"

The further conversation between Yeliseyev and the tax officer is not known, but the fact is that work boiled all that night. In the morning, the sign for the sale of wine was affixed to the other end of the building, looking out into Kozitsky Alley. The wine cellar had a separate entrance, and it was blocked off from the store.

Wines ordered at the store had to be claimed at the Kozitsky Alley entrance, but, of course, this rule did not apply to everyone. Yeliseyev's principal income came from wine. The most expensive wines kept in his cellar were imported by his father on his three sailing ships, which cruised in the first half of the last century between the Gulf of Finland, and the harbors of France, Spain, Portugal, and the Madeira Islands, where Yeliseyev owned wine warehouses.

MYTHOLOGY INCLUDED BOTH BACCHUS AND blind Femida, goddess of the law, with scales in her hands on which, invisible to her and, apparently, everyone else, were weighed people's acts and crimes. Her eyes were blindfolded so there could be no hint of favoritism. Thousands of years had passed since the disappearance of the Olympian gods, but Bacchus's worshippers had not vanished, and his priests had built temples. They also built a temple to Femida, whose duties included weighing the sins of Bacchus's worshippers. She was depicted in temples all over the world with a blindfold. Thus it was in Paris, London, New York, Calcutta, Tambov and Mozhaisk. But in Moscow's Kremlin, in a niche in a vestibule, she had her eyes open wide! When they removed the blindfold is unknown. Maybe she never had one?

In 1864-6, from the very start of judicial reforms, Femida stood in the Kremlin's "Temple of Justice," the building for judicial decrees. The statue was similar to others around the world: scales, a sword for punishment, and thick legal tomes. The goddess lacked only the most important thing, a blindfold. For almost half a century, the sighted Femida stood, and might have remained whole and unchanged to this day. No one paid her any attention. When a reporter wrote a note about this for the liberal newspaper *Russian Gazette*, it was not published. "It can't be done. The shame would go all across Europe."[9]

When Yeliseyev rented his building's third floor, under the same roof as the store, to an arbiter, courtroom-style symbols of the law were put on display: a crest depicted Peter I's decree and a golden post with a crown on top, about which two lines have long been repeated:

In Russia there is no law,
There's a post, and on the post a crown

Here, they put a blindfold on Femida. But they did this, it would seem, so that she could not see the excesses in the nearby Temple of Bacchus, whose worshippers were sometimes brought by the Fates to the Temple of Femida. The goddess of justice had no luck here: a two-ton plaster ceiling with ornate moldings collapsed in the main hall: the ceiling fell at night in an empty building. The Temple of Bacchus stood until the October Revolution. Today, it appears unchanged: it is two-toned, with decorative molding. The difference is that no doorman summons coachmen, and the shop is filled with people buying simple groceries. In the evenings, the same bright lights shine through the mirrored panes.

---

9. A statue of Femida without a blindfold stands outside the Russian Federation's Supreme Court building in Moscow. She carries no sword but has a shield and the traditional scales. Her face and body recall socialist realism. She's a bit hard to spot in Google earth, but fortunately there is a nice photo of the piece on the court's home page: supcourt.ru.

BANYA

THE *BANYA* WAS THE ONE place that no Muscovite avoided. No master tradesman, no grandee, no poor man, no rich man could live without the commercial
baths. In the eighties, the all-powerful "master of the capital," the military Governor-General V.A. Dolgorukov, frequented the Sandunovskiye Baths, where, in an
elegant room, in its seventh section, he bathed in silver basins and tubs. This, despite the fact that his palace had marble baths, which at that time were still a rarity.
Moscow took a while to get used to them, preferring, in the traditional manner,
to steam, use switches, relax in a dressing room, and "scratch their tongues" in
friendly conversation.

Every level of society had its favorite bath. The wealthy and, in general, people
of means visited the gentry section. Workers and the poor went to the common
section for five kopeks. The water, the heat, and the steam were identical, only
the settings were different. *Banyas* are *banyas*![1] A sponge cost 13 kopeks; soap, one
kopek. Many of them stand now as they were then, and in the same buildings as at
the end of the last century. Their clientele is different, and their former managers
and the owners of the baths are no longer there. Stories about them will soon disappear entirely, because there is no one to tell them. There is no literature about
everyday life in Moscow's *banyas*. At the time, all of this was in plain sight, and no
one was interested in writing about something that everyone knew: who would read
about the *banyas*? Only in Dal's dictionary could one find a telling characteristic of
many *banyas*: "Commercial *banyas* are scrubbed clean by others, who themselves are
drowning in filth."[2]

---

1. The plural of *banya* is actually *bani*; we have, however, opted to use *banyas* because it reads better in English.
2. *Explanatory Dictionary of the Living Great Russian Language*, compiled and published in 1863 by Vladimir Ivanovich Dal
   (1801-1872). The work went through multiple editions and then reprints. Even today it is a priceless reference work.

Sandunovskiye Baths.

I judge by my own experience: I worked for half a century as a chronicler of Moscow's everyday life, and it would never occur to me to utter even a word about the baths; although I knew no small amount about them, knew the everyday peculiarities of particular baths, and met there with interesting Muscovites from all levels of society. Moscow had 60 *banyas* of the most varied character; moreover, each of them had regulars who considered themselves real Muscovites. In the first edition of *Moscow and Muscovites*, not once did I say a word and never would have mentioned them now, if it were not for the conditions in which the *banshchiki*[3] lived, if one kind man had not tweaked my nose, as they say, and reminded me of a phrase that I heard somewhere in the deep countryside, maybe Zaraysk, maybe Kolomenskoye. I remember only that the village was near the Oka River, where I often went in the eighties to hunt. There, among the old men, local residents, I heard this phrase more than once:

"We are Muscovites!"

With what pride they said it, sitting on heaps outside their small huts.

"We are Muscovites!"

An unfamiliar, hulking old man with a grey moustache walked up to me.

"I've known you for decades and read your latest books. You will forgive me please for allowing myself to bother you." He looked at me and smiled, "You've got a small debt to pay."

I was more than a little surprised.

"I have no new debts, and as for the old ones, with money lenders, the revolution settled accounts for me, for which I'm grateful," I said to him.

"That's just the thing, there is a debt, and it's got to be paid."

"Whom am I in debt to?"

---

3. Those who work at the *banya*.

"You're in debt to all of Moscow! In your books about Moscow not a single word is written about the baths. Moscow without the baths is not Moscow. You know Moscow, and it's your fault that you haven't written about us, old Muscovites. We ask you not to forget about the baths."

We took turns sharing reminiscences, both carried away by the conversation's theme, each with his own perspective. We spoke disjointedly, one word brought forth another, one detail, another; one man knew something from one side, the other from another. Word after word, detail after detail, we sketched bright pictures and characters. Both of us were focused on one goal, to illuminate a familiar reality from every direction.

"I still have the strength to work, but as soon as I have given Moscow all I can, I'll go back home. We're almost all Muscovites. That's why it's insulting that you have forgotten us. Your audience is much broader than you thought when you titled the book. It's not only those who were born in Moscow, but those from the greater Moscow region as well. Yaroslavl supplied waiters; Vladimir provided carpenters; Kaluga gave bakers. *Banya* workers came from three different areas, but only from two or three parts within each, and not one by one, but more like groups from nests. The Kolomenskoye area had only a few nests for Moscow: folks from Kolomenskoye preferred to work in Petersburg. For ages, Moscow benefited from *banya* workers from the regions of Ryazan, Tula, Kashirsky, and Venevsky. So, from generation to generation, men and women went to Moscow. I was brought there as a 10-year-old boy, as our grandfathers had been, and our fathers, and our children."

Before the railroads, children were brought to Moscow with someone going the same way, on horses. A relative, living in Moscow, would travel in the same way to the village for a visit, dressed in a caftan, a cap with a brim, boots with galoshes, and on his vest a watch with a chain. All his relatives and acquaintances rejoiced, and envied him, listening to tales of good jobs and life in Moscow.

A father, with a 10- or 12-year-old son, would ask for him to be taken to relatives at the baths. They equipped the young boy somewhat sensibly, giving him two pairs of bark shoes, a vest of rough cloth, and two sets of homespun underwear. They took care of his passport, in which they needed to add a year to his age, which cost money.

In Moscow, the boy was delivered to relatives or people from the same village working in a *banya*. Here, they first cut his hair, wash him, and give him a city look. Teaching starts with "geography." First, they show him the *banya* and how to get in through the back door, then the location of the tavern, where to run for hot water, and the bakery. Thus, the future Muscovite assumes his rights and responsibilities. The work done by small boys, except for closing the *banya* and packages, was much the same as the adults, although they did have their specialties. On the two "non-bathing" days of the week – Monday and Tuesday – boys washed bottles

Boys working in Moscow at the turn of the century.

Barber shop in the Kitayskiye Baths.

and helped pour *kvas*, which was sold in the baths. On bathing days, they prepared bunches of switches, which on Sundays and the eve of big holidays, at some *banyas* could mean as many as three thousand pieces. These switches were carted from distant villages, especially from around Gzhel, and tied together loosely in pairs. The boys' job was to untie the switches.

In the *banyas*, the boys worked in the dressing rooms, helped the barbers, and even learned how to clip nails and trim callouses. They also prepared sponges and cleaned them so they scrubbed with little effort. For its devotees, they brought the best sponge, the "baron," tender and soft. They brought them especially for Moscow's bakers; it was three times more expensive than others. On the two non-bath days of the week, tasks were often related to housekeeping. The manager might set them to cleaning the courtyard of his own house, taking out the garbage, or clearing snow from the roof.

The boys got both work assignments and beatings from the "small pieces." These were semi-managers, who were in charge of both men and women who worked at the *banya*. They especially exploited the steam workers, whose working and living conditions were incomparably bad. From five in the morning until 12 midnight, barefoot and naked, except for a small cloth around his waist, a steamer toiled non-stop with every muscle in his body, in awful temperatures, and to make matters worse he was always wet. He dried off only once per day, for half an hour, at midday, when for lunch he threw on a shirt and shower shoes. That's a steamer. He received neither money from the manager, nor a salary. Steamers lived by tips from those who had bathed thanks to their hard labor in the steam, heat, and wet. There were no fixed charges for washing and steaming.

"As much as your kindness allows!" was their usual answer to a question from a washed customer. They gave various amounts. Steamers knew their customers, who gave how much, and tried to adjust their washing and scrubbing accordingly. The

millionaire Solodovnikov, who never asked how much, came to wash at the Sandun-ovskiye baths, and silently gave 40 kopeks, of which the *banshchik* would get only 20.

Steamers received no salary, and to make matters worse, they were required to hand over half of their tip money to the manager or his deputy, the "small piece," the "little manager." Moreover, the steamer was responsible for heating and cleaning the steam room and the washroom. The "small piece"[4] watched when the steamer got something for "tea," he knew his customers and who gave what. Getting the usual 20 kopeks from Solodovnikov, he did not even ask who it was from, but said, "from the millionaire," and cursed.

The "small piece" paid rent to the *banya* manager and hired and fired workers himself, aside from the steamers, whom the manager controlled himself. The "small pieces" lived with their families at the *banyas*, had separate rooms, and paid rent that varied by *banya*, from 20 to 100 rubles per month.

In their turn, the dressing room workers, who also did not receive a salary from the manager, were supposed to pay the "small pieces," from their tips, various charges depending on the number of divans, corners, sheets, and cabins they served. The "small pieces" were supposed to wash the sheets from the divans, pay the work-ers, feed them and the boys, and also answer for the cleanliness of the baths and for the loss of items by bathers in the "gentry" baths.

The 1905 Revolution made its way to the "small pieces." Workers decreed their liquidation, and succeeded. But within two years, due to the intensity of the reac-tion, they appeared again and existed in full strength until 1917.

Some of the baths, especially the "common" *banyas*, faced thefts of underwear, shoes, and occasionally an entire bundle of clothes. There were bands of *banya* thieves who had worked out their own system. They stole underwear and clothes that were drying in the "hot room." This was done in the following way. The thieves fed the stove so that the room was filled with a cloud of hot steam; many who could not take the heat left for the washroom. Taking advantage of their absence, the thieves filched underwear from the benches and hid it right there in the room. In the evening, they would return to the *banya* and pick up what they had hidden. For this, the *banshchiki* had to reimburse customers from their meager earnings.

There also was a theft system practiced in the "gentry" sections of the *banya*, where the "small pieces" answered for items that disappeared. Bathers handed in their clothes in the dressing room and received a rough little number on a loop of string, and sometimes put it around their neck or tied it to their arm, or sometimes just attached it to the handle of the locker and went off to wash and steam. The thief, having watched in the dressing room, replaced the number with his own, left

---

4. Small piece: кусочника.

quickly, recovered the clothes, and disappeared with them. Instead of their own expensive clothes, the bather found rags and scraps.

The *banya* thieves were strong and elusive. Some managers, to save their baths' reputations, even made deals with the thieves, paying them monthly protection.The "bought" thieves guarded them against outside thieves. If they caught one, it ended badly. There was no mercy for competitors; if they did not kill them outright, they scarred them for life. Almost all the baths had wooden posts supporting the ceiling. If a thief was caught, let's say, at seven in the morning, they would tie him to a post close to the exit, half-naked and barefoot. Among those coming to the *banya* were some who had been robbed there, and they often took out their anger on these captives. At midnight, before the *banya* shut down, the beaten thief sometimes, but rarely, was sent to the police. Most often, he was simply driven out of the building with no regard to the weather or season.

Future *banya* workers were trained on the job, starting in childhood. They had significantly fewer runaways than country boys training for other jobs. Boys ran from the beatings of tailors, cobblers, barbers, plasterers, and painters, especially those who worked for small-time managers, "rodents," where they, aside from training in a trade, ran all sorts of errands for their managers and especially for their drunken masters and mistresses. In rags, half-naked, they were sent at all times of day and night with buckets to the trough for water; they got up earlier than everyone in the quarters; they brought in firewood, and put on the samovar in the dark. Suffering from unbearable labor and beatings, with no friends their own age, never hearing a kind word, they ran back to their villages, where sometimes they remained. If their parents returned them to the manager, they would often escape to Khitrovka, and join gangs of thieves their own age; through the slums and prisons, they often were exiled to hard labor.

With the *banshchiki*, this happened rarely. They worked and lived together with their villagers and relatives, watched how they worked, followed their example, and small tips for little services gave them the ability, in their own way, to relax. On holidays, with relatives, they went to festivals in Sokolniki, near Novodevichy Monastery, or on Krasnaya Presnya, or went to sideshows and the circus. They were entranced by rumors from relatives in the village noting some Fedka or Stepka, almost the same age, who had come from Moscow to be married in the village, in boots and, what's more, with a watch and chain, like a real Muscovite. Relatives and folks from home, when the time came, arranged credit for them for clothes and shoes. They sewed underwear in the village out of indestructible home-woven cloth and buttons. For holiday shirts they bought fabric and thread in Moscow. At the market, the *banya* workers bought only boots, the most necessary shoes, which the *banshchiki* could not get by without. At work, they wore only sandals and rags, but everyone had nice holiday clothes.

Calfskin boots and high leather galoshes were the height of style. Ordering such boots was an event: they cost 30 rubles. They wore them for a long time, then had new uppers made, and the leftovers were fixed up and worn in the *banya*.

Their outerwear included a cloth caftan, long "Siberian" pants, a vest with a thick collar, and in winter a sheepskin coat covered with cloth and a ram's wool collar. Like boots, all these items were worn for years, and assembled over the years, first one piece, and then another. Boys naturally wore hand-me-downs, but they prepared for years ahead of time, putting away "capital" for a down payment to the tailor or boot maker, saving kopek after kopek, held by a relative, an older friend, or an "auntie" from the *banya*.

Boys trained until they were 17 or 18. In this time, they learned the ins and outs of the *banya*, how to get along with customers, cut hair, and accurately trim callouses. After learning these skills, an trained teenager would petition the manager to become a candidate for an open position; otherwise, a trip back home to be married was awkward: they would laugh in the village. A new candidate, preparing to marry, would go to Maroseyko Street, where scissors were painted on a sign above the gate and Ion Pavlov, the *banya's* tailor, lived in the courtyard. The candidate and an uncle, an old friend, would show up at Pavlov's.

"Ion Pavlych! This candidate would like to get a sheepskin coat made, a caftan, and all the rest... time to marry him off!"

Ion Pavlych would make him what he needed, just like he did for the other *banshchiki*, and it would last for many years. He only worked with *banyas*, and the *banyas* never knew another tailor like this man, like them, from the country. All his tailoring and materials were done on credit, for installment payments. They paid in crumbs, and a basic account reckoning was done twice a year, at Easter and Christmas. It was the same way with the boot maker. A candidate went with an uncle to Karetny Row, to the village boot maker.

"Peter Kirsanich, measure him please, he's going to get married!"

Peter Kirsanich measures him with a strip of paper, writes something on it and asks:

"A raised heel?"

"To hell with the heel!" the uncle answers for him.

"It would be nice, just a little, Unc, for the honeymoon," the "aspirant" pleads. "The raised heel is more stylish!"

"Fine."

"What's your name?"

"Petrunka."

The boot maker scratches something with a pencil on the size slip, and when saying goodbye, says: "Two Sundays will pass, and I'll deliver on the third Sunday."

Kirsanich has served three generations of *banshchiki*. He does an especially large number of repairs. Customers run up now and again: some need heels, some an insole, some a worn upper, and for the *banshchiki* new red boots on a rubber sole for the moisture, for the woman chiropractor, shoes without heels, and repairs, all kinds of repairs. Just try and finish it all.

Every order was marked, which *banya*, whose shoes. Summer in a cart, and winter in a broken-down sleigh, Peter Kirsanich harnesses up a thick-headed old horse, loads 10 or more large sacks, and sits on them, right behind the coachman, his 10-year-old grandson.

"First things first; to Sandunovskiye, then to Kitayskiye, then to Chelyshevskiye!"

"I know, grandfather, I know, like always!"

Sunday the baths are closed to the public. Workers gather in the dressing room: Kirsanich has promised to deliver. And here he is with a large sack, on it a label written in chalk: "Sandun." A most friendly and lively greeting. Kirsanich carefully unpacks his work and begins to call out: Cruel Ivan! Sad Fyodor! Semyon Shotglass! Sasha the Bubble! Tall Masha!" Family names weren't used at that time among friends, but more often nicknames. Nicknames were given according to one's character, figure, or habits. What's a nickname if it doesn't instantly tell everything about someone? Ivan truly is cruel, Fyodor is always on the edge of tears, Shotglass has a red nose, Masha is tall and thin, and Sasha is small, just like a soap bubble.

They receive their orders. They settle up. A flask appear, glasses, salami with cucumbers. They honor and thank their country friend, Kirsanich. He leaves after drinking his "first reinforcements"[5] to the Kitayskiye Baths. There, the same scene. The same roll-call by nickname, but no one responds to the call for "Shoeless Petrunka." Only when shiny boots with galoshes are pulled out of the bag did a small person with a bright face jump up, and his uncle burst out laughing:

"Shoeless!"

Again, there was a flask, a celebration, and an escort to the Chelyshevskiye Baths. From there, they went further along a well-known route. Late in the evening, they set out for home, but Kirsanich is no longer alone, but with some "Shotglass" or other, both draining their "last reinforcement." They would sleep soundly on the empty sacks in the back of the cart. Kirsanich always ended his working week with this type of celebration.

The Sandunovskiye Baths, like the alley, were named at the start of the last century in honor of the famous actress-singer Sandunova. They are still named the same as they were in Pushkin's time. On the other side of Neglinnaya Street, in Krapivinsky Alley, on an empty lot between two ponds, were the Lamakinskiye

---

5. A few drinks.

Kitayskiye (later Tsentralniye) Baths.

Prusakovskiye Baths.

baths. Their owner was Avdotya Lamakina. The place was a slum, with dirty baths, but because of the name, they were always crowded.

Sandunova and her husband, a well-known actor, Sila Sandunov,[6] whose building faced the neighboring Zvonarsky Alley, also owned a large pond. Here, Sandunova built nice baths and rented them to Lamakina, who, while retaining the older baths that had made her fortune, spared no expense on decorating the new ones. They became Moscow's best. The Sandunova name helped create success: the baths in Krapinivsky Alley remained under the Lamakin name, but the new ones became forever known as Sandunovskiye.

Moscow rushed in, especially to the men's and women's gentry sections, which were built with conveniences unheard of in Moscow: a mirrored dressing room, clean sheets on soft divans tidied by servants, and experienced male and female *banshchiki*. The dressing room became a club where the most varied parts of society met. Each found here a circle of acquaintances and, moreover, a buffet with all types of beverages, from *kvas* to the champagnes Moët and Ay.[7] Griboyedov's and Pushkin's Moscow came here, the same people that went to Zinaida Volkonskaya's salon and the English Club.

When *Journey to Arzrum* appeared in the press, where Pushkin described the baths in Tiflis in such a fascinating way, Lamakina, as a test, hired a Tatar *banshchik* from Tiflis, but he did not have much success with native Muscovites, who loved a hot, high bench in the steam room and hot birch switches.[8] No more Tatars were

---

6. Yelizaveta Semyonova Sandunova (1772-1826). Other sources say the street was named after Yelizaveta's husband, Sila Nikolayevich Sandunov (1756-1820), a famous comic actor.

7. Ay is actually a region where some of the finest champagnes are made, not a brand *per se*.

8. *Journey to Arzrum During the Campaign of 1829* (*Путешествие в Арзрум во время похода 1829 года*), one of Pushkin's prose works, prepared for publication in 1835, was a revision and expansion of a diary he kept, sporadically, during his turn as a volunteer in the Caucasus in 1829.

hired. However, our *banshchiki* took Pushkin's advice and installed, for those who like them, liquid soap dispensers and woolen wash-mittens.

Later, family sections appeared at the baths, where high society ladies brought their dogs. Maids washed the dogs along with their masters. This started at the Sandunovskiye Baths, and slowly spread to other baths with expensive "gentry" and "merchant" sections. Squads of soldiers were brought from their barracks to the "common baths." They took two kopeks from each, and supplied one bundle of switches for 10 men. Still later, in the beginning of the eighties, all the baths decreed that a bundle of switches would cost a kopek, which led to a scene at the Ustinovsky Baths: customers broke a window, and during a fistfight people ran-off naked.

Charging a kopek for the switches, the managers made good money, but did not add any improvements to the baths. In general, the managers used everything, truth and lies, to squeeze out kopeks and rubles wherever possible. Some baths even stole city water. Thus, at the Chelyshevsky Baths, to everyone's great surprise, the pond in the courtyard, which was always full, dried-out unexpectedly and the baths were left without water. But the next day water reappeared, and things went on as before. The secret of the water's disappearance and reappearance was never revealed to the public. The authorities learned nothing about it, and those who knew kept quiet for their own good. It was quite simple: there was a large holding tank on Lubyanskaya Square where street cleaners filled their water tanks. The water came from the My-tishchinsky water pipe, and the guard closed a valve when the tank was full. When Chelyshevsky Pond had to be filled, the guard did not close the valve for the tank, and water flowed through pipes to the *banya*'s pond.

Moscow's baths were almost always built on the banks of the Moscow River, the Yauza, or streams such as Chechery, Sinichky, Khapilovky, or close to spring-fed ponds. The *banyas* were typically built of wood, and were only on one floor, since in those times, with a primitive water supply, it was difficult to get water to a second floor. Baths were split into three sections: the dressing room, the soap room, and the hot room.

Outside the city center the common baths had no conveniences at all. At most of them, even the toilet was somewhere in the courtyard: year round, in rain and winter storms, bathers could get to them only through the open air. There were no true water pipes under the floor: soapy water flowed into pits in the courtyard through wooden gutters, and then followed other gutters to the river, perhaps only only 10 meters lower than where the water was taken. Such baths are depicted in engravings published by Rovinsky. Such were the Serebryanicheskiye Baths on the Yauza.

The *banyas* were heated by "ceramic stoves" in the hot departments and "Dutch Ovens" in the dressing rooms. The most beautiful element of a *banya* was thought to be its ceramic stove. In some *banyas*, it heated both the "hot room" and the "washroom." In the old days, they used only wood for fuel, which was floated in huge piles from the upper reaches of the Moscow River, near Mozhaisk and Ruza, and was landed near Dorogomilov, at Red Meadow. The arrival of the wood was a spring holiday for Muscovites. Thousands of spectators strolled along the river and the Dorogomilovsky Bridge: "The rafts are here!"

Saturdays, and the eves of the biggest holidays, were the most popular bath days, when the *banya* was crowded and lines of bathers, waiting for the faucets, held lightweight linden-wood tubs that had replaced the traditional, heavy oak tubs. In the gentry sections there were drinks, rest, haircuts, shaves, callous removal, *banky*[9] were applied, and even teeth were pulled. The common baths had, one can truly say, "polyclinics" that treated all types of ills. The medical workers included porters, barbers, steamers, and women chiropractors, and here and there they had masseurs, even in the days when the word was unknown.

On the edge of town at the common baths the "polyclinic" presented the following picture. Saturdays, after five or six in the morning, the doors to the *banya* do not close. People flow by endlessly. A barber is hunkered down in a corner of the dressing room and, without any sanitary precautions, cuts hair and shaves customers. In his downtime, he practices medicine: he lets blood, applies *banky* and leeches, and pulls teeth.

The *banya's* washroom was filled with steam: on the bench was a heavy, red, hot body, and a barber bustled nearby with a box of questionable cleanliness, in which were 12 *banky*, pliers, and a small container of kerosene. A wire tipped with a cork was placed in a bottle. All *banky* ready, the barber set fire to the cork, and with its help created a vacuum in a *banka*, and started the application. After two or three minutes a *banka* can pull into itself a centimeter or more of flesh. Barbers had a rule to leave the *banky* for about 10 minutes, so that they could work better, but it turned out in practice in different ways. This time the barber went out for a smoke, and the victim of his art lay quietly, waiting further suffering. Finally, he had run out of patience, and asked those nearby to fetch the barber. "I'll take care of you in just a moment, it's not too long, boss!" rang out in answer.

Finally the barber came back and lit his torch. Inside, the *banka* clung to his flesh, a reddish lump. The "surgeon" took a dirty, rusty blade, held it up against the lump, sliced the skin, manipulated the torch, and reapplied the *banky*. In 3-5 minutes it was full of blood. Each *banka* was removed and the blood dripped to the floor. The *banshchik* poured a bucket of water on the patient, who then went into the dressing room covered with red welts. After this, a consultation usually was held about the effects of the *banky*.

---

9. *Banky, banochky*, plural from *banka, banochka* – a folk treatment that uses a small glass jar (*banka*), affixed to the skin by creating a vacuum inside using the heat of a flame. Banky are used to allegedly draw out "poisons" that interfere with healthy body functions. This folk medicine is still practiced all over Russia.

Aside from the *banky*, the barbers let blood. Back in the 1880s, on the edge of the city, one would run across signs with the words: "Haircuts, shaves, leeches, and blood-letting." Such signs were usually above the entrance, and on their sides were often painted two big, long pictures that showed how this was done. In one, a man sits with a lathered beard. A barber holds the man's nose with an index finger and thumb, raising his head, and leaning toward him, with a razor half-covered with lather, in his right hand. On the other side of the sign sits a large, red-faced *bogatyr*, in a shirt with its sleeves rolled up to his shoulders, with a barber standing before him holding a bloody lancet; showing that the operation is done; a large stream of blood pulses from the *bogatyr*'s arm, like a fountain, and he holds it so that a large bucket is half full of blood. These operations were also done in the washroom, but without a boy with a tub, and the blood fell right to the floor. "Bloodletting" was favored by stevedores, teamsters, cab drivers, clerks starting to put on weight, and aging merchants.

Women's baths had their own "treatments." For face whitening, they cooked herbs, and in the gentry sections women washed their faces with almond flour. Later, other treatments became popular, including washing hair with kerosene to encourage growth. Here, female *banya* workers took care of the bathers. Female chiropractors worked only in the common baths. They helped with treatment of men. Someone, bent over, arrives at the *banya*, goes to the order taker, and requests a chiropractor. "My spine is acting up!" He says the same thing to the woman. She gives him a small container with some sort of liquid, sends him off first to bathe, and then to apply the liquid with a brush, with instructions to come back after the bath. Washed and dressed, the ailing man called for the woman. She directed him to lay down with his belly across the threshold of an open door, put a dry bundle of switches on his waist, and struck him lightly with an axe a few times along the switches while whispering indecipherable incantations. The procedure was called an "intersection."

Women chiropractors played a huge role: it was because of these women that many people went to the *banya*. Bath managers valued them highly: the women corrected jaw problems, fixed hernias, aligned stomachs for both men and women, and added height. Their specialty was midwifery. A few weeks before the event, a pregnant woman would begin to ask:

"Babushka Anisya,[10] don't leave me!"

"Fine, but come to the *banya* more often. It will help set the child on the right path. When I'm needed, I'll be there!"

Long before Gonetsky transformed the Sandunovskiye Baths into a palace, A.P. Chekhov loved to go there: it was comfortable, nothing fancy, no shiny fixtures.

---

10. "Grandmother Anisya": a term of endearment that does not indicate a familiar link.

"Anton, let's go to the *banya*," his brother Nikolai an artist, all stained with paint, would say. "I'd like to go, but I'm nervous. What if we unexpectedly, you remember, run across Sergienko. Last time, I was dressed, and was leaving while he was coming in. He grabbed me and droned on for maybe an hour. What if we see him again? I love Sandun... But the air around it is poor: in dry weather it's dusty, and in the rain filth flows from every building into the Neglinka." A.P. Chekhov at one point was forced by circumstance to live in one of the apartments in the renovated *banya's* courtyard, which had the same air as the former Sandun.

IN THOSE DAYS, BIRYUKOV, THE *banya* king as they called him in Moscow, owned the baths. He came to Moscow as a young boy, in little *lapty*,[11] at the time when the Lamakins were in charge, worked for 10 years, renovated a series of *banyas*, and even owned Sandunovskiye. Later, the building and the *banya* were part of a debt settlement with the gentry millionaire Firsanov. What did Firsanov get? Firsanov invested in large, well-built properties, and managed things so that the building would unavoidably end up his. Many grand mansions and income properties became his prizes. At the time when Sergiyenko buttonholed A.P. Chekhov, Firsanov still only held the mortgage, but within a year he owned it outright. It was an enormous building in Arakcheyev's barracks style, with a luxurious, noble dressing room, a creation of the famous architect of the twenties.

After Ivan Firsanov's death, his daughter Vera became the owner of the baths, 23 buildings in Moscow, and Srednikovo, an estate just outside the city where at one time great writers and poets were guests. Vera Ivanovna lived grandly and happily on Prechistenka Street, in the best of the grand mansions inherited from her father. Golden youths and fashionable *bons vivants* visited, the lions of the capital, and serious people, including powerful judicial officers and lawyers. After the death of her father, Vera Ivanovna conducted major business deals practically alone. She learned what she needed from visiting ministry officials, and ably conducted, from time to time, her own business deals. Around her gathered handsome young people enjoying a good time, solidly wealthy people, government officials, and titled persons hunting for beauty, but most of all for money.

One fine day Moscow gasped: Vera Ivanovna had gotten married! Her husband was a lieutenant in the guards, the son of an army general, Gonetsky. Before the wedding, he was often in Moscow – summers at the races, winters at balls and luncheons. He had made "not a step" toward Vera Ivanovna, although she, through her friends, tried in every way possible to attract him to her group of suitors. Among the friends she instructed to scout Gonetsky, there were some who already knew him.

---

11. Footware made from bast (woven birch bark), see photo, page 35.

They convinced "Verochka" that he was the only heir of an old Polish magnate-millionaire, and that he would soon be awash in money.

The friends got their wish. Vera Ivanovna Firsanova became a Gonetskaya. After the wedding the young couple, to avoid visitors, went to Srednikovo. The new husband completely charmed his young wife by proposing that he busy himself with her commercial affairs and work alongside her. After seeing the income account from the Firsanov buildings, Gonetsky declared: "Khludov's Central Baths has been rebuilt! You should be embarrassed to own the Sandunovskiye ruins; they shame the Firsanova name. The Khludovs ought to be knocked aside."

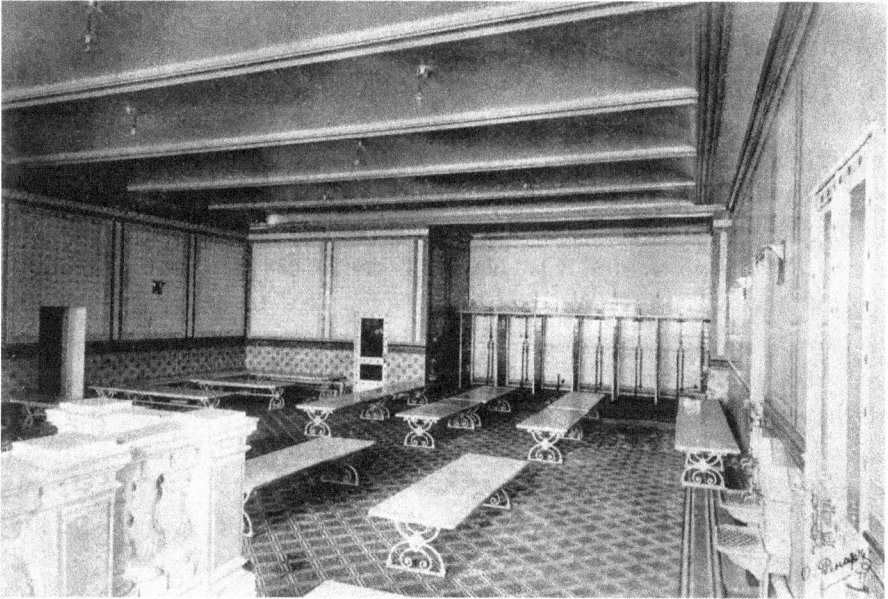

Washroom inside the Sandunovskiye Baths.

After bruising his wife's "merchant pride," Gonetsky pointed out to her the enormous profits earned by the Central Baths. "First, you need to turn the Sandunovskiye Baths into something that Moscow has never before seen, and won't see again. We will replace the ruins with a *banya* palace, do everything according to the latest word in science, and the more money we invest, the more income we will earn. We'll make the Khludovs look like nothing. The press will start to write about our *banyas*, and you will be famous!"

They decided to renovate the old baths. "We need to announce, through the Architecture Society, a competition for designs for the baths," Vera Ivanovna hiccupped. "What? Moscow architects build a *banya*? Why didn't the Khludovs do this? Because they hired a builder from Vienna. Eyebushits, it seems? And he's not among the best. There are more-admired architects. I will not work with Moscow architects. We need to create something new and great, while combining the East and the West in this palace!"

After a tour of Europe's baths, from Turkey to Ireland, there was a pre-construction meeting in the youth palace on Prechistenka Street. Gonetsky led the overall project, and the design was created by the Viennese architect Freidenberg. Taking advantage of the construction of the baths, Gonetsky, in just a few months, had bank checks signed by his wife and submitted for all of his outstanding debts. These disappeared into the malachite stove in the office of a "retired brigadier of the guard" who had given up the luster of guards' parades for commercial millions.

Once, on a hot autumn day, which can happen in September, three short little men marched briskly out of the Tver Gate and up the street, moving past groups of children in shirtsleeves and adults strolling in summer suits. Focused, they noticed no one. Their shaven faces, sweaty and reddened, looked out from the fur collars of warm coats. In their right hands were riding whips, in their left hands, small travelling bags, and one, in a grey lambskin hat pushed up on his brow, carried a bag under his arm and a *banya* bundle of switches. He was a little taller and a bit wider than his fellow travelers. All three were famous jockeys: in the lambskin hat was Voronkov, and the other two were Englishmen, Ambrose and Claydon. In two days, the most lucrative stakes race for two-year-olds would be run. They needed to lose weight, and were returning from the Georgian Baths, where they had been "stretched out" on the benches. They marched briskly, got to All Saints Alley, and went their separate ways home. Claydon lived on Bashkilova Street, and the others in the little track ghetto next to the stables.

"Georgian" baths were a favorite among jockeys and Gypsies living in the Zhivoderk area. The jockeys were the *banya's* favorite customers, they paid a ruble for everything, and most importantly, they sometimes would whisper among themselves about the winning horse at the next day's race. Gypsies, passionate fans of horse racing, took advantage of this information, baking for it in the terrible heat and clouds of steam that the *banshchiki* produced for their generous guests.

AN ACQUAINTANCE WHO KNEW THAT I write about Muscovites once invited me to visit his relative, a *banya* owner. The *banshchik* lived in a *dacha* in Petrovsky Park, and his baths were somewhere on the Yauza River. "He has four name days today: his wife Sofia and three daughters, each a year apart, Vera, Nadezhda, and Lyuba. He was a calculating man: he arranged his daughters births so that in one day, with their mother, he could take care of their name day. The older two daughters were finishing *gymnasium*.

A large room was reserved for the young people: students, those at the *gymnasium*, two or three relatives in blue shirts and pants and tall shiny boots, and two or three quiet, noble women in silk dresses. There was music, singing, and dancing, all accompanied by piano. During the breaks there were poetry recitals and student songs, including *Dubinushka*, student-style. It was the sound of young people celebrating.

Next door, in the reception room, merchants' wives and poor relatives sat motionless, according to social standing, along the wall or in small groups near the three name day girls, who were draped in valuables. They were being served dessert from trays. A few men in coats with and without tails, the former wearing shined boots and the latter in shoes, entertained the ladies.

They went into the next room, where appetizers and drinks covered a large table. They came back, freshened their drinks, and returned to the ladies or went into the next room. There, two tables stood: at one, a quiet game of *preferance*; at the other, *stukolka*.[12] The *preferance* players were older merchants, two solid clerks – one with a medal on his chest, and the host himself, dressed in a suit with tails, with a gold medal on a ribbon around his red neck sticking out of a deep blue silk vest. The *stukolka* players were simpler and younger.

"You, Kirill Makarich, don't let those peepers look at others' cards!"

An office mail boy from the police precinct, a former priest, answered sarcastically:

"What does it say in the rules?"

"What?"

"Well they put it this way: Man, if you want to win, look at the others' cards first, because you'll always have time to look at your own."

From the *stukolka* table was heard:

"Club… Queen of diamonds, King of clubs…"

People eavesdropped. The sound of dishes clinked in the dining room. Lunch was being set. A hot course was served on dishes. This ended with the clink of glasses. Immediately, everyone grew silent. Only for the young people in the next room did things continue at a loud simmer. The scraping of spoons and chewing became so loud that it even rose above the background noise of the young people. Someone burped. His neighbor silently slapped him on the back to help dislodge a fish bone. Sighing, chewing, red faces, sleepy eyes. Two *banshchiki* in blue shirts unwrap bottles, corks shoot to the ceiling, one-ruble Laninskoye champagne sprinkles down on guests like a cold shower.

THE STRELTSOV BROTHERS WERE "ALMOST millionaires," Moscow building owners, Old Believers, apparently from the Preobrazhensky group, and their entire lives were as clear to them as the palm of their hands; each of their steps was known 10

---

12. *Preferance* is an Eastern European card game played with a 32-card deck. *Stukolka*, at one time Russian gamblers' favorite card game, was largely based on luck. The name comes from the light knock on the table (*stuk*) made by players who wished to stay in the game.

years in advance. They both were bachelors and lived in their comfortable home with their niece, who was their whole world: she managed the house, kitchen, and domestic help. For the brothers, life was counted out in days, hours, and minutes. They were almost the same age, one with brown hair and a dark curly beard, the other lighter-colored and greying. The older lent money at high interest rates. The case of Nikifor and Fyodor Streltsov, accused of usury in the first degree, went to court. They were charging 40 percent. In the end, the judge sentenced F. Streltsov to only a few months in prison. He could not wiggle out of it, he had to do his time, but pretended to be sick, and was sent to the prison hospital from which, somehow – it cost ten thousand they say – he was sent home. Sitting there with nowhere to go, he managed his bond portfolio.

This adventure went by unnoticed, and again life flowed on, only they started to lend money not through promissory notes, but with buildings as collateral. The younger brother, Alexei Fyodorovich, while his brother was in the prison hospital – for the one time – decided to charge interest, and lent money for a promissory note to a familiar "member" of the Moscow Racing Society, taking as collateral his racing stable.

A.F. Streltsov, curious to see the borrower's horses run, arrived at the track early one day and became fascinated. His life, to that point tranquil, became filled with conversations about sport. He started to go to the races every day on his own horse. To care for the horse, a stable hand assigned a relative, a young boy from one of the racing stables. Alexei Fyodorovich started to "raise some dust" on his way to the races in a carriage with his driver Lenka, who was both a horse lover and a coachman. Over time, he slowly started to take the reins in his own hands and learned to drive. He replaced his low quality horse with a trained racer, became a real "dust raiser," and flew along the Petersburg highway, starting from the hippodrome's gates and riding as far as the Crossroads tavern where, about two hours before races, all types of sportsmen, just like him, gathered. They raised dust in the same types of carriages and discussed the odds. Drivers sat on the carriages and waited for their masters.

Horse drivers took their masters from the tavern to the start of the races, to comfortable grandstand seats, at the time still made of wood. The drivers stood on their carriages and watched races through the fence. They knew every horse, discussed odds, and even bet, pooling their 40-kopek coins – at the time the minimum bet was a ruble. Sometimes, Alexei Fyodorovich stopped by at the stables of his debtor, who was making his payments promptly. From there he would go to the winners' circle to watch the ride-bys. Sport filled his life, although his domestic routine remained just the same.

The elder Streltsov continued lending at high interest rates and cutting coupons, going to the city during the day on business. Both brothers lunched at home, ate only plain Russian cooking, and neither drank. At eight in the evening, they went to

Savrasenko's on Tverskoy Boulevard, where the most varied people ate inexpensively. In the two back rooms, there were nice billiard tables where Moscow's best players gathered, and, of course, card sharps. Upstairs, were Saracen rooms for couples
from the boulevard. Cardsharps also set up their "mills" upstairs and lured billiards
players, whom they no doubt cheated.

Walking into the tavern, Fyodor sat at the buffet with his friend Kuzma Yegorich and Kuzma's brother Mikhail, the owners. Alexei went into the billiards room,
where he discussed the races, and occasionally played billiards for a ruble a game.
He always managed, even with card sharps, before the game was half over, to raise
the stakes. Alexei rarely lost, although he played not with a regulation cue but with
a thicker stick. Thus, they spent every evening until 11 at Savrasenko's.

The brothers left home together at 10 in the morning, Fyodor on business to
the city, and Alexei to the Chernyshevskiye Baths, with its wooden paneling and
its swept and washed floors. He went to the gentry section's dressing room, sat for
about two hours, received from his assistant the day's cash, and put it in a fireproof
safe. Then he summoned the barber. He was shaved every day – you don't have to
pay your own people, so it was free. At exactly 11, his brother Fyodor arrived, took
the packet of money from the safe while leaving the coins for his brother, and left.

Once his brother was gone, Alexei went across the street, through Brusevsky Alley, to a dirty coach tavern in the Kosourov Building to drink tea. He stayed exactly
one hour, discussing, arguing and handicapping racehorses and drivers. Cab drivers
came here. They, like the horse-loving "dust raisers," knew the horses, but watched
the competition through the fence. Out of tact, each was even-handed about the
odds for the next race. "Look, last time you were approaching the post first, but
Balashov went around you. His horse, Volny, bumped your horse. He galloped by
and pushed you off your line. Balashov urged his ride to charge and won, and you
were disqualified."

By this time, Streltsov was a member of the Racing Society. Without warning,
the owner of the horses that were collateral went bankrupt. Some of the horses
were given to other creditors, but two remained to cover the debt to Streltsov. The
broker holding the horses proposed that Streltsov keep them and ride them in the
sweepstakes. Streltsov attempted the ride-bys successfully. He won a consolation
prize by serendipitously finishing in last place. After a series of losses they finally
gave him attractive odds and a favorable distance. He would have lost badly if not
for one thing that the other riders, out of sympathy, reminded him of constantly.
From the time that he started hating Balashov, he always dreamed of riding around
him. Seasons had passed, and he always finished in the tail of the pack or dead last.
He always wagered on himself and sometimes this was the only ticket on his horse.

The crowd laughed when he rode out to the start, and during the race, heckling Streltsov's profession, they always shouted: "Switches! Give her the switches!"[13]

He continued to hope that his one ticket would beat the odds, but kept finishing last. Even the crowd stopped laughing. Streltsov, in his own way, filled his life with this sport. It was his only joy! Alexei Fyodorovich did not dare tell his brother about his hobby, which he considered a trifle, comparatively inexpensive, and in no way a violation of the usual order of life: money, money, and money. He had no acquaintances, no drinking buddies. The Streltsov brothers did not even read the newspapers: only in taverns did Nikifor sometimes skim through magazines, and Alexei only read the racing sheet.

Once, the police stuck the brothers with two tickets to a charity show, *Demon* at the Bolshoi. Alexei took as his guest Lenka the driver. After returning home, they both cursed, telling Fyodor Fyodorovich: "Again it's all lies! How he shouted, that Volny is the son of Efir; and you, Lenka are poking me in the side and whispering: 'He's lying.' And he was lying. Volny is the son of Legky and Vorozha."[14]

IT WAS NINE IN THE morning on a non-bathing day, but the Sandunovskiye Baths had a liveried doorman at entrance No. 6 on Zvonarsky Alley. The entrance was usually busy with people coming to swim in an enormous second-floor pool. Actors and actresses from the best theaters came to swim in the pool; among them was a nearly 100-year-old actor from the Korsh Theater, whom they admitted in deference to his age. This was Ivan Alekseyevich Grigorovsky, who had worked on the stage in Moscow and at times in the provinces. He had played villains in the old days, roles that he still knew by heart, and had performed as early as the 1840s. He came every day at the same time to swim in the pool before everyone. After bathing he took a small "cheater"[15] out of his pocket, uncorked it, and after drinking half, and sometimes the whole thing, would chase his drink with raisins.

Because of this "cheater," Moscow's famed Doctor Zakharin, who took 300 and 500 rubles for visiting merchants who had overeaten *bliny* on *Maslennitsa*, almost beat him with a cane. The old man, never ill, suddenly felt, he said, "tightness in the chest." They advised him to see Zakharin, but after hearing that an appointment cost 25 rubles, he roundly cursed the whole idea and did not go. They booked him an appointment through an acquaintance, and Zakharin received him. First question:

"You drink vodka?"

"Of course!"

---

13. A reference to the banya, not money lending or racing.
14. In Mikhail Lermontov's *Demon*, the Demon says at one point (Section X), "Тебя я, вольный сын эфира / Возьму в надавёздные края" ("I, the unfettered child of the ether / Will take you to a region beyond the stars"). It is a play on words, here *volny* is an adjective (willful, unfettered), but it might also be the name of a horse.
15. The Russian is жулик, which means a cheater or a rogue; in this case it is a flask.

"Time to time?"

"No, every day."

"A shot? Two?"

"Sometimes by the glassful. And only vodka, I don't drink anything else. I was at three name day celebrations yesterday. I drank maybe 30 glasses, maybe 40."

Zakharin lost his composure. He jumped up from the chair, his eyes bulged, he banged his cane on the floor and shouted:

"Wha-at? F-F-Forty? Did you drink today?"

"Well, I just had half of this," he said, and showed him the "cheater."

"Zakharin struck me on the arm," Grigorovsky told his friends, "but I held my ground."

"Get out of here! Drive him off!"

A servant ran up because of the noise and led me out. But Zakharin continued cursing and yelling. Then he ran and caught up with me.

"Have you been drinking long? How many years?"

"I've been drinking since I was 20. Next year I will be 100."

Sitting in a steam room in the Sandunovskiye Baths, where Gonetsky introduced the sale of red wine, the old man said: "I learned to drink here, in these same baths, when Sandunova herself was still alive. I saw her, I saw Pushkin... He loved hot steam."

"Pushkin?" his audience asked with surprise.

"Yes, right here. These private rooms did not exist back then, the building was long, two-storied, and the gentry section was large, with the same type of soft divans, and the buffet was... ask me whatever you want. Pushkin spent time here. A friend of his taught me how to drink. In front of the divans, at the time, there were little tables. Well, we would sit at the tables after the *banya*, and rest. Dmitriev and I drank bilberry water. The famous Denis Vasiliyevich Davydov[16] came out, limping slightly. His Excellency was staying at Tinkov's, on Prechistenka Street, and Tinkov's wife was my godmother. I became acquainted there with this famous hero. He wrote poems and sometimes recited them at my godmother's.

"Denis Vasiliyevich came out of the steam room, put down a sheet, and sat down with me. Dmitriev said to him, 'Glad you had a good steam, Your Excellency. Would you like some bilberry water? It's tasty!'

" 'Aren't you afraid?' he asked.

" 'What?'

" 'To drink it.' Pushkin says this about it: "Bilberry water, I fear, might not do me any harm," and therefore he usually drank it with *arak*.' [17]

---

16. A hero of the war of 1812 and a poet.
17. A clear, unsweetened aniseed-flavored alcoholic drink, produced and consumed primarily in the Middle East.

"Denis Vasiliyevich winked and the *banshchik* carried in two bottles of bilberry water and one of *arak*. Denis Vasiliyevich started to pour drinks for all: Half a glass of bilberry water, half a glass of *arak*. I tried it – tasty. He recited some lines of poetry about *arak*.

"I can't even remember how I walked home.

"My first time, I got drunk. I didn't know *arak* was so strong.

"Now, every time that I see a Kudryavtsev caramel in a colored wrapper, with a little paper tail on one end, I remember my teacher."

"Small slips of paper were put inside each wrapped candy, with two lines of poetry. I remember I got a slip with:

I fear bilberry water
It would do me no harm

"Later, you could get neither *arak* nor bilberry water! We lived to see the days of 'cheaters.' Cheap but with a kick!"

Grigorovsky loved to talk about the past. He had seen a lot and had a surprising memory. He took pleasure in speaking, loved to talk, and everyone willingly listened. He did not like to talk about himself, but this was, after all, unavoidable at times because he only spoke about events where he was a participant, where you can't exclude yourself. Sometimes he spoke in the third person, as if he was not talking about himself. His recollections were usually dictated by location: when in a tavern – he would speak about old taverns, about how they drank and ate; in a theater among the actors – he would speak about and reminisce about actors and the theater. What didn't he know! Whom didn't he remember!

"Well, Vanya, did you know Sukhovo-Kobylin?," the actor Kiselevsky, ungluing his false sideburns and removing his makeup after *Krechinsky*,[18] asked him once at the Korsh Theater.

"No, but did you ever see Raspluyev?"

"What do you mean Raspluyev? He's a character in a play."

"Well, yes, a character, but he was a real chorister in the theater in Yaroslavl, and a card sharp too. A different family name... Once, I saw him thrown out the window of the Pillar tavern for cheating at cards. Only I forget just by who exactly; maybe Mishka Dokuchaev, maybe Yegorka Bystrov!

For his age, Grigorovsky was quite spry and did not like it when he was reminded of his years. Once, in the restaurant Livorno, Ivan Alekseyevich was telling his friends: "Yesterday, I was the guest of a young woman, a telegraph operator. I had a wonderful time."

---

18. *Krechinsky's Wedding* by A.V. Sukhovo-Kobylin.

Andreyev-Burlak laughed: "Vanya! How you lie! Back when you could have had a good time with young women, the telegraph did not yet exist!"

ONCE, IN THE MORNING, A six-foot-tall colonel came into the dressing room, elegantly dressed, with a moustache down to his chest. Greetings, with formal bows, came from all the divans:

"Hello, Nikolai Ilyich."

"I was in the Rogozhsky precinct all night at a fire. I will bathe, then sleep. About 20 homes burnt down."

This was Colonel N.I. Ogaryov, a relative of the poet, a friend of Herzen.[19] All of Moscow loved him. He was transferred from the guards to the army, with a promotion to colonel, and assigned to the command of Moscow's Governor-General. There, they made him a police chief in Moscow's second department. He had a passion for fires, never missed one, and like all firefighters loved the baths.

In the sixties, he allowed all arrestees to go to the *banya*, even those from secret cells in the police precincts, that is, political criminals, if they were accompanied by "musketeers," unarmed police employees. In 1862, Tverskaya Precinct secretly housed the biggest state criminal of the day, later sentenced to hard labor in exile, P.G. Zaichnevsky.[20] Ogaryov rode by every day on huge fire horses, and got acquainted with Zaichnevsky, also a horse lover, through the windows. Ogaryov later visited him in his cell more than once, and permitted him, accompanied by a soldier, to go to the *banya*.

ON SATURDAYS, MEMBERS OF THE Russian Gymnastics Society usually left the Pedlikh Building on Strastnoy Boulevard after evening classes and went to the nearby Sandunovskiye Baths. I always went to the Palashevskiye Baths, next to the rooms at the England where I lived, mainly because the *banya* was near a small stand where the people's poet Razorenov sold his own *kvas* and salted pickles. His marinade was so aromatic and tasty that it was preferred to even his wonderful *kvas*.

The shop was as small as a crumb, so the old giant Alexei Yermylich could barely turn around when scooping marinade from the barrel or pouring from the tap a big mug of *kvas*. Both cost a kopek. The shop was locked at 11, and I always hurried from the *banya* to avoid being late, so I could find time to gab with the old man about theater and poetry, hear his new poems, and share some of my own.

On the Saturday that I am talking about, I dropped by Sandunovskiye Baths around 10 in the evening. First, I decided to have my haircut. I did not cut my beard or moustache after leaving the stage. The hairstylist, still a boy, cut my hair and started to get ready to shave me, but I refused.

---

19. Nikolai Ilyich Ogaryov (1813-1877), poet and revolutionary, and Alexander Herzen (1812-1870), a noted writer, critic and dissident.
20. Peter Grigoryevich Zaichnevsky (1842-1896), a revolutionary. (See pages 41 and 182.)

Moscow gymnasts.

"Have mercy," he called me by my first name and patronymic, "you always get a shave."

It happened that he was a trainee from the theatrical hairstylist in Penza. I told him that I had left the stage, and the last time I had shaved was before a show in Baku.

"That means you were in the Caucasus? Our *banya* has a worker from the Caucasus. I can call him over if you like."

I was delighted. I had been to the Caucasus during the war, and had ridden all over, but had not made it to the famous baths. Truly, during war there's no time for bathing. The band I rode with through remote villages could not even poke their noses into the city. In Baku, there was no time for baths, and we bypassed Tiflis.

"Abidnov!" he shouted.

An agile and flexible masseur, completely bald, circled, bustled, and gave me pleasure that I had not known until that day. I won't try to write about the session, so unexpected in Moscow. After Pushkin, it's impossible to even try. I quote his *Journey to Arzrum*:

Hasan began by laying me out on a warm stone floor, then flexed my arms and legs, stretched my joints, and pounded me firmly with a fist: I felt not the slightest pain, but a surprising relief (Asiatic *banshchiki* can become ecstatic, jump up onto your shoulders, slide their feet along your ribs and dance on your spine in a half-crouch). After this, and for some time, he massaged me with a bath mitten, and after splashing me with warm water, set to washing me with a soapy towel stretched over a small bottle. The sensation is indescribable: hot soap pours over you, like air! Hasan then put me in the bath, and the session ended.

I sat in the bath until, with sponges and soap in their hands, two handsome, athletic, and flexible men came in, the Durov brothers, members of our gymnastic society. One of them stopped for a moment on the rope rug leading into the "hot" room, executed a back flip, waved his sponge at me in greeting, and followed his brother into the hot *banya*.

These are our guys. Ignoring everyone, our unbeatable fencing teacher, Taras Petrovich Tarasov, with an imposing moustache and switches under his arm, swam through the crowd like a huge catfish. His rough-hewn, athletic figure had already started to accumulate a layer of fat, which, however, only accentuated the magnificence of his biceps and veined calves. There's a model for Hercules!

And here's a model for Mark Antony: our gymnastics instructor, an unsurpassed coach, a famous dancer and horseman. He's the older brother of another excellent gymnast, the now famous surgeon, Peter Ivanovich Postnikov, who at the time was a mere student. The coach stood under a cold shower, stretched, twisting the marble body of a modern-day Greek demigod, working his brilliant muscles, a living network, shown in relief, rippling across his wide back into narrow hips.

I sat in the warm bath. As always, sound filled the room: the smacking of wet, naked flesh, the rush of water exploding from faucets into tubs, the splash of bathers, and the rainy patter of showers, but no human voice. As always, in the dressing room they gossiped, in the washroom they were silent, and in the steam room they laughed. This laughter was audible when the steam room door opened. Suddenly, there was laughter so loud that it trumpeted right through the closed door to the steam room.

"And they say when they finally took him..."

"For a quarter of an hour I sat here, and he was there too. Like a lion roaring in the Libyan desert. He'll cook them all," a clean-shaven old man with curly grey hair combed down to his cheeks said to me from the next tub. He was a retired official of the civil court. He worked for 50 years, thereby earning a pension of three rubles per month, chronic pain in his waist, and a badge for his lapel. "During Mother Catherine's time," he said in an insulted tone, "this badge gave me the right to enter the women's *banya* for free, but now I have to pay even in the men's!"

Then, men started to rush out of the steam room a few at a time. Laughter surged through the open door.

"Oh, ho, ho. Oh, ho, ho."

"Oo-oo-oo-oo."

"Splash some more... Splash... Heat!"

The thrashing of switches could be heard. Those who exited to the washroom rocked back and forth, whinnied, hurried to the showers and rinsed at the faucets.

"Move! Your waist! Your waist!" resounded a thunderous bass.

"That's it! That's it! Move lower! O-o-o-o... ho... ho... You got it! Get my lower back! Lower back!"

Suddenly, "Right now! A! A! A! O! O!.."

Steam rushed out the open door. It grew hot in the washroom. Tarasov appeared first, holding a bundle of switches. Behind him moved a monster with messy hair hanging down to his shoulders, roaring in ecstasy. He made even Tarasov seem small. Both were red, eyes bulging. They rushed to the shower and the monster roared again, like an elephant turned toward the cold rain. I recognized him immediately. We had met dozens of times at ceremonies, and also at the track, where he was a regular. At intermission at the track, he always hid in a remote corner. As he put it, "It's not suitable for a spiritual figure to be at a horse race. The bosses might see, and I'm a horse lover!" He also liked the buffet. Servers would fill his tea glass with vodka, but if one didn't know him and failed to pour, like the others, a full glass, he would immediately blare:

"What are you up to? Huh? Whom are you pouring for? A sparrow might peck at this for communion, but it's not fit for a priest or deacon to drink."

All the servers knew Shekhovtsev from his processional blessings at merchants' weddings, where his performances blew out candles and shook chandeliers.

Tarasov and I went to get dressed. We had friends in the dressing room, including the strapping, long-haired writer Orfanov-Mishel, a bit smaller than Shekhovtsev. It was obvious that scissors had last touched his beard either long before, or possibly never. Next to him was tiny Vasya Vasilyev, shaved like an actor, with a care-worn face, and curly hair. Both were regulars at Chernyshy, on parole, and under surveillance. Both were my old friends!

"How did you end up here? I thought you never went to the *banya*. You're members of the Unwashed Dogs' Club, but here you are!"

Vanya, even back when we worked together at Brenko's Theater, would talk about the sixties in Peter, when there really was such a club, and insist that he had been there, and that he lived on Yertelevy Alley, where the club met. His building and its neighbor were later demolished, and in their place Suvorin built a press for *New Times.*[21]

ONLY TWO POETS DEDICATED A few lines to the Russian *banya*. Each reflected his own era. Both were inspired by Moscow's *banyas*. One was the all-embracing Pushkin.[22] The other was the Moscow poet Shumacher.

21. Alexei Sergeyevich Suvorin (1834-1912), journalist, writer, critic and leading publisher in his era. A close friend and patron of Chekhov.
22. This selection is from Pushkin's *Ruslan and Ludmila* (1820), a fairy tale written in epic poem format. The Prince of Kiev's daughter, Ludmila is abducted and a brave knight, Ruslan, rescues her.

A teenage Khan, a castle keep.
A line of maids awaits, three deep.
A girl takes off his winged helmet,
The next unbuckles armor, plated,
A third the sword, a fourth the shield,
Unclothed, unshod, bare-skinned, unpeeled,
Wrought iron armor thrown down, damned, cursed.
But first the Khan is led down to
a wondrous Russian banya. Out burst
warm waves of steam to clean, renew,
then marvelous silver basins brimming
A fountain shoots-up, burbling, numbing.
The rugs piled thick as they can be,
To soothe the tired young Khan when resting
The steam, so thick inside it's misting,
and veiling his young majesty.
Magnificent, half-nude, and beautiful
Young maidens now the Khan encircle,
They're gentle, sensitive, not proud,
Massage the stress that comes from crowds.
Above the Khan, a girl fans bundles
of lushly green, young birch switches
infuses scents like flowered tundra
Another pours rose water pitchers
To cool and set his knotted limbs loose
And with scented water cleanly sluice
The Khan's so dark and curly hair...

A brilliant line cites "the ecstasy of an intoxicated knight" to extol the marvel of the Sandunovskiye Baths, which he visited with friends every time he was in Moscow. The poet, young, strong, and rugged, "after steaming on a bench with young switches of birch," jumped into the *banya's* ice-water bath, and later went back to the bench, where again "steam rose above him." He relaxed, "clothed in pleasure," in a richly-appointed dressing room, decorated by the builders of Catherine the Great's palaces, where "cool fountains splashed" and "luxurious rugs were thrown."

Half a century passed. New ideas and new aspirations were born. P.V. Shumacher, a liberal poet of the sixties, from his apartment on Meshchanskya Street, went to the Yauza River, to the "common" Volkonskiye Baths. He was overweight and suffered from gout. Turgenev told him, "We're colleagues in literature and in gout."

Shumacher treated his gout, indeed all of his ailments, in the baths.[23] Two *banshchiki* steamed him, taking turns every minute heating the "oven." He especially loved the Sandunovskiye Baths where, after steaming, he rested and even slept for a couple of hours, and always carried a bundle of switches. At home, resting on a divan, he would place the bundle under his head. He spent the last years of his life in a room he kept at the eccentricity-tolerant Sheremetev Building on Sukharevka Square. He lived there in the winter, and summered in Kuskov, where Sheremetev let him use Holland House. Shumacher's poems were published in newspapers and sometimes separately. A *banya* lover, he was the only poet who extolled its marvels tastefully and attractively. Here is a selection from his poem about the *banya*:

> *My skeleton softens, every last vein hums*
> *Whole torrents of sweat roll right off my body*
> *From top to bottom my whole spine burns.*
> *The bath lady states some senseless, confusing concerns*
> *Don't turn me now, my dearest girl Tanya*
> *I'm totally spent from steam in the banya*
> *Gelatinous now, my tight tendon links,*
> *none of my joints now bothered by kinks.*
> *In the baths, switches beat title and rank,*
> *So throw some more dry ones in the prep tank,*
> *Makes them softer, with a nice scent*
> *Smoother, handier, more easily bent.*
> *I climbed up the hot room to the top bench*
> *through soft clouds of steam, raspberry-drenched.*
> *I swung the switches, gave my hide a good beating,*
> *silky and springy, lashes hasten the heating.*

Here is another of his poems on the *banya*:

> *My private hopes, proven dead-end paths,*
> *in helpless anger, in pain, alone,*
> *I went to the public, old hot baths*
> *Steamed on a bench right to the bone.*
> *What can it be now? Oh joy! Oh good!*
> *For my most secret, heart-felt dream,*
> *Freedom, equality, and brotherhood,*
> *I just found, in common public steam.*[24]

---

23. Peter Vasiliyevich Shumacher (1817-1891) was a humorist and poet who specialized in parody and satire. Research failed to uncover a version of the poem cited by Gilyarovsky; however, a poem by Shumacher from 1886, "*Bannaya*," does share several verses. See *Poety-demokraty 1870-1880-kh godov*, Moscow: Sovetsky Pisatel', 1968.
24. No published version of this poem has yet been located.

This poem, like others at the time, simply could not be allowed to exist. They were not approved for printing. They passed from hand to hand and were read with success at illegal parties. I thought of this once in the Sukhonniye Baths, on Bolotny, where there was a 20-kopek gentry section loved by the local merchants. After a fire on Tatarskaya Street, I returned to the Pyatnitskaya Precinct with the firefighters, jumped from the cart, and, smoked through by the fire and covered by ash, I went to the nearby Sukhonniye Baths. I ran into the common section, but it was packed even though it was only 11 o'clock. On the other hand, the 20-kopek gentry section was relatively uncrowded. In the washroom, perhaps 30 men splashed around. The *banshchik* had soaped my head a second time, and with effort scraped the ash from my beard and hair – at the time my hair was still thick. I sat with closed eyes and enjoyed myself. Then, through the noise, the splashing of water, and the switching of bare flesh, I heard a loud shout:

"He's leaving! He's leaving!..."

In that instant, my *banshchik*, not uttering a word, scurried across the wet floor and disappeared. "What?" There was no one to ask. I saw nothing. I felt around for the bucket – and couldn't find it; the *banshchik* had taken it with him, but soap covered my head and face. I wiped-off my eyes and saw: chaos! *Banshchiki* had abandoned their clients, one with a lathered head, one lying soaped on a bench. They hurried to fill tubs of water from the faucets, and stood in two lines by the door to the steam rooms holding the buckets above their heads I understood nothing and had soap in my eyes. Next, the door opened wide, and accompanied by two steamers holding birch switches, proudly and carefully, a mighty bearded figure, hair parted in the middle, with a bowl cut, paraded across the room. *Banshchiki* in turn, one after another, poured buckets of water on him with an adroit flip, so not one drop missed. They spoke happily and respectfully:

"To your healthy, Peter Ionich!"

"Glad you had a good steam!"

Within a minute, the *banshchik* was back washing my head, not even apologizing, as would seem necessary. He said, "Peter Ionovich Gubonin. His home is next to the Pyatnitskaya Precinct, and when he's in Moscow, he comes to us every other day at this time. He gives a ruble tip to every steamer."

TAVERNS

"FOR US, TAVERNS MEAN MORE than anything!" Arkashka Shchastlivtsev says in *The Forest*.[1] For many Muscovites, a tavern was their "first thing." It took the place of the market for traders, who made thousands of deals over drinks, and a dining room for lonely people, and hours of relaxation in friendly discussion for all kinds of people, a place for business meetings and celebration for everyone from millionaires to tramps. In a word, Arkashka is right: "A tavern is the first thing!"

There were three old, purely Russian taverns in Moscow at the start of the last century: Saratov, Gurin's and Yegorov's. There were two Yegorov's: one in the Yegorov building, on Hunter's Row, and another in the millionaire Partikeyev's building, on the corner of Voskresenskaya Street and Theater Square. Yegorev had to part with the latter. In 1868, Gurin's buyer, I.Y. Testov, convinced Partikeyev, who dreamed only of glory, to take the tavern back from Yegorev and give it to him. Well, to his great satisfaction, on the wall of the luxuriously renovated building (by the standards of the time), was a huge sign with letters two feet tall: "Big Partikeyevsky Tavern." And humbly, below: "I.Y. Testov."

Testov opened for business offering Russian cuisine. Merchants and nobles mobbed the new tavern. Business was especially brisk starting in August, when landowners from all across Russia brought their children to Moscow's schools. A custom was established to lunch with your children at Testov's, or in Saratov at Dubrovina's. The famous Anna Zakharovna departed from this building when, with her choir, she "went off to live." Later, they starred at Yar. After their shows, a crowd of theater fans would form a line at Saratov.

---

1. An 1870 comedy written by Alexander Ostrovsky. Shchastlivtsev is the main character.

Slava Testov beat Gurin and Saratov. In 1876, the trader Karzinkin bought the Gurin tavern, demolished it, put up an enormous building, and founded the Syndicate of Large Moscow Hotels. He decorated its large halls, and soon had a hotel with 100 wonderful guest rooms. In 1878, the first half of the hotel was opened. But that did not stop Testov, who added to his sign a crest and the slogan, "Supplier to the Highest Court."

Petersburg's high society, headed by princes, came to Moscow just to dine on Testov's piglet, crab soup with stuffed pasta, and the famous Guryev *kasha*, which, it should be noted, was unconnected with the Guryev tavern, and was created by a mythical Guryev. In addition to private dining rooms, the tavern had two enormous halls where, during the luncheon hours or at breakfast, landed merchants had reserved tables which, until an agreed time, could be occupied by no one else.

On the left side of the room, the far table by the window, starting at 4 o'clock, was reserved for the millionaire Iv. Vas. Chizhev, a clean-shaven, portly, old man, extremely tall. He sat at his table promptly, almost always dined alone, ate for approximately two hours, and napped between courses. His menu included: a portion of cold beluga or osetra caviar with horseradish, two bowls of crab soup, fish or kidney broth with two dumplings, then fried pork, and veal or fish depending on the season. In the summer, he had cold *kvas* soup with salmon, white fish, and dry-ground fish. Then, for the third course, without fail, he had a pan of Guryev's *kasha*. Sometimes, he deviated slightly, replacing the dumplings with a fishing boat pie – an enormous crust with 12 layers, everything from a layer of trout to a layer of marrow in black butter. With this, he drank red and white wine, and, after napping for half an hour, went home to sleep so he could be at the Merchants' Club at 8 o'clock to sip champagne and order meals the entire evening, this time with a large group. He always ordered at the club, and no one from the group contradicted him.

Kitchen staff from Testov's Tavern.

"For me, these various folly-jollies and fricassee-chickasees are not even a consideration. We eat the Russian way. Thus, our bellies don't ache, we don't rush around to doctors, and we don't have to go abroad for treatments."

This gourmet lived until old age in good health. There were many such at Testov's.

I have in front of me a bill from Testov's tavern for 36 rubles, with a canceled stamp, a signed receipt for the money, and the signatures: "V. Dalmatov and O.

Grigorevich." The date, 25 May. The year is not written, but it seems to be from 1897 or 1898. My old stage comrade V.P. Dalmatov and his friend O.P. Grigorevich, a well-known engineer and Muscovite, were visiting from Petersburg. We went to Testov's to have lunch Moscow-style. In the room on the left we were greeted by the waiters' patriarch, the successful manager of 40 years of celebrations, Kuzma Pavlovich.

"If you please, Vladimir Alekseyevich, take Pastukhov's table! Nikolai Ivanovich yesterday left for a fishing trip on the Volga."

We were seated at a nice table, which for 10 years was reserved by Pastukhov, the editor of *Moscow Broadsheet*. In a snow-white shirt, with a beard and hair almost whiter than the shirt, Kuzma froze in an expectant pose before us, after whispering something to two nearby, young waiters.

"Well, sir, Kuzma Pavlovich, we are hosting a famous actor! First let's have a little vodka, and something a bit special, something that the cat won't miss, for an appetizer."

"Yes, sir."

"Tell us what you can offer."

"Don, Yantar, and Kucherga salmon with the scent of wind off the steppe."

"Fine. After that, we'll have white fish with cucumbers."

"It's *manna* from heaven, not whitefish. Ivan Yakovlevich caught and prepared it himself at his *dacha*. We have beluga caviar. Achuyevsky paste caviar and Achuyevsky rolls. Piglet with horseradish."

"I'd like some fried pork with *kasha*," V.P. Dalmatov said.

"So, a cold course won't be needed, sir?" He winked at the busboy. "What will be your main course?"

"Testov's broth, of course," O.P. Grigorevich declared.

"Broth with sturgeon and sterlet – fresh, yellow like gold, whole sterlet."

"Pasta stuffed with trout."

"Next, I would recommend whole cutlets *á la Jardinière*. Veal, white like snow. We get it from Alexander Grigorevich Shcherbatov, sir. Something special."

"I'll have pork with *kasha*, plain, like Raspluyev," V.P. Dalmatov smiled.

"Pork for everyone. Be sure, Kuzma, that a nice bottle of vodka is iced so it will be ready."

"Grilled salmon would be nice between the meat courses," V.P. Dalmatov proposed.

"The salmon is fresh from Petersburg. Would you like it with herbs? Soft, like butter."

"Fine, Kuzma. The rest is up to you... but you won't forget?"

"Please, sir, how many years have I served your table?"

A Merchant's Wake, by Firs Zhuravlyov (1876).

He looked back. At just that moment, two waiters struggled past with enormous trays. Kuzma watched, then vanished into the kitchen.

In a moment, a bottle of chilled Smirnov's on ice, English bitters, berry juice, and Levy's Port No. 50 were placed on the table next to our bottle of wine. Two more waiters brought platters of sliced ham cut in translucent, rosy slices, thin as a sheet of paper. Another tray, with pumpkin and cucumbers, fried marrow steaming on black bread, and two silver servers with grey, grainy caviar and shiny black Achuyevsky paste caviar. Silently, Kuzma appeared with a platter of smoked salmon decorated with lemon ends.

"Kuzma, you forgot after all."

"Not at all, sir. Please take a look." On a third tray stood a bottle of champagne and three glasses.

"How could I forget? My dear sir, have mercy!"

We started toasts "with the herring." "In rhythm," as I.F. Gorbunov used to say: vodka – herring. First the Achuyevsky caviar, then the caviar with tiny stuffed pasta with trout, a glass, first of clear cold Smirnov's with ice, and then the same but colored with a bit of wine. They drank the English bitters with the marrow, and *Zubrovka* with an Olivier salad.[2] After every glass, appetizers were replaced.

Kuzma sliced the steaming ham, other waiters scooped the caviar with silver spoons and served it on plates. The rose-colored, smoked salmon was replaced by

2. *Zubrovka* is a vodka in which various grasses are steeped for added flavor.

amber fish heads. They each had a shot of ale "to settle things." Gradually, the appetizers disappeared and in their place shone expensive china and silver spoons and forks. At the serving table there was steaming broth with small, round, rosy stuffed pasta. "Broth, sir!"

Kuzma threw a napkin across his left shoulder, took a fork and knife, pulled the pie over, waved his puffy, white hands like a dove moves it wings, quickly and silently directed his strokes, and the pie lay in dozens of thin pieces, running from an entire piece of trout in the middle to the thick reddened edge of the crust.

"That's a Chinese rose, not a pie!" Dalmatov was ecstatic.

"If you please, sir, I've been slicing for 40 years," Kuzma said, as if in justification, while starting on the next pie. "Vlas Mikhailovich Doroshevich[3] himself praised the way I sliced a rose pastry."

"Was that long ago?"

"They ate breakfast today. Left just before you arrived."

"They surely had piglet with horseradish?"

"They ordered six hams and vodka. They prefer it with horseradish and sour cream."

The group continued eating, and a player piano sounded out in the adjoining, large hall:

Here's how they lived under Askold,
Our grandfathers and fathers...

Testov's was one of those Russian taverns that was fashionable in the last century, and later came to be called restaurants. At that time, there was only one "restaurant" in the city center, Slavyansky Bazaar, and the rest were known as "taverns," because their primary customers were long-time Russian merchants. Each of the city taverns in the Ilyinka and Nikolsky areas had their own ways, a specialty dish, and their own regular customers. Waiters from Yaroslavl worked in all these taverns, in white shirts made of expensive Dutch fabric, washed to a sheen. They were called "white shirts," "floor men," and "sixes."

"Why 'sixes'?"

"Because they serve aces, kings, and queen, and any card, even a deuce, can beat them," Fedotych, an old waiter, explained. Smiling, he added, "That's nothing! A six of spades can beat an ace!"

But while a "six" was becoming a spade, it endured much suffering. In the old days, waiters were mainly from Yaroslavl, known as "Yaroslavl water drinkers."

---

3. Vlas Mikhailovich Doroshevich (1865-1922), a journalist, publicist and theater critic. One of the most renowned feuilletonists of the end of the nineteenth century. Editor of *Russian Word* from 1902-1917, when it became the largest circulation newspaper in tsarist Russia.

Later, when there were more taverns, waiters appeared from the Moscow Region, Tver, Ryazan, and other neighboring areas. They brought boys to Moscow, to a tavern, Sokolov's, it seems, over near the Tverskaya Embankment, where tavern managers came to find them. Here, there was a market for future "sixes." Parents usually brought their boys, and agreed on a training contract with the tavern managers, typically for about five years. Terms varied, depending on the tavern. Everyone dreamed of working at Hermitage or Testov's, where they took the quickest of hand, the smartest, and the best readers, and started them down the difficult path to the title of waiter.

At the start, a boy would wash dishes for a year. Later, if they found him sensible, he moved to the kitchen to get acquainted with plating food and learn dishes' names. For half a year, the boy sharpened his skills under the experienced leadership of the cooks, and then they dressed him in a white shirt. "He knows all the sauces!" the head cook would compliment him.

Waiter, by Boris Kustodiev (1920).

After this, for no less than four years, he worked as a busboy, carrying plates from the kitchen, clearing dishes, learning to take orders from guests, and finally, in the fifth year of his training, earning a stamp holder and silk belt, from which the stamp holder hung. Then, the boy could work tables in the dining room. By this time he was expected to own pants and half a dozen cotton shirts, always snowy white and never wrinkled, and for those who could afford it, Dutch fabric. Older waiters, sent to pick-up orders at larger restaurants, had cloaks. Only in Slavyansky Bazaar, waiters worked in cloaks and were not called waiters, but "officiants," while guests called them, "Man!" Later "small cloaks" appeared in restaurants at the edge of the city.[4]

Buffet bills were paid with stamps. In the morning, each of the waiters received 25 rubles of bronze stamps, from three rubles to five kopeks each. Handing in a guest's order, the waiter put stamps down for the food, and later exchanged stamps for cash received from the guest. Tips were handed in at the buffet, where they were counted and divided equally. But no one handed in all their money; part of

4. The word Gilyarovsky uses for a waiter is половой (*polovoy*).

Slavyansky Bazaar – its entrance is the ornate construction left of center, before the larger archway.

it, sometimes the larger part, was hidden, put away somewhere. Waiters called this money wedding funds. Why wedding funds? "This is from the old days. Country boys sometimes hid in their huts a few kopeks from their parents, in cracks and crevices, and under moldings," the old men explained.

Waiters did not receive salaries, and also were required to pay the manager a share of their earnings or a fixed sum, starting at three rubles a month and up, or 20 percent of the tips handed in at the till. Saratov was the only exception: there, managers never, not before Dubrovin, and not after Savostyanov, took anything from the waiters and until the tavern shut down paid both the waiters and the boys three rubles per month.[5] "Tips are their good luck. We do not need someone else's good fortune, and we should pay for their service," Savostyanov would say.

Waiters worked countless hours. But it never mattered how much time they spent rushing between rooms, or to and from the kitchen, which sometimes was located on the bottom floor, with the dining room on the third floor. In some taverns, they worked almost 16 hours per day. Work in the "common" taverns was especially difficult, where tea was sold for five kopeks for a pair, that is tea and two pieces of hard sugar for one person, and even then customers tried to save money. Three men might sit down, open their coats, and order: "Two and three!" The waiter brings, for 10 kopeks, two pairs and three settings. The third setting is free, even if they go back for water 10 times.

"The tea is a little weak, please add a bit," a guest might request.

Waiters had to add a bit and also run for hot water.

It was especially difficult to work in coachmen's taverns. There were many of them in Moscow. Their courtyards had wells for the horses, while inside there was a buffet table. The table had everything: beef, fish, and pork. A driver in from the cold wanted something a little rich, like fried eggs; then rolls, big thick hunks of bread, and then, always, pea *kisel*. Many Moscow millionaires, raised from poverty,

---

5. Unclear who Dubrovin and Savostyanov were, likely owners, but perhaps managers.

loved to treat themselves here to remember the old days. If he did not go himself, he sent someone: "Bring me a 40-kopek serving of tripe. And grab a pair of rolls or some bread." During Lent: "Pea *kisel*, with a little extra fat." His Honor sat in a luxurious office or newly renovated warehouse and took pleasure in simple food, remembering his not too distant past. All this time, he discussed million-ruble deals with a foreign trade representative.

Coachmen would come inside the tavern to eat and warm-up. There was no other place for them to rest or eat. Theirs was a life of cold, dry food. Tea and tripe with cucumbers were favored. Rarely, they had a glass of vodka, but never to the point of drunkenness. Twice a day, and when it was cold three times, they ate and warmed up in winter or dried their shirts while wearing them in the fall. All this enjoyment cost only 16 kopeks: Five kopeks for tea, 10 kopeks to eat until you drop, and a kopek to the yard keeper to water the horses and watch them near the well.

The coachmen's favorite taverns were in the city center: London on Hunter's Row, Kolomna on Neglinnaya Street, in Brusevsky Alley, in Greater Kiselny Alley, and the most central in Stoleshnikov Alley, where building No. 6 now stands, and where earlier there was a flock of chickens and a big red courtyard hound, Caesar, who sat by the gate and kept tramps from the yard. Every tavern had a room for coachmen with a tempting buffet. The one who leased the table paid a lot of money to the tavern owner and tried to offer the best food and drink to attract coachmen, so they would say: "We're going to Stoleshnikov's. There's no better buffet!" Coachmen also went to Stoleshnikov's because the fish was fatty and the rolls were

Moscow Tavern, by Boris Kustodiev (1920).

always hot. On holidays, toward evening, it would be packed with drunks – not an empty seat. A waiter would maneuver past the drunken men at tables, turning and bending, juggling a tray above his head on the palm of a hand – and sometimes on the tray he had two and seven, that is, two teapots full of water and seven place settings. As for tips, customers who had only ordered tea left nothing or, perhaps, two or three kopeks, and that only for outstanding service.

"Young one, hurry over to my place on the quiet and tell herself that I won't be eating lunch, I'm going into the city," orders a neighborhood merchant. The "young one," sometimes through rain and mud, or in temperatures far below freezing, after tossing on his head or neck a dirty napkin, wearing only a shirt, hurries across the street for a regular customer whom the boss prizes. There is no time to dress, or he'll get it in the neck from the buffet manager. Or a coachman commands: "Run, now, out on the courtyard and in my sleigh, under a grey blanket, there's a beaver hat. Bring it here. My horse is a bay, you know, with a bald spot." And a poorly-dressed boy runs to and fro among 100 horses in the coachmen's yard to find "a bay with a bald spot" and "a beaver hat under a blanket." So many of them got pneumonia!

Getting money from a drunk was an out-and-out triumph. For half an hour a drunken customer might hold his ground and curse until the waiters could talk sense into him. The experienced ones knew how, and that's how they made money. They knew how to get it.

"Well how'd it go? Set it straight?"

"Peter Kirillich? Such a tiny one. But after all…"

Today, the boot maker Peter Ivanovich, who remembers all this, is still alive. As I described above, the peasant from Uglich, Peter Kirillich, really did exist, and Peter Ivanovich knows because he made him a pair of boots. Peter Ivanovich drinks tea every morning at Lady Glutton, where old waiters gather.

Moscow merchants, who always loved to make fun of someone, told him: "You, Peter, don't pull a Peter Kirillich on me." But Peter Kirillich sometimes answered the merchant – he knew whom to answer and how – in this way:

"It seems I'm on your mind, always me. This is useful. If, as you do your sums, you remember me, look, and you'll find a way to cheat. Also, when you are writing out a tab for a customer, don't forget about me. Give yourself a tip, if you can be so kind."

But it became necessary to give up these merchant pranks.

This calculated manner of poking fun at and browbeating defenseless customers was used by certain waiters. They sometimes pretended to be insulted, and in this way also eked out some additional tip money. One Ivan Seledkin was a waiter at Gurin's. This was his real family name, but he complained rudely when they used it and not his first name.[6] It was not just when they used his family name, but even in cases where a guest ordered herring, he would be wildly angry:

"I'll give you a herring! How about across your face?"

The tavern was always filled with regulars who never took offense. But once he almost had real trouble. This was at Testov's, where he went to work after leaving Gurin's. General Slezkin, promoted to commander of Moscow's gendarme division, walked into the room. He got a table for his group and ordered appetizers. After taking the order, the waiter went to see about the food, and Slezkin shouted after him, in a commander's voice, "Don't forget the herring, the herring!" Unfortunately, at this moment, Seledkin walked in through the other door. He did not see the general, but only heard the word "herring."

"I'll give you a herring, you bastard! You want it across the mug?"

The merchants froze. One stopped with a spoon raised to his mouth. Someone broke a glass. Someone else passed gas and held his breath, afraid to cough. How this *tableau* ended is unknown. I only know that Seledkin kept his job at Testov's.

At Yegorov's, on Hunter's Row, famous for its *bliny* and its fish, and for its prohibition on smoking, because the manager was an Old Believer, there worked a waiter called "Goat." An old man with an enormous, goat-like, grey beard, from Tver to boot, he was nicknamed quite aptly, but he could not stand the word, which folks from Tver generally disliked.[7] Merchants on Hunter's Row often teased him in the following way: they sat at a table, ordered food, and in the middle of the table placed a package. When the old man served the food and moved the package to make room for the dishes, he removed the paper wrapping and found a toy goat! The old man would take the goat and, cursing, throw it on the floor. But if the toy was expensive, from a good shop, he would grab it up, run off, and hide it. The next time, the merchants would again buy a goat. In his elder years, Goat worked at Obukhov's Monetny on Hunter's Row, where in the old days there had been a mint.

In Arsentych there was a waiter who could not abide the word "lemon." They say that he had once stolen a sack of lemons from a display, was celebrating with some girls, they opened the bag, and instead of lemons, rotten potatoes poured out.

There were many such targets for practical jokes but sometimes these jokes ended in grief. Thus, a waiter at Lopashov's, an old man, did not like it when piglet was ordered with a smile. This reminded him of a bitter experience. When he was still young, he had once gone visited his village to see his wife, and brought some guests. The wife lived in a small hut and kept a piglet. Unfortunately, when the husband knocked, the wife was entertaining her lover. Frightened, she hid the lover under the stove and let the husband in, but did not know what to do. She opened the door,

---

6. His family name, Seledkin, is close to the word *seledka*, селедка, "herring."

7. Since at least the early part of the nineteenth century (one likely apochryphal story makes a link to the war of 1812), "goat" has been used as a slur for people from Tver (to call someone a goat is, just as in English, a serious insult).

drove the pig out to the barn, and from the barn to the street, where she yelled to her husband, "The pig escaped! Get him!" Right behind, she too fled. In this confusion, the lover left, but the neighbor saw the entire scene and gossiped, and from there villagers brought the story to Moscow. They teased the unlucky man into his old age. Sometimes he cried.

Lopashov's, on Varvarka Street, was among the oldest taverns. First, it belonged to Martyanov, but after his death it went to Lopashov. Bald, with a clipped moustache, clean shaven, and always dressed in an expensive black suit, Alexei Dmitriyevich Lopashov was widely respected and singularly solicitous with each and every guest. On the tavern's upper floor there was a large dining room called the Russian Hut, decorated with embroidered linens and carved wooden decorations. In the middle of the room was a table set for 12 with a homemade Russian tablecloth and embroidered towels in place of napkins. It was set with antique dishware, glassware, decanters and silver from the time of Peter I and earlier. The menu also pre-dated Peter. Small luncheons were given here for especially important foreigners; French cuisine was not offered, although there were some French wines that they poured into old bottles with the labels Fryazhsky, Falernsky, Malvazia, Greek, etc. An enormous silver tureen, the size of a tub, was used for champagne, which was scooped out with a silver pitcher and served in mugs.

Alexei Dmitriyevich only changed the menu once in the Russian Hut, but that decision saved the day. All of Moscow's Siberians were his faithful customers. The chef, recruited by Lopashov from Siberia, made *pelmeny* and meat dishes.[8] Once, in the eighties, the most powerful Siberian gold industrialists gathered in Moscow and had lunch Siberian-style at Lopashov's in the Hut. The menu listed: "Lunch in the Style of Yermak Timofeyevich,"[9] and on it there were only two entries: first – appetizers, and second – "Siberian *pelmeny*." There were no other courses. 2,500 *pelmeny* with meat, fish, and fruit in rose champagne were prepared. The Siberians scooped them up with wooden spoons.

At Lopashov's, like other expensive city taverns, the most powerful businessmen had their favorite tables. They came with their customers, mostly large provincial wholesalers, and ordered tea first. During Lent, lime honey was served in place of sugar.[10] At that time of year, the Orthodox were forbidden standard sugar: beef bones were used in its production! Drinking this tea, for 15 kopeks, deals were closed for tens and hundreds of thousands of rubles. Only when the deal was done did they move to a private dining room and eat breakfast.

Arsentych's in Cherkasky Alley was another such tavern, praised for its Russian cuisine, boiled ham, and osetra and beluga sturgeon served with horseradish and red

---

8. *Pelmeny* are small meat dumplings considered a mainstay among Siberians.
9. Yermak Timofeyevich (c. 1532-1585), the Russian Empire's Cossack conqueror of Siberia.
10. Honey produced with pollen collected largely from lime flowers.

Tea Drinking in a Tavern, by Victor Vasnetsov (1876).

grain vinegar as an appetizer. Nowhere was it tastier. Arsentych's cabbage soup with brains was amazing. G.I. Uspensky, when he came to Moscow, never missed it. At noon, rich merchants, who on a given day could not go to the tavern, sent servants for ham and the osetra and beluga sturgeon. This was the most respected tavern in Moscow, and there was never anything fancy. If the occasional group enjoyed a glass too many of vodka, owing to the horseradish vinegar and hot ham, then they could wander into Bubnov's office or the Slavyansky Bazaar, or maybe even go straight to Yar. Merchants walked to the tavern, rode to visit with "the ladies," but "wound-up" at Yar or "beyond the gate."[11]

Arsentych's was satisfying and "homey." Yegorov's was the same, but the one difference was that you could smoke there. In Cherkasky Alley, in the eighties, there had been another tavern, Ponomaryov's, in Kartashev's. This little building is long gone. It had a respectable clientele. In the second room of that tavern, in the front corner, under a large icon with a small, lamp, at a separate little table, sat an old man for entire days, uncombed, unshaven, rarely washed, almost a tramp. Respectable people, even rich people, well known in Moscow, stopped by his table. Some he asked to sit. Some left happy, some very upset. He sat and drank long-cooled tea. Occasionally, he took out a bundle of stocks or bonds and clipped coupons.

This was the building's owner, a businessman of the highest caliber, Grigori Nikolayevich Kartashev. His apartment was next to the tavern, he lived there alone, and slept on a bare bed frame with a piece of clothing for a pillow. The apartment's floors were never washed, and the place was never cleaned. He spent nights in the

11. Outside the Ring Boulevard.

cellar, near his money, like a "miserly knight." He rose at 10 in the morning and exactly at 11 walked into the tavern. Arrived. Sat. Summoned over a waiter.

"Are there any of yesterday's sausages left?

"There should be."

"Ask, now, to warm them up… And if there's some *kasha* left, I'll have that."

Food was on the house account, but tea was paid for in cash:

"One tea for six kopeks, and a one kopek cigar."

A debtor arrives. He comes over and sits.

"What do you want?"

"I'd have a cup of tea."

"Well, order it yourself. Pay for your own tea and cigar."

The debtor had to order his own tea for six kopeks. If he asked for a 30-kopek portion, or if he ordered wine or broth – the conversation was over.

"Look at you! How fancy! Get the hell out, I don't lend money to spendthrifts!"

And he would drive him off.

Everyone knew this, and a rich merchant or noble businessman visiting him smoked one-kopek cigars and drank six-kopek tea, and then would borrow tens of thousands of rubles for a promissory note. Kartashev did not like to lend money for small deals. He charged enormous interest rates, but avoided the courts, even though there were cases where debtors lost his money.

In the evening, his watchman, Kvasov, would come and take him home. Kartashev lived like this for decades, not visiting anyone, not even his sister, who was married to old man Obidny, also a millionaire. He later inherited Kartashev's millions. Only after Kartashev's death did it become clear how he had lived: in his rooms, covered by layers of dust, there were packets of bonds, letters of credit, and promissory notes everywhere, on the furniture, behind the wallpaper, in the vents. His primary cash funds were kept in a huge stove to which he had attached something resembling a guillotine: if a thief crawled in he would have been cut right through. Iron trunks stood in the basement, where, together with enormous sums of cash, he kept heaps of half-eaten lumps of sugar, pieces of bread spirited away from the table, rolls, twine, and dirty underwear. Piles of outdated promissory notes and bond coupons were found, as were expensive sable furs chewed by rodents, and nearby, tubs of half-imperial coins, more than 50 thousand rubles worth. In another pile, there were 150 thousand rubles in credit slips and bonds. The total estate exceeded 30 million rubles.

There was one other Russian tavern in the city. This was in the Kazan Court building on Vetoshny Alley, Bubnov's. It took up two floors of the enormous building and the mezzanine with an enfilade of luxuriously appointed private rooms and separate, individual dining rooms. This tavern was for celebrating, especially the private dining rooms, where merchants' sons as well as prosperous, bearded merchants poured out their souls, unlimited debauchery, for an entire week, and then complained, hung-over: "Oh the merchant's life is difficult: a day with a friend, two with customers, three days like this, and, on Sunday, permission for wine and ale, and then they order me to Yar."

They went to Bubnov's after a business breakfast at Lopashov's and Arsentych's, if they had put too much behind the collar.[12] From Bubnov's they went anywhere they wanted, just not home. They would go on a bender for a week. There were many such dissolute people. One, for example, drinks sadly in taverns and dives, acts outrageously, and will only say one phrase, "How much?" He takes out a wallet, pays, and for no apparent reason, takes a bottle of champagne and whips it against the mirror. Noise. Crashing. A servant, a buffet worker, rushes up. The man cold-bloodedly takes out his wallet and in the most businesslike tone asks, "How much?" He pays without bargaining and again beats...

There was another one who lived near the Moscow River who drank only at Bubnov's and wouldn't leave his reserved private dining room for perhaps two days. He once went home late at night in a cab with a friend. The gates were opened for him – the entrance to his grandfather's house was off the courtyard, which was surrounded by a tall wooden fence. He yelled, "I don't want to go through the gate. Break the fence down. I won't enter otherwise."

The owner's word is strong and so is his fist. They closed the gate, broke down the fence, and His Honor triumphantly rode into the courtyard. The next day: no repentance. The bold one is off carousing again. In the morning, his wife begins to compose his punishment, but he is on her with his fists:

"Who's the boss here? Who? If I want something, I get it!"

"You, Makary Pasiyevich, should go to the *banya* and wash-up. It will ease..."

"Let's wash!"

"I'll order the *banya* to be heated."

"I don't want the *banya*. Heat the root cellar!"

And he got them to put a stove in the root cellar and turn it into a makeshift *banya*.

Bubnov's upper floor was at least civil. The lower floor was something unique.

"Why are your eyes closed and your snout sideways?"

"Well that's the way I ended up yesterday."

"Fell in 'the hole,' did you?"

"Aimed for it."

The lower part of Bubnov's was called "the hole." Bubnov's hole. Thanks to this, even the upstairs, clean part of the building was known as "the hole." Beneath the tavern was an enormous underground cellar, to which led a staircase with more

---

than 20 steps. It had ancient pillars, improbably thick, and not a single window. It was gas-lit. Along the sides of the room were wooden booths; these "closets" were gloomy and dirty. In the middle of each stood a table, above which a gas light twinkled through the tobacco smoke. All the tables had the same type of dirty tablecloth and four identical, wooden chairs.

Travelling merchants, looking for "a kopek and more" or "more for a kopek" started their celebrations there with friends and customers at 10 in the morning. There were drunkenness, debauchery, and scenes all day and late into the night. It was hot from the gaslights, and stuffy from the tobacco and the kitchen. Songs, laughter, cursing. You had to shout in someone's ear since talking over the noise, even sitting side by side, was impossible. You could curse as much as you liked – women were not allowed. And new people just kept coming. Why wouldn't you when everything there was so inexpensive? They had enormous portions, a ruble per bottle of vodka, wine also a ruble per bottle, various ports, madeira, Spanish wines made in Moscow, right up to Lanin's two-ruble champagne, about which they sang a song:

With Lanin's wine,
Your head swells and cracks...

They drank and ate because it was cheap, and the police never even peeked in. Any scenes ended right there, and for a merchant the main thing was to keep it "secret." Not a single tavern in Moscow was as noisy as Bubnov's hole. There was no more interesting tavern, except perhaps Martyanich. It operated in the cellars of a municipal building, advertising as much as possible and trading on fame, copying in all respects Bubnov's hole. Only here the debauchery was heightened by admitting women, which did not happen at the hole.

The fashionable Slavyansky Bazaar had expensive guest rooms, where government ministers from Petersburg stayed, as well as Siberian gold producers, and landowners from the steppe, who controlled hundreds of thousands of acres of land, and... con men, Petersburg hustlers, who arranged card games in 20-ruble rooms. The entrance from the guest rooms went straight into the dining room, through a corridor of private dining rooms. "Bless yourself and get married."

The restaurant's lunches and dinners were not especially popular, but its breakfasts, from midnight until three, were fashionable, just like at Hermitage. Groups of merchants, finished with "the labors of the just" at the market, got up here before two, closed million-ruble deals at their tables, and left before three. Those remaining after three finished as "storks." "They breakfasted until the storks" was a common expression.[13] People in the know understood that it meant the breakfast was at Slavyansky Bazaar, where the group, after champagne and coffee with liqueurs, demanded "storks." This was a sealed, crystal decanter, decorated with golden storks, containing a wonderful, 50-ruble cognac. Whoever paid for the cognac received the empty decanter as a keepsake. For a time, there was even competition to collect these bottles. One horse breeder got seven of them and displayed his collection with pride.

The Slavyansky Bazaar's building was constructed in the 1870s, the work of A.A. Prokhovshchikov. Its round, two-tone dining room with a glass roof was beautiful. Two big-time con men sat once in Slavyansky Bazaar eating breakfast. One said to the other:

"Look, on my plate. I see some sort of little grates. What does that mean?"

"It means that you won't avoid prison! It's an omen!"

The plate clearly reflected the frames of the glass ceiling panes.

There were also restaurants just outside the city, and the best were Yar and Strelnya, whose outdoor summer service was known as Mauritania. At the time, Strelnya, founded by I.F. Natruskin, was one of the sites to see in Moscow. It had an enormous winter garden. It had 100-year-old grottos, cliffs, fountains, gazebos, and, as was expected, it was surrounded by private rooms with all kinds of choirs.

Yar was owned by Aksyonov, a fat, clean-shaven man, aptly nicknamed "Orange." He was proud of his Pushkin room, including a bust of the great poet, who had never been there. When Pushkin wrote:

And chilled veal recalls Yar's truffles,

He was referring to the old Yar, located in his day on Petrovka Street.

Beyond the Tver Gate there was another restaurant, El Dorado. Skalkin's Gold Anchor in Ivanovskaya Street was near Sokolniki. The Prague restaurant was where Tarykin combined all of the best from Hermitage and Testov's, and even surpassed the latter, making its stuffed pasta with half sturgeon, half white fish. Prague had the best billiard tables, and you could always find a good game there.

When it became fashionable, many taverns started to call themselves "restaurants." Even Arsentych, which changed ownership, was re-listed in the directory as "Old Cherkasky Restaurant." But people still went to "the tavern" at Arsentych. Later, many restaurants and eateries sprouted in Moscow, such as Italia, Livorno, Palermo, and Tatarsky on Petrovka, which later became the hotel Russia. These places were very cheap and very bad. The one exception was Peterhof on Mokhovaya Street, where Razzhivin introduced cheap daily specials, advertised in the newspapers. "Today, Monday – fish broth with stuffed pasta; Tuesday – pork; Wednesdays and Saturdays – Siberian *pelmeny*... Every day, *shashlyk* from Karachayevsky mutton."

Razzhivin popularized *shashlyk* in Moscow. The first *shashlyk* were Antandilov's, who owned, in the seventies, the first small Caucasian wine cellar with regional wines, in a basement on Sofia Street. Then, Avtandilov moved to Myasnitskaya Street and opened a wine shop. He stopped making *shashlyk* for a long time, until, in the eighties and nineties, in Cherkasky Alley, right above the Arsentych tavern, the Caucasian Slukhanov opened, without a permit, in his own apartment, a Caucasian eatery with *shashlyk* and, secretly, regional wines, especially for travelers from the Caucasus. Later, Russians started to go. He distributed business cards through friends, "K. Slukhanov. Nephew of Prince Argutinsky-Dolgorukov," and his address. Every blessed soul knew why he went by this card. The affair played on, and the hostile competitors eyed one another. It ended with a summons and a closure. Later, Razzhivin invited him to open a kitchen in Peterhof. Business cards again circulated hand-to-hand from the "nephew of Prince Argutinsky-Dolgorukov," and business went magnificently. This was the first *shashlyk* kitchen in Moscow, and after him came hundreds of Caucasians, and *shashlyk* became fashionable.

There were also German restaurants, such as Alpine Rose on Sofia Street, Billo on Greater Lubyanka Street, Berlin on Rozhdestvenka Street, and Dyuso on Neglinnaya Street, but they were atypical of Moscow; nonetheless, the food was good and they served mugs of genuine Pilsner beer.

Among the small restaurants, Venice, on Kuznetsky Street,[14] in the basement of a building near Tverskoy Boulevard, was interesting. There, in a small, separate room with a swinging door, gathered the grandfathers of our revolution. No place was more convenient: at 11, the restaurant locked its doors, the public left, and friendly arguments commenced. The kitchen and buffet were closed, and only the restaurant owner, Vasily Yakovlevich, waited, practically praying for each of the visitors in his small room. Only vodka, beer, and cold foods were served. Sometimes they drank until morning. "It's inspiring and private at my place!" Vasily Yakovlevich would say. People came alone and in pairs, and left the same way through the service entrance, off into the empty night to Kuznetsky Street and Newspaper Alley (at the time, the entire alley from Kuznetsky Street to Nikitskaya Street was known as Newspaper Alley) to Tverskaya Street to Chernyshy or Olsufev's, where they lived and where illegals went to spend the night.

In the "small hall," as this little room was misleadingly called by Vasily Yakovlevich, at a big, gas-lit table, sat the enormous, bearded, hairy figures of P.G. Zaichnevsky, M.I. Mishla-Orfanov, F.D. Nefedov, N.N. Zlatovratsky, and S.A. Priklonsky.

---

14. The literal translation of the street's name is "Kuznetsky Bridge," but we have used "street" to avoid confusion.

Among them was the thin N.M. Astyrev, with the red beard of an *intelligent*, at the time reviewing proofs for his book, *Among the Local Scribblers*. Then there was the tiny, clean-shaven actor Vasya Vasiliyev, who would have ended up in prison in the Trial of the 193, but, by some coincidence, was able to get out of trouble.[15] His real surname, known only to a few, was Shvedevenger. V.A. Goltsev was occasionally here; once, during one of German Lopatin's escapes. The men met here for about two years, then they went their separate ways. Vasily Yakovlevich stayed open and all of those mentioned above, when in Moscow, considered it a duty to stop in, and sometimes take a little money for the road. Once, Vasya Vasiliyev brought by a newly arrived copy of issue No. 6 of *The People's Freedom*, and late at night read it aloud, not hiding anything from Vasily Yakovlevich. When Mishla read a poem published in this issue, P.Ya. Yakubovich's "Mothers," Vasily Yakovlevich, with tears in his eyes, asked to copy it. Vasiliyev gave it to him.

"How much can I pay you, Vasily Vasilyevich?"

"As much as you'd like. The money will go to help political prisoners." ·

"Just a moment."

Vasily Yakovlevich disappeared, returned, and produced a multi-colored, 100-ruble note.

"On behalf of such a great endeavor, please allow me to accept it."

The small restaurant Venice was memorable for one thing only: during the day it served middle class and government workers passing by on Kuznetsky Street. The city's ever-restless dandies did not consider a cheap restaurant worthy of their attention, preferring either a bakery or the neighboring Alpine Rose or Billo.

Moldavia, in the Gruzino neighborhood, was also called a restaurant, and days and evenings served average customers, drinking vodka. In the mornings, however, starting at five, drivers of cabs, pairs and gypsy coaches would arrive. This was a Gypsy tavern. After Yar, Strelnya, and El Dorado closed, the Gypsies, all living in Gruzino, came here to "drink tea" with their admirers.

Not far from Moldavia, on Greater Georgian Street, at Kharlamov's, in the same hours, Yegor Kapkov's humbler tavern grew lively. At six in the morning it was full of cloaked customers. These were waiters from Moscow's restaurants, who had finished their shifts, and arrived to spend time in their own circle: drink tea, or a shot of vodka, and have some broth with cabbage. After seeing their fill of self-important guests at work, they took a turn at it themselves, picking on their white-shirted waiters for any kind of mistake, sometimes even copying someone they had served

---

15. The Trial of the 193 was actually a series of trials in 1877-1878. Officially conducted under the title "Concerning Propaganda in the Empire," the trials prosecuted 193 "revolutionary *narodniki*" for a propaganda campaign that allegedly started in 1873 and was said to be aimed at fomenting "popular unrest." *Narod* is Russian for "the people," so a *narodnik* (plural, *narodniki*) was one who went among the people. This was the largest political trial in the Empire's history and ended in acquital of all but a small percentage of those accused.

only an hour before, pompously summoning the waiter, "Man, this is for you 'for tea.' " And the "man" in the cloak gave 10 kopeks to the man in the shirt. The cloak added his apostrophes. They quizzed the younger waiters. They would serve tea, and an old buffet worker would flick the nail of his index finger against his own front teeth: "Give me iron!" Or he would order, "Punch me in the teeth until smoke comes out!" An experienced boy would hand him the sugar tines, bring cigarettes, and light a match.

On the corner of Ostozhenko and First Zachatevsky Alley, in the first half of the last century, Shustrov's tavern occupied a large building. He and his family lived on the mezzanine. It had an enormous rooftop pigeon coop, Moscow's largest. Clouds of pigeons of all breeds and colors flew above the surrounding area when the Shustrov family was busy with Moscow's favorite sport, pigeon racing. Among the fans was the wealthy restaurateur I.E. Krasovsky. He bought the tavern from Shustrov, and convinced the building's former owner to demolish the wooden structure and build a stone one according to his own plan for the largest tavern in Moscow. The stone building was three stories high, and fronted on two streets. The bottom floor had shops, the second floor had the tavern's "gentry" section with a large number of private dining rooms, and the third floor had a public tavern where the main room, with a low ceiling, was so large that it fit more than 100 people, with the center of the floor still open for dancing. A player piano was located on the first floor and the upper floor had a stage for singers and harmonists. While one musician played, 40 people would dance.

Above the building, like earlier, were clouds of pigeons, because Krasovsky and his sons were just like Shustrov, so they built a pigeon coop under the roof. The tavern was called Pigeon Coop and no one knew any different, although this was not its official name, which appeared in print only once, in a Moscow newspaper in 1905, in a short notice under the title, "Arrest of Revolutionaries at 'Pigeon Coop.'" Long before 1905, the comfortable private dining rooms of Pigeon Coop, safe from police surveillance, served as a place for get-togethers and larger meetings of revolutionaries. In 1905, enormous meetings were held there.

Krasovsky built some very comfortable rooms. Here, in the mornings, starting at five, waiters who had worked at dinners, lunches, and weddings met to split their earnings and drink vodka. Balls were held here, "common" weddings, and "the Knitting" met here. This gang of fixers reduced auctions to a sham, and thereby eliminated customers' willingness to bid: either a good buy would be torn right out of your hands, or they would drive the price on bad goods so high that they would beat out any interest in ever participating again. In their language, this was known as "putting on a cast-iron hat."

In addition to meetings of the less-than-honorable association of the "cast-iron hat," cock fights were held here twice per month. On designated evenings the room was divided, and a fighting ring was laid out in the middle, like a circus. Benches and chairs were placed all around the ring for the audience, specially invited fans of this old Moscow sport. Much like at horse races, there was a type of tote board. Larger bets were held aside for the winner. At the agreed time, rich merchants rode up to Pigeon Coop, but always in cabs, not in the saddle, so they could speak privately. They climbed to the second floor and passed by a row of closed, private dining rooms to the buffet. From there, they climbed an inner staircase to a blocked-off area, and took places around the arena. Behind them, one by one, men with suitcases walked through to a private room. These hunters had brought their birds, English fighters, with no crown or beard, with highly sharpened spurs. The desperate battle began. The arena was bathed in blood. Frenzied viewers, with blazing eyes and grimaces, at times grew quiet and at times roared like beasts. Everyone was there: propertied merchants, important government officials, rich traders from the bazaar, theater owners, and "cast-iron hats."

Bets sometimes reached several thousand rubles. Audience favorites for a long time were imported from England, most notably birds belonging to the flour trader Larionov, who at one time had been convicted for delivering rotten flour to the army. Thanks to his birds, he was once again among the wealthy, who forgave his past because of his "successful bird hunting." These evenings ended in the dining rooms and halls on the tavern's second floor with the most extravagant drinking sessions.

Krasovsky himself was a fan, which brought the tavern enormous revenues. But later, at the end of the century, Krasovsky became mentally ill, spent most of his time at Pigeon Coop, and when there, he wandered through its rooms with unreasoning eyes and sang psalms. He, of course, was cheated: the tavern, once a "gold mine," fell into others' hands to pay debts. Krasovsky finished his life in poverty.

Aside from Pigeon Coop, cockfights were held on the other side of the Moscow River, but the audience there was mixed. Simple Russian roosters fought, English birds were not allowed. This tavern was called Trap. Among dirty piles and heaps of trash was a door to an unheated barn with a ring. Here the audience was even tougher than at Krasovsky's, and more interested in gambling. A third spot for cockfights was Wave on the Garden Ring Road, a criminal den filled with a mix of secretive vagrants.

Among Moscow's taverns was one where, once a year, at the time of the spring rains, when from the upper reaches of the Moscow River rafts landed with timber and logs, one could see the wood floating down the river. This tavern, spacious and dirty, was in Dorogomilov, right near the Borodinsky Bridge on the Moscow River. These few days of the arrival of the rafts in Dorogomilov were a holiday for Muscovites, who filled the bridge and the river banks, marveling at the work of the best lumber drivers, neatly leading rafts under the bridge, every minute risking crashing and drowning.

At the Nikitskaya Gate, at Borgest's, there was a tavern where one of the rooms had swallows in cages covered by paper, and in the evening and early in the morning, from all over Moscow, people gathered who enjoyed their songs. Many taverns had cages with song birds in what was then Newspaper Alley, across from Shcherbakov's, like for example at A. Pavlovsky's on Trubnaya Square, and in the Hunting Tavern on Neglinnaya Street. In this tavern, on Sundays, on their way from Trubnaya Square, where dogs and birds were sold, Moscow's well-known hunters met.

A.T. Zverev owned two taverns, one in Gavrikovy Alley, Grain Market. Wholesaler-millionaires, who controlled the grain market, met there and closed major deals over tea. This was the quietest tavern. Even voices weren't audible. Traders spoke ear-to-ear, or occasionally you might make out, "Payment in kind, 126..."

"And the oats?"

"Eighty..."

Now and then they would receive telegrams about grain prices from their agents in port cities. One might wrinkle his brow after reading a telegram – a loss. But his word was always good, never taken back. You might go bankrupt, but you'd keep your word.

On the tables were small sacks with grain samples. There was a mass of them in the entry hall on the coat rack. During market hours, except for tea, there was nothing on the tables. Later, after "business," they breakfasted and lunched.

Zverev's other tavern was on the corner of Petrovka Street and Rakhmanovsky Alley in the building belonging to Doctor A.S. Levenson, father of A.A. Levenson, later famous as a printer of advertisements and periodicals, and a tenant of state theaters.

"The Knitting," a gang, met here on days when there were auctions in pawnshops or when goods were seized by the courts. This was a group of middlemen, unofficial, but nonetheless real, known to the police but without official authorization, that attended auctions and fixed bids to buy expensive items for next to nothing. They often succeeded.

After every auction, The Knitting met at Zverev's, and one of its rooms would present a strange picture: on the tables were gold, silver and bronze valuables, on the chairs, items under debate; they would take from their pockets, display, and resell watches and necklaces. Here, the Knitting settled accounts and split profits. Other middlemen elbowed into the room, traders from Sukharevka, who were interested in all of the gang's auction purchases. As a result, Zverev's tavern was later closed. The editorial offices of *Russian Word*, at the time still a small newspaper, took its place.

Newspaper and magazine employees did not at that time have their own tavern. Nevertheless, "fabricators of people's books," book traders and publishers from Nikolskaya Street got together in Kolgushkin's tavern on Lubyanskaya Square, and worked for the "enlightenment" of old peasant Russia. Publishers met here: I. Morozov, Sharapov, Zemsky, Gubanov, Manukhin, both Abramovs, Presnov, Stupin, Naumov, Fadeyev, Zheltov, and Zhivarev. Each of these firms annually published 10 or more "titles," with 75 to 600 pages, with garish covers, terrible titling, and prices starting at a ruble and a half per 100. Each was published in no fewer than 6,000 copies.

It was at Kolgushkin's, over tea, that publishers gave orders to "writers." They were known as "writers from Nikolskaya Street." The walls of these taverns had seen even mighty men of literature run to the "publishers from Nikolskaya" in a moment of financial despair. Most writers were government clerks driven from the service, former officers, dropout students, seminarians, and sons of members of literature's pantheon who had rejected the leading writers and officials of the literary world.

A publisher sits by the window with a glass of tea and speaks with one of these writers.

"I might need a new *Battle with the Kabardines*."[16]

"I can do that, Denis Ivanovich."

"I need it soon. Can you write it in a week?"

"Yes, sir. How many sheets?"[17]

"About six. I'll publish it in two parts."

"Fine, sir. Six rubles per sheet."

"Eating a bit rich aren't you? Two!"

"Well, fine, I'll take five."

They closed the deal and the writer delivered the book in two weeks.

At another table, a man with a large estate, but worn boots, sat with a small book.

"You see, Ivan Andreyevich, all of your competitors have an *Ice House*, a *Basurman*, a *Count of Monte Cristo*, a *Three Musketeers*, and a *Yuri Miloslavsky*. But they are in no way what Dumas, Zagoskin, or Lazhechnikov wrote.[18] After all, who the hell

---

16. The 1840 novel *Russia's Battle with the Kabardines*, by Nikolai Zryakhov, is considered the epitome of Russian pulp fiction of the early nineteenth century. It was wildly popular yet literary critics panned it as sentimental and simple.

17. The common measurement used in Russian publishing is the *avtorsky list*, the "author's sheet," roughly equivalent to 22 typewritten pages, or about 6000 words. So the publisher is looking for what we would think of today as a short novel, about 150 pages.

18. Mikhail Nikolayevich Zagoskin (1789-1852), wrote comedies and historical fiction. His historical novel, *Yury Miloslavsky* (1829), was set during Russia's Time of Troubles (Смутное время). This period was between the death in 1598 of the last Tsar of the Rurik Dynasty, Feodor Ivanovich, and the 1613 founding of the Romanov Dynasty. The novel became the first Russian best-seller. Ivan Ivanovich Lazhechnikov (1792-1869), was a Russian writer of historical fiction whose novels include *Basurman*, *The Ice House*, and *The Last Novik*. Both Zagoskin and Lazhnikov wrote during the period that prose fiction was first becoming popular in Russia.

knows how many fabrications are hidden in there? The authors' bones would turn over in the grave if they knew."

"Well, what? I have them too. Everyone has their own *Yuri Miloslavsky*, and their own *Monte Cristo*, and the signatures: Zagoskin, Lazhechnikov, Dumas. That is why I called you. Write *Taras Bulba* for me."

"What do you mean *Taras Bulba*? That's Gogol's after all."

"Well, what of it? You write it just like Gogol, only change just the smallest bit, and make it different and shorter. It will be interesting to everyone because it's Taras Bulba, and not anyone else. Everyone will be pleased that it's a new Taras Bulba! Here, brother, the title's the main thing; the content, spit on it. They'll read it anyway, if they paid money. They can't get you for misstating anything, it's Bulba after all. It's Bulba, only the words are different."

After this conversation, in fact, *Taras Bulba* did appear over the signature of a different author, since Morozov added his own name, which no one could have expected!

In the place where, before 1918, stood the Hotel National, at the end of the last century stood a building pre-dating Peter I, belonging to Firsanov. On its ground floor was a favorite of Hunter's Row traders, Yegor Kruglov's tavern, Balaklava.

"Where's himself?" asks a purchasing agent.

"He's in the cave with a customer."

The Balaklava consisted of two, low-ceilinged, gloomy rooms, and instead of private dining rooms they had two caves, the right and the left. These were strange, enormous niches, reminiscent of old-time stone cells, which they probably were, judging by the unusual thickness of the walls and fixtures, including iron straps, rings, and hooks. Only honored guests were given reservations there.

On the other side of the square, in a narrow alley behind the Loskutina Hotel, was Kogtev's tavern, a dive called Glutton, where shoplifters and petty bureaucrats had tea and two or three of the most respected "loo-yawrs from Iverskoy"[19] received customers. All sorts of people went there to have legal petitions written. This was "the people's law bureau." At his own table sat a man who formerly held an important judicial position. He had been dismissed from the state's judicial service for alcoholism, but drafted documents for wealthy merchants who came to see him. There were times when the well-known lawyer F.N. Plevako visited here with the great obfuscator Nikolai Ivanovich.

Kuznetsky Street, across Petrovka Street, connects to the wide mouth of narrow Kuznetsky Alley. Halfway down the mouth of the alley was an old wooden wing with decorative trim. Such buildings remained only on the edges of the city. Here, surrounded by stone buildings with mirrored glass, were the Tremblé cake shop and

---

19. With the odd pronunciation of "lawyer" Gilyarovsky alludes to both the ignorance of many potential customers and the questionable credentials of some of the practicioners.

Tavern Owner, by Boris Kustodiev (1920).

the Solodovnikovsky shops. This building stood out because of its antiquity. Many decades ago, above its porch, not the entrance as in neighboring buildings, but a wooden decorative porch with four steps and a wooden bannister, glowed a small sign: "Tavern of S.S. Shcherbakov." The owner, Spirodon Stepanovich Shcherbakov, an old man in tails, with a neat beard, was a favorite of all actors. During Lent, Shcherbak's was full of actors and all the best known people invariably visited. They treated Spirodon Stepanovich with respect and he knew everyone by their first name and patronymic. He was very interested in success and inquired about all those who had not yet made it to Moscow for Lent. Giants of the stage came here: N.K. Miloslavsky, N.Kh. Rybakov, Pavel Nikitin, Poltavtsev, Grigorovsky, the Vasilyevs, Dyukov, Smolkov, Laukhin, Medvedev, Grigoryev, Andreyev-Burlak, Pisarev, Kireyev, and well known Moscow actors from the Maly Theater. There were also playwrights and writers of the day: A.N. Ostrovsky, N.A. Chayev, K.A. Tarnovsky. The Kondratiyev brothers, still young, were regulars at Scherbakov's, and a poem went around about them:

One of these brothers
by the name of Ivan,
surname Kondratyev,
titled Ataman.

Old man Shcherbakov was a true friend of actors, and in their moments of despair, usually toward the end of Lent, in addition to credit at his restaurant, he gave them money for the road. No one stayed in debt to him. His tavern was praised for its meat-stuffed pies. For 15 kopeks you could buy a whole plate of *pirozhki*, three fingers deep, and with it, for the same price, a bowl of broth. Toward the end of Lent, when actors' money dried up, they ate only these pies.

Spirodon Stepanovich died. Khomyakov, the owner of a row of stone buildings on Petrovka Street, would have replaced this old wooden wing with a new building much earlier, but he felt sorry for the old man. His heirs proved to be different. After receiving their inheritance, they evicted Shcherbakov's, depriving actors of their traditional refuge.

The enormous property went to the young Khomyakov. He immediately demolished the wing and decided to build in its place a luxurious stone building, but the city council would not approve his plan: it required widening the alley. Khomyakov dug in his heels, "The land is mine after all." The city proposed buying the scrap of land. Khomyakov outright refused to sell: "I don't want to." After blocking off the land with an iron fence, he began construction. At the same time, he planted trees.

The building went up. The trees grew. A new bank office opened with no entrance from the alley. Khomyakov built a sidewalk between the building and his grove, and blocked it from the sidewalk using the same kind of iron fence. In this way, in the middle of Kuznetsky Alley, a triangle was formed, which long went by the name Khomyakov's Grove. No matter how the authorities argued or what friends said, Khomyakov would not give in: "This is my property." He enjoyed the abusive letters he received every day. The press satirized his obduracy.

"Take administrative action," someone advised the mayor. The Chief of Police was summoned. They proposed clearing out the alley, and threatened Khomyakov with exile from Moscow. "You can drive me off," Khomyakov said. "I'll leave, but my property will remain."

The wind rustled the young grove, which probably would have survived to enjoy Soviet protection, but one fine day there was no grove, no fence, and a cobblestone street shone in place of yellow sand. How? Who? What? Moscow did not understand. There were various rumors, but only one was true: Khomyakov ordered the trees felled and alley paved and on that same day went abroad. It was said that he genuinely feared exile from Moscow; it was said that relatives asked him not to shame the family name. I have in my hand a copy of a story from the magazine *Entertainment*, signed by A.M. Pazukhin. A news writer and novelist, and the author of many stories and tales, Pazukhin bet the editors of *Entertainment* that he could get rid of the grove. He got his hands on a photograph of Khomyakov and through a mutual acquaintance sent him a caricature: in a grove wanders a donkey with Khomyakov's face.

Earlier, before Shcherbakov's, the actors' tavern was Barsova's in the Bronnikov building, on the corner of Greater Dmitrovka and Hunter's Row. It contained the famous Hall of Columns. In it gathered the actors and writers mentioned above, who later went to Shcherbak when Barsova's closed and its space was taken by the Artists' Circle. Actors spent days in Shcherbak and evenings at the Artists' Circle. When Shcherbak closed, actors gathered at the restaurant Livorno, located in Newspaper Alley, as it was known at the time, across the intersection from Shcherbak.

From noon until four during Lent, Livorno was full of people. A cloud of tobacco smoke hovered in its small rooms and there was an unimaginable stink. A small cloakroom was filled with fur coats, winter coats, cloaks of the most fantastic colors, and styles. In the restaurant every table was covered with bottles and decanters. Tight circles of clean-shaven actors sat together, colorfully and creatively dressed: the jacket and pants of a vaudeville straight man, horrid collars, ties, vests – some white, some with designs, some of velvet, some of linen. During the first half of Lent, watch chains with bunches of small charms shone on all the vests. On the table sparkled new, small, silver cigarette cases. Those with cigars and watches for the hundredth time told every new face about ovations where audiences had presented them with these things.

For the first three weeks the actors sparkled with gifts, but then things started to change: cigars didn't sit on the table, watches were not taken out, and by then jackets were buttoning a bit more tightly, because even the last bauble, the watch chain with charms, followed the watch into the pawnshop's till. The wardrobe, for which they had paid a lot of money in slowly-saved, hard earned kopeks, went last.

With the switch to Livorno from the solid Shcherbak's, the group of actors became smaller: many of the leading players stopped going, and limited themselves to evening visits to the Actors' Circle or dropped in at the German restaurant Veldt, behind the Bolshoi Theater. Grigorovsky, after moving from Shcherbak's to Veldt spoke about Livorno: "They have some sort of Greek cook-mistress. I ask for appetizer for vodka, and owner proposes: 'Zee bezt abbet-izer – eez Greek trowt.' I try eet – filth."

Actors met at Livorno until it was shuttered. Then they met at Rogov's Tavern in Georgiyevsky Alley, on Tverskoy Boulevard next to the game, meat, and fish sellers. An upper floor of this building had Rassokhin's library and a theater ticket office.

Among the actors there were, of course not a few card and pool players, who spent Lent in the billiards room of Savrasenkov's restaurant on Tverskoy Boulevard, where high stakes games were played. There were well known provincial actors as well. Among them, two were especially well known: Mikhail Pavlovich Dokuchaev, who played tragedies, and Yegor Yegorovich Bystrov, also an excellent actor, who played all types of roles. Yegor Bystrov, a professional gambler, could swindle anyone: he was the origin of the verb, "to yegorate."

THE PIT

FROM TVERSKAYA STREET WE WENT through the Iversky Gate and turned into the deep arch of an old building, a former location of the Governor-General's office. "Well, this is where I live, let's go inside." We walked across the courtyard, ringed by similar old buildings, and went under another arch. A staircase led to the second floor. There was a dark hallway, and deep inside, to the right, there was a door.

"We made it."

The heavy door creaked and behind it was gloom.

"Here we go down a bit, give me your arm..."

I descended into the darkness, holding my acquaintance by the arm. I took a few steps forward but could see nothing. The switch clicked and the bright light of an electric bulb threw a shadow on a pile of trash. Yellow stripes played against book bindings and on pictures above a writing table. I found myself in a large, long room with thick, hanging pipes, and a deep recess for a small, dark, barred window that contrasted with the illuminated wall. It seemed to me that near the window, at the table, a chronicler sat and wrote:[1]

Still one last tale...
and my chronicle is done

It flashed through my mind. I stood and kept silent "This has to be Pimen's cell! You could not imagine a better setting and props," I said. I don't know if this was Pimen's cell, but what was literally here, in this room, was the "pit" where they imprisoned debtors – that's a fact. It was the same "pit" mentioned by Dostoyevsky

---

1. A reference to Pushkin's Pimen. See footnote page *19*.

and Ostrovsky. A horrible prison for those jailed, not for crimes, but for debts. They were victims of bad luck, those unable to manage a business. Sometimes drunks were jailed here too. "The pit" was the nadir of the commercial thirst for revenge. It existed before the revolution, which cleanly swept away this vestige of cruel times.

According to ancient French and German law, a debtor was obligated to work off money owed to the creditor, or was subject to detention in shackles until the debt was paid. The creditor was obligated to "feed not bleed" the debtor. In the days of *Rus*, it was supposed that the "creditor had first claim on the rights and income of a debtor until he is paid back." Under Peter I, debtors' departments were formed, and since that time debtors have done their time in prison together with criminals. Debtors' departments were later consolidated across the Moscow River, to the Presnensky Police Building on the third floor. Despite its third floor location, it was still called "the pit."

Once an old man was there, a former millionaire, Plotitsyn. At the same time, a merchant's wife was there, an older woman, with such sorrow in her eyes that it was sad to see. I went there once on newspaper business. When I was going back down the stairs, I saw an older woman on the porch. She went into the guards' office but quickly left. I grew interested and asked the guard: "She came to do her time but there's no room, it's being renovated. She has seven children and she'll go to prison for her husband's debts." As it happened, "the pit" had a women's section. In Russia, corporal punishment of women was stopped much earlier than for men, but even women could not avoid debtors' prison. An old soldier who had served at "the pit" for many years told me:

It's a pity. It may be legal but it's unconscionable! They put a person in jail, take him away from his family, from small children, and instead of letting him work and perhaps get back on his feet, they keep him behind bars for years for nothing, A young man sat here, he had just been married and the next day he was in prison. A rich creditor had tricked him into a bad deal, and then had him thrown him in jail so he could steal his wife. He stunned the debtor and took his wife.

He is doing time now, and his wife visits with their children: small, smaller, smallest... Tears, so many tears! Legs shaking, they ask the guard to let him out just for the holiday.

Of course, there were cases where arrestees ran off after a day or two at home, but they would catch them and bring them back.

Creditors could saddle their debtors with various hardships. A creditor might suddenly stop paying meal fees. Then the authorities would release the debtor. He would leave happy, joyful, and arrive back home, just start to get settled, and the cruel creditor would pay the fees and receive a frightful document from a judge, an "arrest warrant." A representative of the creditor would show up with the police, and the debtor, just starting to come back to life, was thrown back into "the pit." Sometimes a creditor's agent, after learning about the release of a debtor, would find him at home, break in, often at night, and in front of his wife and children take him to the debtors' prison. They caught debtors on the street, in taverns, as dinner guests, and even leaving church!

But here, like everywhere, some were happy, some were sad. There were cases where a judge ordered a debtor freed, and then in another month would send another order. He was a free man. But someone else, who has no protection and no way to give a bribe, couldn't expect any judicial orders. Would a prison guard, out of simple humanity, let someone go home to their family for a day? They were all victims of arbitrary administrative rules and money-hungry merchants. Most ended up in "the pit" at the whim of a wealthy creditor, angry at the debtor for not paying, and at himself for making a mistake and losing money, or to sweep from the road a bothersome competitor. The creditor grudgingly signed a warrant and paid a meal fee of five rubles, 85 kopeks per month. There were many revenge seekers among Moscow's wealthy merchants, proven by the debtors' prison usual population of almost 30 people.

OLSUFEV'S FORTRESS

ON TVERSKOY BOULEVARD, ACROSS FROM Bryusov Alley, in the seventies and at the start of the eighties, near the Governor-General's residence, stood Olsufev's large building: four stories, with shops and a wine cellar. The shops and cellar had two exits onto the street and the courtyard, and they serviced separate clienteles. The cellar sold out of its back door all night. At that time, this creatively designed building was painted dark grey. There were enormous mezzanine windows, several bays, and tall, cast-iron, grated stairs in a setback leading to the entry. There were no entranceways or vestibules. In the middle of the building there were solid iron gates with the entrance always chained, next to which, day and night, enormous servants stood guard. The building's exterior, decorated with the signs of commercial enterprises, was in complete order. The first and second floors sparkled with the enormous windows of richly appointed shops. Orlov's fashionable hair salon was here, Ovcharenko's photograph studio, and Vozdvizhensky's tailor shop. The upper two stories, as long as anyone could remember, were occupied by Chernysheva's and Kalinina's furnished rooms, which is why they were known as "Chernysh."

Actors, petty clerks, teachers, students, and writers lived in Chernysh. In 1876, a young actor at the Maly Theater, M.V. Lentovsky, lived here in a cheap little fourth-floor room, with two small, floor-level windows looking out onto the courtyard. His possessions included one thin coat, a guitar, and some empty bottles. In apartment No. 45, in the courtyard, lived the building's watchman for as long as anyone could remember. This was Karasev, a former city policeman, a favorite of Governor-General Prince V.A. Dolgorukov, from whom he had become inseparable, sometimes as a messenger, sometimes carrying out personal instructions. The police feared Karasev more than the Prince himself, because in Olsufev's building he poked his nose into everything.

The building's owner, retired Headquarters Captain Dm. L. Olsufev, unrelated to Count Olsufev, did not live there. A former watchman managed the building, a close friend of Karasev's. He received payments from tenants and the owners of the commercial businesses: quite a bit of money. But this was not the primary income for the building's owner. Behind the permanently locked gate was an enormous courtyard, next to which was a row of buildings that looked like the worst slums. The crumbled entrances, with stairs going down into the earth, leading to cellar floors with iron-barred and grated windows, were a horror.

In the middle of the courtyard was an enormous wing. There were also side wings, so there was not a single fence across which one might crawl. There was one exit through a guarded gate. 1,500 people lived there. In short, there was a reason why the building was called "Olsufev's Fortress." In run-down courtyard buildings there were hundreds of apartments and rooms rented by all sorts of artisans. Five days a week it was quiet in the courtyard, but on Sunday and Monday everyone was drunk and wild: the whine of harmonicas, songs, fist fights, hundreds of half-naked apprentices, children crying, apprentices roaring and cursing, beaten for nothing and no reason by their masters, who were beaten the same way when they were apprentices.

Nothing was visible or audible from the street beyond the large courtyard. The gates were locked. Somewhat respectable apartment renters, who dressed a little more cleanly than the rest, occasionally flowed through the gate. Others never left the fortress.

Studios filled the entire, enormous property, and half of the studios held tailors. Half of the tailors were homeless drunks. These were the most profitable, cheapest, and most defenseless workers. Alcoholism here was supported by the owners themselves: it tied people to their places. Where could someone go with no shoes and no clothes? The doorman would not let you out on the street like that, and there's nowhere to complain. "Crab" was the slang word for this type of person. Crabs would sit for years in their little holes, half-dressed, barefoot, with the barest rag as a shirt to run out into the courtyard. Their dream was to go to the tavern, and the means of achieving it – the *banya*. They would buy a cheap chintz shirt and pants, and on the eve of a holiday the yardman would let crabs beyond the gates right across from Brusevsky Alley to the Streltsovskiye Baths. There, they tore off their rags, and after bathing, feeling lighter and clean, would get their hair cut for five kopeks. Then they would go to Kosourova's tavern near the baths, and from there, accompanied by sober companions, would disappear back into the "fortress."

The studios started work on weekdays at six or seven in the morning and end-ed at 10 in the evening. Fifty people worked in a tailor's studio on Vozdvizhenka. Married men lived with their families in apartments on the courtyard, and bache-lors and apprentices slept in the studios, on benches and the floor: for a pillow – a rag under the head or a pair of pants if they were dry.

By six in the morning, a bucket of water was boiling, put on by the apprentices, who had to get up earlier than the rest and go to bed later. Each had his own mug, or sometimes just a jar. Tea was bought by the boss, and even then not everywhere. They had to buy their own bread and sugar. In certain studios, apprentices were given tea only twice a year: a mug on Christmas and one on Easter. "So they don't get spoiled!" Following important holidays, when they drank and were hung over for weeks, they sat at work almost naked, having traded their only shirt for a rag at the tavern, enough only "to cover their shame."

At seven, they poured hot water in mugs without saucers, put glasses on the table, and next to them placed an enormous bronze tea kettle with chicory steeped in the water, to fight cholera. The cook (in studios, they called her the "hostess") gave each a lump of hard sugar and bread cut in thick slices. The boys cleared used plates and served lunch. That was the habit all across Moscow – both in large studios and at the "rodents."

Masters put down their work. Some sat as they worked – "legs like a pretzel" – at the table with their glasses. Those who could not find a place got by standing with the boys, and took turns scooping cabbage soup with large wooden spoons. They did not hurry while eating their lunch. The "hostess" would serve soup a few times, then put sliced beef in the mugs and the oldest of the masters would bang his spoon. In human speech, it meant: "Dig in!" After this, quietly and gradually, they would take one piece of meat at a time in their spoons knowing, that if they took two pieces, the oldest would throw a spoon at their forehead. They ate in silence, placing the spoon back on the table after every swallow, and again, after chewing the meat and the bread completely, would scoop a second. The *kasha* was always buckwheat, with re-processed oil, and during Lent with Lenten oil. Mealtimes were cheerful, but you couldn't even blink, or your spoon would be knocking against the bottom of an empty mug.

After lunch, the boys would clear the table, wipe it down, and the tailors would get right to work. After sewing for an hour, the masters, who had clothes they could wear, went to the tavern to drink tea. Later, around six in the evening, with the others, they drank the owner's tea. After half an hour, they sat down to work until nine. At nine, they had dinner, or more accurately, repeated lunch.

Owners of small enterprises with five or six workers and a few boys with their free labor were called "load carriers." Here, it was even more difficult for the boys: they carried water and chopped wood, ran to the shops, at times for bread, at times

The Newcomer, by Ivan Bogdanov (1893).

for onions for a kopek, at times for salt, and all day long for packages. They also were nannies to the masters' children. They would get up earlier than the rest, and go to bed later.

There was not a spare minute to run out to play, or make friends with other children. In Olsufev's, the boys were less crowded, but they ran off even from there, and runaways from the "rodents" were common. Get acquainted on the streets with young pickpockets, and you could wind up on Khitrovka and fall victim to the slums and prison. Aside from the "Masters' regime," here construction workers and their teams lived with their families and had apartments: carpenters, masons, painters, plasterers, or, as they were called in Moscow, "plodders." There were dozens of sewing shops, tailors, knitters, and laundries. These were the quietest and neatest apartments, filled to capacity with masters and apprentices sleeping in a heap in the studios, barefoot until promoted from apprentice to master. They, like the boys, were brought from the country and apprenticed for 4-5 years with no salary, so they were kept in place. Apprentices who had done their time became masters and mistresses, and stayed to live with their bosses for a meager salary. Some started families.

They lived in Olsufev's for generations. All were acquainted with one another, and were organized by specialty, income, and lifestyle. Drunks (and under this "masters' regime" they were practically the majority) were not accepted in sober family buildings. The courtyard always hummed with kids too young to be apprentices. They did not even think of school. No one taught the little ones. The adolescents, busily apprenticed, had no time to study. The owners' grown daughters, and young women and men becoming masters, and who were already earning a salary, wed. The tribe grew. In Olsufev's, many were related.

On important holidays, parties were organized in the family buildings. But these humble gatherings were only a small part of the widespread, drunken revelry. Universal drunkenness was typical during *Maslennitsa* and the high holy days.

Costumed people went from apartment to apartment with a traditional "goat," and with a drum and a "bear," in a stolen fur coat. A grown man with a fake beard dragged the "bear" on a chain. The "bear," rattling his chains, showed how farmhands stole peas in the field, how the boss danced, how a noble drank vodka, and how a drunk caroused. Of course, they gave the "bear" vodka and after the second or third party it fell down asleep in the hay. If he got a little wild, they sent him to the cellar.

The humble, young working families of Olsufev's Fortress had nothing for their hearts or minds, or even reasonable entertainment – no newspapers or books, and not a single musical instrument. The mezzanine of the Gagarin Palace, with three spacious and luxurious apartments facing the street, was a striking contrast to the extreme poverty and need reigning on the square. On holidays, the sound of music from glittering balls topped the drunken revelry in the courtyard.

In family apartments in the courtyard wings, the only entertainment for the young was dancing, and only one dance, the quadrille.[1] And even that without music. On holidays, when the majority of men left their families for entertainment in taverns and beer bars, young apprentices played in the enormous courtyard, and women stayed home. Young people would gather in one apartment, then another, drink tea, and munch nuts and cheap cookies or sunflower seeds. Conversations covered only the narrow confines of their own specialties or local gossip.

Young people started to yawn. From an open window on the mezzanine, music could be heard from Gagarin's. "Well, what's with you? They started over there already!" With happy faces, neatly dressed cavaliers invited partners: "Allow me to ask you to dance the quadrille." In a trice, the tea table was pushed into a corner, and older mommies and aunties took places along the walls. Six couples lined-up in the middle of a cleanly washed floor, and the dancers sang:

In the grove or the garden
A maiden strolled...

Ever louder and happier, to the song, they went through the first three steps of a dance known all over the world. They did the fourth and the fifth steps to:

The maiden went for water
at a cold spring...

Carpenters, masons, and painters living in work teams at Olsufev's celebrated two holidays with special energy: in the summer, Petrov Day, and in the fall,

---

1. The standard quadrille was danced by four couples arranged in the corners of a square. While one couple danced the others rested. Introduced in France in the 1760s, the dance spread rapidly to other countries.

Pokrov.[2] Hiring was done for the period from Petrov Day to Pokrov, that is from 29 June to 1 October. On Petrov Day, in front of the apartments on the court-yard (and, if it rained, inside the apartments), tables were set up in the morning, and on them were bottles of *sivukhi*, herring, cucumbers, sausage and bread. The team's work boss drank the first glass, and then everyone took a bench, drank, ate, bargained, and right there "by a drunken agreement" committed verbally to terms with the boss. Their word was stronger than a notarized contract. After they had enough to drink, they bargained and traded.

"Andrei Maximovich, how much are you offering?" a drunk carpenter says to the boss.

"You wan' the old deal, fine. You wan' more, I don' need ya. G' back to the village," answers the boss, red as a crab.

"Give me a raise, or let's split!"

"Whaddever ya wan'. Take yer pay now and stop wastin' yer breff!"

They shout, yell, bargain, and fight the whole night. The next day, the entire team stays with the boss. This is Petrov Day, the day for new teams. Tailors, knit-ters, cobblers, and coopers also had their own holiday, Sitting Day, 8 September. They enjoyed just the same carousing, and resorted to the same night in the cellar, where they sometimes bound people for being too wild. On the next day, work until 10 in the evening.

After "sitting," they put their backs into it.

"Sitting" for tailors lasted two days. All sat until 9 September at seven in the evening, legs crossed, near a lit lamp. They light another and sit, pretending to knit. A young boy watches the door.

"He's coming!"

One of the tailors turns the lamp down all the way. The boss comes in.

"Why so dark in here?"

"Kerosene won't light."

"Why would it stop working just like that?"

"You oughta know! The lamps are yours..."

"So... Well, take this to light them!"

He throws three rubles down for a taste, a quarter of the total.

They turn up the light.

In an hour, a quarter has been drunk: again they turn the light down. They sit in silence. They send the boy to the head knitter, and just the same conversation takes place, the same quarter is given. The next day, everyone goes to work.

---

2. Petrov Day, June 29, marked the end of spring and start of summer, as well as the end of the June wedding season. Pokrov, October 1, is an Orthodox feast that celebrates the Intercession with God afforded the faithful by the Virgin Mary. The word has been translated in various ways due to its dual meaning as both "cloak" (or shroud) and "intercession" (or protection). Given the complexity of the various issues involved, it has been left untranslated in the text.

They sit at work, legs pretzled,[3] and their hands shake from hangovers and the cold. Summer vacation is over. After "sitting," there begins the joyless winter of Olsufev's inescapable serfdom, from which you could not even escape in a tavern.

---

3. They sat "ноги калачиком."

ALONG THE ROAD TO PETERSBURG

WHEN I LEFT THE TRAM heading toward the station a young man stopped me.

"Excuse me, I'm in Moscow for the first time. I'm a student. I'd like to know why the tram station on the empty square by the Ring Road is called "Triumphal Gate," and this is "Tver Gate," although in front of me, "Triumphal Gate" stands in all its majesty. Also, what is the significance of the two little buildings with columns?"

I explained that this was the end of Tverskaya Street, and that the gate was built 100 years earlier, in memory of the War of 1812. At one time, on the Ring Road, there had been a wooden "Triumphal Gate." It had been demolished for 150 years, but the place name was kept. I also explained that the two small buildings, in the old days before the railroads, were gate posts and were called guard houses because military guards stood watch there, between the buildings was a gate, etc. The student thanked me, said that he would write an article for his newspaper and would report at his club. They were all interested in Moscow because it was the world's top city.

The student captured my attention. In a half century of living in Moscow, I had gone in and out of these gates on a horse, on the tram, past them in a carriage, and on foot, thinking about everything possible, just not about the gates. This wonderful sculptured grouping of horses and a figure with a wreath in her hands avoided my attention so completely that I did not know whom it represented. I only remembered something I had heard about her: in all Moscow, they said, there are only two sober drivers, here and on the façade of the Bolshoi Theater. Only, according to local slang, this was not a "chariot driver" but "a broad with a bagel." I raised my eyes and finally saw that it was the "Goddess of Victory" with a laurel. In the same type of chariot, another "coachman" stood on the façade of the Bolshoi Theater

Tverskaya's Triumphal Gate, circa 1908. The "Goddess of Victory" rides her chariot atop the structure.

holding a lyre: Apollo. The groupings were similar, since both the gates and the Bolshoi Theater were built by the architect Bove in the 1820s.[1]

The small guardhouses, in my lifetime, were a base for the city's street sweepers, a police guard, and then privileged invalids sitting on the porch under Doric columns, rooting around in sacks of snuff for their customers. Later, one of the buildings housed the city ambulance service and in the other was an office for ambulance attendants and their assistants. Around the building on the right side of the gate, under a light iron stairway long connected to the roof, worked "cold cobblers," who came to Moscow from Tver with an "iron foot," on which they repaired shoes quickly, cheaply, and well. There were always around 10 of them working here and their clients stood by the wall on one leg, the other raised with no shoe, waiting for a repair. I remembered this image because I saw it every time I went by, walking or riding. And I wonder: how can it be that not a single artist thought to paint this lively bit of Moscow?

A tram line started to run past the gate in 1881. In the old days, expensive carriages belonging to fast livers rushed past the gate to the Hippodrome day and night, to restaurants outside the city, for rambles on *troikas*, ringing with bells and buckles, or on sleighs with drivers in ridiculously thick coats of expensive cloth, with silk belts and pointed, colored felt hats. With the end of serfdom, it seems, this type of thing should have been forgotten: gentry and landowners were "put on their feet," deprived of their coachmen and carriage. Luxurious carriages disappeared along with the abolition of serfdom, and lackeys crawled down from their perches.

---

1. Joseph Bove (1784-1834) was a neo-classical architect who supervised the reconstruction of the three-fourths of Moscow that was incinerated in 1812, when Napoleon's troops occupied the capital.

Moscow's streets by this time were paved with cobblestones, and along them rumbled *droshkys*, which got their name because people travelling in them shook feverishly.[2] After the abolition of serfdom, a type of carriage officially known as a "burial chariot," but in common speech dubbed "lucks," disappeared forever from Moscow's streets. It was said that, "If you croak, your 'luck' will take you head first to Iverskoye Cemetery."[3]

Out of a carriage yard's driveway, a pitch-black horse hitched to a black cart with a black post moved along Tverskaya Street. Next to the post was a bench, and on it sat, back to the horse, a convicted criminal in a black robe and hat. He was chained to the post. On his chest hung a blackboard with large chalk lettering listing his crimes: robber, murderer, arsonist, etc. They carted him from the prison along the main streets, across Red Square and the Moscow River to Konnaya Square, where, as late as the sixties, criminals mounted a scaffold and were whipped. If the convicted was from the gentry, an executioner with a red shirt broke a sword above his head, stripping his rank, his titles, and his place among the gentry.

I never had any "Luck," but I never had to "change my shirt." In place of the previous serfs' owners, there were new, wealthy merchants, "nobles without land," who tried to show former serfs their place, both by word and by deed. Drivers had to fill their shirts with cotton wadding again, only twice as thick, since a blow from a merchant's boot is much heavier than a noble's imported shoes or calfskin boots from Piron's.

I remember 1881. On my way to rehearsal once, passing Triumphal Gate, I saw an enormous crowd. Turning their heads, all shouted. On horseback, a man sat with a bottle of vodka. He was shouting out songs. By the gate stood an officer in a magnificent greatcoat, with a silver-embroidered guards' collar. He shouted and waved a fist above his head:

"Get down, low life!"

The singer called, "What are you shouting for? Crawl over here and drink some vodka!"

I remember nothing else clearly from that day at the Triumphal Gate. Perhaps only the pronunciation of the word "Triumphal Gate." Let's say you grab a cab:

"Triumphal!"

"Trukhmalny? Which one? Old or new?"

I myself had gotten used to Moscow slang and automatically said:

"To Trukhmalny."

The deceased actor Mikhail Provych Sadovsky, a Muscovite going back many generations, took great pride in and loved his Moscow accent. He would always say:

---

2. Droshky, from the verb *drozhat*, "to shake."
3. In Russian, the nickname was фортунка. The saying is "Достукаешься, повезут тебя на фотунке, к Иверской затылком."

"Old Trukhmalny. Anglish Club."

In Palashevsky Alley, next to the *banya*, in the eighties, there was a tiny stand where for many years the people's poet I.A. Razorenov, the author of many folk songs, sold his own homegrown vegetables. He wrote the song *Don't Sew Me, Mother, a Red Sarafan*.[4] Surikov had been his friend. Many Moscow poets spent time with him. From Petersburg, A.N. Pleshchev and S.V. Kruglov, would come to visit. I lived for a time in rooms at the England and visited him every day. As a gift, he gave me his booklet, *A Continuation of Evgeny Onegin*. He had signed it and added a clever little poem. He was a very tall old *bogatyr*. He knew almost all of Pushkin by heart, memorized *Evgeny Onegin*, and loved to quote it.

Razorenov had a taller friend, grey-haired, with a silver, curly beard. He was immeasurably powerful. His name was Yermolai, but since childhood everyone had called him Yermak. In those days, the space between the Garden Ring and Tverskoy Gate was considered the Yamskaya Slum. Yermak's ancestors were from Yamskoy going way back. Their home burned down on the day that Napoleon retreated from Moscow across the Tverskoy Bridge. Yermak remembered this home. Whenever, at my request, Razorenov talked about the past, he would recite the lines from *Onegin* where Napoleon hid from sight in Petrovsky Castle:

There, deep in thought,
He looked at the dreadful flames...

Yermak from time to time would sing his favorite song:

Just like in Piter, going down Tverskaya Yamskaya...

From these recollections of a friend I sketched for myself the Tverskoy Gate's past.

The traffic was heavy, especially at winter's start, in the snow, when landowners arrived for the season. Behind their baggage train came carriage loads of landed gentry; stretched out behind them were the humbler travelers.

"Remember? Just like Larina, from *Onegin*." Razorenov would quote the lines about Larina's trip to Moscow, and how they prepared:

Abandoning the sleigh,
Packing things in a cart,
Put in jars, mattresses,
Pillows, cages with roosters

---

4. A traditional dress worn by peasant girls and women in Russia until the twentieth century. Today, it is most often seen as a folk costume for various performances.

and how

they led 18 sleds into the courtyard.

Listening to these tales, I imagine a slowly moving line stretched-out on the other side of the barrier. Finally, one or another traveler, thanks to rank or title, is given a pass. A junior officer walks over from the guardroom porch to command:

"Raise it!"

An invalid pulls the barrier's chain. This lifts a brightly painted timber. After the person passes it is lowered until the next:

"Raise it!"

But now the Petersburg road is filled by the ringing of a little sleigh bell – everyone moves. They clear the right side of the road for a courier or military *troika* rushing through. The invalid does not wait for the command, "Raise it!" and, after raising the log, stands at attention. He knows that this is either the military, a courier, or the transport for a state criminal. Everyone else was obliged to put away their bells when approaching Moscow.

An especially large number of *troikas* went from Peter to Siberia. Yermak drove courier *troikas*. He had endured couriers' whips and switches, and when talking about it sang:

Balconies, lions at the gate
Flocks of birds on the crosses

Razorenov gets carried away describing Tverskoy, but Yermak continues his song:

Faraway a troika rushes
To Kazan on the hard stone road
A little bell, a gift from Valdai[5]
Rings plaintively in the meadow

For a long time, up until they built the Nikolayevskaya Railroad, he drove courier *troikas*. Later, he worked along the Garden Ring, and Vladimirka Road as far as the first station, close to dangerous Guslits.

---

5. Valdai, a small city in the Novgorod region, was incorporated in 1770 but first mentioned in writing in 1495. Located astride the postal route from Moscow to Petersburg, it was known for the production of bells, both large and small. Today, Valdai is the home of Russia's only bell museum.

Tverskaya-Yamskaya, with Triumphal Gate barely visible in the background.

Along Tverskoy-Yamskoy.
With a little bell...

This was the situation until the first half of the last century, with the construction of the Nikolayevskaya Railroad. Nicholas II placed a ruler on a map and drew a straight line from Moscow to Petersburg.

"Don't deviate from that line – I'll hang you!"

A straight line was built. The first to travel it were arrestees. Many from the gentry and the merchants were frightened.

"An unclean power turns the wheels..."

"The devil drives!"

"From one nostril rushes steam, from the other fire and smoke."

At the start, they still transported exiles to Siberia along the Pitersky Tract, but later they were sent on the railroad, and goods went in freight cars. The guard posts closed. They no longer shouted, "Raise it!" Invalids in shackles turned to quietly grating tobacco for snuff.

Razorenov recalled how the Yamskaya Slum became part of the city. He remembered when they replaced the guardhouse. He had not forgotten how the road, until emancipation, passed through these gates, just like the loads of birch switches for punishing serfs – and not serfs alone but everyone from the "crude class of people." They even allowed, until the end of serfdom, corporal punishment, but later they stopped importing switches. Punishments were done every Saturday, except during Holy Week and at the start of Lent.

Tsars went through this Triumphal Gate *en route* to coronations. In 1896, in honor of Nicholas II's coronation, a large fair was organized on Khodynskoye Field, the same place where, in 1882, was held the famous All-Russia Artistic Industrial Exhibition. This was beyond Moscow's border at the time. Bodies of those who perished at Khodynskoye were brought back to the city through the Triumphal Gate. "This is a bad omen. Nothing good will come of this tsar's reign." That was the opinion of the old typesetter from *Russian Bulletin* who had typeset my article on the Khodynskoye catastrophe. No one responded to his words. All fell silent in fear and changed the subject.

IN MY EYES

EXITING THE TRAIN STATION, I climbed into a car with its top down. The first thing I saw was the enormous Triumphal Gate. On top were the same four stallions and, in the chariot, the same statue of Fame with a laurel held high. I remembered... But we were already rushing along noisy Tverskoy Boulevard, through the bustle and hum. Its beautiful surface shines after a passing rain under the bright September sun. The sidewalks are full of busy people. All are in a hurry, some on their way to work, some to the office, some returning from work, from the office, or running errands, but I do not see, as in the past, portly men trying to work up an appetite. I recall the saying: "Now a pot-belly chases after bread, and bread does not chase the pot-belly."[1]

We hurry through the flow of clanging and humming trams, through the banging of carts and tired drivers living out their days. Most of those on horseback don't have even a saddle, they cling to the reins. We pass all the traffic. We go by enormous buses and agile taxis. Traffic is frozen. Finally, we stop at the Ring Road. Nothing moves. Traffic noise dies. Pedestrians hurry straight across Tverskoy Boulevard, dodging between carriages. On the rise, just in front of us, stands a well-dressed police officer, wordless, in a grey helmet, with his hand raised. As soon as he lowers this living semaphore in a white glove, everyone rushes ahead, all the noise starts, rings. Moscow starts booming.

We turned onto the Garden Ring. At a three-minute stop, I came to myself, not entirely, but at least a bit. I had lived for four months in the wonderful silence of the deep forest, and suddenly I was in a boiling pot. We turned left, onto the Garden Ring. How many thousands of times in the past half-century have I gone along it

---

1. Теперь брюхо бегает за хлебом, а не хлеб за брюхом.

or across it! I've done a bit of riding. Memories flash, images of the past. Here we ride quietly. The street is full of trucks that crawl among trams coming one after another from the left, squeezing the cabs to the sidewalk. We have to wait and pick the right moment to pass. The first sight that brought me back to the distant past was a familiar two-story building that reminded me of 1876. But where is the fence in front of it? The view changes every minute. Thoughts and recollections can't keep up. But now, when I write, I have time to think and resurrect the past down to the smallest details.

In April 1876, I bumped into a friend from the stage, the singer Petrusha Molodtsov (he sang the role of Torop at the Bolshoi, and later worked with me in Tambov). He dragged me as a guest to his uncle's in a grey building with a fence, behind which a goat wandered and two little girls, preparing for the *gymnasium*, played. We stopped by the gate to watch their game. They hid in the bushes, tossing a silver 20-kopek coin attached to a thread out onto the sidewalk, and waited. We waited too. From one direction came a fat merchant, and from the other an elderly, poor woman. Both caught sight of the coin and threw themselves at it. The merchant knocked the old woman away and bent over to grab his prize, but the kids pulled the thread and the coin disappeared. The merchant was astonished.

"That's their favorite game. Sometimes it's funny," his grey-bearded uncle explained when we went inside.

That fence is not there anymore, but I saw it last year. In front of the newly-painted building there was a broad asphalt sidewalk and the street was smooth, the cobbles paved over. Uncle Molodtsov remembered what the Garden Ring was like in the days of his youth, in the forties.

"In those days, it was not yet lined with cobbles; instead, it was covered crosswise with logs. After downpours, they floated out of place, turned to the side, and held up traffic."

Wealthy grandees and proud gentry rode in enormous, tall carts with folding stairs by the doors. In the back of the carriages, on footrests and holding to straps, stood two enormous guards, two liveried lackeys, and, on the bottom level, a Cossack on each step. It was their job to run into entrances and announce arrivals, and in bad weather help the bodyguards carry the master and mistress from the carriage to the building entrance. The carriage was hitched to four horses. Especially important people had six horses. On the left front horse sat a look-out, and in front galloped a man on horseback watching the road: could they get through? Along the entire Garden Ring Road, next to the fence rails along the sidewalks were wooden paths with gutters underneath. Especially difficult to get through were the Samoteka and Sukharevka sections of the Ring Road, with their steep drop to the Neglinka River.

Drovers struggled up these hills for hours with their loads. Groups of arrestees were tested here for the first time on their walk to Siberia along the Vladimirka

Ring Road, circa 1934.

Road. They walked from Moscow's transfer prison, Butyrskaya, up Lesser Dmitrovka along the Ring Road to Rogozhsky Gate. The Ring Road, on the day a group walked – sometimes a thousand men or more – was cordoned by a chain of soldiers with weapons. At the head of the group, clinking in hand and leg irons, exiles walked to hard labor wearing grey jackets with a diamond of yellow cloth sewn on the back, and grey cloth caps with no bills covering their half-shaved heads.

Behind them shuffled exiles in leg irons attached to one iron bar: one tripped on a bump and annoyed his neighbors. Next came a crowd of vagrants, and then a line of covered carriages piled high with household items, on which nested woman and children and ill convicts. Convoys faced especially horrible conditions in heavy rain, when the streets were washed out and they waited for hours while the log roads were fixed.

Old Uncle Molodtsov said, "We witnessed these horrors for decades. Over the clanking of shackles we could hear songs about bad luck and mercy. Children would cry in the carriages while a mother in prison clothes got drenched trying to comfort them. The general public cried, giving the unfortunates rolls and bagels, whatever they could."

This was the Ring Road in the first half of the last century. I remember it in the eighties, when a horse drawn tram with shaky cars, roofed against the rain, was hitched to a pair of monstrously large horses. Fifteen people fit in the car sitting back to back. At the bottom of a hill, the driver would stop the horses and shout: "Climb out!" They climbed out and walked through the rain, up to their knees in mud to the top of the hill, climbed back in, and rode until the next uphill.

I remember Muscovites' joy when, in 1880, a horse-drawn tram line was built along Tverskoy to the park. Perhaps two years later one was built on the Ring Road. By then, at the uphill near Samotek and Sukharevskaya, they no longer shouted,

"Get out!" Instead, they stopped the horses, hitched another pair in front, with a young boy for a lookout. They were known as *"falatory."*[2] They rode up the hill, shouting at and whipping the horses with the end of a rein, kicking them in the sides with booted feet that barely reached the stirrups. There were cases when the *falator* fell from a horse. Or a horse might slip and fall, and the *falator*, wearing enormous boots, or *valenki* in the winter, could not be dragged out. No one taught them how to ride. Straight from the village they were put up on a stallion and told, "Ride!" It was not unusual for horses to break their legs climbing a cobbled hill. They were always underfed and in poor health.

Moscow's *falatory*, like the Kalmyks in Astrakhan or on the Don River steppe had lives that matched their horses, marching the same path. At sunrise, they rode out on horseback, in their left hand a rein while their right hand stretched back to steady the huge, awkward rigging that hitched the horses to the carriage. As soon as they got to the square, they started work: trips up the hill, and later, around midnight, they went to sleep in the horse yard. Many of them spent nights in the stable. They watered the horses at the fountain on the square, and drank from the same bucket. In the summer heat they drank a lot of water. Dust moved in clouds down the never-swept streets and squares. In the winter, they froze at stops and warmed back up together climbing the hill. In autumn rain, mixed with sleet, they were worse off than the horses. Jackets made from thick, coarse fabric were soaked right through, frozen, with the consistency of plaster casts; instead of covering the freezing *falator*, jackets left their knees uncovered.

At stops, the horses munched hay, and the *falatory* had to eat whatever they could. In the best case, they went to street vendors who kept their food warm on heaters. They bought canned meat and broth, and sometimes *kasha* with a warm topping: for one kopek, lung; for two kopeks, heart; and for three kopeks the vendor would slice off a piece of liver.

Every *falator's* dream was to work their way up to driver. In the rain, winter cold, and storms, they gazed with envy at drivers sleeping under a carriage tops, now and then enjoying aromatic snuff to keep from falling completely asleep: the wagon shakes, the horse looks up, the streets are empty, there is no one to bother them.

Mikhail Lvovich, a snuff lover, was the head of the Strastnaya Square station since it was built. He always had a large supply of tobacco; a friend who worked in a factory in Yaroslavl sent him whole boxes of it as gifts. Drivers would run to him when they stopped at the station: some with snuff boxes, some with shoe-polish tins. "Pour me some, Mikhail Lvovich!" He never refused. At the time of the revolution, Mikhail Lvovich worked at the Rogozhsky Station. He died from typhoid.

---

2. This comes from the German word *vorreitor*. The proper English term is "postilion" or "post boy."

Falatory dreamed about a coachman's life, but seldom achieved this happiness. Many were permanently dismissed, sent by their management back to a village with no pension. If it was challenged in court, the judge would conclude: "For violating personal safety rules." Many caught cold and died in the hospital. They had no break between six a.m. and midnight, riding up and walking down the hill, or sitting on horseback in the waiting area. The artist Sergei Semyonovich Voroshilov, the best painter in this genre aside from Sverchkov, exhibited a painting of two *falatory* sleeping on nags. This image, taken from Russian magazines, was republished abroad. Underneath, there was an inscription: "Rain washes them, dust covers them."

Streetcars in use at the time were two-storied, a lower section and on its roof another level. The upper level was called an "imperial," and its passengers, "three-kopek imperialists." On the bottom level passengers paid five kopeks per station. A narrow, spiral staircase led to the upper level. Women were not allowed to use it. The question of allowing women in the imperial was raised in a city council commission. One liberal even argued that the prohibition was a violation of women's rights. They decided to vote. A Ukrainian member of the commission who had defended the prohibition, when the vote was proposed, said: "Bud, *day* don't haff pants." With laughter all around, the question was not voted.

WE HURRIED ON AND I kept looking: "Where can that fence be?" At Ugolnaya Square, on the corner of Lesser Dmitrovka, where vegetables, firewood, and samovar fuel were sold and customers haggled, there was a nice little spot with a lacy fence. The yard next to it was always unkempt, but the building was freshly painted. At one time the tavern Volna had been here, a hangout for card sharps, con men, and "businessmen."

In 1905, Volna was occupied by revolutionaries who fired at, first, the police and gendarmes, and later troops. They failed to take it for some time. Finally, late at night, a large squad with a cannon arrived. They planned to attack with grenades. The tavern was brightly lit with lamps. The troops surrounded the building and prepared to fire, but the front door was unlocked. After breaking a few panes of glass with rifle shots, they decided to storm the building. One brave soldier was found to walk in the door. He quickly returned, "No one's there." The tavern was empty. The revolutionaries had learned there would be an attack at midnight and left in time.

I remember another case. For decades a coffin maker rented a ground floor space. His name is connected with the "Deuce of Hearts" gang, which had been talked about all over Moscow. I remember neither the name of the coffin maker nor of the gangster for whom he made a luxurious coffin, upholstered with a nice finish. The deceased lay in his apartment, in one of the alleys off Tverskoy. The Orthodox clerics had finished their singing and had left to escort him to Vagankovo.[3] Leading the procession were choristers in robes, in back there were two carriages and a few young people accompanying the catafalque.

They got as far as the *chic* restaurant Yar, which was across the street from the turn to the cemetery. They stopped. The young people took the coffin and instead of going to the cemetery, to the great surprise of the general public, they carried it right into Yar's entrance. There, no one stopped them, and they proceeded into the largest room, filled with young people. Rising from the coffin after removing his shroud to reveal a fashionable suit, a gangster was met with champagne.

The police started an investigation. The coffin, coffin cover, and the shroud, were bought for next to nothing by the coffin maker. And the next day, they were used for some sort of merchant.

Another case was opened. Relatives who had been left out of the merchant's will decided to sue the primary heirs for insulting the memory of the deceased by burying him in a "used" coffin.

The coffin maker was teased for years. People would run into his shop and ask: "Have any used coffins? A used shroud?"

Later, as time passed, this was all forgotten. I only remembered it when going past on Karetny Row, or on the Ring Road at Samoteka.

We rushed along. Where is the fence? It was here a year ago. It was in fine condition with expensive greenery, with paths. Only the rich had access to gardens, the ones in the most expensive apartments. And there were few such gardens. The majority of these fenced quadrangles senselessly ate up half the street. They were empty lots, overgrown by weeds. Gates were locked so thieves could not get to the first floor. In almost all of them, large trees grew, planted in the old days at the order of the bosses. These same trees come in use now. They form wide alleyways, covered in asphalt, for pedestrians. These alleyways, under a pavilion of green trees, have a beauty and luxury that I had not yet seen in Moscow.

We go down along Samoteka. After seeing the sparkle of innovation, here one feels old Moscow. People congregate on the sidewalks and square, coming from Sukharevka or streaming toward it. They carry a mix of old items: one, used clothes; one, a samovar; another, a lamp or a once-expensive vase with a broken handle. A tramp carries a sack, and bluish meat shines out. People slog through the dirt in clothes still wet from the rain. The ripe smell of the slums hangs in the air.

We turned right. We hurried along Tsvetnoy Boulevard, passing two trams. The boulevard is still fresh and clean, the trees are green with golden flashes of autumn.

---

3. The reference is to the Vagankovskoye Cemetery in Moscow's Krasnaya Presnya District. Vladimir Vysotsky the bard and actor (1938-1980), Vladimir Dal the lexicographer (1801-1872), Sergei Yesenin the poet (1895-1925), Vasily Surikov the painter (1848-1916) and other well-known figures are buried there. Like several other Moscow cemeteries, it was established by Catherine II in 1771, during the plague epidemic.

Hunter's Row, circa 1934.

I remember when empty lots surrounded the just-built circus. At one time here, at night, "anything could happen," and during the day kids played with kites, always attached to noisemakers. At this memory, I imagine I hear them. I reflexively raise my eyes to look for a kite. Above me, three airplanes fly past, one after another, and then are hidden behind the Peasants' Club on Trubnaya Square.

THE PETROVSKAYA TRAM LINE IS paved. Freshly rinsed, Petrovka Street is paved too. In front of a building, a janitor hoses down the street, and two others push the water into a grated drain.

On Theater Square Drive we curve around the Bolshoi Theater and Sverdlovskaya Square, and ride out onto the wide, ever-so-straight, almost "licked" clean Hunter's Row Square. Cars rush by; trams and fat buses trundle along.

Wherever is Hunter's Row?

Stoleshniki, 1934

POEMS AND SONGS IN ORIGINAL RUSSIAN

28

Были когда-то и вы рысаками
И кучеров вы имели лихих...

30

У барыни платье длинно,
Из-под платья...

....

Франт, рубаха -- белый цвет,
А порткам, знать, смены нет.

....

На дворе собака брешет,
А хозяин пузо чешет.

87

...Возле древней башни
На стенах старинных были чуть не пашни.

94

Осенний мелкий дождичек
Сеет, сеет сквозь туман.

99

И чай пил-ла, и б-булк-и ела,
Поз-за-была и с кем си-идела.

115

Видел я архив обжоры,
Он рецептов вкусно жрать
От Кавказа до Ижоры
За сто лет сумел собрать.

132

Да, час расставанья пришел,
День занимается белый,
Бочонок стоит опустелый,
Стоит опустелый "Орел"..

159

Ах ты, сукин сын Гагарин,
Ты собака, а не барин.
Заедаешь харчевые,
Наше жалованье,
И на эти наши деньги
Ты большой построил дом
Среди улицы Тверской
За Неглииной за рекой.
Со стеклянным потолком,
С москворецкою водой,
По фонтану ведена,
Жива рыба пущена...

182

Кругом непрогляднию серою мглой
Степная равнина одета,
И мрачно и душно в пустыне глухой,
И нет в ней ни жизни, ни света.

183

Отважен, силен, сердцем прост,
Его не тронула борьбы житейской буря,
И занял он за это самый высший ноет,
На каланче дежуря.

185

Пожарный

Мчатся искры, вьется пламя,
  Грозен огненный язык
Высоко держу я знамя,
  Я к опасности привык!

Нет неделями покоя,--
  Стой на страже ночь и день.
С треском гнется подо мною
  Зыбкой лестницы ступень.

В вихре искр, в порыве дыма,
  Под карнизом, на весу,
День и ночь неутомимо
  Службу трудную несу.

Ловкость, удаль и отвага
  Нам заветом быть должны.
Мерзнет мокрая сермяга,
  Волоса опалены

Правь струю рукой умелой,
  Ломом крышу раскрывай
И рукав обледенелый
  Через пламя подавай.

На высоких крышах башен
  Я, как дома, весь в огне.
Пыл пожара мне не страшен,
  Целый век я на войне!

190

Вчера угас еще один из типов,
Москве весьма известных и знакомых,
Тьмутараканский князь Иван Филиппов,
И в трауре оставил насекомых.

194

...Вот клубится
Пыль. Все ближе... Стук шагов,
Мерный звон цепей железных,
Скрип телег и лязг штыков.
Ближе. Громче. Вот на солнце
Блещут ружья. То конвой;
Дальше длинные шеренги
Серых сукон. Недруг злой,
Враг и свой, чужой и близкий,
Все понуро в ряд бредут,
Всех свела одна недоля,
Всех сковал железный прут...

196

Меж чернеющих под паром
Плугом поднятых полей
Лентой тянется дорога
Изумруда зеленей...
Все на ней теперь иное,
Только строй двойной берез,
Что слыхали столько воплей,
Что видали столько слез,
Тот же самый...
...Но как чудно
В пышном убранстве весны
Все вокруг них! Не дождями
Эти травы вспоены,
На слезах людских, на поте,
Что лились рекой в те дни,–
Без призора, на свободе–
Расцвели теперь они.
Все цветы, где прежде слезы
Прибивали пыль порой,
Где гремели колымаги
По дороге столбовой.

200

Народ галдел, народ зевал,
Едва ли сотый понимал,
Что делается тут...
Зато посмеивался в ус,
Лукаво щуря взор,
Знакомый с бурями француз,
Столичный куафер.

212

И на обломках самовластья
Напишут наши имена!
....
И пусть у гробового входа
Младая будет жизнь играть,

224

Ночной разбойник, дуэлист,
В Камчатку сослан был, вернулся алеутом,
И крепко на руку нечист...
....
Это с Дона челны налетели,
Взволновали простор голубой,–
То Степан удалую ватагу
На добычу ведет за собой...

225

С паденьем головы удалой
Всему, ты думаешь, конец –
Из каждой капли крови алой
Отважный вырастет боец.

232
Краса инспекции московской
И всей губернии краса -
Иван Иванович Красовский,
Да где же ваши волоса?

236
Бойцы вспоминают минувшие дни
И битвы, где вместе рубились они.

241
Сейте!
«Сейте разумное, доброе, вечное»
Сейте студентов по стогнам земли,
Чтобы поведать все горе сердечное
Всюду бедняги могли.
Сейте, пусть чувство растет благородное,
Очи омочит слеза,–
Сквозь эти слезы пусть слово свободное
Руси откроет глаза,
Пусть все узнают, что нравами грубыми
Стали опять щеголять,
Снова наполнится край скалозубами,
Чтоб просвещение гнать.
Пусть все узнают: застенки по-старому,
И палачи введены,
Отданы гневу их дикому, ярому
Лучшие силы страны.
Вольные степи ветрами обвеяны,
Русь широка и грозна –
Вырастет новое – всюду посеяны
Светлых идей семена.
Те, что упорно и долго не верили
Правде свободных идей,
Ныне поймут – обсчитали, обмерили,
Выгнали их сыновей.
Всех разогнали, а всех ли вы выбили,
Сделавши подлость и срам?
Это свершили вы к вашей погибели.
Память позорная вам!

242
Я видел грозные моменты,
Досель кружится голова...
Шумели буйные студенты,
Гудела старая Москва,
Толпы стремились за толпами...
Свистки... Ура... Нагайки... Вой...
Кругом войска... за казаками
Трухтит жандармов синий строй.
Что улица – картины те же,
Везде народ... Везде войска...
Студенты спрятаны в манеже,
Шумят, как бурная река.
И за студентами загнали
В манеж испуганный народ,

Всех, что кричали, не кричали,
Всех, кто по улице пройдет,–
Вали в манеж!
А дело жарко,
Войскам победа не легка...
Лови! Дави!
Идет кухарка,
Под мышкой тащит судака...
Вскипели храбрые войска!
Маневр... Другой... И победили!
Летят кто с шашкой, кто с штыком,
В манеже лихо водворили
Кухарку с мерзлым судаком...

244
И вырежем мы в заповедных лесах
На барскую спину дубину...

251
Среди рассеянной Москвы,
При толках виста и бостона,
При бальном лепете молвы
Ты любишь игры Аполлона.
Царица муз и красоты,
Рукою нежной держишь ты
Волшебный скиптер вдохновений,
И над задумчивым челом,
Двойным увенчанным венком,
И вьется, и пылает гений.
Певца, плененного тобой.
Не отвергай смиренной дани,
Внемли с улыбкой голос мой,
Как мимоездом Каталани
Цыганке внемлет кочевой.

252
Лук звенит, стрела трепещет.
И, клубясь, издох Пифон;
И твой лик победой блещет,
Бельведерский Аполлон!
Кто ж вступился за Пифона,
Кто разбил твой истукан?
Ты, соперник Аполлона,
Бельведерский Митрофан.

252
Работа кипела под звуки оков,
Под песни – работа над бездной!
Стучались в упругую грудь рудников
И заступ и молот железный.

253
Певцов-итальянцев тут слышала я,
Что были тогда знамениты,
Отца моего сослуживцы, друзья
Тут были, печалью убиты.
Тут были родные ушедших туда,
Куда я сама торопилась
Писателей группа, любимых тогда,
Со мной дружелюбно простилась:
Тут были Одоевский, Вяземский; был
Поэт вдохновенный и милый,
Поклонник кузины, что рано почил,
Безвременно взятый могилой,

257
А на Тверской в дворце роскошном Елисеев
Привлек толпы несметные народа
Блестящей выставкой колбас, печений,
       лакомств...
Ряды окороков, копченых и вареных,
Индейки, фаршированные гуси,
Колбасы с чесноком, с фисташками и
       перцем,
Сыры всех возрастов – и честер, и
       швейцарский,
И жидкий бри, и пармезон гранитный...
Приказчик Алексей Ильич старается у
       фруктов,
Уложенных душистой пирамидой,
Наполнивших корзины в пестрых лентах...
Здесь все – от кальвиля французского с
       гербами
До ананасов и невиданных японских вишен.

260
Гайда, тройка, снег пушистый.
Ночь морозная кругом...

263
В России нет закона,
Есть столб, и на столбе корона.

284
Боюсь, брусничная вода
Мне б не наделала вреда!

289
...В чертоги входит хан младой,
За ним отшельниц милых рой,
Одна снимает шлем крылатый,
Другая–кованые латы,
Та меч берет, та–пыльный щит.
Одежда неги заменит
Железные доспехи брани.
Но прежде юношу ведут
К великолепной русской бане.

Уж волны дымные текут
В ее серебряные чаны
И брызжут хладные фонтаны;
Разостлан роскоши ковер,
На нем усталый хан ложится,
Прозрачный пар над ним клубится.
Потупя неги полный взор,
Прелестные, полунагие,
Вкруг хана девы молодые
В заботе нежной и немой
Теснятся резвою толпой...
Над рыцарем иная машет
Ветвями молодых берез..
И жар от них душистый пышет;
Другая соком вешних роз
Устали члены прохлаждает
И в ароматах потопляет
Темнокудрявые власы...

290
Мякнут косточки, все жилочки гудят,
С тела волглого окатышки бегут,
А с настреку вся спина горит,
Мне хозяйка смутны речи говорит.
Не ворошь ты меня, Танюшка,
Растомила меня банюшка,
Размягчила туги хрящики,
Разморила все суставчики.
В бане веник больше всех бояр,
Положи его, сухмяного, в запар,
Чтоб он был душистый и взбучистый,
Лопашистый и уручистый...
И залез я на высокий на полок,
В мягкий, вольный, во малиновый парок.
Начал веничком я париться,
Шелковистым, хвостистым жариться.

290
Лишенный сладостных мечтаний,
В бессильной злобе и тоске
Пошел я в Волковские бани
Распарить кости на полке.
И что ж? О радость! О приятство!
Я свой заветный идеал–
Свободу, равенство и братство –
В Торговых банях отыскал.

296
Вот как жили при Аскольде
Наши деды и отцы...

306
От ланинского редерера
Трещит и пухнет голова...

307
И с телятиной холодной Трюфли "Яра"
	вспоминать...

315
И один из этих братьев
Был по имени Иван,
По фамилии Кондратьев,
По прозванью Атаман.

318
Еще одно, последнее сказанье
И летопись окончена моя...

325
Во саду ли в огороде
Девица гуляла...
	....
Шла девица за водой
За холодной ключевой...

331
Отселе, в думу погружен,
Глядел на грозный пламень он...

331
Как по Питерской, по Тверской-Ямской...

331
Забвенью брошенный возок, как в обозе
	укладывались домашние пожитки

...Варенье в банках, тюфяки,
Перины, клетки с петухами...

...Ведут во двор восьмнадцать кляч.

332
Балконы, львы на воротах
И стаи галок на крестах...
	....
Вот мчится тройка удалая
В Казань дорогой столбовой...
И колокольчик, дар Валдая,
Гудит уныло под дугой...

333
По Тверской-Ямской
С колокольчиком...

INDEX

GILYAROVSKY'S MOSCOW

This map is based on an 1893 map by Ruddeman Johnston Co., London. It therefore gives a good indication of the outline of major streets and features in Gilyarovsky's day, before the major street transformations of the Soviet era.

It is far from comprehensive, but does indicate most of the major places of interest mentioned by Gilyarovsky in the book. These two pages use an overlay that shows most of the featured places mentioned in the book. The following two pages show the main street names.

For even more links, many annotated, visit **bit.ly/GilyaMap** for a Google Maps mashup map with locations superimposed on a modern map of the capital.

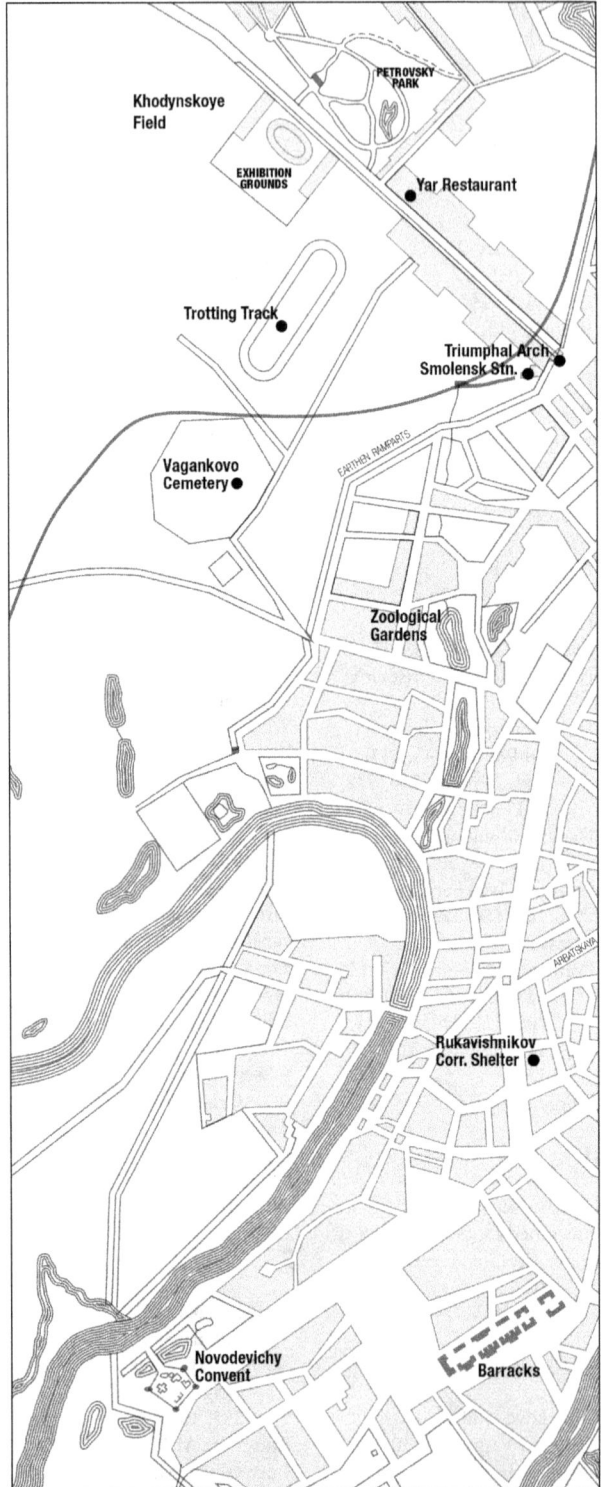

Khodynskoye Field

PETROVSKY PARK

EXHIBITION GROUNDS

Yar Restaurant

Trotting Track

Triumphal Arch
Smolensk Stn.

EARTHEN RAMPARTS

Vagankovo Cemetery

Zoological Gardens

ARBATSKAYA

Rukavishnikov Corr. Shelter

Novodevichy Convent

Barracks

Butyrka Prison

St. Petersburg Station

Yaroslavl Stn.

Ryazan Station

Traktir Volna

Catherine Hospital

GARDEN RING ROAD

Strastnoy Mon.

Naryshkin Square

Hermitage

Trubnaya Sq.

Sukharevka Tower

English Club

Latin Quarter

Merchants' Club

Yeliseyev's

Brenko Th.

Fillipov's

Post & Telegraph

Chebyshy

Hell

Fire Watchtower

Sandunov. Baths

Gov. Gen. Res.

Dresden Hotel

Alpine Rose

Consistory

Secret Police HQ

Olsufyeva's

Central Banya

Shipovsky Fortress

Bolshoi

Lubyanka Sq.

Golitsyn Palace

Metropole

Nikolsky Gate

Hunter's Row

Testov's

Polytech. Mus.

Supreme Court

The Pit

Ilyinsky Gate

Kursk Station

University

RED SQUARE

Slav. Baz.

Tolkuchy Market

Continental

Varvarsky Gate

Prague Rest.

Hunter's Club

Khitrovka

KREMLIN

Foundling Hosp.

Savior's Cath.

Stone Bridge

PRECHISTENKA

KITAI CITY WALL

CHISTIE PRUDY

BOULEVARD RING

Taganka Square

Novospassky Monastery

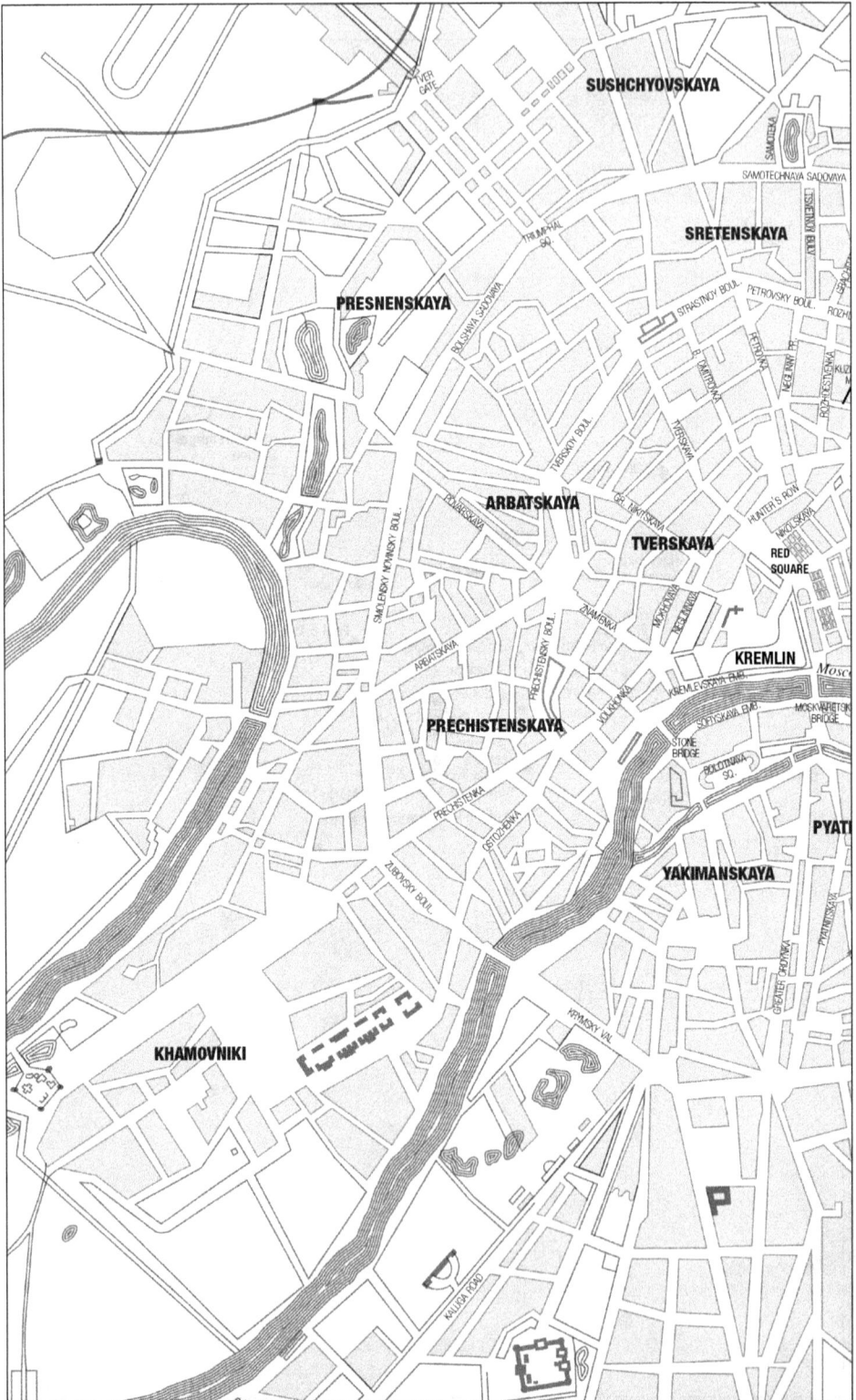

SUSHCHYOVSKAYA

SAMOTECHNAYA SADOVAYA

SRETENSKAYA

TRIUMFAL SQ.

PRESNENSKAYA

STRASTNOY BOUL. PETROVSKY BOUL.

BOLSHAYA SADOVAYA

TVERSKOY BOUL.

ARBATSKAYA

TVERSKAYA

RED SQUARE

HUNTER'S ROW

NIKOLSKAYA

SMOLENSKY MOVNSKY BOUL.

ARBATSKAYA

PRECHISTENSKY BOUL.

ZNAMENKA

MOKHOVAYA

KREMLIN

Mosco

PRECHISTENSKAYA

VOLKHONKA

KREMLEVSKAYA EMB.

SOFIYSKAYA EMB.

MOSKVARETSKY BRIDGE

STONE BRIDGE

BOLOTNAYA SQ.

PYATI

PRECHISTENKA

OSTOZENKA

YAKIMANSKAYA

ZUBOVSKY BOUL.

GREATER POLYANKA

PYATNITSKAYA

KRYMSKY VAL

KHAMOVNIKI

KALUGA TORG

MESHCHANSKAYA

OLKHOVETS

LEFORTOVO

AYA SADOVAYA

TSVETNOY BOUL

SUKHAREVSKAYA SADOVAYA

SRETENKA

BORICEVKA

ROZHDEST. BOUL

NOVAYA BASMANNAYA

RAZGULYAI

RED GATE

SRETENSKY BOUL

STARAYA BASMANNAYA

ROZHDESTVENKA

KUZNETSKY MOST

LUBYANKA

NYESHCHIKY SQ.

CHISTOPRUDNY BOUL.

BASMANNAYA

YAUZSKAYA

POKROVKA

NOVAYA SQ.

STARAYA SQ.

POKROVSKY BOUL.

MYASNITSKAYA

ARE

VARVARKA

SOLYANKA

KITAY CITY WALL

VORONTSOVSKAYA

Moscow River

Yauza River

MOSKVARETSKY BRIDGE

VLADIMIRKA

PYATNITSKAYA

ROGOZHSKAYA SLOBODA

PYATNITSKAYA

B. TATARSKAYA

KLYMETSKAYA

ABOUT THE AUTHOR

Vladimir Gilyarovsky (1853-1935) was an adventurer, raconteur, poet, actor, gourmand, and an indefatigable writer. He is widely acclaimed as "the grandfather of Russian journalism," and wrote hundreds of sketches, reports and exposés. There have been several collections of his work in Russian, but *Moscow and Muscovites* is considered his masterwork and is a treasured classic among Russians, who know him best by the affectionate nickname, "Uncle Gilya."

ABOUT THE TRANSLATOR

Brendan Kiernan is a translator and political analyst. A student of Russian language and literature since 1977, he graduated from Williams College and earned his Ph.D in Political Science from Indiana University, along with an area studies certificate from IU's famed Russian and East European Institute. He is the author of *The End of Soviet Politics: Elections, Legislatures and the Demise of the Communist Party* (Westview).

www.ingramcontent.com/pod-product-compliance
Lightning Source LLC
Chambersburg PA
CBHW060023030426
42334CB00019B/2162